Sheffield Hallam University
Learning and IT Services
Adsetts Centre City Campus
Sheffield S1 1WS

101 914 ___

D1145770

Sheffield Hallam
University
WITHDRAWN

REFERENCE

Palgrave Sourcebooks

Series Editor: Steven Matthews

Published
Simon Bainbridge: **Romanticism**
Lena Cowen Orlin: **The Renaissance**
Steven Matthews: **Modernism**

Forthcoming
Carolyn Collette and Harold Garrett-Goodyear: **Medieval Literature**
John Plunket, Ana Vadillo, Regenia Gagnier, Angelique Richardson, Rick Rylance
   and Paul Young: **Victorian Literature**
Nigel Wood: **The 'Long' Eighteenth Century**

Palgrave Sourcebooks

ISBN 978–1–4039–4277–7 hardback
ISBN 978–1–4039–4278–4 paperback

You can receive further titles in this series as they are published by placing a standing
order. Please contact your bookseller or, in the case of difficulty, write to us at the address
below with your name and address, the title of the series, and the ISBN quoted above.

Customer Services Department, Palgrave Ltd.
Houndmills, Basingstoke, Hampshire, RG21 6XS, England

The Renaissance

A Sourcebook

Lena Cowen Orlin

© Selection of material and editorial matter Lena Cowen Orlin 2009

All rights reserved. No reproduction, copy or transmission of this publication may be made without written permission.

No paragraph of this publication may be reproduced, copied or transmitted save with written permission or in accordance with the provisions of the Copyright, Designs and Patents Act 1988, or under the terms of any licence permitting limited copying issued by the Copyright Licensing Agency, Saffron House, 6–10 Kirby Street, London EC1N 8TS.

Any person who does any unauthorized act in relation to this publication may be liable to criminal prosecution and civil claims for damages.

The author has asserted her right to be identified as the author of this work in accordance with the Copyright, Designs and Patents Act 1988.

First published 2009 by
PALGRAVE MACMILLAN

Palgrave Macmillan in the UK is an imprint of Macmillan Publishers Limited, registered in England, company number 785998, of Houndmills, Basingstoke, Hampshire RG21 6XS.

Palgrave Macmillan in the US is a division of St Martin's Press LLC
175 Fifth Avenue, New York, NY 10010.

Palgrave Macmillan is the global academic imprint of the above companies and has companies and representatives throughout the world.

Palgrave® and Macmillan® are registered trademarks in the United States, the United Kingdom, Europe and other countries.

ISBN-13: 978-0-230-00175-6   hardback
ISBN-10: 0-230-00175-0   hardback
ISBN-13: 978-0-230-00176-3   paperback
ISBN-10: 0-230-00176-9   paperback

This book is printed on paper suitable for recycling and made from fully managed and sustained forest sources. Logging, pulping and manufacturing processes are expected to conform to the environmental regulations of the country of origin.

A catalogue record for this book is available from the British Library.

A catalog record for this book is available from the Library of Congress.

10 9 8 7 6 5 4 3 2 1
18 17 16 15 14 13 12 11 10 09

Printed and bound in China

SHEFFIELD HALLAM UNIVERSITY
REF
820·3
OR
ADSETTS LEARNING CENTRE

Short Contents

In tribute to Joan Thirsk

Detailed Contents

List of Illustrations

Acknowledgments

My first thanks are owed to Steven Matthews for inviting me to edit this collection and for the structure he set out to guide and inspire my work. The editorial hands of Kate Haines and Jocelyn Stockley, at Palgrave Macmillan, have been steady and supportive. Many entries are excerpted from early printed books, as was made possible by the research databases of the Georgetown University Library. I have also consulted the manuscript archives of the Folger Shakespeare Library, the British Library, the National Archives (Public Record Office), the London Guildhall Library, the Corporation of London Record Office, the London Metropolitan Archives, and the Canterbury Cathedral Library and Archives. I am grateful to their staffs, as also for research travel support from the University of Maryland Baltimore County (UMBC), and Georgetown University.

At UMBC, I was fortunate to work through many of these selections with some intrepid undergraduates: Lakshmi Balaji, Julianne Bowen, Joshua Bright, Emily Campbell, Reshma Desai, Michael Donaldson, Jr., Kate Henning, Alison Hill, Jessica Holman, Kevin Johnson, Rabia Khokhar, Shirley Long, John Mason, Jeannine Necessary, John Nguyen, Asynith Palmer, Matthew Prud'homme, Michael Rebok, Meghan Sullivan, Michael Washington, and Emmiline Weeks. At Georgetown, MA candidate Sarah D. Schotland reviewed the entire manuscript with keen intelligence. Carole Levin was an advisor at an earlier stage, Georgianna Ziegler provided important assistance, and Andrew Hadfield was a generous and sympathetic reader for the press. As ever, best thanks are to my husband Glenn.

Notes on Editorial Practice

Most excerpts are derived from original manuscripts and early printed books. For all, spelling, capitalization, and punctuation have been silently modernized. Sources are indicated with the abbreviations listed below, generally with signature and folio numbers but in a few cases, where rectos and versos are not indicated, by page numbers. Dates are given Old Style, with the new year presumed to start on 1 January.

Unlike other Palgrave Sourcebooks, this volume does not correlate individual documents to specific literary texts. These connections are so many and so rich that they are left to the imaginative engagement of the reader.

List of Abbreviations

BL	British Library
Bodleian	Bodleian Library, Oxford
CCAL	Canterbury Cathedral Archives and Library
CLRO	Corporation of London Record Office*
CUL	Cambridge University Library
ESTC	Eighteenth-Century Short-Title Catalogue of Printed Books, 1701–1800
FSL	Folger Shakespeare Library
GL	Guildhall Library, London
HL	Henry E. Huntington Library
HU	Harvard University Library
Illinois	University of Illinois, Urbana-Champaign Library
Michigan	University of Michigan Library
PROB	Probate Records of the Prerogative Court of Canterbury, National Archives of the United Kingdom
SP	State Papers housed in the National Archives of the United Kingdom
STC	Short-Title Catalogue of Printed Books, 1475–1640
Wing STC	Short-Title Catalogue of Printed Books, 1641–1700

---

* CLRO is closed. Its documents are now held at the London Metropolitan Archives, but at the time of this writing it is unknown whether they will be permanently housed at LMA or at the London Guildhall Library.

Series Editor's Preface

For at least twenty-five years, questions about the relation between literature and the historical period in which it was created have formed the central focus and methodology of critics. From the early 1980s, crucially, a range of literary scholars have sought to explore and define the parallels and differences between the representational language deployed in creative texts, and uses of similar rhetorical strategies in other contemporary cultural sources, such as journals, court documents, diaries, and religious tracts. This kind of historicist reconsideration of literature has had far-reaching consequences in the academy and beyond, and the drive better to understand the dialogue established between texts and their originating period has brought new dynamism to ideas of context and contextualization.

The *Sourcebooks* series aims to provide a comprehensive and suggestive selection of original cultural sources for each of the major artistic moments from the medieval period onward. Edited by internationally renowned British and American experts in their chosen area, each volume presents within suitable subsections a panoply of materials relating to everything from historical background, to gender, philosophy, science, and religion, which will be of use both to students and scholars seeking to contextualize creative work in any given period. It has been a particular ambition of the series to put back into circulation ephemeral original texts from magazines, newspapers, and even private sources, in order to offer a more representative sense of any one period's cultural debates and processes. Literature remains the primary focus of the volumes, but each contains documents relating to the broader artistic and cultural context which will be of interest and use to everyone working in the humanities area.

Each volume contains an informative general Introduction giving an overview of pertinent historical and cultural movements and pressures of its time. Each document is edited to a high scholarly standard through the use of headnotes and other supportive apparatus, in order to make the document accessible for further study. This apparatus is not prescriptive in determining the relation between any one literary text and these background resources, although each volume contains instances where documents directly alluded to by major writers are specifically excerpted. Generally, however, the series seeks to further historicist study and research by making available important or intriguing materials which might act to instigate further thought and reflection, so aiding to determine a more substantial picture of any literary work's moment of coming into being.

Steven Matthews

Timeline of Historical Events

1485 Battle of Bosworth and accession of the first Tudor king, Henry VII.

1489 Yorkshire Rebellion against taxes for war in Brittany.

1497 Cornish Rebellion against taxes for war on Scotland.

1499 Peace treaty between England and Scotland.

1509 Death of Henry VII; Henry VIII becomes king and marries Katherine of Aragon.

1512 Henry VIII declares war on France.

1516 Birth of Princess Mary Tudor.

1521 Pope names Henry VIII "Defender of the Faith" for condemning Luther.

1525 English-language New Testament printed in Germany. Resistance to the Amicable Grant to finance proposed war with France.

1530 English-language Pentateuch (first five books of the Old Testament) printed in Belgium.

1533 Henry VIII divorces Katherine of Aragon and marries Anne Boleyn; birth of Princess Elizabeth Tudor.

1534 Act for the Submission of the Clergy to the King's Majesty; Act Concerning the King's Highness to be Supreme Head of the Church (Act of Supremacy); Act of Succession; Treason Act.

1535 Execution of Sir Thomas More and Bishop John Fisher for refusing the Oath of Succession. Act of Union with Wales.

1536 Act for the Dissolution of the Lesser Monasteries. Death of Katherine of Aragon; beheading of Anne Boleyn; Henry VIII marries Jane Seymour. Pilgrimage of Grace against religious change and economic problems.

1537 Birth of Prince Edward Tudor; death of Jane Seymour. Mathew Bible published.

1538 Pope Paul III excommunicates Henry VIII.

1539 Great Bible published. Act for the Dissolution of the Greater Monasteries.

1540 Henry VIII marries Anne of Cleves; marriage annulled; Henry marries Katherine Howard. Beheading of Thomas Cromwell. Every parish church required to have English-language Bible.

1541 Henry VIII declared King of Ireland and Head of the Irish Church by Dublin Parliament.

1542 Execution of Katherine Howard.

1543 Wales made subject to English law. Henry VIII marries Katherine Parr. Mary Stuart crowned Queen of Scots.

1546 Burning of Anne Askew for heresy.

1547 Act for the Dissolution of the Chantries. Death of Henry VIII; accession of Edward VI with Edward Seymour as Lord Protector. Publication of *The Book of Homilies*.

1549 Act of Uniformity authorizes *Book of Common Prayer*. Western Rebellion against new liturgy. Kett's Rebellion against enclosures.

1550 Act for the Dissolution of Diverse Books and Images, ordering destruction of religious iconography.

1552 Second *Book of Common Prayer*; Second Act of Uniformity.

1553 Death of Edward VI; Jane I declared Queen at the Tower of London; Mary I declared Queen in the City of London. Mary I renounces title of Supreme Head of the English Church. Act of Repeal of Edwardian legislation. Licensing required for all printing.

1554 Wyatt's Rebellion against Mary I. Execution of Thomas Wyatt and Jane Grey; imprisonment of Elizabeth Tudor. Mary I marries Philip of Spain. Royal Injunctions restore Catholic practices.

1556 Execution of Thomas Cranmer. Widespread starvation and illness follow bad harvests.

1557 Burning of Protestants in large numbers. All printing in England to be controlled by the London Stationers' Company.

1558 Death of Mary I; accession of Elizabeth I. Mary of Scotland marries Francis II of France.

1559 Acts of Uniformity and Supremacy; Oath of Supremacy. Restoration of Edwardian Prayer Book.

1560 Treaty of Edinburgh: England and France withdraw from Scotland. Protestantism established as the religion of Scotland. Publication of the Geneva or "Breeches" Bible.

1561 England defeated in Ireland.

1562 John Hawkins begins slave trading.

1563 Welsh translation of the Prayer Book undertaken. Statute of Artificers.

1564 Court of High Commission established in Ireland to enforce conversion to Protestantism.

1566 Birth of Scottish Prince James

Stuart; his widowed mother Mary of Scotland returns from France.

1567   Mary of Scotland abdicates in favor of James VI, with Earl of Moray as Regent.

1569   Rebellion of the Northern Earls on behalf of Mary of Scotland for the English throne. Irish rebellion fails.

1570   Pope excommunicates Elizabeth I, calling on English Catholics to depose her.

1571   Every cathedral and collegiate church required to have Foxe's *Book of Martyrs*.

1572   Treaty of Blois between France and England. Huguenots emigrate to England following St Bartholomew's Day Massacre of Protestants in France. Sir Francis Drake plunders Spanish treasure. Poor Relief Act establishes penalties for vagrancy.

1576   Poor Relief Act establishes workhouses and houses of correction.

1579   Spain sends troops to aid Irish revolt.

1580   Sir Francis Drake circumnavigates the earth.

1581   Act to Retain the Queen's Majesty's Subjects in their True Obedience; Act against Seditious Words and Rumors. James VI dispenses with regent to take control of Scotland.

1583   Throckmorton Plot on behalf of Mary of Scotland for the English throne.

1585   English soldiers aid Dutch resistance of Spain. Founding of Roanoke colony in Virginia. Founding of Cambridge University Press.

1586   Death of Sir Philip Sidney in Flanders, in battle against Spain. Printing restricted to London, Oxford, and Cambridge.

1587   Execution of Mary of Scotland.

1588   Destruction of Spanish Armada in storms at sea.

1590   James VI marries Anna of Denmark.

1592   Act to Retain the Queen's Subjects in Obedience (against Puritan nonconformity); Act against Popish Recusants (against Catholic heretics).

1594   Birth of Prince Henry Stuart of Scotland.

1595   Tyrone's Rebellion in Ireland. Apprentice riots in London. Spanish fleet to aid Irish resistance destroyed in storms at sea.

1596   Grain riots in Kent over bad harvests. Blackamoors expelled. Spanish fleet to Ireland fails. Birth of Princess Elizabeth Stuart of Scotland.

1597   Grain riots spread to Sussex and Norfolk. Spanish fleet to Ireland fails. Act for Relief of the Poor.

1599   Defeat of Essex's army in Ireland. Spanish fleet to Ireland is defeated.

1600   Founding of the East India Company. Birth of Prince Charles Stuart of Scotland.

1601   Execution of the Earl of Essex for rebellion. Spanish fleet assists Irish resistance of England.

1602   Irish resistance defeated.

1603   Death of Elizabeth I; accession of James VI of Scotland. Bye Plot in opposition to recusancy fines. Main Plot on behalf of Arabella Stuart for the English throne. James I proclaimed King of Ireland in Dublin but not Cork.

1604   James VI and I styles himself "King of Great Britain." English and Scottish Parliaments reject union of the countries. Bishops and Puritans clash at Hampton Court Conference. Banishment of Jesuit priests. Treaty of London ends war with Spain.

1605   Gunpowder Plot against James VI and I and Parliament. English Catholics required by Penal Laws to take Oath of Allegiance annually.

1606   Bate's Case confirms the king's right to levy duties without parliamentary consent. Treaty of Paris provides for free trade with France.

1607   Midlands riots against enclo-

sures. Founding of Jamestown colony in Virginia.

1608   Scots born after 1603 are made English subjects. Treaty of The Hague for cooperation with the Dutch Republic.

1609   Henry Hudson names the Hudson River. Sir George Somers shipwrecked in Bermuda. Plantation of Ireland planned.

1610   Commons' Petition on Religion requires James VI and I to enforce recusancy laws. Henry Hudson names Hudson's Bay. Thomas Roe sails up the Amazon. Founding of Newfoundland colony.

1611   Authorized or King James Version of the Bible published.

1612   Death of Prince Henry.

1613   Princess Elizabeth marries Frederick, Elector Palantine. Import of tobacco from Virginia.

1614   John Napier invents logarithms.

1616   Walter Ralegh voyages to Guiana.

1618   *Book of Sports* published. Execution of Walter Ralegh.

1619   Death of Anna of Denmark.

1620   Founding of Plymouth colony.

1623   Treaty of Westminster for trade with Russia. Famine in Scotland.

1624   12,000 Englishmen fail to

restore James VI and I's son-in-law to the Palatinate. Unapproved foreign books on religion banned.

1625 Death of James VI and I; accession of Charles I. Treaty of marriage between Charles I and Henrietta Maria of France calls for England to suspend recusancy laws. Treaties of alliance with Denmark and the United Provinces.

1626 Forced Loan to raise funds for war against Spain.

1627 England defeated in war with France. Colonization of Barbados.

1628 Charles I accepts the Petition of Right. Assassination of the Duke of Buckingham. Founding of colonies in St. Kitts and the Leeward Islands.

1629 Dissolution of Parliament; beginning of Charles I's Personal Rule. Peace treaty with France. Founding of New Hampshire colony. Riots in Dublin against planned closure of all Irish monasteries and Catholic churches.

1630 Birth of Prince Charles Stuart. Treaty of Madrid ends war with Spain.

1632 All newsbooks banned.

1633 Charles I crowned in Scotland. Birth of Prince James Stuart. Republication of *Book of Sports*. Founding of Connecticut colony.

1634 Inland districts required to provide Ship Money to fund coastal protection. Founding of Catholic colony in Maryland.

1636 Founding of Rhode Island colony.

1637 Scottish riots against English Prayer Book. Founding of Maine colony.

1638 Founding of New Haven colony.

1639 Charles I launches First Bishops' War against rebellious ecclesiasts in Scotland.

1640 Second Bishops' War. Scotland invades northern England. Root and Branch Petition to abolish the episcopacy. Founding of sugar plantations in Barbados.

1641 Rebellion of Irish Catholics. Dissolution of Star Chamber.

1642 Charles I retreats to Nottingham Castle. Parliament closes public theaters. First battle of the First Civil War. Treaty of London for peace with Portugal. Defeat of Irish rebellion by English and Scottish troops.

1643 Parliament establishes presbyterian church governance.

1644 John Milton protests press censorship. Scotland gains control of northern English cities.

1645 Founding of New Model Army by Parliament. New Directory of Worship replaces Prayer Book. Execution of Archbishop of Canterbury William Laud.

1646   Charles I surrenders to the Scots. Parliament abolishes archbishops and bishops. Colonization of the Bahamas.

1647   Scots deliver Charles I to English Parliament. Charles I escapes to Isle of Wight.

1648   Second Civil War.

1649   Trial and execution of Charles I. End of the monarchy and House of Lords; England declared a Commonwealth. Oliver Cromwell puts down Irish Rebellion. Colonies declare allegiance to Charles II.

1651   Charles II crowned king in Scotland. Cromwell invades Scotland. Colonization of Surinam.

1652   First Anglo-Dutch War. Barbados, Virginia, Maryland, Ireland submit to Parliament.

1653   Oliver Cromwell named Lord Protector. Expulsion of Catholic priests from Ireland; transportation of Irish vagrants to West Indies.

1654   Treaty of Westminster ends First Anglo-Dutch War. Treaties with Sweden, Portugal, Denmark. England declares Union with Scotland.

1655   Jews readmitted to England. Irish Catholics expelled.

1656   Spain declares war on England.

1657   England and France unite against Spain. Act of Union with Scotland.

1658   Death of Oliver Cromwell. Richard Cromwell named Lord Protector.

1659   Richard Cromwell resigns. End of Protectorate.

1660   Charles II promises religious toleration, restoration of Church of England and the episcopacy, separation of England and Scotland. Monarchy and House of Lords restored by Parliament. Charles II crowned King of England and proclaimed King of Ireland. Reopening of London theaters.

Timeline of Literary Events

1495   *Everyman* performed.

1509   Desiderius Erasmus's *The Praise of Folly* published.

1516   Thomas More's *Utopia* published in Louvain.

1522   John Skelton's *Why Come Ye Not to Court?* published.

1531   Thomas Elyot's *The Book Named the Governour* published.

1548   Edward Hall's *The Union of the Two Noble and Illustre Families of Lancaster and York* published.

1553   Thomas Wilson's *The Art of Rhetoric* published.

1557   *Tottel's Miscellany* published.

1559   *The Mirror for Magistrates* published.

1562   Thomas Sackville and Thomas Norton's *Gorboduc* published.

1563   John Foxe's *Acts and Monuments* published in English.

1567   Arthur Golding's translation of the first four books of Ovid's *Metamorphoses* published.

1573   George Gascoigne's *A Hundreth Sundrie Flowres* published.

1576   The Theatre opened.

1577   The Curtain theater opened.

1578   Raphael Holinshed's *Chronicles of England, Scotland, and Ireland* published.

1579   Stephen Gosson's *The School of Abuse* published.
Thomas North's translation of Plutarch's *Parallel Lives* published.

1580   Edmund Spenser's *The Shepheardes Calendar* published.

1581   Philip Sidney's *Old Arcadia* circulated in manuscript.

1582   Philip Sidney's *Astrophel and Stella* circulated in manuscript.

1583   Philip Sidney's *Apology for Poetry* published.

1587   The Rose theater opened.
Christopher Marlowe's *Tamburlaine* performed.

1589   Edmund Spenser's first books of *The Faerie Queene* published.

1591   John Harington's translation of Ariosto's *Orlando Furioso* published.
        Philip Sidney's *Astrophel and Stella* published.

1592   Thomas Kyd's *The Spanish Tragedy* published.

1593   Philip Sidney's *Countess of Pembroke's Arcadia* published.
        William Shakespeare's *Venus and Adonis* published.
        Christopher Marlowe's *Dr. Faustus* performed.

1594   Richard Hooker's first books *On the Laws of Ecclesiastical Polity* published.
        William Shakespeare's *The Rape of Lucrece* published.
        William Shakespeare's *First Part of the Contention between the Two Famous Houses of York and Lancaster* [*Henry VI, Part 2*] published.

1596   Edmund Spenser's further books of *The Faerie Queene* published.

1597   William Shakespeare's *Romeo and Juliet* published.

1598   Christopher Marlowe's *Hero and Leander* published posthumously.
        George Chapman's partial translation of Homer's *Iliad* published.
        John Stow's *Survey of London* published.

1599   The Globe theater opened.

1600   Michael Drayton's *England's Helicon* published.

1603   William Shakespeare's *Hamlet* published.
        John Florio's translation of Michel de Montaigne's *Essays* published.

1604   William Shakespeare's *Othello* performed.

1605   Francis Bacon's *The Advancement of Learning* published.

1606   Ben Jonson's *Volpone* performed.

1608   William Shakespeare's *King Lear* published.
        William Shakespeare's *Coriolanus* published.
        John Webster's *The White Devil* performed.

1609   William Shakespeare's *Sonnets* published.
        William Shakespeare's *Troilus and Cressida* published.

1610   Ben Jonson's *The Alchemist* performed.

1611   John Donne's *First Anniversary* published.
        Aemilia Lanyer's *Salve Deus Judaeorum* published.
        King James Version of the Bible published.

1612   John Donne's *Second Anniversary* published.

1613   William Shakespeare's *Henry VIII* performed.
       Elizabeth Cary's *Mariam* published.

1614   Ben Jonson's *Bartholomew Fair* published.

1616   Ben Jonson's *Works* published.
       George Chapman's translation of Homer's *Iliad* and *Odyssey* published.

1621   Robert Burton's *The Anatomy of Melancholy* published.
       George Sandys's translation of Ovid's *Metamorphoses* published.

1622   John Webster's *The White Devil* published.

1623   William Shakespeare's *Comedies, Histories, and Tragedies* published posthumously.
       John Webster's *The Duchess of Malfi* published.

1624   Thomas Middleton's *A Game at Chess* performed and banned.

1625   Francis Bacon's third edition of *Essays: Counsels Civil and Moral* published.

1633   John Donne's *Poems* published posthumously.
       George Herbert's *The Temple* published.

1634   John Milton's *Comus* performed.

1638   John Milton's *Lycidas* published.

1640   John Donne's *Eighty Sermons* published.
       Ben Jonson's *Timber* published.

1642   Thomas Browne's *Religio Medici* published.
       All public theaters closed by order of Parliament.

1644   Globe theater demolished by Puritans.

Introduction

The Idea of the Renaissance

The period between the Middle Ages and more modern times was not popularly identified as "the Renaissance" until the nineteenth century. History as we now know it was shaped in 1860, when Jacob Burckhardt, a Swiss academic, published his highly influential *Civilization of the Renaissance in Italy*. The term itself, however, can be traced back as far as 1550, when, in *The Lives of the Most Eminent Italian Architects, Painters, and Sculptors*, the Tuscan artist Giorgio Vasari described "the rise of the arts to perfection, their decline, and their restoration – or rather, renaissance." For Vasari and also for Burckhardt, the classical age of Greece and Rome was a golden one; the medieval years represented a descent into darkness; and the era of Leonardo, Alberti, Brunelleschi, and Michelangelo was a rebirth of creative glory.

Together, Vasari and Burckhardt set out some of the parameters for the way in which we continue to think about western culture. One is the idea of "periodization": that is, that history can be divided into blocks of time, each of which has a unifying character. The process has now accelerated, so that we tend to define the more recent past in terms of decades rather than epochs, but our notions about the late twentieth century, for example, demonstrate some of the problems with this way of conceptualizing history. First, what we regard as the distinguishing elements of "the Sixties" – the sexual revolution, the growth of secularism, distrust of authority – were also present in varying degrees in the 1950s and 1970s. History is full of continuities. Second, many people living in the Sixties practiced sexual restraint, were religious, and honored traditional values. A dominant culture is by no means the only culture, and history is experienced differently by the different people who live through it. Third, all characterizations have connotations which make it difficult for us to retain analytical detachment about history. If we accept an uncomplicated view of the Sixties, then our understanding of the decade tends to be dictated by our subjective attitudes towards sexuality, faith, and convention. "The Renaissance," too, is in all these ways a fraught concept. Vasari, Burckhardt, and Burckhardt's followers were confident of the magnificence of the Renaissance, but they would not have been able to make it seem nearly as splendid had they not also been convinced that the preceding years were "dark" ages. Both representations were over-simplifications.

Vasari wrote the first work of western art criticism, and Burckhardt was a founding figure in the field of art history; in consequence, a leading indicator for the Renaissance has always been the visual arts. What lay behind some of the new achievements in painting was the 1415 development by Brunelleschi of a geometrical method for representing visual perspective. But this was just one of many advances in scientific and mathematical understanding. When these fields are foregrounded, rather than the arts, the later Renaissance can be given the alternate periodizing label of "the Scientific Revolution." For this slice of history, important names include Copernicus, who showed that the earth rotated around the sun; Vesalius, who dissected corpses to study human anatomy; Galileo, who invented the telescope through which he saw the moons of Jupiter; William Harvey, who described the circulation of blood; and Sir Isaac Newton, who experimented with earth's gravity. In this period, when the foremost mathematicians were to be found in the Middle East, mathematical advances came to the West in consequence of increasingly internationalized mercantile trade. These same European searches for new import and export markets also motivated many of the ventures that have given the Renaissance a third name, "the Age of Exploration." This label recognizes the men who found a route from Portugal to India under Vasco da Gama; others who sailed to the Americas, led by Christopher Columbus, Vasco Núñez de Balboa, John Cabot, Ponce de León, and Jacques Cartier; and those who circumnavigated the globe with Ferdinand Magellan and Sir Francis Drake.

Although the Renaissance as conceived by Burckhardt was concentrated in a collection of Italian city states and Vasari focused especially on Florence, many regions throughout Europe contributed to the cultural advances usually associated with this period of "rebirth." Critically, however, in different countries these came at different times. Change occurred first in Italy, and is often associated not only with Vasari's great painters and architects but also with the poets Dante and Petrarch, writing in the thirteenth and fourteenth centuries, and with such fifteenth-century philosophers as Marsilio Ficino, Lorenzo Valla, and Giovanni Pico della Mirandola. From there, new ideas and attitudes spread slowly northwards. England did not experience its own "Renaissance" until the sixteenth and seventeenth centuries. The English Renaissance is so closely tied to the establishment of a national, Protestant church in the 1530s that it carries the fourth periodizing label of "the Age of the Reformation." It proceeded also from the intellectual movement known as "humanism." In a search for truth based in knowledge rather than faith, humanists sought out and translated ancient Greek and Roman texts on the arts, the sciences, and philosophy. The leading humanist Desiderius Erasmus was Dutch, but he spent many years in England and dedicated his most important work, *The Praise of Folly* (1509), to one of his closest friends, an English humanist with an international reputation, Sir Thomas More. For most people the names most indelibly associated with the English Renaissance, however, are those of the great dramatist William Shakespeare, and the queen who ruled England for most of his writing life, Elizabeth I.

Many present-day historians avoid the term "the Renaissance" as a product of nineteenth-century enthusiasm. They prefer the designation "early modern." The two labels can be roughly interchangeable for northern Europe; for Italy, where the creative Renaissance occurred so much earlier, they do not coincide. As a period between the Middle Ages, on the one hand, and the Industrial Revolution, on the other, the "early modern" in England stretches into the eighteenth century. One advantage of the term is that it is readily inclusive of social, economic, and political factors, in addition to the arts. It also suggests that this period was foundational for the common culture of the West, because the traditions and innovations of the "early" modern helped to constitute "modern" life. Literary masterworks are part of the heritage of the early modern, but so, too, are capitalism, the nation-state as we know it, and scientific inquiry. In particular, Anglo-American social identity is often thought to have developed out of the two landmarks of the English Reformation in the sixteenth century and the English Civil Wars of the seventeenth century. One is seen to have led to contemporary notions of selfhood; the other to more participatory government.

Still, the label has its own detractors. To characterize a period as "early" modern is to place priority on the modern. This is one strand of what has been called "presentism": a tendency to define the past in terms of those things which lead to the present, to imagine that these developments happened inexorably and progressively, and thus to suppress the past's alternative realities and possibilities. Revisionist historians, for instance, have emphasized that both the English Reformation and the Civil Wars were far from inevitable. These epochal events depended on countless unpredictable factors that could have come together very differently. Neither our idea of individualism nor our experience of democracy, in other words, was the result of a manifest destiny. Similarly, while the scientific discoveries of the seventeenth century were essential first steps for much contemporary knowledge, it must also be remembered that early modern scientists took many other steps in directions that for our purposes led nowhere. Isaac Newton, for example, has been lastingly influential in the fields of mechanics, gravitation, mathematics, and optics, but he also conducted experiments in alchemy. This project to turn lead into gold seems scarcely to merit the designation of "science" today. Thus, the belief that human history is a matter of steady advancement is false in two senses: it is triumphalist about the present and it is misrepresentative of the past. The past cannot properly be limited to a source of the modern, and so perhaps it should not admit of such colonization as the term "early" modern can imply. It was stranger and less purposive than the label admits.

Today, even scholars who hold profound reservations about periodizing and characterizing history nonetheless acknowledge that the names "Renaissance" and "early modern" continue to have convenience and recognition value in public and academic discourse. With all the reservations noted, this volume, too, employs the familiar terms. But some of the documentary selections that are included here seek to counterbalance the problematic ideas of history these

labels incapsulate. Although many are concerned with the discoveries and
achievements that are customarily emphasized, others demonstrate that the
Renaissance had its dark sides and that the early modern can seem immeasur-
ably remote from the modern. "The past is a different country," wrote the novel-
ist L. P. Hartley in 1953; "they do things differently there."

The State of England

If the past is a different "country," how different was England *as* a country in the
past? How did it locate itself on the world map, for example? One starting point
for the English Renaissance was 1485, when the first of the Tudor monarchs,
Henry VII, took the throne as King of England and France and Lord of Ireland.
At the time there was no "Great Britain": England, Scotland, and Wales
remained separate countries, with England and Scotland often at war. England
had conquered Wales in the thirteenth century, but, because Wales had not
previously figured itself as a sovereign state, it was never listed among the
English monarch's principalities; instead, Wales was acknowledged in the title
"Prince of Wales," for the heir to the throne. The English had insisted on their
right to the French crown from the early fourteenth century, and Henry V had
famously invaded in the early fifteenth, calling himself the "Heir of France" and
marrying a French princess. Their son Henry VI, who succeeded to the throne in
1422, was the only English king to be acknowledged by the French themselves
as their rightful monarch. Thirty-four years later, Henry VI was displaced from
all entitlement in France except for the northernmost French town, Calais; in
1558, Calais, too, was lost. (In 1800, English rulers finally ceased to insist on
their futile claim to the throne of France.)

Henry VII passed the titles of King of France and England and Lord of Ireland
to his son. During Henry VIII's reign, English subordination of Wales continued.
A formal union of the two countries was effected in 1536, and over the course
of the next seven years Welsh law was replaced by English law, Welsh lands were
divided into counties on the English model, and Wales was given a seat in the
English Parliament. By the end of his reign, Henry VIII was also called "King of
Ireland," having been so proclaimed by the Irish Parliament in 1541.

Henry VIII's son Edward VI retained his father's titles as ruler of England,
France, and Ireland. So also did the fourth Tudor to rule, Henry's daughter Mary
I. She then married a Spanish prince, Philip; together, the two of them shared
the style of King and Queen of England, France, Naples, Jerusalem, and Ireland.
With the death of Philip's father a few years later the list came also to include
Spain, Sicily, and eventually Portugal. These political unions were dissolved by
Mary's death in 1558, and Mary's sister Elizabeth I inherited only the native
titles of England, France, and Ireland. The next successor to the English throne
was the King of Scotland, James VI; as King of England he was also known as
James I. Although James VI and I joined two countries in his person, and began

Figure 1 Map of England, from John Speed's *Theatrum Imperii Magnae Britanniae* (1616). Courtesy of The British Library.

In 1616, the "Kingdom of England" included Wales but not Scotland or Ireland. John Speed embellished his map with a chart numbering the cities, bishoprics, market towns, castles, parishes, rivers, bridges, chases, forests, and parks in every English and Welsh "shire," or county. (Both chases and parks were used for hunting, but chases were unfenced and parks were enclosed.) Speed also added marginal illustrations of the costumes appropriate to "A Lady" and "A Nobleman," "A Gentleman" and "A Gentlewoman," "A Citizen's Wife" and "A Citizen" (or city trader), and "A Countryman" and "A Countrywoman."

to call himself King of Great Britain, the formal union of the English and Scottish Parliaments did not occur until 1707.

Throughout this period, there were seeds of the British Empire in Irish rule and New World colonization. But the more important stories of the sixteenth century were domestic ones: the consolidation of monarchic power, the development of a central government staffed by a class of educated professionals, and the growth of nationalism. To a large extent, English identity was a creation of

Henry VIII's reign. Henry had first to deal with the fact that his father had inaugurated Tudor rule in 1485 by deposing the sitting monarch, Richard III. No less an eminence than Thomas More assisted him by writing the *History of King Richard III* (1513), which promulgated the "Tudor myth" that Henry VII had saved the country from an evil despot and restored its virtue. Many English men and women were happy to accept the victor's version of events because the Tudor rebellion put an end to the disastrous thirty-year "War of the Roses," and, by the sixteenth century, had re-established domestic tranquility. More's *Richard III* also demonstrated the ability of written history to effect a common culture. It was succeeded by many other chronicles by authors such as Edward Hall, Raphael Holinshed, and John Stow. Thanks to the development of a printing and publishing industry, these circulated widely.

In the 1530s, Henry VIII faced another crisis of popular opinion when he instituted a Church of England that was independent of papal authority in Rome. This was less a change of doctrine than of leadership. Ironically, Thomas More was put to death for refusing to acknowledge Henry's supremacy in matters spiritual, but with others Henry was successful in making the case that England was for the English, in religion as in politics. Thus, when Henry VIII's Catholic daughter married the powerful prince of Spain and acquired title to so many European lands, this was more a cause for suspicion than a point of pride. Given the prevalent notion that wives were subordinate to their husbands, Mary I's gender aggravated public fears that England would be subjected to Spanish rule. It did not help when she also yielded her ecclesiastical authority to that of the Roman Pope and when Calais fell to the French during her reign. Thirty years after her death, in 1588, her husband sought to conquer England by dispatching his "Invincible Armada" northwards. Much of Elizabeth I's popularity can be credited to the victory of her navy against a foreign enemy, because the shared threat established a common cause. Tudor propaganda and historical chronicles successfully created the idea of England as a proud sovereign nation and world power.

The reigns of the monarchs provide alternative ways of naming the English Renaissance. Henry VII founded the Tudor dynasty in 1485, and the last of the Tudors, Elizabeth I, died in 1603. This "long" sixteenth century, as it can be called, is also known as the Tudor Age. The period is further divisible into the Henrician years, for Henry VIII's rule (1509–47); Edwardian, for Edward VI's (1547–53); Marian, for Mary I's (1553–8); and Elizabethan, for Elizabeth I's (1558–1603). When Elizabeth I died childless, the new family that came to the English throne had the surname Stuart. The Stuart Age lasted from 1603 to 1714. The Stuart reigns that are usually held to coincide with the Renaissance are the Jacobean, for James VI and I (1603–25), and the Caroline, for his son King Charles I (1625–49). Stuart rule was interrupted by the Civil Wars of the 1640s. These have also been called a Revolution, as leading Puritans replaced the monarchy with a parliamentary government.

This way of periodizing can produce a history that is described as "top-down," since it seems to suggest that all the events that are worthy of note originated among those with the greatest power, exerting their influence on everyone below them. Unarguably, many of the phenomena associated with the English Renaissance – the centralization of government, the nationalization of religion, and the politicization of ideology – were products of Tudor and Stuart monarchy. It is a story told in royal proclamations, parliamentary statutes, and other official documents. One concern of this collection, however, is to supplement the state-sponsored texts with some which represent the concerns of early moderns who had less wealth and authority. Life experiences varied significantly by class, gender, region, and other factors. This is why each person's Renaissance was different from any other's, and why those who lived in the provinces as farmers and petty craftsmen seem scarcely to have had a "Renaissance" at all. In a time when literacy was far from universal, voices from below are not always easy to recapture. Alternative genres include private letters, diaries, legal records, and reports of religious dissidence and popular protest.

Taxonomies

"Taxonomy" is another nineteenth-century term, developed in the sciences of botany and zoology for the classification of plants and animals on the basis of their observed relationships. By the 1960s, the word was being used more loosely for other systems of categorical thought, as well. Here, the object is a taxonomy of cultural history. This volume has ten sections covering important fields of knowledge about the English Renaissance: "Key Historical Events," "Society, Economy, and Class," "Families, Gender, and Sexuality," "Religion and Belief," "Philosophy and Ideas," "High Culture," "Everyday Life and Popular Culture," "Literary Production and Reception," "Trade and Exploration," and "Science and Medicine."

The first part, "Key Historical Events," reproduces the political framework outlined above, giving some information about each of the reigns between 1485 and 1642 – that is, from the beginning of the Tudors to the start of the Civil Wars. This way of approaching the period is true to its time in important ways. While one early modern dating system was much like ours, indicating (for example) that the English navy defeated the Spanish Armada in 1588, another, which counted by regnal years, would have specified that the same event took place in 30 Elizabeth I, the thirtieth year of the reign of Elizabeth I. Even though early modern people clearly thought in terms of the reigns of their kings and queens, it may nonetheless seem like a taxonomic mismatch to define Vasari's artistic "Renaissance" in its English context with start points and end points that refer to political events. Burckhardt, however, began *The Civilization of the Renaissance in Italy* with a section on "The State as a Work of Art." The idea that monarchy and statecraft changed in this period, developed a self-consciousness about their roles, their performances, and their propaganda, was always for him a key ingredient in the story of the Renaissance, and many scholars have followed him.

In England, further, the artistic and political spheres intersected at important points. Many of the most remarkable creative achievements were in the drama, and plays developed for such public theaters as the Globe and the Rose were also performed at court and were licensed and censored by government officials. James VI and I was the principal patron for Shakespeare's acting company, who therefore were entitled to call themselves "the King's Men." But the Puritan members of Parliament who took over the government during the Civil Wars, deposing James's son Charles I, also forced all the public theaters to close in 1642. Thus, the stagecraft practiced by Shakespeare and other great writers came to an end along with the monarchic form of government. When the Stuart line was reinstated and the theaters were reopened, in 1660, there was both a different balance of power between king and Parliament and also a new approach to dramatic performance. For just one example, all roles were played by men on the Renaissance stage; after the Restoration, there were female actors, as well. The political and the theatrical institutions of the seventeenth century in this fashion had coincident histories, so that the chapters on "Political Events" and "Literary Production and Reception" are closely related.

This is just one of many ways in which cultural taxonomies are necessarily inexact. As has already been indicated, the visual arts were revolutionized by the introduction of geometry to create the effects of visual perspective. Music, too, was understood to be a mathematical art. For this reason and others, the borders between the categories of "high culture" and of "science and technology" can be difficult to draw. Then there is the impact of "trade and exploration" on "high culture." The lag between southern and northern Renaissances meant that many new ideas about architecture and design came to England from their sources in Italy and France. They were imported along with French wines, Middle Eastern spices, Italian silks, Asian dyes, Russian furs, Spanish swords, and the seeds for such exotic produce as artichokes and asparagus. Around objects which were new to the English market, there developed innovative methods of agriculture and manufacture to reproduce them at home. Thus, "trade and exploration" had a direct effect on "science and technology." The fad for symmetrical façades in elite building was introduced in architectural books written by such Continental authors as Alberti, Serlio, and Palladio, meaning that "high culture" was also a product of "literary production." Leading intellectuals thought actively about the place of learning in public life and the effect of new discoveries on world views, so that "philosophy" was deeply engaged with "society" and "science."

Many of these connections are obvious, and to some extent, of course, taxonomic categories are as much a convenience for organizing knowledge as is the name of "the Renaissance." But other overlaps get to something important about Renaissance society. Every aspect of early modern life, for example, was shaped by "religion and belief." Religion was at the heart of many "key historical events," as Henry VIII established a national Protestant church, Edward VI reformed the liturgy along more strongly Protestant lines, Mary I turned the country Catholic again, Elizabeth I restored Protestantism, and Protestants James VI and I and Charles I sought to contain the militant Puritans who would eventually unseat Stuart rule. Popular religious discourse was preoccupied with the subject of "families, gender, and sexuality," dictating that the purpose of sexual congress was to enlarge the Christian commonwealth, and preaching the proper roles of men and women in rearing observant members of "society." Most "philosophy and ideas," which sought to reconcile classical knowledge with the teachings of the Christian Bible, were informed by religion. The parish church was at the center of "everyday life," as a source for news, community, social discipline, and charity. For some involved in "trade and exploration," the spread of Christian doctrine to other societies was a motivation; for others it was a useful (and much-cited) pretext. To create a category for "religion," thus, is in some ways to misrepresent how pervasive it was in early modern society.

Nor is it possible to extricate "philosophy and ideas" from all other chapters, because ideology informed every sphere of knowledge. So did the technological "science" of movable type, which for some is the single most revolutionary development of the age. It democratized access to knowledge because books in every field could be printed in quantity (instead of handwritten individually) and sold in the public market (rather than being restricted to monastic and university libraries). The topic of an expanding economy comes up in many categories, as well, and so does that of social mobility. In the end, the themes that appear to cut across the categories are those that can be most helpful for developing an idea of what it was that uniquely characterized "the Renaissance." None is more debated than the notion that the Renaissance was midwife to the birth of "the individual."

The Renaissance Subject

Periodization is always retroactive. No one in 1550 read Vasari's *Lives of the Artists* (to give its short title) and was excited to discover himself to be living in "the Renaissance." It is nonetheless of great significance that Vasari and many of his contemporaries felt that they had made a break with those who preceded them. Perhaps what most distinguishes this period from earlier ones is the fact that it seems to have possessed a sense, in its own time, that horizons of expectation had changed in terms of artistic ambition, economic opportunity, scientific possibility, world geography, and human agency.

Many scholars believe that subjectivity as we now know it was discovered – or, some might say, invented – in the Renaissance, providing yet another name for the period as that of the "Rise of Individualism." This is explained in many ways. The new philosophy of learning, known by its practitioners as "humanism," through its very name suggested its commitment to the worth and capability of the earthly individual. Reliance on scientific experimentation and observation, rather than on abstract theory and received ideas, involved direct engagement with the natural world as humanly encountered. The art of perspective sought to reproduce the visual experience of the embodied viewer. The technology of print widened the circle of persons who had access to the forms of interiority nurtured by knowledge. In these ways and more, it appears, value was placed on the individual in unprecedented and transformative ways.

Here, too, there are skeptics. No area of history has been more contaminated with presentism than that dealing with human psychology. In fact, it is not difficult to demonstrate that early modern understandings could be very alien from our own; one need look no further than the dominance of humoral theory in early modern medicine. This was a concept first propounded by the ancient Greek physicians Hippocrates and Galen, and thus, in a time of classical rediscovery, formidably authoritative. The idea was that the body contains four substances: black bile, yellow bile, phlegm, and blood. In the healthy individual, these were believed to be in optimal balance. The cause of every human disease was thought to be humoral imbalance – not infection, organ malfunction, poor nutrition, or any of the conditions we recognize today. Furthermore, the Greek Theophrastus used this medical symptomology as a basis for determining personality types: anyone with a predominance of black bile was described as melancholic; of yellow bile, choleric; of phlegm, phlegmatic; of blood, sanguine. For us, the most foreign aspect of this system of thought is that it acknowledged no separation between mind and body. Neither emotion nor reason was believed to function independently of the material condition of the humors.

Writing plays such as *Every Man Out of His Humor* (1599) and *Every Man In His Humor* (1601), the dramatist Ben Jonson certainly expected his audience to know the basic terms and concepts of humoral theory, but there were also biological discourses that were more esoteric. Some of the most educated and intellectualized medical theoreticians argued, for example, that men and women were anatomically identical, that the female genital organs were inverted versions of the male, and that female organs had failed to descend because women possessed insufficient heat. The "one sex" model of human anatomy was premised on the belief that women were underdeveloped men. This was a medical discourse that operated at a fairly high level of abstraction and at some remove from everyday life.

Vasari, Burckhardt, and indeed most modern scholars have focused upon those aspects of the Renaissance that were products of learning and leisure, both rare commodities in sixteenth- and seventeenth-century life and both more available to wealthy men even than to wealthy women. Some of the prime indicators for early modern subjectivity are located in letters, diaries, and such conduct books as Erasmus's *Education of a Christian Prince* (1516), Baldassare Castiglione's *The Book of the Courtier* (1528), and Sir Thomas Elyot's *Book Named the Governour* (1531). From the titles alone, it is evident that these volumes were intended for the elite readership of rulers and courtiers. The discourses of "the Renaissance" were conducted among a small, highly internationalized group of men living in large cities or at major universities, a world away from the urban craftsmen, provincial farmers, and working women who made up the greater proportion of the early modern population. What does it mean, to define an age in terms of its most privileged persons?

And yet, if there is a case to be made for the democratization of Renaissance ideas, it would be in England. The Reformation was an event of boundless consequence, not only because the religion that was nationalized in England placed so much emphasis on individual responsibility for faith, but also because of the precise way in which the change occurred. First, there were the rapid transitions from Henrician and Edwardian Protestantism to Marian Catholicism and then back to Elizabethan Protestantism – so many changes in so few years that any person of faith, no matter the denomination, was challenged to establish his or her own subjective relationship to spirituality. Second, what motivated the Reformation was what Henry VIII described as a crisis of conscience in his private life. With this, he opened a public dialogue that justified behavior in terms of personal ethics. Both he and his daughter made martyrs of those who were willing to die rather than violate their own religious principles. Third, the disbanding of many Catholic institutions produced a massive realignment of wealth in England, creating unprecedented opportunity for people to rise on the basis of personal merit rather than through heredity.

These were the ways in which England may have had the most broadly based Renaissance of any European country. Many of the authors who are associated with the explosive creativity of the period – William Shakespeare, Edmund Spenser, John Donne, and others – were products of these ingredients for individualism. Like Vasari, they presumably thought they experienced a Renaissance, too. Shakespeare, for example, came from a small Midlands town, received a modest grammar school education, and yet discovered a medium through which he was able to portray human psychology in a fashion that has since found common ground among people of many places and eras. The point of a collection of documents, as opposed to a historian's redaction of them, is to encounter a time long past through the eyes of those for whom, to quote Shakespeare's Miranda, it was a "brave new world" of human experience.

1

Key Historical Events

In *Richard III*, Shakespeare dramatized England's transition from the medieval to the early modern. Civil wars for the throne, conducted among the leading aristocratic families, had begun in 1455. They concluded thirty years later, when the young Henry Tudor defeated King Richard III at the Battle of Bosworth and was crowned King Henry VII. The year 1485 is one of the more important turning points of English history, inaugurating a Tudor line that held the throne until 1603. One of the new royal family's first successes was to employ history itself for propaganda purposes, purveying a "Tudor myth" that the insurgence against Richard III was a national deliverance rather than an act of rebellion. Shakespeare prudently subscribed to this view.

Under the Tudors, the monarchy grew more powerful as an institution. No longer was the king the chief among a collection of powerful noblemen; instead, there emerged a concept of the monarch as supreme head. This change did not occur without controversy and conflict, as the Tudors and then their seventeenth-century successors, the Stuarts, faced revolts against their own authority.

The First Tudor: Henry VII

Henry VII ruled from 1485 to 1509, surviving the Yorkshire Rebellion of 1489 and the Cornish Rebellion of 1497. These uprisings broke out when he demanded subsidies; by law, the king could tax his people only for such extraordinary purposes as war and even then only with the consent of Parliament. In 1496 Henry joined the "Holy League," a coalition of European leaders, headed by Ferdinand of Aragon, who opposed a French invasion of Italy. The "Catholic Kings" of Spain, Ferdinand and his wife Isabella of Castile, are also remembered for funding the voyages of Christopher Columbus.

Henry had already made another strategic alliance with Ferdinand and Isabella. Within two years of the birth in 1486 of his son Arthur, he had begun negotiations to marry the boy to their daughter Katherine. The wedding of Katherine of Aragon and Arthur of England occurred in 1501, but Arthur died unexpectedly in 1502. To preserve the strategic alliance with Spain, Katherine was then pledged to Henry's second son, who had been born in 1491 and who was named for his father. Although Arthur had boasted of his sexual precocity, Katherine insisted her

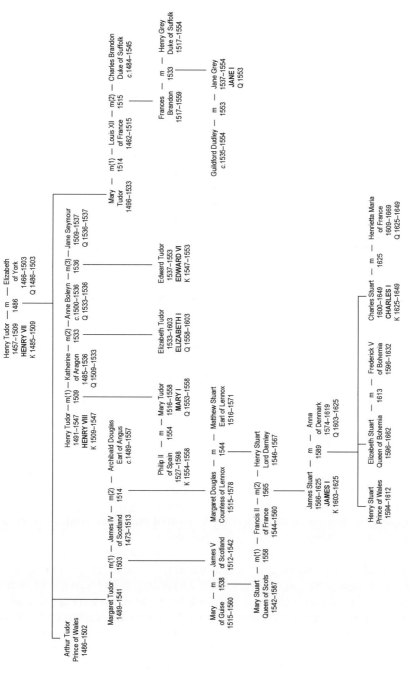

Figure 2 The Tudor and Stuart Monarchs of Renaissance England

first marriage had never been consummated. Otherwise, the wedding to the younger Henry would have been regarded in sixteenth-century terms as incestuous. To be safe, a papal dispensation authorized the new match.

Great Matters: Henry VIII

Henry VII's second son was both crowned king and married in 1509. Within five years, however, Henry VIII began to contemplate an annulment, convinced that the blessing of a son was withheld from him because the marriage to Katherine was invalid. The birth of daughter Mary in 1516 did not reassure him. In 1527 he demanded that the papacy admit its error in having granted the marital dispensation. Unfortunately for Henry, Katherine of Aragon had her own sphere of international influence. Her nephew Charles V was now king of Spain and of the Germanic states known as the Holy Roman Empire. His good will was more important to Pope Clement VII than was that of a ruler in the remote island nation of England. The Vatican procrastinated and finally, for political reasons more than moral or religious ones, in 1533 reconfirmed the sanctity of Henry's marriage.

During the early years of his reign, Henry VIII's principal advisor was the powerful Lord Chancellor, Cardinal Thomas Wolsey. When Wolsey failed to resolve Henry's succession crisis, his era of influence ended. Thomas Cromwell, Earl of Essex, then became the master strategist of what was called the king's "Great Matter." Theorizing that Henry had a royal supremacy not only in state affairs but also in ecclesiastical ones, Cromwell engineered a "Submission of the Clergy" in 1532: he required English churchmen to surrender their legislative and administrative powers to the king. At this, Henry's new Lord Chancellor, Sir Thomas More, resigned in protest. In 1534, Parliament endorsed Cromwell's Act of Supremacy, creating a Church of England that was independent from the Vatican. Both Thomas More and the prominent theologian John Fisher were executed for refusing to pledge loyalty to Henry VIII, rather than the Pope, as their spiritual head. The break with Rome had far-reaching consequences, including the state appropriation of properties that had formerly belonged to England's 800 monasteries, nunneries, and friaries. A rebellion in the northern counties, the Pilgrimage of Grace, failed to halt the royal plunder of church lands, buildings, libraries, and precious art objects.

Had Henry not been so determined to secure a legitimate male heir, he might simply have made Anne Boleyn, the daughter of an English merchant, his mistress. Instead, the couple wed secretly in January 1533, even before Henry's marriage to Katherine was officially annulled in May. Despite intense public hostility, Anne was crowned queen in June. To make room for the child she was expecting, Henry declared Katherine's daughter Mary a bastard. But the baby born to Anne in September was another girl, Elizabeth. When Anne's second child was stillborn, in 1536, Henry concluded that this marriage, too, was cursed. He turned again to Thomas Cromwell for a solution. Charges were manufactured that Anne had committed adultery with a number of men, including her own brother. She and five of her falsely accused lovers were beheaded.

In 1536 Henry married Jane Seymour, the Englishwoman who was finally to provide him with the desired male heir. Edward's legitimacy was indisputable because Katherine of Aragon's death in 1536 preceded his birth in 1537. When Jane died in childbed, another political alliance seemed advisable. Henry agreed to a match with the Princess of Cleves, a small country strategically located between the Netherlands and Germany. He soon convinced himself, however, that Princess Anne's earlier contract with François, Duke of Lorraine, invalidated their union. The 1540 wedding of Henry and Anne was probably unconsummated and was annulled within six months. Anne of Cleves, who would never be permitted to remarry, was given lands, incomes, and the incongruous title "the King's Sister," while Cromwell, who was held responsible for Henry's displeasure, was executed. This created space for the rise of Thomas Cranmer as Henry's third principal advisor. It was Cranmer who secured evidence that Henry's fifth wife, Katherine Howard, committed the crimes of which Anne Boleyn had been unjustly accused six years earlier. Howard was executed in 1542 along with her paramours. Henry married for a final time in 1543 to Katherine Parr, who outlived him.

Some of the turns in Henry's domestic life were matched by realignments in international affairs. Like English kings before him, he claimed title to France. He waged war there twice, in 1512–14 and 1543–6. Generally, Henry could count on Spain to keep France in check, but in 1538 a temporary peace between the superpowers prompted England's search for a new ally through the union with Cleves. The Franco-Spanish truce soon ended, and, with the crisis concerning Katherine of Aragon also past, Charles V was Henry's partner in invading France in 1544. There were persistent hostilities with Scotland: in 1513 the Earl of Surrey turned back Scottish invaders at the Battle of Flodden Field, and in 1536 Scotland again provoked English anxiety by allying with France. England's control over Dublin and adjoining lands led to Henry's being declared King of Ireland in 1541. His most lasting accomplishment was a project to anglicize Wales.

Henry's dying "Order of Succession" was approved by Parliament in 1544. Edward Tudor was, necessarily, first in line to the throne. Next came Edward's potential heirs. Henry then restored his delegitimated daughters, Mary and her heirs followed by Elizabeth and hers. For the rest, he skipped his older sister Margaret, who had married James IV of Scotland, to favor his younger sister Mary's descendants. These included Henry's niece, Frances Grey, and Frances Grey's daughter Jane.

The Boy King: Edward VI

Edward Tudor was nine years old when crowned in 1547. Effectively, the kingdom would be run by his maternal uncle Edward Seymour, Duke of Somerset, who seized the lead over fifteen other members of the Privy Council. Another uncle, Thomas Seymour, jockeyed for power by marrying Henry VIII's widow Katherine Parr and, after her death, courting Henry's daughter Elizabeth Tudor. Although Seymour was executed on fabricated treason charges in 1549, the rivalry between the brothers weakened Somerset's position. So also did two uprisings that summer. Kett's Rebellion protested governmental mismanagement, and the Western Rebellion flared on religious grounds as the Protestant liturgy was instituted. John Dudley, Earl of Northumberland, capitalized on this unrest to take control of the Council, and Somerset was executed in 1552.

Northumberland negotiated peace with France and Scotland, but Edward's 1549 Act of Uniformity in religion provoked an international crisis when England refused Charles V's demand that Mary Tudor be allowed to celebrate the traditional Catholic mass rather than the new Protestant services. In 1553, ill with tuberculosis, Edward subverted Henry VIII's line of succession. Mary's staunch Catholicism was an obvious concern, but Edward also bypassed the Protestant Elizabeth for fear she might marry a Catholic foreign prince. He preferred the as-yet-unborn male descendants of Frances Grey, Duchess of Suffolk. Under the influence of Northumberland, Edward came to favor first the potential "heirs male" of Frances's oldest daughter Jane and then Jane herself. Northumberland arranged for his own Protestant son, Guildford Dudley, to marry Jane Grey. She was to be known as the "Nine Days' Queen."

Bloody Mary: Mary I

Crucially, Parliament did not endorse Edward's "Devise of Succession." Henry VIII's oldest child, Mary Tudor, rallied her supporters and took back the throne in a spectacularly executed coup in 1553. Northumberland was executed; so, too, was the Protestant reformer Thomas Cranmer. At first Mary I showed mercy towards Jane Grey, but, when challenged by Wyatt's Rebellion in 1554, she saw the need to eliminate her contender. Jane I was beheaded. The life of Elizabeth Tudor was spared, even though Mary suspected her half-sister of approving Sir Thomas Wyatt's plot on her behalf. Elizabeth was confined to the Tower and isolated from other potential followers.

Mary I restored Catholicism as the official religion of England and disclaimed her own supremacy by reinstating obedience to the Pope in Rome. Executing more than 300 Protestants for resisting these changes, she became known as "Bloody Mary." England might have remained a Catholic nation had Mary not succumbed to stomach cancer after just five years as queen, or had she produced an heir. This was a preoccupation for her as it had been for her father. In childhood she had been pledged to François I of France, James V of Scotland, and her cousin Charles V of Spain; in 1554, despite parliamentary resistance, she wed Charles's son Philip. She failed to foresee that this marriage would lastingly link Catholicism with foreignness in the popular imagination. Common as political alliances were, in Mary's case her gender provoked alarm that the country might be subjected to alien rule. Although Philip's powers were strictly limited by Parliament, such fears were borne out when Mary dispatched her navy to aid Philip in his Italian wars. More catastrophically for public pride, in 1558 England lost control of Calais, its last foothold in France.

The Virgin Queen: Elizabeth I

Elizabeth Tudor was twenty-five when she came to the throne in 1558. With the "Elizabethan Settlement," the moderate Protestantism of Edward VI was restored. This disappointed some who had wished for a more radically reformed church, but Elizabeth was suspicious of such extremists as the Calvinist John Knox. She was also tolerant of those who maintained Catholic beliefs privately so long as they recognized her political authority publicly; she had no desire, she said, to "make windows into men's souls." Nonetheless, she was confronted with the Rebellion of the Northern Earls, a Catholic rising, in 1569, and was excommunicated by Pope Pius V when she quelled it. The conspirators behind the Ridolfi Plot of 1569–70 aimed to replace Elizabeth with the Catholic queen of Scotland, Mary Stuart, who had been forced to resign her own throne in favor of her son James and who fled to England in 1568. Mary's intended husband, Thomas Howard, Duke of Norfolk, was beheaded in 1572, but Elizabeth refused to execute a kinswoman and sister sovereign until 1587, in the wake of another intrigue on Mary's behalf, the Babington Plot.

Because Elizabeth was the last of the Tudors, there was concern about the succession from the moment she acceded to the throne. Fears flared as she suffered a near-fatal bout of smallpox in 1562 and as she declined each of her many suitors: Philip II of Spain (her sister Mary's widower); James Hamilton, Earl of Arran in Scotland; Erik XIV of Sweden; Ferdinand and Charles, Archdukes of Austria; Henry and Francis, Dukes of Anjou and Alençon in France. The last of these courtships continued into 1581, when Elizabeth's child-bearing years were long past.

Other diplomatic ventures included a truce with Scottish Reformers in 1560 and, after England provided armed aid to French Protestants in 1562, with France in 1564. English forces also supported the Dutch in their Eighty Years War against Spanish occupation. Spain was further provoked by English privateers such as Sir Francis Drake, who preyed on Spanish trading ships. In 1588, Philip II dispatched his "invincible" Armada to England. With the help of bad weather, the English navy defeated the invaders, but war with Spain continued till the end of Elizabeth's reign. Struggles in Ireland climaxed with a rebellion in 1597 that was not put down until 1601.

The first of Elizabeth's personal favorites was Robert Dudley, whom she created Earl of Leicester. Another favorite, Robert Devereux, Earl of Essex, betrayed her by rebelling, unsuccessfully, in 1601. Like her father, Elizabeth was also associated with a number of powerful advisors and administrators, princi-pally including her able Lord Treasurer, William Cecil. Cecil was succeeded by his son Robert. The succession solution favored by Robert Cecil – and allegedly authorized by Elizabeth I on her deathbed – was that the crown should go to James Stuart, a great-great-grandson of Henry VII and son of the Scottish queen whom Elizabeth had executed.

The First Stuart: James VI and I

Born in 1566, Mary Stuart's son was installed as James VI of Scotland when just a year old. After a long period of political instability brought on by a series of regencies and disputes among Scotland's powerful noblemen, James had come into his own around 1581. For leading Englishmen, it was important that James had royal experience, that he had been removed from his Catholic mother's influence as a child and raised as a Protestant, and that by 1603 he was already furnished with two sons. This seemed finally to ensure an orderly succession. Thus he became the first English king to be named James and the first of the Stuart royal family; he is usually referred to as James VI and I for his titles in the two kingdoms of Scotland and England. Parliament rejected his 1607 proposal to unite the countries, which were to remain independent until the eighteenth century. James succeeded, however, in achieving a peace with Spain that lasted between 1604 and 1624; he also made an alliance with France.

James VI and I is remembered less for his advisors than for his male favorites, who included Esme Stuart in Scotland and then, in England, Robert Carr, Earl of Somerset, and George Villiers, Duke of Buckingham. Like Elizabeth I, James disappointed both Catholics and radical Protestants by steering a moderate course in religion. In 1605 he escaped a Catholic assassination attempt, the Gunpowder Plot. He had already dismissed most Puritan petitions at the Hampton Court Conference in 1604, endorsing only the proposal for a new English translation of the Bible. This was to become known as the King James Version.

The Martyr King: Charles I

Henry, the oldest son of James VI and I, predeceased his father in 1612. The second boy, born in 1600, was crowned Charles I in 1625. From the first, Charles was an unpopular figure. His mother, Anna of Denmark, had been raised Lutheran but had converted to Catholicism while married to James. After contemplating marriage to the Catholic infanta of Spain, Charles wed a Catholic princess of France, Henrietta Maria, in his accession year.

Leading members of Parliament were firmly committed to a Protestant nation, and their relationship with Charles deteriorated over a series of financial, political, and religious controversies which in 1642 sparked civil war. The Puritan Oliver Cromwell, holding Charles responsible for the war dead, was eventually persuaded that the execution of "that man of blood" was necessary. Charles was beheaded in January 1649 and Cromwell was named Lord Protector of the English Commonwealth. Although Charles's son was crowned in Scotland in 1650, he soon fled to France. The parliamentary government of the "Interregnum" – the years "between reigns" – ended in 1660, when Charles II finally returned to London in triumph.

Political History

Shakespeare recognized that the history of the monarchy was full of drama. He and other playwrights, poets, and chroniclers have shaped our idea of the royal personalities: Richard III as a murderous usurper, Henry VII as a divinely-sanctioned redeemer, Henry VIII as a serial spouse and frustrated scion, Mary I as a "bloody" executioner, and Elizabeth I as the celebrated "Gloriana." But England's sixteenth- and seventeenth-century succession crises, wars, and rebellions are just three of many themes in these tumultuous reigns. Under each monarch, there were also important stories of trade and exploration, social upheaval and economic advancement, achievements in the arts and literature, and innovations in science and industry. These are the subjects of subsequent chapters.

1.1   Richard III's Proclamation against Henry Tudor (23 June 1485)

From *The Reign of Henry VII from Contemporary Sources*, ed. A. F. Pollard, 3 vols (London: Longmans, Green, 1913–14), 1: 3–6.

This is an excerpt from the statement Richard III issued when he learned of Henry Tudor's rebellion. Although France had an established royal family, English kings claimed sovereignty there, and one of Richard's accusations was that Henry had ceded English rights to the French king in order to secure his support. Richard also argued that Henry was a bastard, that he had no right to the throne, that he would redistribute the lands of the church and the nobility, and that he posed an immediate and personal danger to the lives and goods of every English man and woman.

To the intent that the said Henry Tudor might the rather achieve his false intent and purpose by the aid, support, and assistance of the King's said ancient enemy of France, he hath covenanted and bargained with him and all the Council of France to give up and release in perpetuity all the right, title, and claim that the kings of England have, had, and ought to have to the crown and realm of France.

. . . The said Henry Tudor and others the King's rebels and traitors aforesaid have extended [*intended*] at their coming, if they may be of power, to do the most cruel murders, slaughters, and robberies and disinheritances that ever were seen in any Christian realm.

For the which and other inestimable dangers to be eschewed, and to the intent that the King's said rebels, traitors, and enemies may be utterly put from their said malicious and false purpose and soon discomfited [*defeated*], if they enforce to land [*invade*], the King our Sovereign Lord willeth, chargeth, and commandeth all and every [*each*] of the natural and true subjects of this his realm to call the premises [*aforementioned matters*] to their minds, and like good and true Englishmen to endeavor themselves with all their powers for the defense of them, their wives, children, and goods and hereditaments [*properties*] against the said malicious purposes and conspiracies which the said ancient enemies have made with the King's said rebels and traitors for the final destruction of this land.

1.2 Henry Tudor's Speech at the Battle of Bosworth (22 August 1485)

From Edward Hall, *The Union of the Two Noble and Illustrate Families of Lancaster and York* (1548), STC 12721 (HL copy), kk1ᵛ–kk2ʳ.

The decisive point in Henry Tudor's insurrection was the Battle of Bosworth. Henry rallied his troops by repeating the rumor that Richard III had murdered his brother Clarence and his nephews Edward and Richard (all of whom had been ahead of him in the line of royal succession). Henry also alleged that Richard's soldiers were forcibly conscripted. By the end of the battle, King Richard III was dead and the rebel was able to claim the title of King Henry VII.

If ever God gave victory to men fighting in a just quarrel, or if he ever aided such as made war for the wealth and tuition [*safe-keeping*] of their own natural and nutritive country, or if he ever succored them which adventured their lives for the relief of innocents, suppressing of malefactors and apparent offenders – no doubt, my fellows and friends, but he of his bountiful goodness will this day send us triumphant victory and a lucky journey over our proud enemies and arrogant adversaries. For if you remember and consider the very cause of our just quarrel, you shall apparently [*clearly*] perceive the same to be true, godly, and virtuous. In the which I doubt not but God will rather aid us, yea, and fight for us, than see us vanquished and profligate [*overthrown*] by such as neither fear him nor his laws nor yet regard justice or honesty. Our cause is so just that no enterprise can be of more virtue both by the laws divine and civil, for what can be a more honest, goodly, or godly quarrel than to fight against a captain being an homicide and murderer of his own blood and progeny, an extreme destroyer of his nobility, and to his and our country and the poor subjects of the same a deadly mall [hammer], a fiery brand, and a burden untolerable? . . . I assure you that there be yonder in that great battle men brought thither for fear and not for love, soldiers by force compelled and not with good will assembled, persons which desire rather the destruction than salvation of their master and captain, and, finally, a multitude whereof the most part will be our friends and the least part our enemies. For truly I doubt which is greater, the malice of the soldiers toward their captain or the fear of him conceived of his people. For surely this rule is infallible: that as ill men daily covet to destroy the good, so God appointeth the good to confound the ill, and of all worldly goods the greatest is to suppress tyrants and relieve innocents, whereof the one is ever as much hated as the other is beloved.

1.3 Henry VIII's Letter to Pope Clement VII (1532)

From BL Ms Harleian Vitellius B.13:168, edited by Gilbert Burnet, *The History of the Reformation of the Church of England* (1681), Wing STC B5798 (HL copy), 108–10.

In 1521, when Henry VIII wrote a book condemning Martin Luther, Pope Leo X named him "Defender of the Faith." By 1528, relations between England and the Vatican had deteriorated dramatically. Pope Clement VII dispatched his legate, Lorenzo Campeggio, to review the "Great Matter" of Henry's desire for a divorce. Campeggio reported back that "if an angel was to descend from heaven, he would not be able to persuade" Henry that the marriage to Katherine of Aragon was valid. Knowing that the Church stood to lose either England or Spain in this controversy, Campeggio eventually adjourned the commission without reaching a decision. Indignant to have been denied his hearing, Henry wrote to Clement, insisting on his right of conscience.

Never was there any prince so handled by a pope as Your Holiness hath entreated [treated] us. First, when our cause was proposed [presented] to Your Holiness, when it was explicated and declared afore the same, when certain doubts in it were resolved by your counselors and all things discussed, it was required that answer might be made thereunto by the order of the law. There was offered a commission, with a promise also that the same commission should not be revoked and whatsoever sentence should be given should straight without delay be confirmed. The judges were sent unto us, the promise was delivered to us, subscribed with Your Holiness' hand, which avouched to confirm the sentence and not to revoke the commission nor to grant anything else that might let [hinder] the same. And finally, to bring us in a greater hope, a certain commission decretal [by papal decree], defining the cause, was delivered to the judges' hands. If Your Holiness did grant us all these things justly, ye did injustly revoke them, and if by good and truth the same was granted, they were not made frustrate nor annihilate without fraud. So as if there were no deceit nor fraud in the revocation, then how wrongfully and subtly have been done those things that have been done! Whether will Your Holiness say that ye might do those things that ye have done, or that ye might not do them? If ye will say that ye might do them, where then is the faith which becometh a friend, yea, and much more a pope to have, those things not being performed which lawfully were promised? And if ye will say that ye might not do them, have we not then very just cause to mistrust those medicines and remedies with which, in your letters, ye go about to heal our conscience, especially in that we may perceive and see those remedies to be prepared for us not to relieve the sickness and disease of our mind but for other means, pleasures, and worldly respects? And as it should seem profitable that we should ever continue in hope or despair, so always the remedy is [attempered],[1] so that we being always a-healing, and never healed, should be sick still.

And this truly was the chief cause why we did consult and take the advice of every learned man, being free, without all affection [*any partiality*], that the truth (which now with our labor and study we seem partly to have attained) by their judgments more manifestly divulged, we might more at large perceive. Whose judgments and opinions it is easy to see how much they differ from that that those few men of yours do show unto you, and by those your letters is signified. . . . Now the universities of Cambridge, Oxford, in our realms; Paris, Orléans, Bituricen [*Bourges*], Andegaven [*Angers*], in France; and Bonony [*Bologna*] in Italy by one consent (and also diverse other of the most famous and learned men, being freed from all affection, and only moved in respect of verity, partly in Italy and partly in France) do affirm the marriage of the brother with the brother's wife to be contrary both to the law of God and nature, and also do pronounce that no dispensation can be lawful or available to any Christian man in that behalf. . . .

No princes heretofore have more highly esteemed nor honored the See Apostolic [*papacy*] than we have, wherefore we be the more sorry to be provoked to this contention, which to our usage and nature is most alienate and abhorred. Those things so cruel we write very heavily, and more glad would have been to have been silent if we might, and would have left your authority untouched with a good will. And, constrained to seek the verity, we fell, against our will, into this contention. But the sincerity of the truth prohibited us to keep silence, and what should we do in so great and many perplexities? For truly if we should obey the letters of your holiness, in that they do affirm that we know to be otherwise, we should offend our God and our conscience, and we should be a great slander to them that do the contrary, which be a great number as we have before rehearsed.

---

1 [*attempered*]: adulterated.

. . . God is the truth to whom we are bound to obey rather than to men, and nevertheless we cannot but obey unto men also, as we were wont to do, unless there be an express cause why we should not, which by those our letters we now do to Your Holiness. And we do it with charity, not intending to spread it abroad nor yet further to impugn your authority, unless ye do compel us.

1.4 An Act Concerning the King's Highness to be Supreme Head of the Church of England (3 November 1534)

From *Acts Made in the Session of this Present Parliament* (1534), STC 9386 (BL copy), A2ʳ.

Henry VIII's wish to divorce Katherine of Aragon came to be linked with other English interests, such as distrust for the power and wealth of the Catholic Church, sympathy for Protestant reforms taking place on the Continent, and the mounting nationalism to which this statute explicitly appeals in rejecting "foreign laws" and "foreign authority." The authority was that of the papacy itself, with Henry's succession crisis leading to a religious and political revolution that inseparably conjoined the English church and the English state, independent of Rome. The king sought validation elsewhere, in Parliament, which passed this statute known as the Act of Supremacy. Previously, heresy had involved theological opinions or doctrines that differed from those of the established church; now, it encompassed opposition to the will of the monarch.

Albeit the King's Majesty justly and rightfully is and oweth [*ought*] to be the supreme head of the Church of England, and so is recognized by the clergy of this realm in their Convocations, yet nevertheless for corroboration and confirmation thereof, and for increase of virtue in Christ's religion within this realm of England, and to repress and extirp [*root out*] all errors, heresies, and other enormities [*transgressions*] and abuses heretofore used in the same, be it enacted by authority of this present Parliament that the King our sovereign lord, his heirs and successors, kings of this realm, shall be taken, accepted, and reputed the only supreme head in earth of the Church of England called *Anglicana Ecclesia*, and shall have and enjoy annexed and united to the imperial crown of this realm as well the title and style thereof, as all honors, dignities, pre-eminences, jurisdictions, privileges, authorities, immunities, profits, and commodities [*benefits*] to the said dignity of supreme head of the same Church belonging and appertaining. And that our said sovereign lord, his heirs and successors, kings of this realm, shall have full power and authority from time to time to visit, repress, redress, reform, order, correct, restrain, and amend all such errors, heresies, abuses, offenses, contempts, and enormities, whatsoever they be, which by any manner, spiritual authority, or jurisdiction ought or may lawfully be reformed, repressed, ordered, redressed, corrected, restrained, or amended, most to the pleasure of Almighty God, the increase of virtue in Christ's religion, and for the conservation of the peace, unity, and tranquility of this realm – any usage, custom, foreign laws, foreign authority, prescription, or any other thing or things to the contrary hereof notwithstanding.

1.5   Edward VI's Chronicle (1547–52)

From BL Ms Cotton Nero C.x, edited by Gilbert Burnet, *The History of the Reformation of the Church of England* (1681), Wing STC B5798 (HL copy), 36–7, 39, 41–2, 45.

As tutor to the third Tudor, the famous humanist Sir John Cheke recommended regular writing to develop communications skills and personal discipline. Cheke thus inspired the first surviving royal diary. By the time Edward VI was twelve, he was recording information about matters of state, international relations and diplomacy, English coinage and the problem of inflation – and also Sir Thomas Palmer's allegations that Edward Seymour, Duke of Somerset, planned to assassinate John Dudley, Earl of Warwick, and William Parr, Marquess of Northampton, as a prelude to seizing the Tower of London and raising a rebellion. In 1551, Edward VI dispassionately noted daily revelations about the widening circle of alleged conspirators associated with the man who had been named Protector of the Realm during his minority, his uncle Edward Seymour. The Earl of Warwick, soon to be named Duke of Northumberland and increasingly Edward VI's most trusted advisor, was the man who stood to benefit from the fall of Somerset.

7 October.   Sir Thomas Palmer came to the Earl of Warwick [and] in my Lord's garden he declared [*revealed*] a conspiracy. How at St. George's Day[2] last, my Lord of Somerset . . . went to raise the people [*instigate a rebellion*], and the Lord Grey went before to know who were his friends. Afterward, a device [*plot*] was made to call the Earl of Warwick to a banquet with the Marquess of Northampton and diverse others and to cut off their heads. Also, [if] he found a bare [*unarmed*] company about them by the way, to set upon [*attack*] them.

11 October.   He declared also that Master Vane had 2,000 men in readiness. Sir Thomas Arundel had assured my Lord that the Tower was safe. Master Partridge should raise London and take the Great Seal[3] with the apprentice[s] of

---

2 *St. George's Day*: 23 April, the feast day of the patron saint of England. Catholic saints' days were still commonly referenced in Protestant England.
3 *Great Seal*: A principal symbol of the monarchy and instrument of office, the seal was a metal disk engraved on one side with an image of the enthroned sovereign and on the other with an image of the ruler on horseback. It was used to make impressions on the lumps of wax with which state documents of the highest importance were authenticated.

London.[4] Seymour and Hammond should wait upon him, and all the horse of the gendarmes [*cavalrymen*] should be slain.

14 October.   The Duke [of Somerset] sent for the Secretary Cecil[5] to tell him he suspected some ill. Master Cecil answered that if he were not guilty he might be of good courage; if he were, he had nothing to say but to lament him. Whereupon the duke sent him a letter of defiance and called Palmer who, after denial made of his declaration, was let go.

16 October.   This morning none was at Westminster of the conspirators. The first was the Duke [of Somerset], who came, later than he was wont [*accustomed to*], of himself. After dinner he was apprehended. Sir Thomas Palmer [was taken] on the terrace, walking there. Hammond, passing by Master Vice-Chamberlain's door, was called in by John Piers to make a match at shooting, and so taken. Newdigate was called for as from my Lord his master and taken. Likewise were John Seymour and David Seymour. Arundel also was taken, and the Lord Grey, coming out of the country. Vane, upon two sendings [*summonses*] of my Lord in the morning, fled at the first sending; he said my Lord was not stout [*valiant*], and if he could get home he cared for none of them all, he was so strong. But he was found by John Piers in a stable of his man's at Lambeth, under the straw. These went with the Duke to the Tower this night, saving Palmer, Arundel, and Vane, who were kept in chambers here, apart.

17 October.   The Duchess [of Somerset], Crane and his wife, with the chamber keeper, were sent to the Tower for devising these treasons; James Wingfield also, for casting of bills seditiously. Also Master Partridge was attached [*arrested*] and Sir James Holcroft.

18 October.   Master Bannister and Master Vaughan were attached and sent to the Tower, and so was Master Stanhope.

19 October.   Sir Thomas Palmer confessed that the gendarmes on the muster day should be assaulted by 2,000 footmen of Master Vane's, and my Lord's hundred horse, besides his friends which stood by and the idle people which took his part. If he were overthrown he would run through London and cry "Liberty, liberty," to raise the apprentices. . . . If he could, he would go to the Isle of Wight or to Poole.

[26 October].   Crane confessed the most part, even as Palmer did before, and more also; how that the place where the nobles should have been banqueted and their heads stricken off was the Lord Paget's house, and how the Earl of Arundel knew of the matter as well as he, by Stanhope who was a messenger between them. Also some part how he went to London to get friends once in August last, feigning himself sick. Hammond also confessed the watch he kept in his chamber at night. Brend also confessed much of this matter. The Lord Strange

---

4 *apprentices of London*: Young men training to learn a craft were thought to be quick to assemble and riot.

5 *Secretary Cecil*: William Cecil, one of Somerset's two leading secretaries, prudently realigned himself with the Duke of Northumberland and survived to become Elizabeth I's principal minister.

confessed how the Duke [of Somerset] willed him to stir me to marry his third daughter, the Lady Jane,[6] and willed him to be his spy in all matters of my doings and sayings and to know when some of my Council spoke secretly with me. This he confessed of himself.

1 December. The Duke of Somerset came to his trial at Westminster Hall. . . . The lawyers rehearsed how to raise men at his house for an ill intent (as to kill the Duke of Northumberland[7]) was treason, by an act (Anno Tertio of my reign[8]) against unlawful assemblies, for to devise the death of the lords was felony. To mind [*plan for*] resisting his attachment was felony, to raise London was treason, and to assault the lords was felony. He answered he did not intend to raise London and swore that the witnesses were not there. His assembling of men was but for his own defense. He did not determine to kill the Duke of Northumberland, the Marquess [of Northampton], etc., but spoke of it and determined, after, the contrary – and yet seemed to confess he went about their death. . . . The Lords acquitted him of high treason and condemned him of treason felonious, and so he was adjudged to be hanged.

22 January. The Duke of Somerset had his head cut off upon Tower Hill between eight and nine o'clock in the morning.[9]

1.6 Mary Tudor's Letter to Members of Edward VI's Privy Council (9 July 1553)

From *The History of Mary I, Queen of England, as Found in the Public Records*, ed. J. M. Stone (London: Sands, 1901), 220–1.

When she received word of her brother's death on 6 July 1553, Mary fled to a safe haven in Norfolk and from there wrote to the most powerful men in England. She employed the royal "we" to make her royal claim. Edward's Privy Councillors replied that Mary was "illegitimate and unheritable" in consequence of her mother's divorce, and John Dudley, Duke of Northumberland, set out with a small army to capture her. In his absence from London, however, the scheme to replace Mary with Jane Grey unraveled. Mary had shrewdly sent copies of her letter to many others, and her statement of intent aroused widespread support. She was proclaimed queen on 19 July.

My lords,
    We greet you well and have received sure advertisement that our dearest

---

6 *Lady Jane*: Somerset's daughter, Jane Seymour (not Northumberland's daughter, Jane Grey).

7 *Duke of Northumberland*: John Dudley, Earl of Warwick, was made Duke of Northumberland on 11 October 1551.

8 *Anno Tertio of my reign*: in the third year of the reign of Edward VI.

9 Sir Thomas Arundel, Sir Miles Partridge, Sir Michael Stanhope, and Sir Ralph Vane were also executed.

brother the King our late sovereign lord is departed to God's mercy. Which news, how woeful they be unto our heart, he only knoweth to whose will and pleasure we must and do humbly submit us and our wills.

But in this so lamentable a case, that is, to wit, now after His Majesty's departure and death, concerning the crown and governance of this realm of England with the title of France and all things thereto belonging, what hath been provided by Act of Parliament and the testament and last will of our dearest father (beside other circumstances advancing our right), you know, the realm and the whole world knoweth. The rolls and records appear by the authority of the King our said father and the King our said brother and the subjects of this realm, so that we verily trust that there is no true good subject that is, can, or would pretend to be ignorant thereof. And of our part, we have of ourselves caused and, as God shall aid and strengthen us, shall cause our right and title in this behalf to be published and proclaimed accordingly.

And, albeit this so weighty a matter seemeth strange, that our said brother, dying upon Thursday at night last past, we hitherto had no knowledge from you thereof, yet we consider your wisdom and prudence to be such that having eftsoons [afterwards] amongst you debated, pondered, and well weighed this present case with our estate, with your own estate, the commonwealth, and all our honors, we shall and may conceive great hope and trust with much assurance in your loyalty and service, and therefore for the time interpret and take things not to the worst and that ye will, like noblemen, work the best.

Nevertheless, we are not ignorant of your consultations to undo the provisions made for our preferment, nor of the great bands and provisions forcible wherewith ye be assembled and prepared – by whom and to what end God and you know, and nature can but fear some evil. But be it that some consideration politic, or whatsoever thing else hath moved you thereto, yet doubt you not, my lords, but we can take all these your doings in gracious part, being also right ready to remit and fully pardon the same, and that freely, to eschew bloodshed and vengeance against all those that can or will intend the same. Trusting also assuredly you will take and accept this grace and virtue in good part as appertaineth, and that we shall not be enforced to use the service of other our true subjects and friends which in this our just and right cause God, in whom our whole affiance [confidence] is, shall send us.

Wherefore, my lords, we require you and charge you, and every [each] of you, that of your allegiance which you owe to God and us and to none other, for our honor and the surety of our person, only employ yourselves and forthwith upon receipt hereof cause our right and title to the crown and governance of this realm to be proclaimed in our city of London and other places as to your wisdom shall seem good and as to this case appertaineth, not failing hereof, as our very trust is in you. And this our letter signed with our hand shall be your sufficient warrant in this behalf.

1.7   Elizabeth I's First Speech to Parliament (10 February 1559)

Version One from BL Ms Lansdowne 94, 14: 29; Version Two from William Camden, *Annals: The True and Royal History of the Famous Empress Elizabeth Queen of England, France, and Ireland* (1625), STC 4497 (HL copy), E2ʳ–E3ʳ.

Three months after Mary I died, the new queen responded to parliamentary requests that she marry immediately for the sake of an orderly succession. Elizabeth took the occasion to formulate a view of the balance of her power with Parliament's. One version of her speech is gathered from contemporary manuscript transcriptions (which themselves have slight variations). The second was recorded by the antiquarian William Camden, who translated Elizabeth's words into Latin in 1615 and then back into English (as given below) in 1625. Camden had the benefit of hindsight, knowing, as no one in 1559 believed, that Elizabeth was to fulfill this very early profession of lifelong virginity.

Version One

As I have good cause, so do I give you all my hearty thanks for the good zeal and loving care you seem to have, as well towards me as to the whole state of your country. Your petition, I perceive, consisteth of three parts, and mine answer to the same shall depend of two.

And to the first part, I may say unto you that from my years of understanding, sith [*since*] I first had consideration of myself to be born a servitor[10] of almighty God, I happily chose this kind of life in which I yet live – which I assure you for mine own part hath hitherto best contented myself and I trust hath been most acceptable to God. From the which, if either ambition of high estate offered to me in marriage by the pleasure and appointment of my prince[11] (whereof I have some records in this presence, as you our Lord Treasurer[12] well know); or if the eschewing [*escaping*] of the danger of mine enemies; or the avoiding of the peril of death, whose messenger, or rather continual watchman, the prince's indignation,[13] was not little time daily before mine eyes (by whose means although I know, or justly may suspect, yet I will not now utter); or if the

---

10 *servitor*: The dual meaning of this word – servant and also assistant – was undoubtedly intended.
11 *prince*: It was common for the English monarch to be referred to as a "prince." Using the title for her sister, Elizabeth made her own claim for a royal status undiminished by gender.
12 *Lord Treasurer*: William Paulet, first Marquess of Winchester, replaced Edward Seymour, Duke of Somerset, as Lord Treasurer in 1550 and continued in that position through the remainder of Edward VI's reign, the whole of Mary I's reign, and the first fourteen years of Elizabeth I's reign (dying in office).
13 *the prince's indignation*: Elizabeth alludes to the dangers she encountered as a princess; according to Proverbs 16:14, "the prince's indignation is death."

whole cause were in my sister herself (I will not now burden her therewith, because I will not charge the dead) – if any of these, I say, could have drawn or dissuaded me from this kind of life, I had not now remained in this estate wherein you see me. But so constant have I always continued in this determination. Although my youth and words may seem to some hardly to agree together, yet it is most true that at this day I stand free from any other meaning that either I have had in times past or have at this present. With which trade [way] of life I am so thoroughly acquainted that I trust God, who hath hitherto therein preserved and led me by the hand, will not now of his goodness suffer me to go alone.

For the other part, the manner of your petition I do well like of and take in good part, because that it is simple and containeth no limitation of place or person. If it had been otherwise, I must needs have misliked it very much and thought it in you a very great presumption, being unfitting and altogether unmeet for you to require them that may command, or those to appoint whose parts are to desire,[14] or such to bind and limit [restrict] whose duties are to obey, or to take upon you to draw my love to your likings or frame my will to your fantasies. For a guerdon [reward] constrained and a gift freely given can never agree together.

Nevertheless, if any of you be in suspect [suspicious] that, whensoever it may please God to incline my heart to another kind of life, ye may well assure yourselves my meaning is not to do or determine anything wherewith the realm may or shall have just cause to be discontented. And therefore put that clean out of your heads. For I assure you – what credit my assurance may have with you I cannot tell, but what credit it shall deserve to have, the sequel shall declare – I will never in that matter conclude anything that shall be prejudicial to the realm, for the weal [welfare], good, and safety whereof I will never shun to spend my life. And whomsoever my chance shall be to light upon, I trust he shall be as careful for the realm and you – I will not say as myself, because I cannot so certainly determine of any other – but, at the leastways, by my good will and desire he shall be such as shall be as careful for the preservation of the realm and you as myself.

And albeit it might please almighty God to continue me still in this mind to live out of the state of marriage, yet it is not to be feared but he will so work in my heart and in your wisdoms as good provision by his help may be made in convenient time, whereby the realm shall not remain destitute of an heir that may be a fit governor and peradventure more beneficial to the realm than such offspring as may come of me. For although I be never so careful of your well-doings – and mind [intend] ever so to be – yet may my issue grow out of kind[15]

---

14 *unmeet for you to require them that may command, or those to appoint whose parts are to desire*: improper for you to make demands of them who may command, or those to ordain whose roles are to entreat.

15 *kind*: Here, the character derived from birth and descent; in other words, any child Elizabeth might have would not necessarily breed true or prove an equally fit ruler.

and become, perhaps, ungracious. And in the end this shall be for me sufficient: that a marble stone shall declare that a queen, having reigned such a
time, lived and died a virgin. And here I end, and take your coming unto me
in good part, and give unto you all eftsoons [*again*] my hearty thanks, more yet
for your zeal and good meaning than for your petition.

Version Two

"In a thing which is not much pleasing unto me, the infallible testimony of your
good will and all the rest of my people is most acceptable. As concerning your
instant [*urgent*] persuasion of me to marriage, I must tell you I have been ever
persuaded that I was born by God to consider and, above all things, do those
which appertain unto his glory. And therefore it is that I have made choice of
this kind of life which is most free and agreeable for such human affairs as may
tend to his service only. From which, if either the marriages which have been
offered me by diverse puissant [*powerful*] princes or the danger of attempts made
against my life could no whit divert me, it is long since I had any joy in the
honor of a husband. And this is that I thought, then [*when*] that I was a private
person. But when the public charge of governing the kingdom came upon me,
it seemed unto me an inconsiderate folly to draw upon myself the cares which
might proceed of marriage. To conclude, I am already bound unto an husband,
which is the kingdom of England, and that may suffice you. And this," quoth
she, "makes me wonder that you forget, yourselves, the pledge of this alliance
which I have made with my kingdom." And therewithal, stretching out her
hand, she showed them the ring with which she was given in marriage and inaugurated to [*installed in*] her kingdom in express [*explicit*] and solemn terms. "And
reproach me so no more," quoth she, "that I have no children, for every one of
you and as many as are English are my children and kinsfolks, of whom, so long
as I am not deprived and God shall preserve me, you cannot charge me, without
offense, to be destitute.

"But in this I must commend you, that you have not appointed me an
husband. For that were unworthy the majesty of an absolute princess[16] and the
discretion of you that are born my subjects. Nevertheless, if God have ordained me
to another course of life, I will promise you to do nothing to the prejudice of the
commonwealth, but, as far as possible I may, will marry such an husband as shall
be no less careful for the common good than myself. And if I persist in this which
I have proposed unto myself, I assure myself that God will so direct my counsels
and yours that you shall have no cause to doubt of a successor which may be more

---

16 *absolute princess*: This construction undoubtedly reflects the seventeenth-century date of its composition, for "absolute," meaning unlimited by any constitution or parliament, was a term used
unapologetically by the Stuarts, and Elizabeth customarily referred to herself as a "prince" (not a
"princess").

profitable for the commonwealth than him which may proceed from me, sithence [*since*] the posterity of good princes doth oftentimes degenerate.

"Lastly, this may be sufficient both for my memory and honor of my name, if, when I have expired my last breath, this may be inscribed upon my tomb: 'Here lies interred Elizabeth, a virgin pure until her death.' "

1.8 Elizabeth I's Speech to Parliament regarding Mary of Scotland (12 November 1586)

From BL Ms Lansdowne 94, 35b: 84–5.

On 14 October 1586 Mary Stuart was found guilty of treason. Parliament petitioned that she be put to death "for the continuance of the Christian religion, quiet of the realm, and safety of Her Majesty's most royal person." In this excerpt from the first of two addresses on the subject, Elizabeth demonstrates her reluctance to endorse Parliament's request. During her trial Mary had insisted "that she was no subject, and rather would she die a thousand deaths than acknowledge herself a subject." Whatever Elizabeth's personal feelings about her distant cousin, politically she recognized Mary as a sister sovereign and upheld the prerogatives of sovereignty. Finally, on 1 February 1587 Elizabeth yielded and signed the warrant of execution.

Albeit I find my life hath been full dangerously sought and death contrived by such as no desert procured it, yet am I thereof so clear from malice (which hath the property to make men glad at the falls and faults of their foes and make them seem to do for other causes when rancor is the ground) yet I protest it is and hath been my grievous thought that one not different in sex, of like estate, and my near kin should be fallen into so great a crime. Yea, I had so little purpose to pursue her with any color of malice that as it is not unknown to some of my lords here (for now I will play the blab), I secretly wrote her a letter upon the discovery of sundry treasons, that if she would confess them and privately acknowledge them by her letters unto myself, she never should need be called for them into so public question. Neither did I it of mind to circumvent [*entrap*] her, for then I knew as much as she could confess, and so did I write. And if even yet, now the matter is made but too apparent, I thought she truly would repent . . . I would most willingly pardon and remit this offense. . . .

I have had good experience and trial of this world: I know what it is to be a subject, what to be a sovereign, what to have good neighbors, and sometimes meet evil willers. I have found treason in trust, seen great benefits little regarded, and, instead of gratefulness, courses of purpose to cross.[17] These former remembrances,

---

17 *courses of purpose to cross*: actions or practices intended to thwart or oppose.

present feeling, and future expectation of evils, I say, have . . . taught me to bear with a better mind these treasons than is common to my sex – yea, with a better heart, perhaps, than is in some men. . . . We princes, I tell you, are set on stages, in the sight and view of all the world duly observed. The eyes of many behold our actions; a spot is soon spied in our garments; a blemish quickly noted in our doings. It behooveth us therefore to be careful that our proceedings be just and honorable.

But I must tell you one thing more, that in this late Act of Parliament you have laid an hard hand on me that I must give direction for her death, which cannot be but most grievous and an irksome burden to me. . . . But for that this matter is rare, weighty, and of great consequence, and I think you do not look for any present resolution, the rather for that, as it is not my manner in matters of far less moment to give speedy answer without due consideration, so in this of such importance I think it very requisite with earnest prayer to beseech His Divine Majesty so to illuminate mine understanding and inspire me with his grace, as I may do and determine that which shall serve to the establishment of his church, preservation of your estates, and prosperity of this commonwealth under my charge. Wherein, for that I know delay is dangerous, you shall have with all conveniency our resolution delivered by our message.

1.9   Elizabeth I's Speech to the Troops at Tilbury (9 August 1588)

From BL Ms Harleian 6798, 18: 87.

On 19 July 1588, Philip II's fleet of 122 ships was spotted off Land's End (in western-most Cornwall) and was successfully met by two English naval forces. Amid fears that the Spanish invaders would make a second assault up the Thames, Elizabeth I rode on horseback to address her army, stationed on the estuary banks at Tilbury (east of London). The concern was unfounded; Philip's "Invincible Armada" had admitted defeat. Elizabeth's speech at Tilbury, long thought apocryphal, is now believed to be genuine, a triumph of will over reality in constructing the country (not yet as important on the world stage as she declares), her people (the men she saluted were mostly hired soldiers), and an heroic queenship.

My loving people: I have been persuaded by some that are careful of my safety to take heed how I committed myself to armed multitudes, for fear of treachery. But I tell you that I would not desire to live to distrust my faithful and loving people. Let tyrants fear; I have so behaved myself that under God I have placed my chiefest strength and safeguard in the loyal hearts and good will of my subjects. Wherefore I am come among you at this time but for my recreation and pleasure, being resolved in the midst and heat of the battle to live and die amongst you all, to lay down for my God and for my kingdom and for my people mine honor and my blood even in the dust. I know I have the body but of a weak and feeble woman, but I have the heart and stomach of a king – and of a king of England, too – and take foul scorn that Parma or any prince of Europe should dare to invade the borders of my realm. To the which rather than any dishonor·shall grow by me, I myself will venture my royal blood; I myself will be your general, judge, and rewarder of your virtue in the field. I know that already for your forwardness [*readiness*] you have deserved rewards and crowns, and I assure you in the word of a prince you shall not fail of[18] them. In the meantime, my lieutenant general shall be in my stead, than whom never prince commanded a more noble or worthy subject. Not doubting but by your concord in the camp and valor in the field and your obedience to myself and my general, we shall shortly have a famous victory over these enemies of my God and of my kingdom.

1.10   The Gunpowder Plot against James VI and I (5 November 1606)

From John Williams, *The History of the Gunpowder-Treason Collected from Approved Authors* (1678), Wing STC W2705 (HL copy), B4^r–C2^v.

Although the accession of the first Stuart king was peaceable, Catholic dissidents remained. In 1605 a coalition of country-gentry recusants smuggled barrels of gunpowder into cellars under the Parliament building, instructing their agent Guy Fawkes to ignite the barrels when James VI and I made an address there. In public reports of the assassination attempt, James was represented as the detective who averted disaster. For the forty-five years of Elizabeth I's reign, her accession day, 17 November, had been celebrated annually. The foiling of the "Gunpowder Plot" was the occasion for a new autumn commemoration; 5 November is still remembered with bonfires in which effigies of the "Guy" are burned.

One [conspirator], having a kindness for the Lord Monteagle, eldest son to the Lord Morley, sent this note to him:

My Lord,
    Out of the love I bear to some of your friends, I have a care of your preservation. Therefore I would advise you, as you tender [*value*] your life, to devise some excuse to shift off [*shirk*] your attendance at this Parliament. For God and man have concurred to punish the wickedness of this time. And think not slightly of this advertisement, but retire yourself into your country [*county*] where you may expect [*await*] the event in safety. For though there

---

18 *fail of*: be disappointed with; i.e., she promises reward for service.

be no appearance of any stir [*insurrection*], yet I say they shall receive a terrible blow this Parliament and yet they shall not see who hurt them. This counsel is not to be contemned [*dismissed*], because it may do you good and can do you no harm. For the danger is past as soon as you shall have burned this letter. And I hope God will give you the grace to make good use of it – to whose holy protection I commend you.

The letter was without date or subscription,[19] and the hand in which it was writ[ten] was hardly legible, and the contents of it so perplexed [*obscure*] that the Lord knew as little what to make of it as whence it came. But yet, however, since it respected [*concerned*] more than himself, he thought not fit to conceal it and presently repaired to Whitehall and put it into the hands of the Earl of Salisbury, principal Secretary of State. . . . The earl presented [the king] with it and told him how it came to his hands.

After the reading of it, the king made a pause and then, reading it again, said that there seemed somewhat in it extraordinary, and what was by no means to be neglected. The earl replied that it seemed to him to be written by a fool or a madman, for who else could be guilty of saying, "The danger is past as soon as you have burnt the letter"? For what danger could there be in that which the burning of the letter would put an end to? But the king, considering the smartness [*vigor*] of the style and withal what was said before – that "they should receive a terrible blow and yet should not see who hurt them" – did conclude, as he was walking and musing in the gallery, that the danger must be sudden and like the blowing up by gunpowder. For what else could the Parliament be in danger of? . . .

The secretary admired the king's great sagacity . . . and on Saturday it was resolved that the houses and rooms thereabouts should be searched. . . . They found in a vault [*cellar*] underground great store of billets, faggots,[20] and coal, brought thither (as Master Whinyard told them) for the use of Master Percy, and [they] spied Fawkes standing in a corner of the cellar, who said that he was Master Percy's servant and left there by him for the keeping of his house. Upon the naming of Percy, the Lord Monteagle told the chamberlain that he now vehemently suspected Master Percy to be the author of that letter, both from his inclination to the Romish religion and the intimacy that had been betwixt them. . . .

It was resolved that further search should be made, what was under that great pile of fuel in such a house where Percy had so little occasion to reside. . . . At midnight [Sir Thomas Knevet] repaired thither and found Fawkes standing at the door booted and spurred,[21] whom he presently apprehended [*arrested*]. Then

---

19 *subscription*: the lines at the end of the document that usually include the writer's signature.
20 *billets, faggots*: Billets are thick pieces of wood cut for fuel, and faggots are light sticks and twigs bundled together for kindling.
21 *booted and spurred*: prepared to flee.

Figure 3 Portrait of James VI and I (early seventeenth century). Courtesy of the National Portrait Gallery, London.

In this engraving, James VI and I is shown wearing coronation garb: the imperial crown, the royal scepter in his right hand, the royal orb in his left hand, and a cape trimmed with ermine and topped with a chain of gold and jewels.

proceeding, he first lighted upon one of the smaller and after discovered the rest of the barrels. Upon which, causing Fawkes to be searched, he found about him three matches,[22] a tinderbox,[23] and a dark lantern.[24] Being thus taken in the fact, he both confessed and defended it . . . declaring that he was not at all sorry for what he had designed, but only that he failed in the execution of it, and that the Devil and not God was the discoverer. . . . He was brought to the Tower and showed the rack, upon the sight of which he began to relent and after some days' examination disclosed the whole.

The news of this discovery flew like lightning. It was what rejoiced the heart of every good subject and daunted that of the rebels.

1.11   James VI and I's Speech to Parliament regarding Monarchy (21 March 1610)

From STC 14396 (BL copy), A4^v–B1^r, B2^r–B3^r, B3^v, B4^r–B4^v.

James VI and I's initial delight in England's comparative wealth turned into dismay at its conservative funding structure. His tax "impositions" aroused alarm, and here, in 1610, he pledges Parliament that he will rule according to law rather than as a tyrant. The speech was not entirely reassuring, nor did it solve the revenue crisis, and in 1614 he called another Parliament to deal with continuing financial problems. He angrily dissolved the session when he realized that internal conflicts and suspicions would preclude any constructive action out of what was to become known as the "Addled Parliament."

The state of monarchy is the supremest thing upon earth. For kings are not only God's lieutenants upon earth and sit upon God's throne, but even by God himself they are called gods. There be three principal similitudes [*analogies*] that illustrate the state of monarchy, one taken out of the word of God and the two other out of the grounds of policy and philosophy. In the Scriptures kings are called gods, and so their power after a certain relation compared to the divine power. Kings are also compared to fathers of families, for a king is truly *parens patriae*, the politic father of his people. And lastly, kings are compared to the head of this microcosm[25] of the body of man.

---

22 *matches*: pieces of cord, cloth, or other flammable material dipped in melted sulphur to prepare them to be ignited with a flint.

23 *tinderbox*: small box containing a substance that takes fire quickly from a spark.

24 *dark lantern*: a lantern with a sliding panel that can be closed to hide the light, here used for covert purposes.

25 *microcosm*: In a complex set of analogies, the human individual was regarded as embodying in miniature (microcosm) the ordering principles of the entire universe (macrocosm).

Kings are justly called gods for that they exercise a manner or resemblance of divine power upon earth. For if you will consider the attributes of God, you shall see how they agree in the person of a king. God hath power to create or destroy, make or unmake at his pleasure; to give life or send death; to judge all and to be judged nor accountable to none; to raise low things and to make high things low at his pleasure. And to God are both soul and body due. And the like power have kings: they make and unmake their subjects; they have power of raising and casting down, of life and of death; judges over all their subjects, and in all causes, and yet accountable to none but God only. They have power to exalt low things and abase high things, and make of their subjects like men at the chess: a pawn to take a bishop or a knight, and to cry up or down any of their subjects, as they do their money. And to the king is due both the affection of the soul and the service of the body of his subjects. . . .

As for the father of a family, they had of old under the law of nature *patriam potestatem* [*patriarchal power*], which was *potestatem vitae et necis* [*power of life and death*] over their children or family. I mean such fathers of families as were the lineal heirs of those families whereof kings did originally come, for kings had their first original from them who planted and spread themselves in colonies through the world. Now a father may dispose of his inheritance to his children at his pleasure; yea, even disinherit the eldest upon just occasions and prefer the youngest, according to his liking; make them beggars or rich at his pleasure; restrain or banish out of his presence, as he finds them give cause of offense; or restore them in favor again with the penitent sinner. So may the king deal with his subjects.

And lastly, as for the head of the natural body, the head hath the power of directing all the members of the body to that use which the judgment in the head thinks most convenient. It may apply sharp cures or cut off corrupt members, let blood[26] in what proportion it thinks fit and as the body may spare, but yet is all this power ordained by God *ad aedificationem, non ad destructionem* [*for constructive, not destructive use*]. For although God have power as well of destruction as of creation or maintenance, yet will it not agree with the wisdom of God to exercise his power in the destruction of nature and overturning the whole frame of things, since his creatures were made that his glory might thereby be the better expressed. So were he a foolish father that would disinherit or destroy his children without a cause, or leave off the careful education of them. And it were an idle head that would in place of physic[27] so poison or phlebotomize[28] the body as might breed a dangerous distemper[29] or destruction thereof. . . .

---

26 *let blood*: a purgative medical practice in which a vein was opened to let blood flow freely.

27 *physic*: either medical treatment in general or a medical compound specifically; here presumably the latter, since the contrast is made to an administered poison.

28 *phlebotomize*: draw blood for diagnostic or therapeutic purposes.

29 *distemper*: disturbance, with specific reference to the theory of the four "humors," which were thought to govern the body and which could become imbalanced.

And so the king became to be *lex loquens* [*a speaking law*] after a sort, binding himself by a double oath to the observation of the fundamental laws of his kingdom: tacitly, as by being a king, and so bound to protect as well the people as the laws of his kingdom, and expressly, by his oath at his coronation. So as every just king in a settled kingdom is bound to observe that paction [*covenant*] made to his people by his laws. . . . As for my part, I thank God I have ever given good proof that I never had intention to the contrary. And I am sure to go to my grave with that reputation and comfort, that never king was in all his time more careful to have his laws duly observed, and himself to govern thereafter, than I.

1.12　A Description of Henry Stuart, Prince of Wales (1607)

From the report of Venetian ambassador Nicolò Molin to the Doge and Senate of Venice, 1607, in the *Calendar of State Papers and Manuscripts Relating to English Affairs, Existing in the Archives of Venice: Vol. 10 (1603–1607)*, ed. H. F. Brown (London: HMSO, 1900), 513–14.

A Venetian diplomat documented the promise and charisma of the boy he believed would one day be crowned King Henry IX. The older son of James VI and I modeled himself on such celebrated Elizabethans as Sir Walter Ralegh and Sir Philip Sidney, men of action as well as intellect. He also maintained a respectful relationship with the rising Puritan movement. Then, at the age of eighteen, Henry predeceased his father. Reports such as this are poignant reminders of how different history might have been, had he lived.

The eldest [son], Henry, is about twelve years old, of a noble wit and great promise. His every action is marked by a gravity most certainly beyond his years. He studies, but not with much delight and chiefly under his father's spur, not of his own desire, and for this he is often admonished and set down. Indeed, one day, the king, after giving him a lecture, said that if he did not attend more earnestly to his lessons the Crown would be left to his brother the Duke of York, who was far quicker at learning and studied more earnestly. The prince made no reply, out of respect for his father. But when he went to his room and his tutor continued in the same vein, he said, "I know what becomes a prince. It is not necessary for me to be a professor, but a soldier and a man of the world. If my brother is as learned as they say, we'll make him Archbishop of Canterbury." The king took this answer in no good part. Nor is he overpleased to see his son so beloved and of such promise that his subjects place all their hopes in him; and it would almost seem, to speak quite frankly, that the king was growing jealous.

1.13   Charles I's Scaffold Speech (30 January 1649)

From Wing STC C2792aA (HL copy), 4–6.

The younger brother who succeeded in Prince Henry's stead had a far less successful public personality. Charles I, crowned in 1625, adopted his father's belief in royal sovereignty, and in 1629 he set out to dispense with Parliament entirely by refusing to call sessions. He embarked instead on what has been called his "personal rule" and "the Eleven Years' Tyranny." When forced to summon Parliament again in 1640 and 1641, he was confronted by a series of demands from the House of Commons known as the Ten Propositions and the Nineteen Propositions. Finally, in 1642, the conflicts escalated to civil war. On 30 January 1649 Charles I was beheaded.

I could hold my peace very well, if I did not think that holding my peace would make some men think that I did submit to the guilt as well as to the punishment. But I think it is my duty, to God first and to my country, for to clear myself both as an honest man and a good king, and a good Christian. . . . Believe it, you will never do right nor God will never prosper you until you give God his due, the king his due (that is, my successors), and the people their due. I am as much for them as any of you. . . . truly I desire their liberty and freedom as much as anybody whomsoever. But I must tell you that their liberty and freedom consists in having of government those laws by which their life and their goods may be most their own. It is not for having share in government, sir, that is nothing pertaining to them. A subject and a sovereign are clean different things. And therefore until they do that – I mean, that you do put the people in that liberty as I say – certainly they will never enjoy themselves.

Sirs, it was for this that now I am come here. If I would have given way to an arbitrary way, for to have all laws changed according to the power of the sword, I needed not to have come here. And therefore I tell you, and I pray God it be not laid to your charge, that I am the martyr of the people.

1.14   An Act Abolishing the Kingly Office in England, Ireland, and the Dominions thereunto Belonging (17 March 1649)

From Wing STC E1086A (HL copy), 1–3.

With the statute excerpted here, Parliament declared the end of monarchic rule in England. The discourse of treason, which since the reign of Henry VIII had criminalized an increasing number of threats to the king, now achieved a radical redefinition, as the king himself was judged guilty of treason. The parliamentary government created by Oliver Cromwell and his Puritan allies lasted until 1660.

Whereas Charles Stuart, late King of England, Ireland, and the territories and dominions thereunto belonging, hath, by authority derived from Parliament, been and is hereby declared to be justly condemned, adjudged to die, and put to death for many treasons, murders, and other heinous offenses committed by him, by which judgment he stood and is hereby declared to be attainted of high treason, whereby his issue [*descendants*] and posterity and all others pretending title under him are become uncapable of [*disbarred from*] the said crowns, or of being king or queen of the said kingdom or dominions or either or any of them: Be it therefore enacted and ordained . . . that all the people of England and Ireland . . . are discharged of all fealty, homage, and allegiance which is or shall be pretended to be due unto any of the issue and posterity of the said late king. . . . And whereas it is and hath been found by experience that the office of a king in this nation and Ireland, and to have the power thereof in any single person, is unnecessary, burdensome, and dangerous to the liberty, safety, and public interest of the people, and that for the most part use hath been made of the regal power and prerogative to oppress, impoverish, and enslave the subject, and that usually and naturally any one person in such power makes it his interest to encroach upon the just freedom and liberty of the people and to promote the setting up of their own will and power above the laws that so they might enslave these kingdoms to their own lust [*pleasure*]: Be it therefore enacted and ordained by this present Parliament and by the authority of the same that the office of a king in this nation shall not henceforth reside in or be exercised by any one single person, and that no one person whatsoever shall or may have or hold the office, style, dignity, power, or authority of king of the said kingdoms and dominions, or any of them, or of the Prince of Wales, any law, statute, usage, or custom to the contrary thereof in any wise notwithstanding.

2

Society, Economy, and Class

There were about six million people in England in 1300 but, two centuries later, little more than two million. We do not know all the reasons for this catastrophic decline in the late medieval population, with healthy births failing to offset deaths, but food shortages caused by bad harvests, and pandemics like the bubonic plague, clearly played their parts. Other diseases such as smallpox, measles, influenza, and typhoid tended to affect the young disproportionately, which meant that the population failed to renew itself. Not until the 1520s did the numbers begin to increase again. Although the sixteenth century had its share of epidemics and famines, there were also countervailing factors. Some couples seem to have married younger and thus produced larger families. The survival rate for infants was still grievously low by modern standards, but it had improved over earlier centuries. Even the split from Rome played a role in demographic growth, since Protestant clergy were not required to be celibate. By 1650 the population had rebounded to an estimated five and a quarter million. The boom was biggest in London, which went from 50,000 residents in 1500 to more than 400,000 in 1650, outstripping even Paris and Naples, and nearly matching Constantinople.

One of the great administrative innovations of Henry VIII's advisor Thomas Cromwell, in 1538, was to order each parish to document its population by recording baptisms, weddings, and burials. An amendment of 1598 stipulated that these records be kept on long-lasting parchment. Parish clerks were directed to recopy old paper versions, but they were allowed to begin with 1558, the first year of Elizabeth's reign, rather than with 1538. For this reason, many registers before 1558 do not survive. Later registers have been lost, too, to fire, water damage, or neglect. Thus, the demography of the Renaissance is an inexact science. The evidence for a sixteenth- and seventeenth-century population explosion includes social and economic symptoms that often accompany growth, such as overcrowding, food scarcity, unemployment, and inflation. All were features of the Tudor and Stuart years.

Occupations

In a pre-industrial age, the great majority of English men and women worked the land, often living in the nucleated settlements of small villages surrounded by their fields and pastures. By tradition, villagers shared common grounds as well as the tasks of building fences and ditches, maintaining dykes, and sowing and reaping. The perils of bad weather and poor harvests were communal experiences, too. Of necessity, farming families knew all the skills to feed, clothe, and house themselves: they thatched roofs, spun wool, baked bread, brewed beer, made cheese, slaughtered pigs, and manufactured candles and soap. In this barter economy, rents owed by tenant farmers to the lord of the local manor were often paid in provisions and service.

After many generations of intermarriage, a provincial village would have seemed like a large extended family. Those sharing a roof, however, were generally parents and children only, with a few laborers or servants. In cultures where extended families cohabit, households tend to operate at a subsistence level. But in England the predominance of the nuclear family meant that most were able to produce surplus goods which were marketable. Country women, for example, knitted stockings for sale, produced specialty condiments, or raised extra chickens in order to supply eggs to neighboring gentry.

Men were customarily identified either by class (John Doe, gentleman) or, if they were below the level of the land-owning gentry, by occupation (John Doe, husbandman – that is, farmer). Women were nearly always identified by marital status (Jane Doe, singlewoman; wife of John Doe; or Jane Doe, widow). In reality, individual labor histories were often far more versatile than was officially recognized with these labels. The highest degree of work specialization was to be found in cities, where people entered training in their teens, women often as maidservants and men learning the trades they would be legally entitled to pursue at the end of seven-year indentures. In 1563 the Statute of Artificers sought to regularize labor practices by setting out the terms of apprenticeship and fixing wages. Even in urban areas, however, many men and women had secondary occupations, the so-called "by-employments." John Doe might be a tavern keeper as well as a carpenter, and Jane Doe might be a nurse as well as a housewife. Townswomen kept shops, ran lodging houses, did service work like sewing, mending, and laundering, and were businesswomen in their own right.

Social Structure

Early modern society had a complex hierarchy informed by birth, degree of wealth, source of wealth, relation to land, profession, and life style. William Harrison wrote in 1577 that these ingredients combined to form four basic "sorts" of men. The top 2 percent were aristocrats and gentry, whose own ranks were finely discriminated (in descending order): king, princes, dukes, marquesses, earls, viscounts, barons, knights, esquires, and, finally, "mere" gentry who had land but no hereditable titles. Next were wealthy business people, including the rising professional class of lawyers and administrators. The third category included yeomen, or farmers of substance. Finally, fourth,

Harrison listed craftsmen and wage laborers. He neglected to mention a fifth group, even though it was the largest. The poor, the unemployed, and the homeless may have constituted as much as 50 percent of the population. Nor did Harrison feel the need to acknowledge gender as a category of subordination within every class.

All early moderns knew their given place in the social scheme. Rank was reinforced every Sunday, as men and women took their appropriate pews in church. During civic processions, the rules of precedent were as clear as is alphabetical order. The system came under pressure, however, in the transitional economy of the sixteenth century, which was increasingly based in cash transactions rather than, as previously, in personal patronage and barter. As it became newly possible for entrepreneurial people to live above their birth stations, the central government struggled to maintain social distinction in recognizable ways, passing highly detailed "sumptuary" laws that dictated which fabrics, colors, and styles each class was permitted to wear (see document 6.6). The penalty for violating these restrictions was forfeit of the offending garment and a prohibitive fine for each day it was worn. Those below the level of knight who wore silk in their hats, nightcaps, or stockings could also spend up to three months in prison. But legislative efforts such as these failed to keep the rising classes in their old places.

Upward Mobility

The "middling sort" had never experienced as much economic opportunity as in the Tudor and Stuart years. An important avenue of advancement was the expanding central government, with its many offices for a new professional cohort of educated men. There was also a revolution in land ownership. Until the sixteenth century, land sales were rare. Instead, property passed down within families, or moved into private hands through grants from the monarch to his supporters, or was bequeathed to the Church by those seeking grace on their deathbeds. It has been estimated that the Church as a whole owned as much as a third of the land in England in the early sixteenth century. Following the break with Rome, these assets were transferred to royal control as Henry VIII closed monasteries, friaries, and nunneries. At the time, land seemed less a long-term investment than a source of short-term income from rents and the sale of timber, ores, and other natural resources. For the king, however, these revenues could not offset the administrative costs of managing property on such a large scale. He immediately gave some of the seized estates to men who had demonstrated loyalty or whose loyalty he sought to ensure. Then he and his advisors recognized the potential bonanza to be realized through selling off some of the vast acreage.

Thus, for the first time in English history, there was a flourishing land market that was accessible to anyone with money – not just aristocrats, but also minor gentry, merchants, urban professionals, and wealthy yeomen. This was an important way in which old boundaries between the classes became permeable. Meanwhile, members of the middle ranks of society had more discretionary income than had ever before been the case. Many small-farmers benefited from the fact that rent expenses were fixed by law while earning power increased, because food prices rose as population growth created demand. People above the poverty line enjoyed higher standards of living. They improved and enlarged their houses, bought more personal possessions, violated the sumptuary regulations, and consumed finer foodstuffs.

Poverty

For others, though, rising costs were disastrous. In 1600, the most basic foods were six times as expensive as they had been in 1500. While many landlords were prohibited from raising rents, they could hyperinflate the "entry fines" charged new tenants. Landowners had also discovered that pasture was more profitable than arable land, because woolen cloth was England's principal international export. When common grounds were enclosed for gentry to graze their own herds of sheep, workers lost both farmland and livelihood. Those who became untethered from traditional social structures included the so-called "masterless" men, soldiers who fought Elizabeth's foreign wars in the 1580s but who were never paid and who failed to find work when they returned to civilian status. Some of the homeless became itinerant peddlers. "Subsistence" migrants also included vagrants in search of seasonal agricultural employment. The London population exploded as "betterment" migrants left the countryside with dreams of steadier work in the city.

Relief efforts were generally administered through the parish church. This represented an attempt to bind the poor to a place, to restrain them from itinerancy. Every parish had impoverished residents who received support in the form of subsidized housing or allowances of bread. But nothing compensated for the loss of the monasteries, which had traditionally relieved the pressures of poverty by offering temporary lodgings and doles of food. Their closing exacerbated the problem by adding as many as 10,000 former religious to the ranks of the dispossessed. Parish officers were known always to be on the watch against adding more dependants to their roster. A poor pregnant woman might not even find a bed in which to give birth unless there were guarantees that she would hold the parish "harmless" of further responsibility for her unborn child.

Beginning in 1576, works projects provided some training for the unemployed, especially in cloth manufacturing. As often as not, though, poverty was criminalized instead. Contrasts were drawn between the "impotent" poor, who were disabled, very old, or very young; the "worthy" poor, who were in temporary financial distress; and the "idle" poor, who were believed to be capable of work but who were assumed to prefer lives as beggars and thieves. A series of

Poor Laws mandated that those in the last category should be whipped, mutilated, imprisoned, or, in cases of repeat offenses, executed. Economic distress resulted in the scapegoating of the "idle" poor, of unmarried mothers, of indigent older widows who were sometimes accused of witchcraft, and of European refugees who were accused of taking jobs away from English workers. Elizabeth acknowledged these protectionist fears by ordering all Africans to leave the country in 1601. As had already proven true for Jews, removed in 1290, expulsion laws were not entirely successful; in the 1590s, there were secret Jewish communities in London and Bristol. The Africans who nonetheless remained also ensured that English society was less homogeneous than was intended.

A Transitional Economy

At the beginning of the sixteenth century, most transactions involved bartering for goods and services. A hundred years later the situation was very different, because the newly internationalized consumer culture was cash-based. Ironically, some of the cash-strapped were those of highest status: their wealth was concentrated in the traditional way on land ownership, but their land returned them fixed rents that might be paid in farm goods and labor rather than money. Like her father, Elizabeth I sold off many crown properties for immediate profit and then suffered the loss of regular rental incomes. Without tax authorizations to provide a consistent source of revenue, she and James VI and I were inventive about gathering funds by selling patents and exclusive trading rights, or monopolies. The cash economy provided another source of opportunity for wealthy merchants, who came under heavy pressure to lend money and who charged interest when doing so. A series of usury acts, citing biblical injunctions against making money from money, reflected the anxieties of an old guard about the ways in which economic structures were inexorably changing.

There were strong centripetal forces in early modern culture, as the central government expanded, a national church was formed, and a national identity was celebrated in sermons, chronicles, and plays. But there were also centrifugal forces, as the gaps between rich and poor grew greater and familiar systems of patronage and service were eroded by changing industries, new professions, proto-capitalism, and consumerism. These meant that the social experience of Renaissance men and women was less settled and predictable than ever before.

2.1 Sir Thomas Wilson, "The State of England" (1600)

From SP 12/280.

In this report on England's volatile social structure, Thomas Wilson airs a personal (and not uncommon) complaint about the prevailing system of primogeniture, which

Figure 4 Portrait of Sir Henry Unton, detail (c.1596). Courtesy of the National Portrait Gallery, London.

Henry Unton's mother was a countess who married much beneath her. Unton himself was a second son who unexpectedly inherited a gentleman's estate when his older brother died childless. His wife commemorated this life of social mobility and serendipity in a portrait she commissioned after Unton's death. Scenes from his biography begin in the lower right-hand corner of the painting, where his mother holds him as a swaddled infant. Above this, Unton is shown completing his education, first reading at Oxford University and then touring in Italy. At the center top of the portrait he appears as a soldier in the Netherlands, and a traveler to France. Below, the large central scene of life in an English country house features Unton in his garret study, Unton playing the viol with friends, and Unton seated at a banquet table watching a mythological masque. The left-hand scenes of the painting show Unton on his deathbed with a doctor taking his pulse after letting blood, and then, beneath, a convoy bringing his body to burial. Lady Dorothy Unton may have asked for Unton to be shown at his writing desk because he corresponded regularly with Elizabeth I as her Ambassador to France.

disadvantaged younger sons as well as all daughters. Wilson's older brother had been bequeathed all the family property, leaving Wilson to make his own way. With a Cambridge education and the patronage of Elizabeth's principal advisors, William and Robert Cecil, Wilson had every reason to hope he would achieve status and prosperity in the new economy. Instead, after difficult and sometimes dangerous work as an intelligence officer in Italy and Spain, he was appointed Keeper of the Records at Whitehall Palace at the modest annual salary of £30. His unpublished manuscript on the numbers, ranks, and incomes of turn-of-the-century Englishmen, intended to showcase his talents for a potential employer, described landed wealth in the old way, in terms of yearly rental incomes.

The ability and state of the common people of England

It cannot be denied but the common people are very rich, albeit they be much decayed from the states they were wont to have, for the gentlemen, which were wont to addict themselves to the wars, are now for the most part grown to become good husbands [*farmers*] and know well how to improve their lands to the uttermost as the farmer or countryman, so that they take their farms into their hands as the leases expire, and either till themselves or else let them out to those who will give most. Whereby the yeomanry of England is decayed and become servants to gentlemen, which were wont to be the glory of the country for good neighborhood and hospitality, notwithstanding there are yet some store of those yeomen left who have long leases of such lands and lordships as they hold. Yea, I know many yeomen in diverse provinces in England which are able yearly to dispend betwixt three or five hundred pound yearly by their lands and lease[s] and some twice and some thrice as much. But my young masters, the sons of such, not contented with their states of their fathers to be counted yeoman and called "John" or "Robert" (such an one), but must skip into his velvet breeches and silken doublet and, getting to be admitted into some Inn of Court or Chancery [*for training in the law*], must ever after think scorn to be called any other than gentlemen. Which gentlemen indeed, perceiving them unfit to do them that service that their fathers did, when their leases do expire turn them out of their lands – which was never wont to be done, the farmer accounting his state as good as inheritance in times past – and let them to such as are not by their bad pennyworths [*bad bargains*] able to gentleman it as others have done.

Commonalty

Notwithstanding this – that the great yeomanry is decayed – yet by this means the commonalty is increased twenty [times] now perhaps with their labor and diligence, living well and wealthily of that land which our great yeoman held before, who did no other good but maintain beef and brews for such idle persons as would come and eat it, a fine daughter or two to be married after with £10,000 to some covetous mongrel. Of these yeomen of the richest sort which are able to lend the queen money (as they do ordinarily upon her letters called "privy seals" whensoever she hath any wars defensive or offensive or any other enterprise), there are accounted to be about 10,000 in country villages besides citizens [*city traders*].

There are, moreover, of yeomen of meaner ability which are called freeholders (for that they are owners of lands which hold by no base service of any lord or superior), such as are able to keep ten or eleven or eight or six milch kine [*dairy cattle*], five or six horses to till their ground, besides young beasts [*cows*] and sheep, and are accounted to be worth each of them in all their substance and stock betwixt three and five hundred pounds sterling more or less. Of these, I say, there are reckoned to be in England and Wales about the number of 80,000, as I have seen in sheriffs' books.

Copyholders[1] and cottagers

The rest are copyholders and cottagers, as they call them, who hold some land and tenements of some other lord which is parcel of the demesne of his seigniory [*estate in feudal possession*] or manor at the will of the lord. And these are, some of them, men of as great ability as any of the rest. And some poor, and live chiefly upon country labor, working by the day for meat and drink and some small wages. These last are they which are thrust out to service in war, the richer sort of yeomen and their sons being trained but not sent out of the land, but kept to defend against invasion at home unless they will go voluntary, as many do. Notwithstanding, the captain will sometimes press them to the end to get a bribe to release them.

The number of this latter sort is uncertain because there is no books or records kept of them, unless it be in private stewards' hands, which is impossible to be gathered altogether. . . .

The state of citizens

These, by reason of the great privileges they enjoy, every city being as it were a commonwealth among themselves, no other officer of the queen nor other having authority to intermeddle amongst them, must needs be exceeding well to pass. They are not taxed but by their own officers of the[ir] own brotherhood, every art having one or two of his own which are continually of the Council of

---

1 *Copyholders*: holders of lands that are part of a manor (with tenure "copied" into the manorial court roll), as distinct from freeholders, who own property outright, and leaseholders, who have tenancy for a fixed rent, often for twenty-one years.

the city in all affairs to see that nothing pass contrary to their profit; besides they are not suffered to be idle in their cities as they be in other parts of Christendom, but every child of six or seven years old is forced to some art whereby he gaineth his own living and something besides to help to enrich his parents or master. I have known in one city (viz., Norwich) where the accounts having been made yearly what children from six to ten years have earned towards their keeping in a year, and it hath been accounted that it hath risen to £12,000 sterling which they have gained, besides other keeping, and that chiefly by knitting of fine jersey stockings, every child being able at or soon after seven years to earn four shillings a week at that trade which the merchants uttered [*sold*] at London (and some trading therewith with France and other parts). And in that city I know in my time twenty-four aldermen which were esteemed to be worth £20,000 apiece, some much more, and the better sort of citizens the half. But if we should speak of London and some other maritime places we should find it much exceeding this rate. It is well known that at this time there are in London some merchants worth £100,000, and he is not accounted rich that cannot reach to £50,000 or near it. . . .

The state of the nobility and the number

I have seen diverse books which have been collected by secretaries and counselors of estate which did exactly show the several revenues of every nobleman, knights, and gentlemen through the realm. . . .

[Of] earls some daily decay, some increase, according to the course of the world. But that which I have noted by perusing many of the said books, and of the later sort, is that still the total sum groweth much to one reckoning, and that is to £100,000 rent yearly, accounting them all in gross to avoid prolixity. If a man would proportion this amongst nineteen earls and a marquess it would be no great matter, to every one £5,000 rent, but as some exceed that much, so many come short of it.

The thirty-nine barons and two viscounts do not much exceed that sum; their revenue is reckoned together to amount to £120,000 yearly.

The bishops' revenues amount to about £22,500 yearly altogether, whereof three of them (viz., Canterbury, Winchester, and Ely) receive rent per annum betwixt £2,000 and £3,000, the rest betwixt £1,000 and £500 and some less. . . . This must be understood, that the state of the clergy is not altogether so bare as may perhaps be conjectured by the smallness of their revenue, for that they never raise nor rack their rents nor put out tenants as the noblemen and gentlemen do to the uttermost penny, but do let their lands as they were let one hundred years since, reserving to themselves and their successors some commodities besides the bare rent, as corn, muttons, beef, poultry, or such like. But to say the truth, their wings are well clipped of late by courtiers and noblemen, and some quite cut away, both feather, flesh, and bone.

These are the states of the nobility, both clergy and lay, which are called *nobilitas major*; there rests to touch those of the meaner nobility, which are termed *nobilitas minor* and are either knights, esquires, gentlemen, lawyers, professors and ministers, archdeacons, prebends, and vicars.

The state and number of knights

There are accounted to be in England about the number of 500 knights as I have reckoned them . . . such as are chief men in their countries [*counties*] both for living and reputations, though many of them know scarcely what knighthood means, but are made knights for the credit of their country and to induce them to live in a more honorable manner, both for their own credit and the service of their prince and country, than otherwise perhaps they would do. These for the most part are men for living betwixt £1,000 and £2,000 yearly, and many of them equal the best barons and come not much behind many earls . . . who are thought to be able to dispend yearly betwixt £5,000 and £7,000 of good land.

The number and state of gentlemen

Those which we call esquires are gentlemen whose ancestors are or have been knights, or else they are the heirs and eldest of their houses and of some competent quantity of revenue fit to be called to office and authority in their country where they live. Of these there are esteemed to be in England, as I have seen by the book of musters [*military register*] of every several shire, to the number of 16,000 or thereabout, whereof there are of [them] in commissions of the peace about 1,400 in every province – in some forty, in some fifty, some thirty, more or less. These are men in living betwixt £1,000 and £500 rent. Especially about London and the counties adjoining, where their lands are set to the highest, he is not counted of any great reckoning unless he be betwixt 1,000 marks [*£666*] or £1,000, but northward and far off a gentleman of good reputation may be content with £300 and £400 yearly. These are the elder brothers.

The state of great younger brethren

I cannot speak of the [number] of younger brothers, albeit I be one of the number myself, but for their estate there is no man hath better cause to know it nor less cause to praise it. Their state is of all stations for gentlemen most miserable, for if our fathers possess £1,000 or £2,000 yearly at his death, he cannot give a foot of land to his younger children in inheritance, unless it be by lease for twenty years or for three lives (or unless his land be socage tenure, whereof there is little, or gavelkind, such as is only in one province, in Kent),[2] or else be purchased by himself and not descended. Then he may demise as much as he thinks good to his younger children, but such a fever hectic hath custom brought in and inured amongst fathers, and such fond desire they have to leave a great show of the stock of their house, though the branches be withered, that they will not do it but my elder brother forsooth must be my master. He must have all, and all the rest that which the cat left on the malt heap – perhaps some small annuity during his life or what please our elder brother's worship to bestow upon us if we please him and my mistress his wife. This I must confess doth us good some ways, for it makes us industrious to apply ourselves to letters or to arms, whereby many times we become my master elder brothers' master, or at least their betters in honor and reputation, while he lives at home like a mome [*dolt*] and knows the sound of no other bell but his own.

The estate of common lawyers

This sort and order of people . . . by the ruins of neighbors' contentions are grown so great, so rich, and so proud, that no other sort dare meddle with them. Their number is so great now that to say the truth they can scarcely live one by another, the practice being drawn into a few hand of those which are most renowned, and all the rest live by pettifogging [*dealing with petty causes*], seeking means to set their neighbors at variance, whereby they may gain on both sides. This is one of the greatest inconveniences in the land, that the number of the lawyers are so great they undo the country people and buy up all the lands that are to be sold, so that young gentlemen or others newly coming to their living, some of them prying into his evidence, will find the means to set him at variance with some other, or some other with him, by some pretense or quiddity [*quibble*], and when they have half-consumed themselves in suit they are fain to sell their land to follow the process and pay their debts, and then that becomes a prey to lawyers. . . . There are in number of sergeants about thirty, counselors about 2,000, and as many attorneys, besides solicitors, and pettifoggers an infinite number, there being no province, city, town, nor scarce village free from them, unless the Isle of Anglesey, which boast they never had lawyers nor foxes.

2.2   James Bankes's Advice to his Children (1611)

From *The Early Records of the Bankes Family at Winstanley*, ed. Joyce Bankes and Eric Kerridge, Chetham Society, 21 (1973), 16–37.

---

2 Socage tenure derived from a royal grant for service. It allowed for "partible" inheritance, meaning that a father could divide his estate among his heirs. A variant in Kent, known as gavelkind, mandated equal division among all sons. Elsewhere, however, "descent" was by law of "primogeniture," with an estate inherited whole by the oldest son.

James Bankes became sufficiently wealthy as a London goldsmith to purchase the manor of Winstanley in Lancashire in 1596. Modestly referring to it as a "poor house," he attempted to avoid a display of unseemly pride in his achievements. For a "new" or self-made man, he was unusually attentive to old ways, refusing to capitalize fully on his property if it meant breaking moral covenants with tenant families. The detailed notes he left his heirs show how close the connections could be between a landlord and those who made a living on his land – and also how his subjective opinion could determine their material circumstances.

My dear children, unto whom it shall please God to enjoy this poor house of Winstanley,

I would advise you in God's most holy name that you would not in any wise deal hardly with any tenant otherwise than in this order and sort, that is to say: I would have every man to enjoy his tenement during his lease and his wife's life, so after to his son if he have any. And the lease being ended, I would have you, because your rents is small and not sufficient to maintain your home and family, to let his son that is next unto it to make him a lease of the said farm in this order and sort as hereafter followeth, that is to say: if the farm be worth twenty pounds a year, as there is some, I would have you to take but sixteen pounds a year rent and so to make him a lease either son or daughter that was born upon the same farm, paying sixteen pounds a year for rent for the same which is worth twenty pounds a year. And likewise if a farm shall fall to you worth sixteen pounds a year I would have you to take twenty marks a year [£13 6s. 8d.] and to make him likewise a lease of the same farm as above, either son or daughter. . . . Be very kind and loving unto your tenants, and so they will love you in good and godly sort, the which I pray God long to continue to his most glorious will and pleasure. And in observing this order and rule, both you and your house shall live in worship and credit to the glory of God and the joy and comfort of your wives and children from age to age. . . .

William Barton of the coal pit.[3] His tenement containeth about thirty acres or more and is worth a year above the rent £20, so that a lease of the same is worth for 21 years £120. And therefore, my children, if at any time you can buy the said tenement for money, not hurting any of his sons by the same, and lay the same to your demesne,[4] you may be bold to give for the same £100. For so it is worth very well.

Humphrey Winstanley. His tenement containeth twenty-six acres and is

---

3 *William Barton of the coal pit*: as with all others named in this extract, a Winstanley tenant. The number of tenants named "Barton" bears witness to the long histories of stable populations in many rural areas.

4 *lay the same to your demesne*: recover the acres in question as part of the estate fully held by the owner himself, not occupied by any tenant.

worth twenty marks a year above the rent, so that a lease is worth a hundred pounds very well, and therefore take no less. This said Humphrey Winstanley most deceitfully did go about as he confesseth at such time as the land was to be sold, and therefore deserveth no favor. . . .

Margaret Ranford. Her tenement contains about eight acres and is worth about £5 6s. 8d. . . . In any wise do no wrong to the house of Ranford or to any of his children, because the name of the father and the sons have done good service to this house of Winstanley. And if you can buy the same, place them in some other tenement in God's name, of the like or better in any wise. . . .

Gilbert Barton. His tenement containeth about ten acres and is worth a year if it be marled [fertilized] at the least £5 . . . place him at some other tenement as well as you can. There is about two or three acres that was taken from the demesne; therefore, if ever the lease be determined in any wise, take the same three acres again to the demesne again. . . .

Rafe Berre hath a cottage in the side of the demesne and of the demesne. I would likewise have you to take the same into your hands at his death and his wife's, and all the cottages about the mill, for they do hinder this house more than a man would think. . . .

William Barton of the Brown Heath. His tenement containeth about sixteen acres right and smooth land and is worth a year £4 above the rent. The said William is a bad man and hath deceived me in taking of his tenement of Master Winstanley but his son may prove well – and therefore be good to his child. . . .

There is another tenement wherein one William Crones did take, over a poor man's head, to his undoing of him and his wife and children, whereupon the poor man's wife died for very grief, the which Crones put them out by the sheriff. And so the poor man Barton, [as his] name was, was constrained to make a poor cabin without [outside] the house and enforced to lie upon the ground a whole winter, still in hope of some relief at the said Crones' his hand, but no peat [turf used as fuel] would he give her in any sort. And in the behalf of the poor man, his neighbors in the end relieved him with begging. Otherwise he should have been enforced to have begged for want [lack] of relief. Therefore my son, if you can, buy in this lease and let the poor man have the said house again during his life if he shall live after me your father, in God's most holy name. He desireth but a dozen acres thereof during his life. This said William Crones hath a lease during his life and for fourscore years if he live so long. The said lease Master Winstanley bestowed it on him without any penny for the same. Therefore in regard it cost him nothing, he might have given some relief to the said poor man, but his heart would not suffer him to do so much good. . . . In God's name, please them with as much as there be worth and rather the more; so shall you please both God and them.

2.3   John Hales's Charge to a County Commission Investigating Enclosures (1548)

From John Strype, *Ecclesiastical Memorials* (1721), ESTC T146402 (BL copy), 56–7.

Enclosure, the conversion of common ground and wasteland into privately controlled pasture, deprived many small-scale farmers of their livelihood. Although the practice was illegal through most of the sixteenth century, enforcement was generally lax. As a Member of Parliament, John Hales was the rare advocate of rural reform, and in 1548 he was appointed to head a Midlands commission to investigate violations. He censured large landowners for putting private profit over public good, and he exposed their strate-gies for disguising their grazing enclosures so that they would appear to be actively tenanted farms. In Buckinghamshire, support for the commission was so ardent that it led to riots, for which Hales was blamed. When his ally the Duke of Somerset fell from power as Edward VI's Lord Protector in 1549, Hales was sent to the Tower. After his release in 1550, he sold most of his own land and emigrated to Europe.

As there be many good men that take great pains to study to devise good laws for the commonwealth, so be there a great many that do, with as great pains and study, labor to defeat them and, as the common saying is, to find gaps and start-ing holes [*loopholes*]. But first, to declare unto you what is meant by this word *enclosures*: it is not taken where a man doth enclose and hedge in his own proper ground, where no man hath commons. For such enclosure is very beneficial to the commonwealth; it is a cause of great increase of wood. But it is meant thereby when any man hath taken away and enclosed any other men's commons, or hath pulled down houses of husbandry [*farmhouses*] and converted the lands from tillage to pasture. This is the meaning of this word, and so we pray you to remember it.

To defeat these statutes, as we be informed, some have not pulled down their houses but maintain them – howbeit no person dwelleth therein, or, if there be, it is but a shepherd or a milkmaid – and convert the lands from tillage to pasture. And some [with] about one hundred acres of ground, or more or less, make a furrow and sow that, and the rest they till not but pasture with their sheep. And some take the lands from their houses and occupy them in husbandry but let the houses out to beggars and old poor people. Some, to color the multitude of their sheep, father them on their children, kinsfolks, and servants.[5] All which be but only crafts and subtleties to defraud the laws, such as no good man will use, but rather abhor. For every good man will direct his study to observe the laws rather than break them and say with himself thus: "I know the makers of these laws

---

5 A statute of 1534 sought to limit the number of sheep an individual could own. But, as Hale recog-nizes, the law was easy to circumvent by putting ownership in the names of others (thus "fathering" them falsely).

meant good to the commonwealth. Men be but men; they cannot see all things. They be no gods; they cannot make things perfect. Therefore, I will rather do that they meant, although without danger of the law I might do otherwise, and I will with all my heart do good to my country, albeit it be against my private profit, rather than hurt it." And therefore if there be any such that use these tricks, albeit they be not comprehended in the letter of the law, I pray you let us know him and present you his name [*charge him before the commission*].

2.4 Sir Roger Wilbraham's Account of Enclosure Riots (June 1607)

From *The Journal of Sir Roger Wilbraham . . . for the Years 1593–1616*, ed. Harold Spencer Scott, *Camden Miscellany*, 10 (1902), 91–5.

As enclosures continued, so did opposition to them, both at the highest levels of government and among the lowest levels of the provincial poor. James VI and I and his advisors were especially concerned about the rural depopulation and crop shortfalls that followed from lost farmland. The form of resistance known to the dispossessed, however, was civil unrest – which England's rulers would never countenance, as is clear from this account of enclosure riots in the East Midlands. The extract is translated from the original Latin.

Beggars and vagrants in the town of Northampton, angered at the enclosures made near the town, in bands during the night threw down [*demolished*] a part thereof. And inasmuch as they are not put down [*quelled*], their numbers increase – both from this town and diverse towns in the county and in the counties of Warwick, Leicester, etc. – and for twenty days their numbers continue to increase, till 300 or more in one place night and day are throwing down the new enclosures. Nor do they desist, in spite of two proclamations made by the king on different occasions that they should have justice and mercy if they desisted. And yet they continue until Sir A[ntony] Mildmay with some horsemen using force slew some ten in hot blood, and thus they were put down. Afterwards, at the assizes of the before-mentioned several counties [*local civil and criminal courts*], two or three were hanged as an example, so that, as the king says, the punishment of a few may impress the majority with fear. Moreover, the proclamation says that it is not a legal course for subjects to remedy their grievances by force, but that they should petition the king to be relieved according to justice. And the judges of assize, in order to satisfy the common people, inveigh against enclosers and depopulators and inquire concerning them and promise reformation at the hands of justice. And this puts courage into the common people, so that with mutterings they threaten to have a more violent revenge if they cannot be relieved. On this the [Privy] Council appoints select commissioners, learned in the law, in the six counties, to inquire concerning the acts of depopulation and conversion of arable into pasture land. And they report to the Council on 6 December 1607 to this effect: that in the counties of Lincoln, Leicester, Northampton, Warwick, Huntingdon, Bedford, and Buckingham, about 200 or 300 tenements have been depopulated and a great number of acres have been converted from arable into pasture land. To wit, 9,000 acres in Northamptonshire and a great number in the other counties. . . .

On this, directions were given to the learned counsel that the most notorious enclosers in each county should be summoned this Christmas for Hilary Term before the Star Chamber,[6] and justice and mercy shown to them, so that they should not despair. Nor should the common people insult them or be incited to make rebellion, whereof they are greatly suspected. Also, the mayor of Northampton, the sheriff, and the neighboring justices who did not repress the outrages at the beginning should also be brought before the Star Chamber by reason of their remissness. And it is hoped that this public example may stay [end] the fury of the common people. These deliberations I reported to the king at Newmarket on 8 December by order of the Council. And he seems to approve of this course, for the manifestation of his justice and the speedy reformation of oppression.

2.5   A Memorandum Regarding the Statute of Artificers (1573)

From SP 12/93: 26.

Five years into Elizabeth's I reign, Parliament created a comprehensive work policy for craftsmen, fixing wages and regulating trade practices. Basketmakers, ironmongers, pewterers, shoemakers, tailors, weavers, and others were licensed to produce and sell goods only after a period in training. The crafts were called "mysteries" to emphasize that they involved specialized skills passed across the generations personally, from a master to his apprentice. The Statute of Artificers insisted that these traditional procedures be followed in full, and also that those born into husbandry should not be trained in the crafts.

In [1563], there was an Act made touching diverse orders for artificers, laborers, servants of husbandry, and apprentices, which Act concerneth the good education of youth and good government of the greatest number of people. And therefore if it were duly observed and executed, it would no doubt avoid many occasions of evil. But for that the good regard and observation thereof is neglected, a multitude of inconveniences groweth among artificers, to the

---

6 High courts were in session four times during the year. Hilary Term was from 23 January to 12 February. The Court of Star Chamber, maintained by the King's Councillors, developed a reputation for unfair proceedings and harsh punishment, but, as is suggested here, it originally functioned as a court of appeal with a reputation for fairness.

impoverishing, decay, and utter ruin of many [of] them, their wives, children, and family, which causeth great increase of rogues, vagabonds, and thieves. As more at large, by certain special notes following, collected out of the said statute being thoroughly examined and considered of, it will appear.

If an artificer occupy husbandry [farming] with his occupation, he cannot take an apprentice to his occupation.

For one man to be both an husbandman and an artificer is a gathering of diverse men's livings into one man's hand, and therefore the law doth not allow such a one to keep or instruct apprentices in any occupation to withdraw from artificers the occasion of their livings, which have no other trade to live by but only their occupations.

Every artificer must be an householder before he can take an apprentice.

Householders are burdened with diverse charges in the commonwealth, which such as keep no houses are not charged with. And therefore it appeareth needful that householders should have a further prerogative in keeping of apprentices to help to get their livings than those that are no householders should.

The master must be full twenty-four years old at the least before he can take an apprentice.

Until a man grow unto the age of twenty-four years, he (for the most part, though not always) is wild, without judgment, and not of sufficient experience to govern himself. Nor (many times) grown unto the full or perfect knowledge of the art or occupation that he professeth. And therefore had more need still to remain under government, as a servant and learner, than to become a ruler, as a master or instructor.

The master in most occupations must dwell in a city, town corporate, or market town.

Cities and great towns are only or for the most part to be maintained by manual arts, occupations, mysteries, and sciences. And therefore it appeareth convenient that apprentices should be there brought up and instructed in the said arts and sciences, and not in such other towns and places where men ought to live by husbandry and laboring of grounds. But yet contrary to the meaning of the law, a number of apprentices are brought up and taught occupations in husbandmen's houses, which turneth to a superfluous increase of artificers and to the decay and ruin of such cities and towns as should set forth the honor and strength of the realm.

The father of the apprentice must be an artificer not occupying husbandry nor being a laborer.

It is a more easier thing for the children of husbandmen and laborers to become artificers than for the children of artificers to become husbandmen and laborers. Therefore, when husbandmen and laborers do put their children to learn occupations, then artificers' children are driven to be rogues and vagabonds. But the Parliament as well for the better service to be done in husbandry (whereunto the children of husbandmen and laborers are most apt) as for the avoiding of other inconveniences that groweth by the evil education of artificers' children, hath provided that each sort of such children should be applied to the trades that their parents were of before them, which no doubt would work great commodity in the commonwealth.

The father of the apprentice must dwell in the same city or town corporate where the apprentice is bound [indentured], or in some other suchlike city or town corporate if the apprentice shall be bound in any city or town corporate.

The inhabitants of cities and great towns that have increase of children should be assured of services for them, if that their neighbor were not furnished from other places out of the country by husbandmen's children. Which would be a good relief to such as have great charge, and so avoid much evil education of youth and many other occasions of miseries in such cities and towns.

If the prentice be bound in a market town not corporate, then the father of the prentice must dwell in the same market town or in some other market town within the same shire.

That which is before said touching cities and towns corporate may also be said touching market towns.

The prentice must be bound for seven years at the least.

The prentice that is bound for less than seven years doth not commonly prove to be an expert artificer, so that thereby ignorance and imperfection in diverse arts and occupations do enter. Yet many are bound for five, four, three, yea, two years or less, and then take upon them to bring up others under them, whom they make as evil and as unskillful workmen as themselves. Which doth not only impair good and perfect workmanship or knowledge in occupations but also is a means whereby the number of artificers do so multiply that one of them do as it were eat and consume another. . . .

The prentice should be bound for so many years that he should be full twenty-four years of age at the least before the end of his apprenticeship.

If this order were well observed many occasions of evil would be avoided, and both the master and the prentice should receive great commodities thereby. The master for that he should have the longer service of his prentice which must needs turn to his great profit, for one year's service at the latter end is more worth than four at the beginning. The servant for that he should grow into greater knowledge and perfection in the art or occupation that he was brought up in, and also should be of a more riper or better judgment to guide or rule himself, and so might the easilier avoid diverse dangers and inconveniences which young men when they come to their own hands or government at nineteen or twenty years of age oftentimes fall into. For it is to be noted that when young men come out of their apprenticeships at those ages, many of them set up their occupations and undo their masters that brought them up, whereby they, their wives, and children fall into ruin and great distress. Also some of those young men lead a licentious and riotous life. Some take wives and before they are twenty-four years of age have three or four children, which often they leave to the parish where they dwell, to be kept. . . . If this point of the statute were well observed, so many ancient householders should not fall into decay and distress as do, nor be driven to live upon the alms of parishes as they are, for then the aged should be guides unto youth, and young men should work to sustain the aged who were their bringers up and should themselves enjoy the like commodity by those that should rise under them. By which means the aged state should never be unprovided for, whereas now young artificers do undo themselves, and drive the old on begging also. . . .

The effectual execution of the said Statute for Artificers will be a very good means and help to advance husbandry, to banish idleness, to reform the unadvised rashness and licentious manners of youth, to avoid many untimely and discommendable marriages, to bring the aged artificer to a staid [*settled*] state of living, to yield unto the hired person both in the time of plenty and in the time of scarcity a convenient proportion of wages, to observe duty between the master and the servant. And so will be a great occasion whereby the commonwealth shall not be in such sort burdened as now it is with lusty beggars, rogues, and vagabonds, whereby those that are poor and impotent [*physically weak*] indeed may be the better relieved and sustained.

2.6   A Petition to the Mayor and Jurats of Sandwich in Kent (1593)

From *Acts of the Privy Council*, ns 24, ed. John Roche Dasent (London: HMSO, 1901), 352–3.

No law was effective without enforcement, but sometimes officials showed mercy, too. Men in the town of Sandwich recognized that if Repent Hubbard was prosecuted for violating the Statute of Artificers they would condemn him to poverty – and perhaps burden themselves with supporting his family. Their petition on his behalf shows the social and economic value of reputation in the early modern period.

There is one Repent Hubbard of that town who (as we are given to under-stand) hath been heretofore a man of good substance and ability and become very poor by great losses at sea and otherwise. And not being able to follow his trade which before his decay he did use, having (as it would seem) a very honest care to live to maintain himself, his wife, and children, hath betaken himself to the occupation of a baker and hath used baking almost for these two years. And because he was never bound apprentice to that science he is threatened (as is alleged unto us) to be sued upon the statute made in the fifth year of Her Majesty's reign concerning apprentices. We have thought good, considering this poor gentleman hath an honest intent to live by his handy labor and not meaning to charge or burden the town with his wife or chil-dren, to pray you to call such persons before you that have or shall have at any time hereafter any purpose to sue him upon the foresaid statute, and to entreat and require them in our names that they will be contented to tolerate him and not to trouble or molest him by course of law. But that in respect of his great losses he may be permitted to use the said faculty, whereby he may be better able to maintain him, his poor wife, and children. And so not doubt-ing but they will show themselves herein conformable, being for so charita-ble a cause as this is.

2.7   Female Apprentices in London (14 March 1570)

From Minute Book 8 of the Drapers' Company of London, 97^r.

Apprenticeships were administered by "livery" companies, guilds which maintained city business standards. Some of the resistance to female apprenticeships came from the fact that a woman who had trained in one company might eventually take trade secrets into marriage with a man from another company. An elder in the London Drapers' Company knew of women who had been indentured in the past, but by 1570 this was a distant memory.

Question and resolution concerning the binding [indenturing] of a maiden apprentice in this Company or any other

Before they went to dinner a question was moved to Master Dummer whether a maiden servant willing to be bound apprentice to a master and mistress for term of years might not be presented in our [Company] Hall and also enrolled in the Chamber of London as other apprentice[s] are and thereby to enjoy also the freedom of the city [*license to trade*]? Who answered, "Yes," and that thereof they have precedents in the Chamber of London for more than a hundred years past. And that the self-same oath which is ministered to all other apprentices that are made free is also ministered to them. And further that their indentures ought also to be made in such manner and form as they are for other apprentices in this city. . . . Which question rose upon a maiden which Master Calverley brought to be presented before the Masters the Wardens to be bound to him and to his wife, which thing they refused for that they had not seen the like heretofore.

2.8 A Female Apprentice in Southampton (23 June 1577)

From *Books of Examinations and Depositions, 1570–1594*, ed. Gertrude H. Hamilton, Southampton Record Society, 16 (1914), 51.

In other places and circumstances, girls did serve apprenticeships, even in manual trades like masonry and blacksmithing. Southampton officials recognized that an apprenticeship in shoemaking solved problems for a displaced couple, a poor orphan, and their own overburdened charities.

Charles Pointdexter and Collet his wife did agree and submit themselves to keep and find [*support*] well and honestly Elizabeth Darvall, the daughter of Nicholas Darvall, deceased, for six pence by the week until the feast of the Nativity of St. John the Baptist [*24 June*], which shall be in the year of Our Lord God 1578. And from thence to keep her freely at their own charge and thereof to discharge [*disburden*] the town in all respects, and then to receive her as their apprentice for the space of twelve years. In consideration whereof, both the said Charles and Collet his wife are permitted and suffered to remain in the town and to set up the occupation of a cobbler for the town's part; otherwise to depart.

2.9 Clais van Wervekin's Letter to his Wife in Belgium (21 August 1567)

From *The Walloons and their Church at Norwich*, ed. William John Charles Moen, Publications of the Huguenot Society of London, 1 (1887), 220.

London's explosive growth came mostly from English men and women seeking oppor-
tunity, but other newcomers included Protestant refugees from the Continent's religious
wars. The capital was not the only destination for immigrants, however. By the mid-
seventeenth century, 40 percent of those living in Norwich were non-native. Although
Europeans faced legal and institutional impediments to free trade, they were often so
highly skilled that they found eager buyers for the wares produced in their covert, unli-
censed workshops. Hatmaker Van Wervekin wrote enthusiastically from Norwich to his
wife still in Belgium.

You would never believe how friendly the people are together, and the English
are the same and quite loving to our nation. If you come here with half our property, you would never think of going to live in Flanders. Send my money and the
three children. Come at once and do not be anxious. When you come, bring a
dough trough [*wooden bowl for kneading*], for there are none here. Know that I
await you and doubt me not; send me Catelynken, Saerle, and Tonyne. Bring
also our long hooks to hang your linen cords on. Buy two little wooden dishes
to make up half pounds of butter, for all Netherlanders and Flemings [*in England*]
make their own butter, for here it is all pigs' fat.

2.10   The Complaint of the London Company of Goldsmiths to the King's Solicitor, Sir Robert Heath (7 January 1622)

From SP 14/127: 12.

London's leaders relied upon the livery companies as organizational units through
which they could disseminate royal proclamations, recruit soldiers, raise subsidies,
maintain city infrastructures, and enforce social order. In turn, this gave the livery
companies considerable power in city affairs – as in 1622, when the Goldsmiths,
Coopers, Clockmakers, and Leatherdressers coordinated a protectionist protest effort.
This complaint to the King's Solicitor included a list of 183 foreigners practicing gold-
smithing in the city, outside the Company's control. The nationalities of the aliens are
not specified, but beside three of the names is added the notation "Jew."

By reason of their great and increasing number in buying, selling, and making
of gold and silver wares, jewels, precious stones, and other employments within
this city and suburbs solely and properly belonging to the goldsmith's profession
free of [*licensed in*] this city, the said aliens and strangers do take away a great
part of the living and maintenance of the free goldsmiths of this city who are
thereby exceedingly impoverished and disabled in their estates to bear public
charges.

That the said aliens and strangers in their habitations are dispersed into many lanes and remote places of this city and suburbs, working in chambers, garrets, and other secret places, where the wardens of this Company may not have convenient access and recourse to search [*examine to maintain standards*]. By which means besides the unlimited number of servants and apprentices, aliens kept by the said aliens and strangers (in which particular they usurp and enjoy more privilege than the freemen of this city), they make and sell many deceitful jewels, pearls, counterfeit stones, and other goldsmiths' wares of gold and silver to the great deceit of the nobility and people of this kingdom, it being partly the means that the use and exercise of other mean trades are crept into the goldsmiths' row in Cheap and Lombard Street to the great disgrace of this city.

For reformation of which inconveniences: We conceive it to be the fittest course by the wisdom of the state to provide that the great multitude of such aliens and strangers may be reduced to a far less number. And that they may not take any servants or apprentices but by the approbation and allowance of the wardens of the Company of Goldsmiths of this city and be subject unto them and their ordinances in all matters of government concerning their mystery, as in former ancient times they have been accustomed and in all other well-governed cities in foreign parts is used. . . . We conceive it will be very material and necessary in these times that the statute laws of this realm and Common Council [*legislative branch*] of this city now in force concerning aliens and strangers be duly and strictly put in execution.

2.11   A Proclamation Licensing Casper van Senden to Deport Negroes (January 1601)

From Salisbury (Hatfield House) Ms 91/15.

The terms "Negro" and "blackamoor" were used loosely in the early modern period, referring sometimes to racial, sometimes to ethnic, and sometimes to religious identity. In the 1560s England joined the maritime trade that furnished New World ventures with African slave labor. At home, meanwhile, it became a status symbol for wealthy Tudors to have an African servant or entertainer. Purportedly acting on common beliefs that foreigners drained native resources and threatened common culture, this edict rewarded the German merchant Casper van Senden with an exclusive contract to traffic deported African immigrants – that is, to enter them into slavery in the Americas. However, because the "proclamation" seems not to have been published and may never have been enforced, the black population continued to grow, especially in London.

Whereas the Queen's Majesty, tendering the good and welfare of her own natural subjects, greatly distressed in these hard times of dearth, is highly discontented to understand the great numbers of Negars and Blackamoors which (as she is informed) are crept into this realm since the troubles between Her Highness and the King of Spain, who are fostered and powered here to the great annoyance of her own liege people that want [*lack*] the relief which these people consume, as also for that the most of them are infidels having no understanding of Christ or his gospel: [therefore she] hath given especial commandment that the said kind of people should be with all speed avoided [*removed*] and discharged out of this her Majesty's dominion. And to that end and purpose hath appointed Casper van Senden, merchant of Lubeck [*in Germany*], for their speedy transportation, a man that hath very well deserved of this realm in respect that by his own labor and charge he hath relieved and brought from Spain diverse of our English nation who otherwise would have perished there.

2.12   An Act for Relief of the Poor (1597)

From *The Statutes of the Realm*, vol. 4, part 2 (London: G. Eyre and A. Strahan, 1819), 896–902.

The 1530s closure of monasteries, which had provided safety nets for the poor, provoked a crisis in public policy. A 1531 law licensed the "impotent" to beg but criminalized the "sturdy." A program for collecting donations from each parish was begun in 1535. In 1547 brutal physical punishments were authorized for the chronically homeless and unemployed. Charity was made compulsory in 1562, and training and apprenticeship programs were introduced in 1576. The Poor Law of 1597 consolidated all these provisions for relief and discipline into a comprehensive program.

Be it enacted by the authority of this present Parliament that the churchwardens of every parish and four substantial householders there . . . shall be called Overseers of the Poor of the same parish. And they or the greater part of them shall take order from time to time, by and with the consent of two or more such Justices of Peace, for setting to work of the children of all such whose parents shall not by the said persons be thought able to keep and maintain their children. And also all such persons married or unmarried as, having no means to maintain them, use no ordinary and daily trade of life to get their living by. And also to raise weekly or otherwise, by taxation of every inhabitant and every occupier of lands in the said parish, in such competent [*adequate*] sum and sums of money as they shall think fit, a convenient stock of flax, hemp, wool, thread, iron, and other necessary ware and stuff to set the poor on work. And also competent sums of money for and towards the necessary relief of the lame, impotent, old, blind, and such other among them being poor and not able to work. . . .

And be it also enacted that if the said Justices of Peace do perceive that the inhabitants of any parish are not able to levy among themselves sufficient sums of money for the purposes aforesaid, that then the said Justices shall and may tax, rate, and assess as aforesaid any other of other parishes or out of any parish within the hundred [*a subdivision of the county*] where the said parish is to pay such sum and sums of money to the churchwardens and overseers of the said poor parish for the said purposes as the said Justices shall think fit. . . .

And that it shall be lawful for the said churchwardens and Overseers (or any of them), by warrant from any such two Justices of Peace, to levy as well the said sums of money of every one that shall refuse to contribute according as they shall be assessed, by distress and sale of the offender's goods. . . . And in defect of such distress, it shall be lawful for any such two Justices of the Peace to commit him to prison, there to remain without bail or manprize [*surety*] till payment of the said sum or stock. . . .

And be it further enacted that it shall be lawful for the said churchwardens and Overseers (or the greater part of them), by the assent of any two Justices of the Peace, to bind [*indenture*] any such children as aforesaid to be apprentices, where they shall see convenient, till such man child shall come to the age of four and twenty years and such woman child to the age of one and twenty years. . . .

And to the intent that necessary places of habitation may more conveniently be provided for such poor impotent people, be it enacted by the authority aforesaid that it shall and may be lawful for the said churchwardens and Overseers (or the greater part of them), by the leave of the lord or lords of the manor whereof any waste or common [*uncultivated lands*] within their parish is or shall be parcel [*a component part*] . . . to erect, build, and set up . . . convenient houses of dwelling for the said impotent poor. And also to place inmates or more families than one in one cottage or house. . . .

And forasmuch as all begging is forbidden by this present Act, be it further enacted by the authority aforesaid that the Justices of Peace of every county or place corporate (or the more part of them) in their general sessions to be holden next after the end of this session of Parliament, or in default thereof at the Quarter Sessions to be holden about the feast of Easter next, shall rate every parish to such a weekly sum of money as they shall think convenient. So as no parish be rated above the sum of sixpence nor under the sum of an half-penny weekly to be paid, and so as the total sum of such taxation of the parishes in every county amount not above the rate of twopence for every parish in the said county. Which sums so taxed shall be yearly assessed by the agreement of the parishioners within themselves or, in default thereof, by the churchwardens and constables of the same parish (or the more part of them) or, in default of their agreement, by the order of such Justice or Justices of Peace as shall dwell in the same parish or, if none be there dwelling, in the parts next adjoining.

2.13   A Proclamation against Vagabonds and Unlawful Assemblies (9 September 1598)

From STC 8266 (Bodleian copy).

Not long after the legislative effort of 1597, this proclamation acknowledged its failure to cope with the pressures of poverty, especially among the "masterless" men who failed to find work after serving in the queen's armies.

Forasmuch as it is seen that notwithstanding the good laws provided for the restraining of idle people and vagabonds, yet for want of due execution thereof by the Justices of Peace and other ministers authorized thereunto, there are in many parts of the realm and specially about the city of London and Her Majesty's court manifestly seen wandering in the common highways, to the annoyance of the common people both in their goods and lives, multitudes of able men, neither impotent nor lame, exacting money continually upon pretense of service in the wars without relief, whereas many of them never did serve. And yet such as have served, if they were maimed or lamed by service, are provided for in the countries [*counties*] by order of sundry good laws and statutes in that behalf made and provided. For reformation whereof, Her Majesty straitly [*strictly*] commandeth all justices and officers to have better regard than heretofore they have had and to appoint upon certain days in the week monthly (for some convenient season) watches and privy searches in places needful, and thereby to attach and imprison such idle vagabonds and to send the lame and maimed into the countries according to the said statutes. And doth further notify hereby to all her subjects that because the disorder of those vagrant persons is, through neglect of her ordinary officers of justice, grown to such unruliness and undutifulness that there hath been of late diverse routs and unlawful assemblies of rogues and vagabonds, coloring their wandering by the name of soldiers lately come from the wars, who, arming themselves with shot and other forbidden weapons, have not only committed robberies and murders upon Her Majesty's people in their travel from place to place but also resisted and murdered diverse constables and others that have come to the rescue. Her Majesty therefore, being compelled to look with the eye of severity into these growing outrages, and being minded to provide for her good and dutiful subjects by cutting off in the beginning such lewd and notorious offenders, meaneth for that purpose to appoint a provost marshal with sufficient authority to apprehend all such as shall not be readily reformed and corrected by the ordinary officers of justice, and them without delay to execute upon the gallows by order of martial law. And these Her Majesty's commandments she willeth to be duly observed upon pain of her indignation.

3

Families, Gender, and Sexuality

As the basic unit of early modern society, the household was much more than a private institution. The state relied upon it as the site where the population renewed itself, where labor was produced, where property was transmitted, and, especially, where social acculturation was performed. Thus, the household had a dual nature. On the one hand, it was the locus for such practical, everyday necessities as shelter and sustenance. On the other hand, it was an object of ideological myth-making.

Love, Obedience, and Patriarchalism

A popular construct was that "love goeth downward, duty goeth upward" – that is, the husband, at the top of the family pyramid, should express his benevolent care for those in his charge, while all others should offer him their obedience. Like the kingdom, the church, any school, each livery company, and social groups of all sorts, the family was understood to be patriarchal in nature. Every member of a household – wife, child, servant – was believed to owe obedience to the man who had undivided powers as husband, father, and master. He was like a king, it was said, in the little world of his house.

The early humanist writings of Erasmus and Vives, the Protestant homily on "The State of Matrimony," and the Counter-Reformation catechism of the Roman Catholic Church unanimously agreed that marriage had three purposes: to furnish a man with a companion and helpmeet, to afford a legitimate outlet for his sexual desire, and to ensure him lawful procreation. As importantly, marriage served to establish a man as a mature member of society, in possession of political authority.

In the reformed state, with a less authoritarian church, there was emphasis not only on individual responsibility for salvation but also on the householder's responsibility for the well-being and behavior of those under his roof. The early modern domestic unit is generally called a "household" because it typically included more than the nuclear family. By the time they reached their mid-teens, most men and women had left their birth families to live within other families, where they were trained in service or in apprenticeship. In theory, all household relationships were binary ones and these binaries were unequal:

husbands and wives, with husbands over wives; parents and children, with parents over children; and masters and servants, with masters over servants. The presence of servants and apprentices was one source of pressure on the family structure – they were often of the same class as their masters and would be social equals when they reached adulthood – so a widely promulgated belief in political hierarchy was necessary to hold them in place.

In a booming print culture, many books catered to the domestic market, providing men with guidelines for choosing partners, rearing children, supervising servants, and achieving "peace" in the household through "right rule." The subordination of women, a frequent topic, was justified as a necessary consequence of Eve's disobedience: both marriage and childbirth were understood to be punitive and painful for all women because the first woman had fallen. Always, the emphasis was on male enfranchisement, heterosexual alliances, hierarchical relationships, and the dissemination of doctrine across lines of age, gender, and rank.

Making a Match

In practice, the inception of marriage was less straightforward than the guidebooks acknowledged. Church authorization took one of two forms. A couple might have their intentions announced three times on successive Sundays. Any objections to the union were to be lodged publicly at the reading of these "banns." Alternatively, a couple could obtain a license from a church official, who would have privately assured himself that there was no impediment to the marriage. In either case, marriage was prohibited if it was discovered that one party was already married, that one party was already betrothed, or that the two had a forbidden degree of "consanguinity." (Connections by marriage as well as by blood could be considered incestuous.) With either a license or the unopposed pronouncing of the banns, a parish minister was authorized to perform the church ceremony that sanctified marriage.

At the same time, however, there were binding forms of union that were contracted outside church. A couple could simply pledge themselves to each other, using what were widely known as "words of the present tense" – for example, "I take you to be my wife." It was also legally valid if a couple promised themselves in words of "the future tense," so long as the relationship was soon consummated. Of course, many such vows spoken in the heat of passion were later regretted. But because betrothal was as binding as a church ceremony, the pledge violated by one person might still constrain the other, making him or her unmarriageable except by the betrothed. Any later union would be considered bigamous. Thus, broken "spousals" were frequent causes of appeal to church courts, as were attempts to trap a person in marriage by falsely claiming a verbal contract. Church officers gathered information about other signs of betrothal: perhaps a couple had betrayed an intent to marry by exchanging gifts, or discussing wedding plans, or undertaking to set up housekeeping. These might go to suggest that the complaint should be honored and a contract should be enforced. Women seem generally to have had the upper hand at this stage. More often than not, it was the man who went to court, alleging that a woman had set him aside and asking that she be required to honor her commitment.

Parental influence in marriage was eroded by the fact that so many people of marriageable age lived and worked away from their birth homes. They sought counsel from friends, employers, and neighbors instead. The disincentive for marrying without approval, however, was that a couple might forfeit financial support. Young men and women generally began housekeeping with the help of "portions" they received from their parents, in addition to what they had earned. The prime requirement for marriage was that the couple be financially capable of establishing an independent household. This was the reason that most early moderns married later than we might assume, men between twenty-five and twenty-seven and women between twenty-three and twenty-five. With the system for service and apprenticeship, family productivity did not usually depend on child labor. Thus, most couples had little need to marry young and produce children who would contribute to the household economy. Second marriages, which were common because of mortality rates, were even more likely to be pragmatic. Then, people were asked – or asked themselves – if they could "learn to love" or "find in their heart to love" their proposed partners.

Exceptions to these general rules were to be found among the peerage and the gentry, where parents were concerned with the allegiances they could forge through marriage. For this reason, they played a stronger role in arranging the marriages of their children. Members of the landed classes married younger because their principal life responsibility was to protect the family estate. This they could do by producing legitimate heirs to whom property could rightly descend.

Home Truths

Although it was frequently said that the early modern household was a "commonwealth," a political organism, in important ways it was more like a corporation, an association based in shared economic purpose. The purpose might be advancement or sheer survival. Nor was the household naturally orderly. Family interactions were multifaceted and complex, sexual desire was not always contained within marriage, and women were repeatedly enjoined to be submissive because they so rarely were. Women had considerable authority in the private sphere, where they were solely responsible for most household functions including, often, the supervision of servants.

A large percentage were pregnant at their church weddings. Servants and apprentices were expected to remain single, and many preferred to live with food and lodgings provided until pregnancy gave the signal that it was time to marry and go out on their own. Women in these committed relationships suffered no social stigma. The situation was very different, however, for women who were sexually abused by their masters. Since conception was widely understood to require female orgasm, pregnancy was believed to disprove any allegation of rape. Women could also become innocent victims of the double standard if their intended partners died, moved, were forbidden to marry by their parents, or otherwise changed their minds. Illegitimate birth was not only a moral issue, it was an economic threat, making an implicit demand on parish charity. There was small sympathy for unwed mothers.

By law, women were regarded as either married or "to be married." However, as many as 40 percent of adult women were single at any one time, and, while some were in short-term service and some were widows, some would never wed. In many ways, men were more reliant on women than women on men, because men needed women to run the households on which their social standing depended, while most women were capable of supporting themselves, even if only at a subsistence level. This may be one reason why men were the more frequent pleaders for matrimonial enforcement in the church courts.

Written records about family matters – court cases, marriage contracts, last wills and testaments – are full of practical concerns. This does not mean, though, that personal relationships in the period were as empty of emotional content as has sometimes been alleged. In less official documents, including letters and diaries, there is ample evidence of deep attachments between husbands and wives, parents and children, and sisters and brothers. The comedies of Shakespeare and other dramatists may have been idealized, but they fully represented a culture that wanted to believe in romantic love and that witnessed instances of it.

Same-sex relationships were common in the period, although information about them can be harder to find. For one thing, early moderns are not known to have self-identified as homosexual or heterosexual; these reifications of sexuality trace to the nineteenth century. For another, the church and the state chose to regulate sexual relationships that had economic consequences, such as those that added to the poor rolls or that jeopardized the orderly transfer of property. There was no reason to police non-reproductive sex, unless child abuse was involved. Sodomy laws dealt with atheism and bestiality as well as anal sex, and were rarely enforced. Thus, both gay and lesbian relationships have tended to disappear into the common practice of same-sex bedsharing, into more open sexual experimentation, and into the language of passionate friendship. Like many private matters, this is a history that was suppressed by the insistence of public ideology upon the social, political, and personal value of marriage.

3.1 "An Homily of the State of Matrimony" (1563)

From *The Second Tome of Homilies of Such Matters as were Promised*, STC 13664 (BL copy), Lll1ᵛ–Lll6ʳ.

In 1547, under Edward VI, twelve authorized sermons, or "homilies," were issued to be read regularly in Reformed churches. Elizabeth I continued her brother's unfinished work, in 1563 issuing a second volume of sermons that she herself edited before publication. Thus, this sermon on marriage was supervised by a Virgin Queen.

The word of Almighty God doth testify and declare whence the original beginning of matrimony cometh and why it is ordained. It is instituted of God, to the intent that man and woman should live lawfully in a perpetual friendly fellowship, to bring forth fruit, and to avoid fornication. By which means, a good conscience might be preserved on both parties in bridling the corrupt inclinations of the flesh within the limits of honesty. For God hath straightly [*directly*] forbidden all whoredom and uncleanness and hath from time to time taken grievous punishments of this inordinate lust, as all stories and ages hath declared. Furthermore, it is also ordained that the Church of God and his kingdom might by this kind of life be conserved and enlarged, not only in that God giveth children by his blessing, but also in that they be brought up by the parents godly, in the knowledge of God's word, that this, the knowledge of God and true religion, might be delivered by succession from one to another, that finally many might enjoy that everlasting immortality.

Wherefore, forasmuch as matrimony serveth as well to avoid sin and offense as to increase the kingdom of God, you, as all other which enter that state, must acknowledge this benefit of God with pure and thankful minds, for that he hath so ruled your hearts that ye follow not the example of the wicked world, who set their delight in filthiness of sin, where both of you stand in the fear of God and abhor all filthiness. For that is surely the singular gift of God, where the common example of the world declareth how the devil hath their hearts bound and entangled in diverse snares so that they in their wifeless state run into open abominations without any grudge of their conscience. Which sort of men, that liveth so desperately and filthily: what damnation tarrieth for them?

Saint Paul describeth it to them, saying: "Neither whoremongers, neither adulterers shall inherit the kingdom of God." This horrible judgment of God ye be escaped through his mercy, if so be that ye live inseparately according to God's ordinance. But yet I would not have you careless, without watching. For the devil will assay [*try*] to attempt all things to interrupt and hinder your hearts and godly purpose, if ye will give him any entry. For he will either labor to break this godly knot once begun betwixt you, or else at the least he will labor to encumber it with diverse griefs and displeasures.

And this is his principal craft, to work dissension of hearts of the one from the other, that whereas now there is pleasant and sweet love betwixt you, [he] will in the stead thereof bring in most bitter and unpleasant discord. And surely that same adversary of ours doth, as it were from above, assault man's nature and condition. For this folly is ever from our tender age grown up with us, to have a desire to rule, to think highly by ourself, so that none thinketh it meet to give place to another. That wicked vice of stubborn will and self-love is more meet to break and to dissever the love of heart than to preserve concord. Wherefore married persons must apply their minds in most earnest wise to concord and must crave continually of God the help of his holy spirit, so to rule their hearts and to knit their minds together that they be not dissevered by any division of discord. . . .

But to this prayer must be joined a singular diligence, whereof Saint Peter giveth his precept, saying: "You husbands, deal with your wives according to knowledge, giving honor to the wife as unto the weaker vessel, and as unto them that are heirs also of the grace of life, that your prayers be not hindered." This precept doth particularly pertain to the husband. For he ought to be the leader and author of love in cherishing and increasing concord, which then shall take place if he will use measurableness and not tyranny, and if he yield some things to the woman. For the woman is a weak creature, not endued with like strength and constancy of mind. Therefore they be the sooner disquieted and they be the more prone to all weak affections and dispositions of mind more than men be, and lighter they be, and more vain [*foolish*] in their fantasies and opinions. These things must be considered of the man, that he be not too stiff, so that he ought to wink at [*disregard*] some things, and must gently expound [*explain*] all things, and to forbear. . . . Yea, he sayeth more: that the woman ought to have a certain honor attributed to her, that is to say, she must be spared [*dealt with leniently*] and borne with, the rather for that she is the weaker vessel, of a frail heart, inconstant, and with a word soon stirred to wrath. And therefore, considering these her frailties, she is to be the rather spared. By this means, thou shalt not only nourish concord but shalt have her heart in thy power and will. For honest natures will sooner be retained to do their duty rather by gentle words than by stripes. But he which will do all things with extremity and severity, and doth use always rigor in words and stripes, what will that avail in the conclusion? Verily, nothing but that he thereby setteth forward the devil's work. He banisheth away concord, charity, and sweet amity, and bringeth in dissension, hatred, and irksomeness, the greatest griefs that can be in the mutual love and fellowship of man's life. . . .

Now as concerning the wife's duty. What shall become her? Shall she abuse the gentleness and humanity of her husband and at her pleasure turn all things upside down? No, surely, for that is far repugnant against God's commandment. For thus doth Saint Peter preach to them: "Ye wives, be ye in subjection to obey your own husband." To obey is another thing than to control or command, which yet they may do to their children and to their family. But as for their husbands, them must they obey and cease from commanding and perform subjection. . . . And they shall not do this only to avoid strife and debate, but rather in the respect of the commandment of God as Saint Paul expresseth it in this form of words: "Let women be subject to their husbands, as to the Lord. For the husband is the head of the woman as Christ is the head of the Church." Here you understand that God hath commanded that ye should acknowledge the authority of the husband and refer to him the honor of obedience. . . .

Truth it is, that they must specially feel the griefs and pains of their matrimony in that they relinquish the liberty of their own rule, in the pain of their travailing [*in childbirth*], in the bringing up of their children. In which offices they be in great perils and be grieved with great afflictions, which they might be without if they lived out of matrimony. But Saint Peter sayeth that this is the chief ornament of holy matrons, in that they set their hope and trust in God, that is to say, in that they refused not from marriage for the business [*labor*] thereof, for the griefs and perils thereof, but committed all such adventures to God in most sure trust of help, after that they have called upon his aid. O woman, do thou the like, and so shalt thou be most excellently beautified before God and all his angels and saints, and thou needest not to seek further for doing any better works. For, obey thy husband, take regard of his requests, and give heed unto him to perceive what he requireth of thee, and so shall thou honor God and live peaceably in thy house.

3.2   John Dod and Robert Cleaver, *A Godly Form of Household Government for the Ordering of Private Families* (1598)

From STC 5383 (HL copy), F4^v, L4^v–L5^r.

The playwright Ben Jonson joked that a gentlewoman slept with the clergyman John Dod hoping for "the procreation of an angel or saint," only to suffer "an ordinary birth." Dod may have been one source for the Jonson character Ananias (a fanatical Puritan in The Alchemist*). He was himself so radical that, in 1614, James VI and I prohibited him from preaching. His earlier work with fellow-Puritan Robert Cleaver was more conventional, however. Advice such as this, on the place of women in marriage, was frequently repeated.*

If she be not subject to her husband, to let him rule all household (especially outward affairs), if she will make head against him and seek to have her own ways, there will be doing and undoing. Things will go backward, the house will come to ruin, for God will not bless where his ordinance is not obeyed. This is allowable: that she may in modest sort show her mind, and a wise husband will not disdain to hear her advice – and follow it also, if it be good. But when her way is not liked of, though it be the best way, she may not thereupon set all at six and seven, with "What should I labor and travail: I see my husband taketh such ways that he will bring all to nothing." This were nothing else but, when she seeth the house falling, to help to pull it down faster. . . .

The husband ought not to be satisfied that he hath robbed his wife of her virginity, but in that he hath possession and use of her will, for it sufficeth not that they be married, but that they be well married, and live Christianly together, and very well contented. And therefore the husband that is not beloved of his wife holdeth his goods in danger, his house in suspicion, his credit in balance, and also sometime his life in peril, because it is easy to believe that she desireth not long life unto her husband, with whom she passeth a time so tedious and irksome. . . . The best rule that a man may hold and practice with his wife, to guard and govern her, is to admonish her often and to give her good instructions, to reprehend her seldom, never to lay violent hands on her, but, if she be good and dutiful, to favor her, to the end she may continue so.

3.3   William Whately, Two Marriage Tracts (1617–24)

From STC 25296 (FSL copy), D2^{r-v}, and STC 25299 (Illinois copy), A3^v–A4^v.

Ben Jonson also satirized Puritan fanaticism in his play Bartholomew Fair. *He specified that the character Zeal-of-the-Land Busy preached in Banbury, a town famously identified with Dod, Cleaver, and William Whately. By trivializing household business, as he does here, Whately participated in the historic devaluation of women's work. Elsewhere, he insisted that it was lawful for a man to beat his wife if she disobeyed him and that the innocent partner of an adulterer or deserter should be permitted to remarry. (When he was called before the High Commission, he was forced to recant his defense of divorce – but not his endorsement of domestic violence.)*

A Bride-Bush, Or A Wedding Sermon (1617)

In commanding, it must be regarded that authority descend not unto low, mean, and trivial things which are not of any moment or importance in the family. The life of the head must be derived even unto the feet; so, the husband's authority doth indeed guide all, even the meanest things in the family, but the head is not always actually stooping unto the foot, for then the body would grow crooked and ill-shapen. So must not the husband be charging, bidding, and intermeddling by strict commandments in the small matters of the family, putting his hand (as it were) to every matter. For that garment which is much worn must needs become threadbare. And this power of commanding is like a vesture for high days,[1] to be put on for some special and needful occasions. When the husband will be housewife and all, and be dealing with brewing, baking, washing, and the particulars of these and the like businesses, it comes to pass that his wife can help in nothing because he will do all things. When the man will bid and charge so eagerly in a thing of nothing, as if his whole estate did depend upon serving the swine or washing the buck,[2] etc., this devalues his word and

1 *vesture for high days*: apparel for holy or feast days, with an echo of the rich "vestments" worn by monarchs and priests.
2 *washing the buck*: doing the laundry, specifically laundry that involves steeping or boiling linens to bleach them.

makes his charge of no regard. In such things he should let his wife rule under him and give her leave to know more than himself, which hath greater matters and more nearly [*demanding*] concerning the family to exercise his knowledge. And if he see any thing in these and the like matters done disorderly, it were his part to advise and counsel rather than command. He that will be drawing out his commandments for every light thing shall find it at length regarded in nothing.

A Care-Cloth, Or A Treatise of the Cumbers and Troubles of Marriage (1624)

I will make bold to foretell those that will enter into marriage that they must make account in changing their estate to change for the less easeful, and will advise him that will follow mine advice (if not, let him follow his own mind and say, ten years after, whether [*which*] was the better counsel) to go unto matrimony with fear of the worst, and to know beforehand that there grow briars and thorns in this way, whereon he must needs tread that will travail in it. Yet is not this written by me to make any man forbear marriage whom God calleth unto it, nor to make men hazard themselves to wickedness for fear of the cumbers of matrimony, but . . . to make men careful not to marry before God calls them to it and withal, being called, to fit themselves for it. . . . When doth God call a man to marriage? I answer: First, when he sets him in such a condition that he may marry without wronging any other person – that is, when he is now become his own man, not bound by covenant to continue another man's servant. For God never crosseth himself: whom he hath called for a certain time to be servant unto a master, him he doth not call during that time to break from that service without his master's liking and to think of making himself a master before he have fulfilled the duty of a servant. Secondly, when God furnisheth a man with some convenient means to maintain a wife and family, and not before. For God calleth no man to any place until he have granted him some means of discharging the duties of that place, and it is one part of an householder's duty to provide for them of his household. The Lord sends not soldiers into the field to fight without some weapons – nor men to housekeeping without some means to keep house.

3.4 William Gouge, *Of Domestical Duties: Eight Treatises* (1622)

From STC 12119 (FSL copy), V3^r, V4^v–V5^r, ¶3^v–¶4^r.

Preaching twice each Sunday and lecturing every Wednesday, the "Arch Puritan" William Gouge compiled a formidable portfolio of sermons which he grouped into such categories as "common mutual duties betwixt man and wife," "wives' particular duties," "husbands' particular duties," "children's duties," "parents' duties," "servants' duties," and "masters' duties." There are seventy-four sermons just on "wives' particular duties"; numbers twenty-three and twenty-six are excerpted below. In the dedicatory epistle to the Duties, *Gouge reveals that he sometimes encountered resistance to his methodical exposition of the various ways in which females should be expected to demonstrate subjection.*

Of a Wife's Restraint in Disposing Goods without Consent of Her Husband, and of the Ground of that Restraint

Whether a wife may privily [*secretly*] and simply, without or openly and directly against her husband's consent, distribute such common goods of the family as her husband reserveth to his own disposing, there being no extraordinary necessity? The most ancient and common answer unto this question hath been negative, namely, that a wife hath not power so to do – whereunto I for my part subscribe. The ground of this answer is taken from that primary law of the wife's subjection, "Thy desire shall be unto thine husband" (Genesis 3:16). How is her desire subject to her husband, if in the case propounded she stand not upon his consent? It is further confirmed both by the forenamed and also by all other proofs that might be produced out of the Scripture concerning the subjection of wives unto their husbands. If in ordering the goods of the family she yield not subjection, wherein *shall* she yield it?

Of Human Laws which Restrain Wives from Disposing Goods without or against their Husbands' Consent

Now, our law sayeth that every gift, grant, or disposition of goods, lands, or other thing whatsoever made by a woman covert, and all and every obligation and feoffment made by her, and recovery suffered, if they be done without her husband's consent, are void.[3] . . . And though she have inheritance of her own, yet can she not grant any annuity out of it during her coverture, without her husband; if any deed be made to that purpose without his consent, or in her name alone, it is void in law. . . . And if she sell anything, the sale is void, except she be a merchant, where, by the custom, she is enabled to merchandise. Finally, she cannot make executors without the consent of her husband, nor a devise

---

3 *a woman covert . . . are void*: By the doctrine of *coverture*, married women were legally under the "cover" of their husbands' authority and protection. They were not entitled to independently buy, sell, or bequeath property. (This obtained only in the common law; there were other forms of law in use.) Gouge refers to an exception: the wives of merchants were entitled to trade as "femes sole" rather than "femes covert," that is, as autonomous businesswomen. Coverture did not apply to adult single women or to widows.

[*bequest of property*], or will. If she make a will, and thereby devise her own inheritance, and her husband die, and she after die without any new publication of it, it is of no force because it was void at first. These and many other like cases which might be alleged evidently show that by law a wife hath not power of herself, without her husband, to dispose the common goods of the family.

The Epistle Dedicatory to his Parishioners in the Precinct of Blackfriars, London

I remember that when these *Domestical Duties* were first uttered out of the pulpit, much exception was taken against the application of a wife's subjection to the restraining of her from disposing the common goods of the family without or against her husband's consent. But surely they that made those exceptions did not well think of the cautions and limitations which were then delivered and are now again expressly noted, which are that the foresaid restraint be not extended to the proper goods of a wife, no, nor overstrictly to such goods as are set apart for the use of the family, nor to extraordinary cases, nor always to an express consent, nor to the consent of such husbands as are impotent [*disabled*] or far and long absent. If any other warrantable caution shall be showed me, I will be as willing to admit it as any of these. Now, that my meaning may not still be perverted, I pray you, in reading the restraint of wives' powers in disposing the goods of the family, ever bear in mind those cautions. Other exceptions were made against some other particular duties of wives. For many that can patiently enough hear their duties declared in general terms cannot endure to hear those generals exemplified in their particular branches. This cometh too near to the quick and pierceth too deep. But (to interpret all, according to the rule of love, in the better part) I take the main reason of the many exceptions which were taken to be this: that wives' duties (according to the Apostle's method) being in the first place handled, there was taught (as must have been taught, except the truth should have been betrayed) what a wife, in the uttermost extent of that subjection under which God hath put her, is bound unto *in case* [*if*] her husband will stand upon the uttermost of his authority. Which was so taken, as if I had taught that an husband might and ought to exact the uttermost, and that a wife was bound in that uttermost extent to do all that was delivered as duty, whether her husband exact it or no. But when I came to deliver husbands' duties, I showed that he ought not to exact whatsoever his wife was bound unto (in case it were exacted by him) but that he ought to make her a joint governor of the family with himself, and refer the ordering of many things to her discretion and with all honorable and kind respect to carry himself towards her. In a word, I so set down an husband's duties as, if he be wise and conscionable in observing them, his wife can have no just cause to complain of her subjection. That which maketh a wife's yoke heavy and hard is an husband's abuse of his authority, and more pressing his wife's duty than performing his own, which is directly contrary to the Apostle's rule. This just apology I have been forced to make that I might not ever by judged (as some have censured me) an hater of women.

3.5   Rachel Speght, *A Mouzell for Melastomus . . . Or an Apologetical Answer*[4] *to that Irreligious and Illiterate Pamphlet Made by Jo[seph] Sw[etnam]* (1616)

From STC 23058 (HU copy), C2^r, C2^v–C3^r, C3^v, D4^v, E1$^{r–v}$.

The European "querelle des femmes" – a debate about women, their nature, and their place in society – provoked a pamphlet war in England, too. In 1615 the misogynistic Arraignment of Lewd, Idle, Froward, and Unconstant Women *was published under the pseudonym "Thomas Tel-troth." In her rebuttal, the nineteen-year-old Rachel Speght identified the "truth-teller" as Joseph Swetnam. Because later contributors to the debate also used pen names, Speght's erudite "muzzle for blackmouth" is the only pamphlet known certainly to have been written by a woman. In 1620 a play by Thomas Heywood,* Swetnam the Woman-Hater Arraigned by Women, *ended with the title character tried, muzzled, and tormented.*

The work of Creation being finished, this approbation thereof was given by God himself: that "All was very good." If all, then woman, who, excepting man, is the most excellent creature under the canopy of heaven. But if it be objected . . . that woman, though created good, yet by giving ear to Satan's temptations, brought death and misery upon all her posterity . . . I answer that Satan first assailed the woman because where the hedge is lowest, most easy it is to get over, and she being the weaker vessel was with more facility to be seduced, like as a crystal glass sooner receives a crack than a strong stone pot. Yet we shall find the offense of Adam and Eve almost to parallel, for as an ambitious desire of being made like unto God was the motive which caused her to eat, so likewise was it his. . . . And if Adam had not approved of that deed which Eve had done, and been willing to tread the steps which she had gone, he being her head would have reproved her and have made the commandment a bit to restrain him from breaking his Maker's injunction. For if a man burn his hand in the fire, the bellows that blowed the fire are not to be blamed but himself rather, for not being careful to avoid the danger. Yet if the bellows had not blowed, the fire had not burnt; no more is woman simply to be condemned for man's transgression, for, by the free will which before his fall he enjoyed, he might have avoided and been free from being burnt or singed with that fire which was kindled by Satan and blown by Eve. It therefore served not his turn a whit afterwards to say, "The woman which

---

4 *an Apologetical Answer*: a defense or vindication, in this case of the female gender.

thou gavest me gave me of the tree and I did eat." For a penalty was inflicted upon him as well as on the woman, the punishment of her transgression being particular to her own sex and to none but the female kind. But for the sin of man the whole earth was cursed. And he, being better able than the woman to have resisted temptation because the stronger vessel, was first called to account, to show that to whom much is given, of them much is required, and that he who was the sovereign of all creatures visible should have yielded greatest obedience to God. . . . The offense therefore of Adam and Eve is by Saint Augustine thus distinguished: the man sinned against God and himself; the woman, against God, herself, and her husband. Yet in her giving of the fruit to eat had she no malicious intent towards him but did therein show a desire to make her husband partaker of that happiness which she thought by their eating they should both have enjoyed. . . .

And if God's love even from the beginning had not been as great toward woman as to man, then would he not have preserved from the deluge of the old world[5] as many women as men. Nor would Christ after his resurrection have appeared unto a woman first of all other, had it not been to declare thereby that the benefits of his death and resurrection are as available by belief for women as for men. For he indifferently died for the one sex as well as the other. Yet a truth ungainsayable is it that the "man is the woman's head," by which title yet of supremacy no authority hath he given him to domineer or basely command and employ his wife as a servant, but hereby is he taught the duties which he oweth unto her. For as the head of a man is the imaginer and contriver of projects profitable for the safety of his whole body, so the husband must protect and defend his wife from injuries. For he is her "head, as Christ is the head of his Church," which he entirely loveth, and for which he gave his very life, the dearest thing any man hath in this world. . . .

Thus, if men would remember the duties they are to perform in being heads, some would not stand a-tiptoe as they do, thinking themselves lords and rulers, and account every omission of performing whatsoever they command, whether lawful or not, to be matter of great disparagement and indignity done them. Whereas they should consider that women are enjoined to submit themselves unto their husbands no otherways than as to the Lord, so that from hence, for man, ariseth a lesson not to be forgotten, that as the Lord commandeth nothing to be done but that which is right and good, no more must the husband. For if a wife fulfill the evil command of her husband, she obeys him as a tempter, as Saphira did Ananias.[6] But lest I should seem too partial in praising women so much as I have (though no more than warrant from Scripture doth allow) I add to the premises [*the foregoing*] that I say not all women are virtuous, for then they should be more excellent than men.

---

5 *deluge of the old world*: Speght refers to the biblical flood and Noah's ark.
6 *as Saphira did Ananias*: Speght refers to Acts 5. Saphira knew about a lie her husband Ananias told; both dropped dead when exposed.

HIC MVLIER:

OR,

The Man-Woman:

Being a Medicine to cure the Coltish Difeafe of
the Staggers in the *Mafculine-Feminines*
of our Times.

Exprest in a briefe Declamation.

Non omnes poffumus omnes.

Miftris, will you be trim'd or truff'd?

Loncon printed for J.T. and are to be fold at Chrift Church gate. 1620.

Figure 5 Title pages from *Hic Mulier* (1620) and *Haec Vir* (1620). Courtesy of the Huntington Library.

Early modern gender wars were played out in two anonymous pamphlets published within a week of each other in 1620. *Hic Mulier* deliberately misused a masculine demonstrative pronoun with a feminine noun to deride "this mannish woman," the woman who forgets that long hair is the "ornament of her sex, and bashful shamefastness her chief honor." The title page shows a woman being

HÆC-VIR:
OR
The Womanish-Man:

Being an Anſwere to a late Booke intituled
Hic-Mulier.

Expreſt in a briefe Dialogue betweene *Hæc-
Vir* the Womaniſh-Man, and *Hic-Mulier* the
Man-Woman.

London printed for *I.T.* and are to be ſold at Chriſt Church gate. 1620.

barbered while another consults a mirror to admire her own short hair and mannish hat. *Haec Vir* employed a feminine demonstrative pronoun with a masculine noun to condemn "this womanish man." The pamphlet opens with a scene illustrated on the title page: Hic Mulier and Haec Vir meet and mistake each other's gender. "Is she mad or doth she mock me?" she asks herself; "What doth he behold in me, to take me for a woman?" he wonders. The two androgynes eventually conclude that they will reform their dress and style to live like "true men and true women," Hic Vir and Haec Mulier.

3.6   Magdalen Gawyn's Punishment for Cross-Dressing (19 April 1575)

From CLRO X109/143, Repertories of the London Court of Aldermen 18, 372^r.

Two notorious contributions to the gender debate were Hic Mulier, *or* The Manish-Woman *(1620) and* Haec Vir, *or* The Womanish-Man *(1620), about people who defied gender norms in behavior and dress. Cross-dressing was not just a device to sell pamphlets, as shown in this case of a real-life "hic mulier." Magdalen Gawyn was publicly re-feminized ("her hair hanging over her shoulders") before being incarcerated in London's house of correction.*

It was ordered and adjudged by this Court that Magdalen Gawyn, a young woman of the age of twenty-one years, for that she, contrary to all honesty of womanhood, appareled herself in man's clothing and went abroad the streets of this city disguised in that sort, shall tomorrow at eight of the clock in the forenoon be set on the pillory in Cheapside there to remain until eleven of the clock, having her hair hanging over her shoulders and appareled in the attire wherewith she is now clothed. And afterwards to be committed to Bridewell.

3.7   Richard Rogers's Diary (12 January 1588)

From *Two Elizabethan Puritan Diaries*, ed. M. M. Knappen (Chicago: American Society of Church History, 1933), 73–4.

The son of a carpenter, Richard Rogers studied at Cambridge, received an MA in 1574, became a Puritan lecturer, and married twice. In this extract from his diary, he imagines losing his wife in childbirth and, thinking perhaps of the inventories of personal goods and valuables compiled at any death, itemizes her worth to him.

By occasion of the strange visitation of one of our neighbors, Mistress A.,[7] I, seeing by much pain in wife and near childbirth many likelihoods of our separation, considered how many uncomfortablenesses the Lord had kept from me hitherto by those which I then saw must needs come if he should part us, that I might more thankfully use the benefit if it should be continued and acquaint myself with thinking on some of them before (that they might not be altogether sudden). But, alas, this latter is hard.

---

7 *Mistress A.*: In the margin, Rogers notes that after "lying like one senseless, no cheer, nor words," she died on 5 January 1588.

First, the fear of marrying again, dangerous as second marriages are.

Want of it[8] in the meanwhile.

Forgoing so fit a companion for religion, housewifery, and other comforts.

Loss and decay in substance [*material worth*].

Care of household matters cast on me.

Neglect of study.

Care and looking after children.

Forgoing our boarders.

Fear of losing friendship among her kindred.

These are some. The Lord may cast me down with them also in sickness.

3.8 Edward Alleyn's Letter to his Wife Joan Alleyn (August 1593)

From Dulwich College Archives Ms I f13.

Amid the discourses of gender hierarchy, there was also evidence of mutual feeling, as in the letters exchanged by Edward Alleyn and his wife. Alleyn was a celebrated actor with the company called Lord Strange's Men. In plague times, when London's public theaters were closed for fear that contagion would spread rapidly among the crowds of playgoers, acting companies went on tour; here, Alleyn wrote home from Bristol.

My good sweet mouse,

I commend me heartily to you and to my father, my mother, and my sister Bess, hoping in God though the sickness be round about you, yet by his mercy it may escape your house – which by the grace of God it shall. Therefore, use this course: keep your house fair and clean, which I know you will, and every evening throw water before your door and in your backside. And have in your windows good store of rue and herb of grace.[9] And with all the grace of God which must be obtained by prayers and so doing, no doubt but the Lord will mercifully defend you. Now, good mouse, I have no news to send you but this: that we have all our health, for which the Lord be praised. I received your letter at Bristol by Richard Couley, for the which I thank you. I have sent you by this bearer, Thomas Pope's kinsman, my white waistcoat, because it is a trouble to me to carry it. Receive it with this letter and lay it up for me till I come. If you send any more letters, send to me by the carriers of Shrewsbury or to Westchester or to York to be kept till my Lord Strange's Players come. And thus, sweetheart, with my hearty commendations to all our friends, I cease. From Bristol this

---

8 *Want of it*: lack of sexual congress.

9 *rue and herb of grace*: the bitter leaves of evergreen plants used medicinally.

Wednesday after Saint James his day [*25 July*], being ready to begin the play of *Harry of Cornwall*. Mouse, do my hearty commendations to Master Grigs his wife and all his household and to my sister Phillips. Your loving husband, E. Alleyn.

Mouse, you send me no news of any things. You should send of your domestical matters such things as happens at home, as how your distilled water proves, or this or that, or anything what you will.

And Jug, I pray you, let my orange tawny stockings of woolen be dyed a very good black against I come home, to wear in the winter. You sent me not word of my garden, but next time you will but remember this in any case, that all that bed which was parsley in the month of September you sow it with spinach, for then is the time. I would do it myself but we shall not come home till All Hallows Tide [*1 November*]. And so sweet mouse, farewell, and brook [*endure*] our long journey with patience.

3.9   Joan Alleyn's Letter to her Husband Edward Alleyn (21 October 1603)

From Dulwich College Archives Ms I f52^{r-v}.

By 1603 Edward Alleyn was affiliated with the Lord Admiral's Men (principal rivals of Shakespeare's Lord Chamberlain's Men). His wife Joan Woodward was the stepdaughter of theatrical entrepreneur Philip Henslowe. In another of their surviving letters, she reveals that the couple shared a thorough knowledge of the playing profession, domestic and business interests, and love.

My entire and well-beloved sweetheart,

Still it joys me, and long I pray God may I joy to hear of your health and welfare, as you of ours. Almighty God be thanked, my own self, your self, and my mother and whole house are in good health, and about us the sickness doth cease and likely more and more by God's help to cease. All the Companies be come home and well, for ought we know, but that Brown of the Boar's Head is dead and died very poor; he went not into the country at all. And all of your own Company are well at their own houses. My father is at the Court, but where the Court is I know not. I am of your own mind that it is needless to meet my father at Basing, the incertainty being as it is, and I commend your discretion. It were a sore journey to lose your labor beside expenses. And change of air might hurt you; therefore you are resolved upon the best course. For your coming home I am not to advise you – neither will I; use your own discretion. Yet I long and am very desirous to see you. And my poor and simple opinion is: if it shall please you, you may safely come home. Here is none now sick near us. Yet let it not be as I will but at your own best liking. I am glad to hear you take delight in hawking, and though you have worn your apparel to rags, the best is you know where to have better. And as welcome to me shall you be with your rags as if you were in cloth of gold or velvet; try and see.

I have paid fifty shillings for your rent for the wharf, the lord's rent. Master Woodword, my lord's bailiff, was not in town but [ap]pointed his deputy, who received all the rents. I had witnesses with me at the payment of the money and have his quittance [*receipt*], but the quittance cost me a groat [*fourpence*]. They said it was the bailiff's fee. You know best whether you were wont to pay it; if not, they made a simple [*foolish*] woman of me. You shall receive a letter from the joiner himself and a printed bill. And so, with my humble and hearty commendations to your own self, Master Chaloners and his wife, with thanks for your kind usage, with my good mother's kindest commendations with the rest of your household . . . I end, praying Almighty God still to bless us for his mercy's sake.

And so, sweetheart, once more farewell till we meet, which I hope shall not be long.

This 21 of October 1603. . . .

Your faithful and loving wife Joan Alleyn.

3.10   An Anonymous Poem of Same-Sex Desire (c.1586)

From Poem XLIX in *The Maitland Quarto Manuscript*, ed. W. A. Craigie, Scottish Text Society, ns 9 (1920), 160–2.

Mary Maitland twice signed her name on the title page of a manuscript collection of poems, probably indicating ownership, not authorship. Some verses were by her father, Sir Richard Maitland of Lethington, but the writer of the poem excerpted below is unknown. The author's persona is that of a woman who longs to be transformed into a man so that she can marry the female object of her passionate love. Maitland herself went on to wed Alexander Lauder of Hatton.

> Would mighty Jove grant me the hap
> With you to have your Brutus' part,
> And metamorphosing our shape
> My sex into his vail [*might*] convert,
> No Brutus then should cause us smart
> As we do [*fare*] now, unhappy women
> Then should we both with joyful heart
> Honor and bless the band of Hymen.[10]

> . . .

10 *Hymen*: Roman god of marriage.

And as we are, though, till our woe,
Nature and fortune do conjure [*command*],
And Hymen also be our foe,
Yet love of virtue does procure
Friendship and amity so sure
With so great fervency and force,
So constantly which shall endure
That naught but death shall us divorce.

And though adversity us vex
Yet by our friendship shall be fain [*gladness*]
There is more constancy in our sex
Than ever among men has been,
No trouble, torment, grief, or teen [*harm*],
Nor earthly thing shall us dissever
Such constancy shall us maintain
In perfect amity forever.

3.11 King James VI and I's Letter to his Favorite George Villiers, Duke of Buckingham (1623)

From Bodleian Ms Tanner 72:14.

George Villiers had a good marriage and four children with his wife, Lady Katherine Manners. As a favorite of James VI and I, he advanced rapidly: in 1615 he was made Gentleman of the Bedchamber; in 1616, Master of the Horse; in 1617, Earl of Buckingham; in 1623, Duke of Buckingham. James defended the relationship to Parliament: "Jesus had his John, and I have my George." But their intimacy was not at issue; the favorite's corruption, nepotism, and abuse of power were. After James's death, in 1628, Buckingham was assassinated by an outraged soldier who believed he thus did his country "a great service."

My only sweet and dear child,
    Notwithstanding of your desiring me not to write yesterday, yet had I written in the evening if, at my coming in out of the park, such a drowsiness had not come upon me as I was forced to sit and sleep in my chair half an hour. And yet I cannot content myself without sending you this present [*letter*], praying God that I may have a joyful and comfortable meeting with you and that we may make at this Christmas a new marriage ever to be kept hereafter. For God so love me, as I desire only to live in this world for your sake, and that I had rather live banished in any part of the earth with you than live a sorrowful widow's life without you. And so God bless you, my sweet child and wife, and grant that ye may ever be a comfort to your dear dad and husband.
    James R.

3.12 Abortionist Peter Stone's Punishment (2 April 1572)

From CLRO X109/142, Repertories of the London Court of Aldermen 17, 296^{r-v}.

Some of the women faced with the terrible social consequences of bearing illegitimate children abandoned their newborn infants; others, like Alice Tyler, sought remedies to terminate unwanted pregnancies. The city officers who publicly disciplined this abortionist also punished the father named by Tyler.

This day one Peter Stone, who practiceth physic as though he were a physician and is indeed utterly unlearned, for that it did manifestly appear to the court that he was a common minister [*dispenser*] of wicked medicines to maidens that chance to be with child, to the destructions either of the children or of the maidens or of both, and for that the matter was very apparently proved that he had practiced with one Randall Plympton, who had gotten one Alice Tyler with child, to destroy her child, and gave her certain medicines as antimony and such like for that purpose, it is ordered that he shall be set on a horseback with his face to the horse tail, being naked from the middle upward, and to be well whipped by two men with whips, on each side the horse one [*one on each side of the horse*]. And to be led from Bridewell round about the Conduit in Fleet Street, and so down from Fleet Street through Cheapside to the stocks, and round about the little Conduit there and so to the Compter in the Poultry . . . and he to have a paper over his head in this wise written: "Ministering of medicines to the destruction of mankind."

3.13 Mary Day's Fertility Treatment (2 April 1575)

From Minutes of the London Court of Bridewell, BCB-02, 107^{r-v}.

Mary Day was presented to the governors of the Bridewell for her unorthodox solution to the problem of marital infertility. Telling them she received sixpence for room rent ("and no more"), she sought to forestall an indictment for prostitution. The governors also punished the woman who provided her with the room.

Mary Day confesseth that about Michaelmas last past, she being in her chamber and sitting in her window at work [*needlework*], was beckoned over by one James Forman, dwelling over against her in the parish of Whitechapel without Aldgate, who beckoned to her three times. Whereupon she went unto him, thinking his wife had not been well, and knew no other cause. And so she went with him into his house, and, being in the hall, he said unto her, "Mary, how doest thou?

Where is thy husband?" Who answered, "He is gone a-shooting." Whereupon she asked how Mistress Forman did, who answered, "She is well, and she is gone into London."[11] And then she asked him, "Sir, what is your pleasure?" And he said he had called her a good while, and asked her if she saw him not, who said she saw him not, for if she had she would have come sooner. And then he said, "Mary, I have had a good mind to thee a good while, this twelvemonth and more, and I could never speak with thee till now." And then she asked him where all his folks [*servants*] were, and he said his wife was gone into London, and his folks were in the garden drying of clothes. And then he drew her into the parlor and said he would have his pleasure of her before she went. Whereupon she said she by fair words entreated him and deferred the same till another time. And he said to her that if he might have his pleasure of her he would be bound in a hundred pounds to get her with child, either a boy or a girl. And so she sayeth she consented unto him when time and place would serve. . . . And about three weeks after, they came to Jackson's house and they went up into the chamber. And then he there had the use of her body, and so in the same house and place he had the use of her body twice after. And at every time he gave her sixpence and no more, which she sayeth she gave unto Jackson's wife when she came down.

3.14   Nehemiah Wallington's Family Life (1630–54)

From FSL Ms V.a.436, 13–14, 29b; and GL Ms 204, 408–9.

Another aspect of parenthood in the early modern period was the high rate of infant mortality. Nehemiah Wallington and his wife Grace had six children, but only one lived to adulthood. Wallington was a London craftsman who was given to bouts of depression and thoughts of suicide. His father had encouraged him to marry (in 1621) in hopes that responsibility would settle him. Clearly Grace, too, was concerned about Nehemiah's emotional balance.

An Extract of the Passages of My Life (1654)

This year, 1622, my family increasing and now having a wife, a child, a manservant, and a maidservant, and thus having the charge of so many souls, I then bought Master Gouge's book *Of Domestical Duties*, that so every one of us may learn and know our duties and honor God every one in his place

---

11 *into London*: The parish of Whitechapel was called "*without* Aldgate" because it was outside the city walls; to go into London was to go inside the walls.

where God had set them. For I was resolved with Joshua that I and my house will serve the Lord.[12] . . . In the beginning of the year 1625 the Lord did take away my maidservant Ann Exersail, which at her death praised God that ever she did come in my house and did see my face, for, sayeth she, if I had died in the country, I had died in ignorance and in my sin. But since I came to you I praise God I know more, and so this did yield to me some comfort to hear her say so.

A Record of God's Mercies, or A Thankful Remembrance, wherein is set down my miserable and sad condition of my corrupt nature with some of the many mercies of God to my soul and body to the year 1630

[On 8 October 1625], in the afternoon, [Wallington family maidservant] Ruth told my wife that she had a pricking in her neck, which words put us all in fear, and toward night she went to bed. And about eight o'clock at night my wife was in the kitchen washing of dishes; my daughter Elizabeth, then being merry, went unto her mother and said unto her, "What do you here, my wife?" And at night when we were abed says she to me, "Father, I go abroad tomorrow and buy you a plum pie." These were the last words that I did hear my sweet child speak. For the very pangs of death seized upon her on the Sabbath day morning, and so she continued in great agonies (which was very grievous unto us the beholders) till Tuesday morning, and then my sweet child died at four o'clock in the morning, being the eleventh day of October, and was buried that day at night. The grief for this child was so great that I forgot myself so much that I did offend God in it; for I broke all my purposes, promises, and covenants with my God, for I was much distracted in my mind and could not be comforted, although my friends spake so comfortably [*comfortingly*] unto me. And my wife said unto me, "Husband, I am persuaded you offend God in grieving for this child so much. Do but consider what a deal of grief and care we are rid of, and what a deal of trouble and sorrow she is gone out of, and what abundance of joy she is gone into. And do but consider it is your daughter's wedding day: and will you grieve to see your daughter go home to her husband Christ Jesus, where she shall never want, but have the fullness of joy for evermore? Consider how willingly Abraham went to offer up his only son Isaac, although he were to be his own executioner."[13] Then said I unto my wife, "Do you not grieve for this child?" "No, truly, Husband, if you will believe me, I do as freely give it again unto God as I did received [*sic*] it of him."

---

12 *resolved with Joshua . . . will serve the Lord*: Wallington refers to Joshua 24:15.
13 *fullness of joy . . . executioner*: Wallington refers to Psalms 16:11 and Genesis 22.

3.15   Allegations of Slander, Domestic Violence, Fornication, and Broken Betrothal in Kent (1587–1600)

From Consistory Court of Canterbury Deposition Books CCAL X.11.1, 159^{r-v}, X.11.6, 198^{v}–200^{r}, 215^{v}–217^{r}, 220^{v}–221^{r}; X.11.3, 75^{r-v}; X.11.4, 4^{r}–6^{r}.

Church courts heard evidence of how many people failed to live their lives as advised. The cases represented here include, first, Joane Nowre's complaint that her reputation had been damaged by allegations of immorality; second, Mary Tress's appeal for divorce on the grounds of her husband's cruelty; third, Peter Colbrand's complaint that a man named Crench had sexually slandered him; and, fourth, Nicholas Fell's request that Agnew Bowes honor a compact of marriage. The oral testimony of witnesses was recorded by an ecclesiastical scribe who inserted such legal language as "the said," "the articulate," and "precontestant," to clarify the identity of those being referred to. In many church-court cases the rulings are unknown, sometimes because out-of-court settlements were reached, sometimes because complainants were satisfied to have a public airing of their personal grievances.

Joane Nowre *contra* Roger Clinton and Joane Clinton *for defamation (1587)*

Deposition of John Naylor, tapster: This deponent . . . heard Roger Clinton articulate standing in his yard and looking in at a window into the parlor of the house of the said Nowre. This deponent being abed, [Clinton] said unto this deponent these words or the like in effect, viz.: "John Naylor, rise and fetch your dame out of the shop, for there is William Harris and she together." . . . Whereupon this deponent did rise and went into the hall and found there the said Joane Nowre standing in the middle thereof, and William Harris sitting by the chimney, and this deponent asked the said Joane Nowre what stir [*fuss*] there was there, and she said she could not let them to talk [*prevent them from talking*], whereupon this deponent went to bed again. . . . On a Tuesday at night happening a sevennight after the time by this deponent predeposed, Joane Clinton articulate stood in her yard and looked into the house of the said Joane Nowre at a window, and Joane Nowre said unto the said Clinton, "What mean you to eavesdrop my house?" And Joane Clinton said she would stand in her own ground and look into the house of the said Nowre, whereupon Joane Nowre called for a dish of water and flung into the face of the said Joane Clinton. And the said Clinton being moved therewith, said . . . "Thou art a whore[14] and William Harris his whore [*William Harris's*

---

14 *whore*: an inflammatory term of insult often (though not in this case) used without specific accusation of sexual transgression.

whore] and the cart[15] cometh for thee and William Harris might have been taken out of thy breech."[16] . . . Whereupon this deponent standing by them, said unto Joane Clinton, "It is a shame for to abuse the woman in this order."

Mary Tresse *contra* Walter Tresse *for matrimonial separation (1593)*

Deposition of Catherine Goldock, wife of John Goldock: At the time when this deponent dwelt with the said Tresse, he the said Tresse would have dealt carnally with this deponent which, because she this deponent denied him, he very much misused her this deponent and beat her and turned her out of his service and would not pay her her wages. . . . [On one occasion] this deponent being gone to milking of kine [*cows*], the said Mary Tresse alias Gawnte[17] came running into the field where this deponent milked, crying and saying that her husband had beaten her out of doors. And indeed the said Mary was so beaten about the face that her face was black with the blows a long time after. . . . This deponent hath heard the said Tresse say that if any of his wife's friends did ever anger or trouble him he would be revenged upon his wife, saying that another country was as good for him as this.

Deposition of Catherina Ridson, wife of Robert Ridson: About three days before All Saints' Day last was two years last past, the said Mary Gawnte alias Tresse came to this deponent's house in Holborne aforesaid, her face being all black with beating. And within a day after, the said Walter Tresse came to this deponent's house to inquire for his said wife. With whom this deponent and her husband reasoning of his beating of his said wife, he said these words as this deponent remembreth: "What if I did give her a blow? Who hath to do with it?" . . . She [this deponent] verily believeth and is persuaded that the said Mary Gawnte alias Tresse cannot live without danger of her life together with the said Walter Tresse her husband.

Deposition of Thomas Newton, weaver: This deponent hath heard the said Mary Gawnte alias Tresse diverse times say that she hath been afraid at night when she hath gone to bed that she should not live until morning, for she hath said that her said husband Walter Tresse hath hanged a sword by his bedside which she hath feared he would have killed her withal.

Deposition of Jane Newton, wife of Thomas Newton: Diverse times since the said Tresse brake out of prison aforesaid this deponent hath heard him say that he would cut his wife's throat and that he would slit her nose and mark her for

---

15 *cart*: a vehicle in which immoral women were placed for public humiliation.
16 *breech*: buttocks; another deponent in this case quoted (more lucidly), "William Harris must be pulled out of thy breech."
17 *Mary Tresse alias Gawnte*: Tresse was Mary's married name; Gawnte, her name either from birth or from a previous marriage.

a whore.[18] And when he was toward [*approaching*] any trouble he would commonly say that he would be avenged upon his wife's blood or the like. . . . [He] would not be contented with her life alone without the loss and damnation of her soul.

Peter Colbrand *versus* Crench *for defamation (1598)*

Deposition of William Alcock, gentleman: On a day happening about the feast of Whitsuntide last past, about ten of the clock in the forenoon of the same day, he this deponent and his precontestant Master Thomas Boys walking together in the body of Christ Church in Canterbury, there came by them Crench articulate, whom Master Boys aforesaid called unto him and charged him that he had abused [*had intercourse with*] his maidservant, meaning Elizabeth Purfry articulate, who then was the said Master Boys his servant. And the said Crench desired the said Master Boys to give him leave and then he would tell him the whole truth. And so began and told him that he the said Crench, the said Colbrand, and Elizabeth Purfry articulate had been walking together, and being come home to the said Master Boys his house, the said Colbrand and Purfry stayed together in the entry, and he the said Crench went in and lighted a candle and went up into his chamber and there pulled off his shoes and came down in his hose [*stockings*] and heard the said Colbrand and Purfry rumbling against the walls and blowing [*panting*] in the entry, and heard the said Colbrand say, "Oh, sweet Bess, sweet Bess." Then said Master Boys aforesaid, "What of all this?" – or the like in effect. To whom Crench again replied, and said that the said Colbrand did there occupy [*have intercourse with*] the said Elizabeth Purfry. Quoth Master Boys, "How canst thou tell?" Then said Crench, "I hope you will not seek advantage of me; I did not say he occupied her, but I think he did, for," said he, "when they were gone out of the entry I fetched a candle to lock the door and there I saw his nature [*semen*] lie upon the ground."

Nicholas Fells *contra* Agnes Bowes *for matrimonial enforcement (1600)*

Deposition of Daniel Snoden, tailor: On a day happening about a week before Christmas last past there came to this deponent's shop, being a tailor's shop in Milton near Sittingbourne, Fells and Bowes the parties articulate, and entreated this deponent being a tailor to go with them to buy a wedding gown cloth, as they termed it, for her the said Agnes Bowes. Whereupon this deponent went

---

18 *mark her for a whore*: There was a common belief that a whore should be lastingly recognizable as such by her scarred nose, and it was traditionally the prerogative of the injured wife to take revenge on her husand's mistress by so marking her.

with them and chose a piece of French green cloth and lining thereunto fitting for a wedding gown for the said Agnes. And they both paid their monies towards the same and so likewise they bought a wedding hat, this deponent thereupon presuming that they meant very shortly to marry together, the common report also going thereupon. And the rather he sayeth he is so persuaded for that the said Fells hired a house of this deponent to here dwell in in Milton after their marriage, and she the said Agnes Bowes was very earnest with this deponent for the same, desiring him that they (meaning herself and the said Fells) might not be disappointed upon their marriage of a house.

Deposition of Robert Smith, laborer: On a day happening about Christmas last past he this deponent spake unto Agnes Bowes articulate (who then was at the house where her father died in the parish of Borden) to have bought some bacon of her which was left in the house where her father died. But she the said Agnes denied to sell any to him this deponent, saying that she should shortly have occasion to use it herself. And this deponent asking her how, she answered and told him this deponent that she and Nicholas Fells articulate should marry together and, said she, "He is a collar maker and meaneth to keep a couple of men and a boy to his trade, and then I shall have occasion to use my bacon myself."

Deposition of Joan Thimble, wife of Eustace Thimble, metalman: That Agnes Bowes articulate, after the death of her father (who died about six weeks after Michaelmas last past), was very conversant with her this deponent and lay at her this deponent's house. And in the absence of her this deponent's husband lay in bed with this deponent, by reason of which their familiarity this deponent was somewhat the more acquainted with her matters. And this deponent sayeth that on New Year's Eve last past she this deponent and her contestant Goodwife Thornton being together with the said Fells and Bowes at the house where the said Agnes Bowes her father died, she the said Agnes Bowes made a motion to go to some of her friends in Sheppey. And the said Fells desired her not to go until they were married, to whom the said Agnes Bowes answered, saying, "We will go to my friends first and be married after our coming back again, and whatsoever I have promised you in the way of marriage I will perform, whatsoever my friends say. And when we return from them, which shall be upon Wednesday next, we will go to Maidstone the next day after and buy a wedding ring and be asked in the Church the next Sunday following, and for we will be married at Shrovetide," or the very like in effect. And further this deponent sayeth that she the said Agnes Bowes in the presence of this deponent hired a maidservant to serve her after her marriage with the said Fells. And further she sayeth that she knoweth that the wedding apparel and the wedding hat for the said Agnes was by her and the said Nicholas Fells bought and provided and the hens set up to be fatted against the wedding time aforesaid.

4

Religion and Belief

The Christian religion was so central to early modern life that it informed all social and intellectual discourse regarding the purpose of family, the nature of community, the reason for political organization, the uses of education, and the objectives of scientific knowledge. Attendance at church was expected weekly, and the life passages of birth, marriage, and death were observed there. For many men and women, governance outside the home was provided most immediately not by the sovereign, a city mayor, or a county Justice of the Peace, but by their parish churchwarden. Churchwardens were laymen elected to monitor church-going, mediate disputes, collect local taxes, and dispense poor relief, among other things. They reported transgressions to judicial courts which regulated moral behavior, betrothals, adultery, domestic cruelty, sexual slander, and the validity of wills. Church-court decisions led to church-supervised punishments and public penances. The parish church was also a main source of news and ideology.

Church and state were inseparable in the sixteenth and seventeenth centuries. Kings and queens were regarded as earthly deputies of the Christian god, and the Bible was read in political ways, with the falls of Lucifer and of Adam and Eve, for example, treated as allegories of disobedience. Promulgating authorized sermons, Edward VI began a tradition of using the parish church as a principal organ of state propaganda. The Crown also held the power to appoint top ecclesiasts and punish heresy. Even with these powerful weapons against unorthodox belief, however, difference nonetheless flourished. In addition to all the conforming Protestants under Elizabeth I and James VI and I, there were such Protestant sectarians as Puritans, Anabaptists, Antinomians, Quakers, and Presbyterians; Roman Catholics; and also magical thinkers and atheists.

Traditional Religion

At the center of Roman Catholic practice was celebration of the mass, performed by a priest wearing ecclesiastical vestments, speaking in Latin, facing the altar rather than churchgoers, and separated from them by a divider called the rood-screen. During the mass, bread and wine were understood to change into the body and blood of Christ, in the miracle known as transubstantiation.

Parishioners played the part of witnesses, except during communion, when they joined in consuming the consecrated bread. Otherwise, their principal interactions with the clergy came during confession, where they detailed their sins and were assigned to pray, fast, or go on pilgrimage. Despite these acts of penitence, no matter the number of good works performed, and even though the Church, the clergy, and the saints were regarded as intercessors on man's behalf with God, salvation was understood never to be immediately achievable. Much of the Church's income was derived from those who paid for intercessory masses to be celebrated after their deaths so that they might advance from the intermediate state of purgatory to afterlives in heaven. One fourteenth-century Archbishop of Canterbury, William Courtenay, provided for over forty years' worth of daily masses – 15,000 of them.

By the sixteenth century, the Church had grown wealthy through deathbed bequests of land to support such masses (called "chantries") and through the granting of pardons and indulgences, which provided remission from punishment of sin (too often for a sizable fee). Increasingly, there were complaints about the "abuses" and excesses of the clergy. Only among some radical groups was there discontent on doctrinal grounds, as well, though their numbers were small. For most, the Roman religion was highly effective in building a sense of community. At the end of the mass, a tablet inscribed with a sacred image, the paxbred, was passed around for each parishioner to kiss. Members of the church would take turns providing a loaf of bread, which the priest cut up and distributed. The calendar was defined by shared feast days like Candlemas, Rogentide, Corpus Christi, and, above all, the holy week of Palm Sunday, Maundy Thursday, Good Friday, and Easter Sunday. Even the practice of requiem masses was public-spirited, because a mass performed for one individual was understood to benefit all the souls in purgatory. Through the idea of purgatory, people felt a continued connection to their dead, too, as part of the Catholic community.

The Reformed Church

The Lollards, followers of the fourteenth-century theologian John Wyclif, were the first in England to argue against masses, saints, pilgrimages, images, shrines, intercessory rituals, and the doctrine of transubstantiation. Others came to be influenced by Martin Luther, who in 1517 nailed his Ninety-Five Theses to the door of the Castle Church in Wittenberg, attacking such priestly practices as the granting of indulgences and pardons. Despite these signs that new ideas were taking root in educated circles, and despite complaints against the clergy, the English Reformation did not result from widespread, popular desire for religious change. It was a top-down phenomenon, imposed by the Crown in the interest of the Crown.

This interest was not, at the outset, theological. Henry VIII was intent on transforming ecclesiastical governance rather than religious doctrine. He bridled at being bound by a clergy that answered to the Pope. Nor was his Dissolution of the monasteries, friaries, convents, and chantries motivated by a desire for clerical reform. The break-up of the land-owning institutions of the Church was not a wholly original idea; Lady Margaret Beaufort and Cardinal Thomas Wolsey had already dissolved some small abbeys, for example, using their confiscated properties to endow colleges at Oxford and Cambridge. But Henry closed all the religious houses with an eye to personal profit rather than alternative foundations. His first step was to have his agents compile information about the revenues he could expect to seize – an order fully revealing of his true intent – and at the same time he had them gather reports of monastic scandal with which to incite public support. Thomas Wolsey, a notorious exploiter of the Church's rich pickings, had been succeeded as Henry's principal advisor by Thomas Cromwell, Earl of Essex, who knew how to link the persistent distrust of ecclesiastical power with a lingering fear of foreign rule, and thus to encourage popular enthusiasm for Henry's split with the Pope in Rome. Others accepted the Dissolution because they stood to gain by acquiring some of the lands and valuable goods formerly held by the Church.

Almost in spite of Henry, however, the English Church eventually became more distinctively Protestant. Reformed theology held that Catholic rituals did not help sinning humankind; instead, they were destructive, because they were spiritually misleading. In this view, the Pope was not only a false cleric, he was the agent of Satan, the Antichrist. Purgatory did not exist, and the intercessory claims of the Church were fraudulent promises, mere tricks to procure wealth. Thus, in a movement known as "iconoclasm," all the elements of intercessory faith were disassembled during the Reformation. Shakespeare wrote of the "bare ruined choirs" of monasteries with their lead roofs stripped off and stone walls pulled down; the materials were put to use in other building projects. In parish churches, altars were broken, crucifixes and other religious statuary were removed, stained-glass representations of the saints' tales were destroyed, and priestly vestments were converted to cushion covers. Romanists had thought that the veneration of images encouraged faith, but reformers believed it incited superstition.

The liturgy of the new church emphasized words delivered to the congregation from a pulpit, rather than ritual gestures performed before an altar. The preacher's principal text was the Bible, newly translated into English. Under Edward VI and again under Elizabeth I, the state also issued the set of sermons known as the *Homilies*. In parishes without preaching clerics, curates could safely read the approved sermons. In parishes with preaching ministers, the homilies established the doctrine with which clergy were expected to comply.

There continued to be heated arguments about whether worshippers should kneel to receive communion (now understood as a symbolic action rather than a miracle) and whether the sign of the cross should be used in baptism, and there were always competing pressures from those who preferred high-church observance versus those who advocated Puritan strictness. Some Protestants believed in salvation through prayer and good works, some in justification by faith, some in predestination, some in reliance on God's mercy. One way in which the reformed religion seemed more personal was that there were so many varieties of belief.

The Bible

The Protestant religious experience was individualized through direct reading of scripture. The Bible had been translated from its original Hebrew into Greek in the third century BCE and then into Latin at the turn of the fifth century CE. The Roman Catholic Church adopted this Latin text, known as the "Vulgate" (from "versio vulgata," for "common translation"). The Vulgate was available only in manuscript copies until the mid-1450s, when mass production via movable type constituted a first step in making the Bible accessible to a wider readership. A second step was the fresh translation of the New Testament into Latin, completed in 1516 in Cambridge by the great Dutch humanist Erasmus. This was the basis for the first New Testament in a modern European language, Luther's 1522 retranslation from Latin into German. In 1523 Luther also brought out a German version of the first five books of the Old Testament, known as the Pentateuch.

When the Oxford-trained William Tyndale sought approval for an English translation, the Bishop of London, Cuthbert Tunstal, withheld it. The Bishop was fighting a losing battle. In self-imposed exile in Wittenberg, Hamburg, and Cologne, Tyndale consulted Hebrew and Greek texts as well as Erasmus's Latin and Luther's German. Both his English New Testament of 1525 and his English Pentateuch of 1530 were published on the Continent. Smuggled into England in 1526, the first copies of the English New Testament were burned at London's central open-air pulpit, Paul's Cross. Then, in 1535 in Cologne, Miles Coverdale published a Bible assembled out of Tyndale's New Testament, Tyndale's Pentateuch, and Coverdale's own translation of the rest of the Old Testament. This was reprinted in England in 1537.

In 1538 Cromwell required every English church to have an English-language Bible. Coverdale's second edition of 1539, known as the "Great Bible" for its large size, was the approved version. Most copies were destroyed, as ordered by Mary I, when she succeeded to the crown in 1553 and reinstated Catholic practices and Latin Bibles. In 1559, with Elizabeth I on the throne, all churches were again furnished with English Scriptures. The translation process then resumed, with the "Bishops' Bible" published in 1568. The first version with books divided into reader-friendly chapters and verses, the "Geneva" or "Breeches Bible," was issued in Switzerland in 1560 and in England in 1576. The Catholic Counter-Reformation resulted in an English translation based on the Vulgate, known as the "Rheims/Douai" version. The New Testament was also translated into Welsh in 1567, with a complete Welsh Bible following in 1588. Sir Philip Sidney and his sister Mary Sidney were among those who translated the Psalms into verse.

At a 1604 assembly known as the Hampton Court Conference, clergy argued that yet another translation was required. Psalm 28, John Rainolds pointed out, was widely given as "they were not disobedient" rather than, as was correct, "they were not obedient." An example that appealed to political interests was well chosen, and the king commissioned a new translation. This was to bear his own name, the King James Version. James ordered his team of fifty-four translators to base their work on the conservative Bishops' Bible (and then, in descending order of priority, Tyndale, Coverdale, and Geneva). In the end, the translation that was to have incalculable influence on culture, literature, and habits of thought in all English-speaking countries was, in large part, that of the man who had been burned at the stake for heresy in Belgium in 1536, William Tyndale.

Dissidence

Beginning in 1574, the diminished number of Roman Catholic clerics in England was supplemented by the arrival of "seminary" priests who had trained on the Continent. With about a hundred in residence by 1580, their ranks were too few to effect many conversions to the old religion; their purpose was to minister to those who remained true to it. Twenty-five percent of English Catholics were "recusants" and refused to go to Anglican churches. The rest were "church papists," meaning that they held traditional beliefs even while they attended reformed parish services and maintained social connections with Protestant neighbors. Most importantly, from the government's point of view, the latter group was politically loyal to the queen rather than the Pope, even though Pius V had excommunicated Elizabeth I in 1570 and had authorized her subjects to disobey her.

In the countryside especially, there were people who paid no attention at all to doctrinal controversies and ecclesiastical hierarchies. They understood their lives in terms of magical thinking and folk superstitions. But for those who attended to religious matters, the sixteenth century was a tumultuous time. Men and women were first required to recognize Henry VIII as their spiritual head, then to adopt a reformed liturgy under Edward VI, next to return to Roman Catholic worship under Mary I, and finally to take up Protestant practices again under Elizabeth I and James VI and I. It is not surprising, therefore, that many came to dissent from the authorized religion. Henry VIII's marital difficulties had created a public discourse of private conscience. With the end of the confessional, with the introduction of homilies that used rhetoric and reason rather than ritual, and with the call for personal study of the Bible, early moderns were encouraged to take responsibility for their own spiritual well-being – and, even though not always in ways the authorities had intended, many did so.

4.1   William Roper, *The Mirror of Virtue in Worldly Greatness; or, The Life of Sir Thomas More* (c.1553)

From STC 21316 (HU copy, 1626), F6^r–F8^r, G3^r–G6^r.

Sir Thomas More, Henry VIII's Lord Chancellor and the author of Utopia *(1516), did not contest the Royal Supremacy, but he did not endorse it, either, and on 6 July 1535 he was beheaded for committing high treason. In 1553, when Mary I re-established Roman Catholicism, William Roper finally felt the climate was right for a memoir of his father-in-law's death that described it as martyrdom. Henry VIII had depicted his own divorce as a crisis of conscience; More's life and death made conscience a matter for all.*

There came unto him [*More*] the Lord Chancellor, the Dukes of Norfolk and Suffolk, with Master Secretary [*Thomas Cromwell*] and diverse of the Privy Council, at two several times, who used all possible policy to procure him either precisely [*expressly*] to confess the Supremacy or directly to deny it. Whereunto, as appeareth by the book of his examinations, they could never bring him or justly tax him for the contrary.

Shortly hereupon, one Master Rich (created afterwards Lord Rich), that then was newly made the King's Solicitor . . . pretending friendly discourse with him [*More*], amongst other things, of set purpose[1] as it seemed, said thus unto him: "Forasmuch as it is well known, Master More, that you are a man both wise and well-learned, as well in the laws of the realm as otherwise, I pray you therefore, let me in courtesy and goodwill be so bold to put you this case. Admit there were, sir," quoth he, "an Act of Parliament that all the kingdom should take me for king. Would not you, then, Master More, take me for king?"

"Yes, marry," quoth Sir Thomas More, "that would I."

"Then I put case further," quoth Master Rich. "Admit there were an Act of Parliament that all the realm should take me for Pope. Would not you, then, Master More, take me for Pope?"

"For answer," quoth Sir Thomas More, "to your first case: the Parliament may well, Master Rich, meddle with the state of temporal princes.[2] But to make answer to your later case: suppose the Parliament would make a law that God should not be God. Would you, Master Rich, then say that God were not God?"

"No, sir," quoth he, "that would I not."

"No more," quoth Sir Thomas More (as Master Rich after reported of him), "could the Parliament make the king supreme head of the Church."

---

1 *set purpose*: not a casual conversation; it is implied that More was a victim of attempted entrapment.
2 *temporal princes*: secular rulers, but with a sly double meaning that the monarch is in power only temporarily, for the length of a mortal life.

And so Master Rich with the rest departed.

Now, upon the only report of[3] this speech Sir Thomas More was indicted of treason upon the statute whereby it was made treason to deny the king to be supreme head of the Church.

. . . So remained he in the Tower more than eight days after his condemnation. . . . Early in the morning there came unto him Sir Thomas Pope, his singular good friend, with a message from the king and Council that he must before nine of the clock the same morning suffer death, and that he should forthwith prepare himself thereto.

"Master Pope," quoth he, "for your good tidings I most heartily thank you. I have always been much bound to the King's Highness for the many benefits and honors that he hath still from time to time most bountifully heaped upon me, especially that it hath pleased His Majesty to put me here in this place, where I have had convenient [*suitable*] time and leisure to remember my last end. And now most of all am I bound unto His Grace that I shall be so shortly rid out of the miseries of this wretched life. And therefore will I not fail to pray earnestly for His Grace, both here and in the other world also."

"The king's pleasure is further," quoth Sir Thomas Pope, "that at your execution you shall not use many words."

"Master Pope," quoth he, "you do well to give me warning of the king's pleasure, for otherwise I might have offended His Majesty against my will. I had indeed purposed at that time to have spoken somewhat, but of no matter of offense to His Grace. Nevertheless, whatsoever I intended, I am ready to conform myself obediently to his commandment."

. . . Whereupon Sir Thomas Pope, taking his leave, could not forbear weeping. Which Sir Thomas More perceiving, comforted him in this wise: "Quiet yourself, good Master Pope, and be not discomforted. For I trust we shall one day see each other in heaven, where we shall be sure to live and love together in joyful bliss eternally."

. . . Then was he by Master Lieutenant brought out of the Tower and from thence led towards the place of execution. . . . Then desired he all the people about him to pray for him and to bear witness that he should now there suffer death in and for the faith of the Holy Catholic Church. Which done, he kneeled down and, after his prayers said, he turned to the executioner and with a cheerful countenance spake thus merrily unto him: "Pluck up thy spirits, man, and be not afraid to do thine office. My neck is somewhat short. Therefore, take heed thou strikest not awry, for saving of thine honesty [*professional reputation*]. But if thou dost, upon my word, I will not hereafter cast it in thy teeth." So, at one stroke of the executioner, passed Sir Thomas More out of this world to God upon the same day which himself had most desired, 6 July 1535.

---

3 *upon the only report of*: solely upon the report of.

4.2   Michael Sherbrook, "The Fall of Religious Houses" (c.1591)

From BL Add. Ms 5813, 19ᵛ–21ʳ.

Between 1536 and 1539, Henry VIII ordered the Dissolution of all monasteries, friaries, convents, and chantries. The large-scale seizure of lands and goods has been called "the great plunder" of England. Yorkshire rector Michael Sherbrook was a child at the time but in later years recorded his memoirs of this epochal event. The redistribution of Church holdings showed "policy," Sherbrook writes, for no one who had acquired seized properties would want to return them: "by that mean every one both in Parliament and forth of Parliament will be against the setting them up again howsoever the religion doth change." He himself bought some of the furnishings of a parish church that was stripped of its holdings.

In the plucking down of which Houses for the most part this order was taken: that the Visitors[4] should come suddenly upon every House . . . to the end to take them napping, as the proverb is, lest if they should have had so much as any inkling of their coming they would have made conveyance [*removal*] of some part of their own goods to help themselves withal when they were turned forth of their Houses. . . . So soon as the Visitors were entered within the gates, they called the Abbot and other officers of the House and caused them to deliver up to them all their keys, and took an inventory of all their goods, both within doors and without. For all such beasts, horses, sheep, and such cattle as were abroad in pastures or grange places, the Visitors caused to be brought into their presence. And when they had so done, turned the Abbot with all his covent[5] and household forth of the doors.

Which thing was not a little grief to the covent, and all the servants of the house departing one from another, and specially such as with their conscience could not break their profession [*religious vows*]. For it would have made an heart of flint to have melted and wept to have seen the breaking up of the House, and their sorrowful departing, and the sudden spoil that fell the same day of their departure from the House. . . . Such persons as afterward [brought] their corn or hay or such like[6] found all the doors either open or the locks and shackles plucked away, or the door itself taken away, went in and took what they found, filched it away. . . . It would have pitied any heart to see what tearing up of the lead there was, and plucking up of boards, and throwing down of the spars

---

4 *Visitors*: those commissioned to visit religious establishments for the purposes of inspection, supervision, or, as in this instance, suppression.

5 *covent*: an early form of the word *convent*, for those living together in a religious order, in this period referring to monks and friars as well as nuns.

6 *corn or hay or such like*: farm goods brought in payment of tithes owed to the Church, another source of income seized by the Crown.

[*rafters*] . . . and the tombs in the church all broken . . . and all things of price[7] either spoiled, carped [*taken*] away, or defaced to the uttermost.

For the better proof of this my saying, I demanded of my father, thirty years after the Suppression, which had bought part of the timber of the church and all the timber in the steeple, with the bell frame . . . whether he thought well of the religious persons and of the religion then used?

And he told me, "Yea. For," said he, "I did see no cause to the contrary."

"Well," said I, "then how came it to pass you was so ready to destroy and spoil the thing that you thought well of?"

"What should I do?" said he. "Might I not as well as others have some profit of the spoil of the abbey? For I did see all would away, and therefore I did as others did."

4.3　"A Fruitful Exhortation to the Reading and Knowledge of Holy Scripture" (1547)

From *Certain Sermons or Homilies Appointed by the King's Majesty to be Declared and Read by All Parsons, Vicars, or Curates, every Sunday in their Churches*, STC 13641.9 (FSL copy), ¶4ʳ–B1ᵛ.

As Archbishop of Canterbury from 1533 to 1556, Thomas Cranmer was England's leading prelate. He proposed a set of authorized sermons, or Homilies, *in 1539, but these were not approved under Henry VIII. They were finally published in 1547, when Edward VI came to the throne. Cranmer himself wrote four of the twelve sermons, including this first one which urged even the unlearned to undertake personal encounters with scripture. Although he was deprived of the See of Canterbury in 1555 and burned at the stake in 1556, his* Homilies *lived on, to be revived by Elizabeth I in 1559.*

Unto a Christian man there can be nothing either more necessary or profitable than the knowledge of Holy Scripture, forasmuch as in it is contained God's true word, setting forth his glory and also man's duty. And there is no truth nor doctrine necessary for our justification and everlasting salvation but that is or may be drawn out of that fountain and well of truth. Therefore, as many as be desirous to enter into the right and perfect way unto God must apply their minds to know Holy Scripture, without which they can neither sufficiently know God and his will, neither their office and duty. And as drink is pleasant to them that be dry and meat to them that be hungry, so is the reading, hearing,

---

7 *all things of price*: materials reused in other building projects, including lead for roofs, boards and rafters for carpentry, and stone from tombs.

searching, and studying of Holy Scripture to them that be desirous to know God or themselves, and to do his will. . . . Let us diligently search for the well of life in the books of the New and Old Testament, and not run to the stinking puddles of men's traditions, devised by man's imagination for our justification and salvation. . . . In these books we may learn to know ourselves, how vile and miserable we be, and also to know God, how good he is of himself and how he communicateth his goodness unto us and to all creatures. We may learn also in these books to know God's will and pleasure, as much as for this present time is convenient for us to know. . . .

These books, therefore, ought to be much in our hands, in our eyes, in our ears, in our mouths, but most of all in our hearts. For the Scripture of God is the heavenly meat of our souls; the hearing and keeping of it maketh us blessed, sanctifieth us, and maketh us holy. It converteth our souls; it is a light lantern to our feet; it is a sure, a constant, and a perpetual instrument of salvation. It giveth wisdom to the humble and lowly hearted; it comforteth, maketh glad, cheereth, and cherisheth our consciences. It is a more excellent jewel or treasure than any gold or precious stone; it is more sweeter than honey or honeycomb; it is called the best part which Mary did choose,[8] for it hath in it everlasting comfort. The words of Holy Scripture be called words of everlasting life, for they be God's instrument, ordained for the same purpose. They have power to convert through God's promise, and they be effectual through God's assistance, and, being received in a faithful heart, they have ever an heavenly spiritual working in them. They are lively, quick, and mighty in operation, and sharper than any two-edged sword, and entereth through even unto the dividing asunder of the soul and the spirit, of the joints and the marrow. Christ calleth him a wise builder that buildeth upon his word, upon his sure and substantial foundation. . . . And there is nothing that so much establisheth our faith and trust in God, that so much conserveth innocency and pureness of the heart, and also of outward godly life and conversation, as continual reading and meditation of God's word. For that thing – which by perpetual use of reading of Holy Scripture and diligent searching of the same is deeply printed and graven in the heart – at length turneth almost into nature. . . .

And if you be afraid to fall into error by reading of Holy Scripture, I shall show you how you may read it without danger of error. Read it humbly, with a meek and a lowly heart, to the intent ye may glorify God and not yourself with the knowledge of it. And read it not without daily praying to God that he would direct your reading to good effect, and take upon you to expound it no further than you can plainly understand it. . . .

He that asketh shall have, and he that seeketh shall find, and he that knocketh shall have the door open. If we read once, twice, or thrice, and understand

---

8 *which Mary did choose*: a reference to Luke 10, in which a village woman named Mary chose to listen to the words of Jesus.

not, let us not cease so, but still continue reading, praying, asking of other. And so, by still knocking, at the last the door shall be opened, as Saint Augustine[9] sayeth. Although many things in the Scripture be spoken in obscure mysteries, yet there is nothing spoken under dark mysteries in one place but the selfsame thing in other places is spoken familiarly and plainly, to the capacity both of learned and unlearned. And those things in the Scripture that be plain to understand and necessary for salvation, every man's duty is to learn them, to print them in memory, and effectually to exercise them. And as for the obscure mysteries, to be contented to be ignorant in them until such time as it shall please God to open those things unto him.

4.4   Anne Askew, *The First Examination of the Worthy Servant of God, Mistress Anne Askew, Lately Martyred in Smithfield by the Romish Pope's Upholders* (1548)

From STC 852 (FSL copy), A2^r–A8^v.

Reading the Bible, Anne Askew became a more radical Protestant than Henry VIII's government was prepared to tolerate. She abandoned her husband and children and embarked on a spiritual quest that caused her to be charged with heresy in the last months of Henry's reign. After refusing many opportunities to recant, she was burned at the stake at London's Smithfield Market in 1546. The playwright and Protestant martyrologist John Bale had Askew's report of her trial printed in Cleves in 1546. He added "elucidations" which pointed out her familiarity with contemporary doctrinal issues, her rhetorical skill as she parried the attempts of her questioners to catch her out, and her sly manipulation of gender expectations. The account of her "examination" was finally printed in England in 1547; the second edition of 1548, excerpted here, omitted Bale's annotations.

To satisfy your expectation, good people (sayeth she), this was my first examination in the year of our Lord 1545 and in the month of March. First, Christopher Dare examined me at Saddlers' Hall, being one of the quest [*inquest*], and asked if I did not believe that the sacrament hanging over the altar was the very body of Christ really. Then I demanded this question of him: "Wherefore [*why*] Saint Stephen was stoned to death?" And he said he could not tell. Then I answered that no more would I assoil [*resolve*] his vain question.

Secondly, he said that there was a woman which did testify that I should read how God was not in temples made with hands. Then I showed him the seventh

---

9   *Saint Augustine*: The profoundly influential early Christian thinker (354–430 CE) is best known for his *Confessions* and for *The City of God*.

and seventeenth chapter of the Apostles' Acts, what Stephen and Paul had said therein. Whereupon he asked me how I took those sentences? I answered that I would not throw pearls among swine, for acorns were good enough.

Thirdly, he asked me wherefore I said that I had rather to read five lines in the Bible than to hear five masses in the temple. I confessed that I said no less. Not for the dispraise of either the epistle or gospel, but because the one did greatly edify me, and the other nothing at all – as Saint Paul doth witness in the fourteenth chapter of his First Epistle to the Corinthians, whereas he doth say: "If the trumpet giveth an uncertain sound, who will prepare himself to the battle?"

Fourthly, he laid unto my charge that I should say: "If an ill priest ministered, it was the devil and not God." My answer was that I never spake such thing. But this was my saying: "That whatsoever he were which ministered unto me, his ill conditions could not hurt my faith. But in spirit I received nevertheless the body and blood of Christ." . . .

Then they had me thence unto my Lord Mayor. And he examined me as they had before, and I answered him directly in all things, as I answered the quest afore. Besides this, my Lord Mayor laid one thing unto my charge, which was never spoken of me but of them. And that was whether a mouse eating the Host[10] received God or no? This question did I never ask, but indeed they asked it of me, whereunto I made them no answer, but smiled.

Then the Bishop's Chancellor rebuked me, and said that I was much to blame for uttering the Scriptures. For Saint Paul (he said) forbade women to speak or to talk of the word of God. I answered him that I knew Paul's meaning so well as he, which is (1 Corinthians 14) that a woman ought not to speak in the congregation by the way of teaching. And then I asked him how many women he had seen go into the pulpit and preach. He said he never saw none. Then I said he ought to find no fault in poor women, except they had offended the law.

Then my Lord Mayor commanded me to ward [*the Counter, a jail*]. I asked him if sureties[11] would not serve me, and he made me short answer that he would take none. Then was I had to the Counter, and there remained twelve days, no friend admitted to speak with me. But in the meantime there was a priest sent to me, which said that he was commanded of the Bishop to examine me and to give me good counsel, which he did not. But first he asked me for what cause I was put in the Counter? And I told him I could not tell. Then he said it was great pity that I should be there without cause, and concluded that he was very sorry for me.

Secondly, he said it was told him that I should deny the sacrament of the altar. And I answered him again that that I had said, I had said.[12]

Thirdly, he asked me if I were shriven;[13] I told him no. Then he said he would

---

10 *Host*: "bread" or consecrated wafer; by the doctrine of transubstantiation, the body of Christ.

11 *sureties*: bonds ensuring that Askew would not flee but would answer the charges.

12 *that I had said, I had said*: that is, I have said all I intend to say on the subject.

13 *shriven*: that is, if she had taken confession and received absolution (a Catholic practice).

bring one to me for to shrive me. And I told him so that I might have one of these three – that is to say, Doctor Crome, Sir William, or Huntington – I was contented, because I knew them to be men of wisdom. "As for you or any other, I will not dispraise because I know ye not." Then he said: "I would not have you think but that I or another that shall be brought you shall be as honest as they. For if we were not, ye may be sure the king would not suffer us to preach." Then I answered by the saying of Solomon (Proverbs 1): "By communing with the wise, I may learn wisdom, but by talking with [a] fool, I shall take skathe" [*harm*].

Fourthly, he asked me if the host should fall, and a beast did eat it, whether the beast did receive God or no? I answered: "Seeing you have taken the pains to ask this question, I desire you also to assoil it yourself. For I will not do it, because I perceive ye come to tempt me." And he said it was against the order of schools that he which asked the question should answer it. I told him I was but a woman, and knew not the course of schools. . . .

Then laid my Lord [Bishop] unto me that I had alleged a certain text of the Scripture. I answered that I alleged none other but Saint Paul's own saying to the Athenians, in the seventeenth chapter of the Apostles' Acts: that "God dwelleth not in temples made with hands." Then asked he me what my faith and belief was in that matter? I answered him: "I believe as the Scripture doth teach me." Then enquired he of me: "What if the Scripture doth say that it is the body of Christ?" I believe (said I) like as the Scripture doth teach me. Then asked he again: "What if the Scripture doth say that it is not the body of Christ?" My answer was still: "I believe as the Scripture informeth me." And upon this argument he tarried a great while to have driven me to make him an answer to his mind. Howbeit I would not, but concluded this with him, that I believed therein and in all other things as Christ and his Holy Apostles did leave them.

Then he asked me why I had so few words? And I answered: "God have given me the gift of knowledge but not of utterance." And Solomon sayeth (Proverbs 19): that "a woman of few words is a gift of God."

4.5   Preface to *The Book of Common Prayer* (1549)

From STC 16270 (BL copy), A2^{r-v}.

Thomas Cranmer produced not only the homilies but also the volume that established the Protestant liturgy in language that is still familiar today. The Book of Common Prayer *was first authorized by Parliament in 1549 and then again in 1552, when a revised version was issued. It abolished old "ceremonies," including celebrations of the mass, prayers for the dead, and private confession. These Catholic rituals were revived in 1553 by Mary I, and the Prayer Book was abandoned. In 1559, under Elizabeth I, ceremonies were again revoked, there was a new Act of Supremacy and Uniformity, and every parish church was required to have a* Book of Common Prayer.

The people by daily hearing of Holy Scripture read in the church should continually profit more and more in the knowledge of God and be the more inflamed with the love of his true religion. But these many years past this godly and decent order of the ancient fathers hath been so altered, broken, and neglected by planting in uncertain stories, legends, responds,[14] verses, vain repetitions, commemorations, and synodals[15] that commonly when any book of the Bible was begun, before three or four chapters were read out, all the rest were unread. . . . And moreover, whereas Saint Paul would have such language spoken to the people in the church as they might understand and have profit by hearing the same, the service in this Church of England these many years hath been read in Latin to the people, which they understood not, so that they have heard with their ears only, and their hearts, spirit, and mind have not been edified thereby. . . .

These inconveniences [*offenses*] therefore considered, here is set forth such an order whereby the same shall be redressed . . . and is ordained nothing to be read but the very pure word of God, the Holy Scriptures, or that which is evidently grounded upon the same, and that in such a language and order as is most easy and plain for the understanding both of the readers and hearers. It is also more commodious [*convenient*], both for the shortness thereof and for the plainness of the order, and for that the rules be few and easy. Furthermore, by this order the curates shall need none other books for their public service but this book and the Bible, by the means whereof the people shall not be at so great charge for books as in time past they have been.

And where heretofore there hath been great diversity in saying and singing in churches within this realm . . . now from henceforth all the whole realm shall have but one use.

4.6 John Foxe, The Martyrdoms of Nicholas Ridley and Hugh Latimer (1563)

From *Acts and Monuments of Martyrs, with a General Discourse of these Latter Persecutions, Horrible Troubles, and Tumults Stirred Up by Romish Prelates in the Church*, STC 11222 (HL copy), 1376–9.

The Roman Catholic Church was rich in legends of saints who were regarded as mediators between the individual and God, but the English Church stripped away these objects of "idolatry." John Foxe developed a massive alternative history of faith and suffering to provide Protestants with new sources of inspiration; the first edition of his Acts and Monuments *(1563) had 1,800 pages. Foxe described two notable martyrdoms from 1555. Hugh Latimer, Bishop of Worcester, was one of the earliest to demand English church services and an English Bible. Nicholas Ridley, Bishop of London, was the most*

---

14 *responds*: anthems sung in alternating verses by soloist and choir.
15 *synodals*: offices or prayers appointed by clerical "synods," or ecclesiastical assemblies.

Figure 6   The Burning of Nicholas Ridley and Hugh Latimer, from John Foxe's *Acts and Monuments of Martyrs* (1563). Courtesy of Brighton and Hove Museums.

This woodcut shows Mary I's men preparing Nicholas Ridley and Hugh Latimer for their martyrdom. Latimer cries, "Father of heaven, receive my soul," and Ridley repeats his frequent call "Into your hands, Lord" ("I commend my spirit"). Meanwhile, the preacher Smith lectures, "If I yield my body to the fire to be burnt, and have not charity, I shall gain nothing thereby." Like all early modern executions, this was a public event. A member of the crowd of witnesses vows, "Master Ridley, I will remember your suit."

charismatic preacher among the early reformers; people were said to have "swarm[ed] about him like bees." The collection popularly known as Foxe's Book of Martyrs *was placed in every cathedral and collegiate church in 1570.*

Doctor Ridley and Master Latimer kneeled down upon their knees towards my Lord Williams of Tame, the Vice-Chancellor of Oxford, and diverse other commissioners appointed for that purpose, which sat upon a form [*bench*] thereby. Unto whom Master Ridley said, "I beseech you, my lord, even for Christ's sake, that I may speak but two or three words." . . . The bailiffs and

Doctor Marshal, [the] Vice-Chancellor, ran hastily unto him and with their hands stopped his mouth and said, "Master Ridley, if you will revoke your erroneous opinions and recant the same, you shall not only have liberty so to do but also the benefit of a subject – that is, have your life."

"Not otherwise?" said Master Ridley.

"No," quod Doctor Marshal. "Therefore, if you will not do so, then there is no remedy but you must suffer for your deserts" [*as you deserve*].

"Well," quod Master Ridley, "so long as the breath is in my body I will never deny my Lord God and his known truth: God's will be done in me." And with that he rose up and said with a loud voice, "Well, then I commit our cause to Almighty God, which shall indifferently judge all."

To whose saying, Master Latimer added his old posy [*motto*], "Well, there is nothing hid but it shall be opened." . . .

Then Master Ridley, standing as yet in his truss [*a close-fitting jacket*], said to his brother, "It were best for me to go in my truss still."

"No," quod his brother, "it will put you to more pain, and the truss will do a poor man good."[16]

Whereunto Master Ridley said, "Be it in the name of God," and so unlaced himself [*unfastened his jacket*]. Then, being in his shirt, he stood upon the foresaid stone and held up his hands and said, "O heavenly Father, I give unto thee most hearty thanks for that thou hast called me to be a professor of thee even unto death. I beseech thee, Lord God, take mercy upon this realm of England and deliver the same from all her enemies."

Then the [black]smith took a chain of iron and brought the same about both Doctor Ridley's and Master Latimer's middles. And as he was knocking in a staple [*securing the chain to a post*], Doctor Ridley took the chain in his hand and shaked the same, for it did gird in [*encircle*] his belly. And looking aside to the smith, said, "Good fellow, knock it in hard, for the flesh will have his course."

Then his brother did bring him gunpowder in a bag and would have tied the same about his neck. Master Ridley asked what it was; his brother said, "Gunpowder."

"Then," said he, "I will take it to be sent of God. Therefore I will receive it as sent of [*from*] him. And have you any," said he, "for my brother?" (meaning Master Latimer).

"Yea, sir, that I have," quod his brother.

"Then give it unto him," said he, "betime, lest ye come too late." So his brother went and carried the same gunpowder unto Master Latimer.

. . . Then brought they a faggot kindled with fire and laid the same down at Doctor Ridley's feet. And when he saw the fire flaming up toward him, he cried with a wonderful loud voice, "*In manus tuas, Domine, commendo spiritum meum.*

---

16 *the truss will do a poor man good*: that is, it can be recycled to clothe a poor man.

Domine, recipe spiritum meum."[17] And after repeated this latter part often in English: "Lord, Lord, receive my spirit," Master Latimer crying as vehemently on the other side, "O Father of heaven, receive my soul!" who received the flame as it were embracing it. After, as he had stroked his face with his hands and as it were bathed them a little in the fire, [he] soon died (as it appeared) with very little pain or none.

But Master Ridley, by reason of the evil [*faulty*] making of the fire unto him, because the wooden faggots were laid about the gorse [*a prickly shrub*], and over-high built, the fire burned first beneath, being kept down by the wood. Which when he felt, he desired them for Christ's sake to let the fire come unto him. Which when his brother-in-law heard but not well understood, intending to rid him of his pain (for the which cause he gave attendance) as one in such sorrow, not well advised what he did, heaped faggots upon him that he clean covered him, which made the fire more vehement beneath that it burned clean all his nether [*lower*] parts before it once touched the upper. And that made him leap up and down under the faggots and often desire them to let the fire come unto him, saying, "I cannot burn." Which indeed appeared well, for after his legs were consumed by reason of his struggling with the pain (whereof he had no release, but only his contentation [*spiritual satisfaction*] in God), he showed that side towards us clean, shirt and all untouched with the flame. Yet in all this torment he forgot not to call unto God still, having in his mouth, "Lord, have mercy upon me" intermeddling this cry, "Let the fire come unto me, I cannot burn." In which pangs he labored till one of the standers-by with his bill [*broadsword*] pulled off the faggots above, and where he espied the fire flame up he wrested himself unto that side. And when the flame touched the gunpowder, he was seen [to] stir no more, but espied burning on the other side by Master Latimer. Which some said happened by reason that the chain loosed. Other said that he fell over the chain by reason of the poise of his body and the weakness of the nether limbs. . . .

Signs there were of sorrow on every side. Some took it grievously to see their deaths whose lives they held full dear; some pitied their persons, that thought their souls had no need thereof. His brother moved many men, seeing his miserable case, seeing (I say) him compelled to such infelicity that he thought then to do him best service when he hastened his end. Some cried out of fortune to see his endeavor (who most dearly loved him and sought his release) turn to his greater vexation and increase of pain. But whoso considered their preferments in time past, the places of honor that they sometime occupied in this commonwealth, the favor they were in with their princes, and the opinion of learning they had in the university they studied, could not choose but sorrow with tears to see so great dignity, honor, and estimation, so necessary members sometime

---

17 *In manus tuas, Domine, commendo spiritum meum. Domine, recipe spiritum meum*: "Into your hands, Lord, I commend my spirit. Lord, receive my spirit."

accounted, so many godly virtues, the study of so many years, such excellent learning to be put into the fire, and consumed in one moment.

4.7   Injunctions Given by the Queen's Majesty (1559)

From STC 10099.5 (BL copy).

Religious matters were at the forefront of fifty-three regulations set out during the first year of Elizabeth I's reign: the virtues of the new liturgy, the Homilies, *and public charity; the iniquity of icons, pilgrimages, and foreign authority. In fact, the Injunctions touched on every aspect of early modern life, including social, political, intellectual, and educational ideas and practices (another extract from the Injunctions is included as document 8.2).*

The first is that all deans, archdeacons, parsons, vicars, and all other ecclesiastical persons shall faithfully keep and observe and (as far as in them may lie) shall cause to be observed and kept of other all and singular laws and statutes made for the restoring to the Crown the ancient jurisdiction over the state ecclesiastical, and abolishing of all foreign power repugnant to the same. And furthermore, all ecclesiastical persons having cure of soul shall, to the uttermost of their wit, knowledge, and learning, purely, sincerely, and without any color or dissimulation, declare, manifest, and open four times every year at the least, in their sermons and other collations, that all usurped and foreign power, having no establishment nor ground by the law of God, is for most just causes taken away and abolished. And that therefore no manner of obedience or subjection within Her Highness's realms and dominions is due unto any such foreign power. And that the queen's power within her realms and dominions is the highest power under God, to whom all men within the same realms and dominions by God's laws owe most loyalty and obedience, afore and above all other powers and potentates in earth.

2.   Besides this, to the intent that all superstition and hypocrisy crept into diverse men's hearts may vanish away, they shall not set forth or extol the dignity of any images, relics, or miracles, but, declaring the abuse of the same, they shall teach that all goodness, health, and grace ought to be both asked and looked for only of God, as of the very author and giver of the same and of none other.

3.   Item, that they the persons above rehearsed shall preach in their churches and every other cure they have, one sermon every month of the year at the least, wherein they shall purely and sincerely declare the word of God. And, in the same, exhort their hearers to the works of faith, as mercy and charity, specially prescribed and commanded in Scripture. And that works devised by man's fantasies besides Scripture, as wandering of pilgrimages, setting up of candles, praying upon beads, or such-like superstition, have not only no promise

of reward in Scripture for doing of them but, contrariwise, great threatenings and maledictions of God, for that they be things tending to idolatry and superstition, which of all other offenses God Almighty doth most detest and abhor, for that the same diminish most his honor and glory.

4. Item, that they the persons above rehearsed shall preach in their own persons once in every quarter of the year at the least one sermon, being licensed specially thereunto, as is specified hereafter. Or else shall read some homily prescribed to be used by the queen's authority, every Sunday at the least, unless some other preacher sufficiently licensed (as hereafter) chance to come to the parish for the same purpose of preaching.

5. Item, that every holy day through the year when they have no sermon, they shall immediately after the Gospel openly and plainly recite to their parishioners in the pulpit the Paternoster, the Creed, and the Ten Commandments[18] in English, to the intent the people may learn the same by heart, exhorting all parents and householders to teach their children and servants the same as they are bound by the law of God and conscience to do.

6. Also that they shall provide within three months next after this visitation [*ecclesiastical inspection*], at the charges of the parish, one book of the whole Bible, of the largest volume in English. And within one twelvemonths next after the said visitation, the *Paraphrases of Erasmus*[19] also in English upon the Gospels, and the same set up in some convenient place within the said church that they have cure of, whereas their parishioners may most commodiously resort unto the same and read the same, out of the time of common service. . . . And they shall discourage no man from the reading of any part of the Bible either in Latin or in English but shall rather exhort every person to read the same with great humility and reverence. . . .

7. Also the said ecclesiastical persons shall in no wise at any unlawful time nor for any other cause than for their honest necessities, haunt or resort to any taverns or alehouses. And after their meats they shall not give themselves to drinking or riot, spending their time idly by day or by night at dice, cards, or tables playing, or any other unlawful game. But at all times as they shall have leisure they shall hear or read somewhat of Holy Scripture or shall occupy themselves with some other honest study or exercise, and that they always do the things which appertain to honesty and endeavor to profit the commonwealth, having always in mind that they ought to excel all other in purity of life and should be examples to the people to live well and Christianly.

---

18 *the Paternoster, the Creed, and the Ten Commandments*: The Paternoster is the Lord's Prayer ("Our father, which art in heaven . . ."); the Creed is the Apostles' Creed or concise statement of Reformed tenets ("I believe in God, the Father Almighty, the Creator of heaven and earth, and in Jesus Christ, His only Son, our Lord . . ."); the Ten Commandments are Old Testament imperatives ("Thou shalt have no other gods before me . . .").
19 *Paraphrases of Erasmus*: popular commentary on the Gospels, written by Erasmus in Latin and later translated into English. The book was first placed in parish churches during the reign of Edward VI.

8.   Also that they shall admit no man to preach within any their cures but such as shall appear unto them to be sufficiently licensed thereunto by the Queen's Majesty or the Archbishop of Canterbury or the Archbishop of York. . . .

10.   Also that the parson, vicar, or curate and parishioners of every parish within this realm shall in their churches and chapels keep one book or register wherein they shall write the day and year of every wedding, christening, and burial made within the parish for their time, and so every man succeeding them likewise. And also therein shall write every person's name that shall be so wedded, christened, and buried. And for the safekeeping of the same book, the parish shall be bound to provide of their common charges one sure coffer with two locks and keys. . . .

12.   And to the intent that learned men may hereafter spring the more for the execution of the premises [*aforementioned matters*], every parson, vicar, clerk, or beneficed man within this deanery, having yearly to dispend in benefices [*clerical appointments*] and other promotions of the church an hundred pounds, shall give £3 6s. 8d. in exhibition to one scholar in any of the universities. And for as many £100 more as he may dispend, to so many scholars more shall give like exhibition in the university of Oxford or Cambridge,[20] or some grammar school. Which after they have profited in good learning may be partners of their patrons' cure and charge, as well in preaching as otherwise in execution of their offices, or may when need shall be otherwise profit the commonwealth with their counsel and wisdom. . . .

14.   Also that the said parsons, vicars, and clerks shall once every quarter of the year read these Injunctions given unto them openly and deliberately before all their parishioners at one time or at two several times in one day, to the intent that both they may be the better admonished of their duty and their said parishioners the more moved to follow the same for their part. . . .

17.   Also that the vice of damnable despair may be clearly taken away and that firm belief and steadfast hope may be surely conceived of all their parishioners being in any danger, they shall learn and have always in a readiness such comfortable places and sentences of Scripture as do set forth the mercy, benefits, and goodness of Almighty God towards all penitent and believing persons, that they may at all times, when necessity shall require, promptly comfort their flock with the lively word of God, which is the only stay of man's conscience. . . .

23.   Also that they shall take away, utterly extinct, and destroy all shrines, covering of shrines, all tables [*painted boards*], candlesticks, trindles [*wax tapers*], and rolls of ware [*textiles*], pictures, paintings, and all other monuments of feigned miracles, pilgrimages, idolatry, and superstition, so that there remain no memory of the same in walls, glasses, window, or elsewhere within their churches and houses, preserving nevertheless or repairing both the walls and

20 *Oxford or Cambridge*: The principal curriculum at the universities was Divinity.

glass windows. And they shall exhort all their parishioners to do the like within their several houses.

24.   And that the churchwardens at the common charge of the parishioners in every church shall provide a comely [*pleasing*] and honest [*plain*] pulpit to be set in a convenient place within the same and to be there seemly kept for the preaching of God's word.

25.   Also they shall provide and have within three months after this visitation a strong chest with a hole in the upper part thereof . . . to the intent the parishioners should put into it their oblations and alms for their poor neighbors . . . knowing that to relieve the poor is a true worshipping of God. . . .

29.   Item, although there be no prohibition by the word of God nor any example of the primitive church but that the priests and ministers of the Church may lawfully, for the avoiding of fornication, have an honest and sober wife . . . yet because there hath grown offense and some slander to the Church by lack of discrete and sober behavior in many ministers of the Church both in choosing of their wives and in undiscreet living with them . . . it is thought therefore very necessary that no manner of priest or deacon shall hereafter take to his wife any manner of woman without the advice and allowance first had upon good examination by the bishop of the same diocese and two justices of peace of the same shire, dwelling next to the place where the same woman hath made her most abode before her marriage, nor without the good will of the parents of the said woman (if she have any living) or two of the next of her kinsfolks, or, for lack of knowledge of such, of her master or mistress where she serveth. . . .

31.   Item, that no man shall willfully and obstinately defend or maintain any heresies, errors, or false doctrine contrary to the faith of Christ and his Holy Scripture.

32.   Item, that no persons shall use charms, sorcery, enchantments, witchcrafts, soothsaying, or any like devilish device, nor shall resort at any time to the same for counsel or help.

33.   Item, that no person shall, neglecting their own parish church, resort to any other church in time of common prayer or preaching, except it be by the occasion of some extraordinary sermon in some parish of the same town.

34.   Item, that no innholders or alehouse keepers shall use to sell meat or drink in the time of common prayer, preaching, reading of the homilies or Scriptures.

35.   Item, that no persons keep in their houses any abused images, table, pictures, paintings, and other monuments of feigned miracles, pilgrimages, idolatry, or superstition. . . .

41.   Item, that all teachers of children shall stir and move them to the love and due reverence of God's true religion, now truly set forth by public authority. . . .

49.   Item . . . the Queen's Majesty neither meaning in any wise the decay of any thing that might conveniently tend to the use and continuance of the said science [of music] . . . it may be permitted that in the beginning or in the end of common prayers, either at morning or evening, there may be sung an hymn or

such-like song to the praise of Almighty God, in the best sort of melody and music that may be conveniently devised, having respect that the sentence of the hymn may be understanded and perceived.

50.   Item, because in all alterations and specially in rites and ceremonies there happeneth discord amongst the people, and thereupon slanderous words and railings, whereby charity, the knot of all Christian society, is loosed: the Queen's Majesty being most desirous of all other earthly things that her people should live in charity both towards God and man, and therein abound in good works, willeth and straightly commandeth all manner her subjects to forbear all vain and contentious disputations in matters of religion. And not to use in despite or rebuke of any person these contentious words: *papist*, or *papistical heretic*, *schismatic*, or *sacramentary*, or any such-like words of reproach. But if any manner of person shall deserve the occupation [*use*] of any such, that first he be charitably admonished thereof. And if that shall not amend him, then to denounce the offenders to the ordinary [*ecclesiastical official*] or to some higher power having authority to correct the same.

4.8   The Conversion of London Blackamoor Mary Fillis (3 June 1597)

From GL Ms 9234/6, 257^r–258^r.

Elizabeth's "Injunctions" emphasized the importance of the church register, a volume documenting all baptisms, marriages, and burials performed in a parish. The register of Saint Botolph Without Aldgate, a large London suburb, includes this report of the advanced-age christening of a servant described as a "black Moor," or blackamoor (a dark-skinned person from Africa, perhaps Ethiopia) whose family had once lived among Moriscos (Moors forcibly converted to Christianity in Spain). Nine named persons attended the christening, with "diverse others." It is an open question whether the baptismal ritual represented an act of faith or Mary Fillis's aspiration to assimilate socially.

Mary Fillis of Morisco, being a blackamoor: She was of late servant with one Mistress Barker in Mark Lane, a widow. She said her father's name was Fillis of Morisco, a blackamoor, being both a basket maker and also a shovel maker. This Mary Fillis being about the age of twenty years and having been in England for the space of thirteen or fourteen years and as it was not christened, and now being become servant with one Millicent Porter, a seamster dwelling in the liberty of East Smithfield, and now taking some hold of faith in Jesus Christ, was desirous to become a Christian. Wherefore she made suit by her said mistress to have some conference with the curate of this the parish of Saint Botolph Without Aldgate, London. Which curate named Master Christopher Threlkeld demanding of her certain questions concerning her faith, whereunto she answering him very

Christian-like, and afterwards she being by the said Master Christopher Threlkeld our curate willed to say the Lord's Prayer and also to rehearse the articles of her belief, which she did both say and rehearse very decently and well, confessing her faith. Then the said curate demanded of her if she were desirous to be baptized in the said faith, whereunto she said, "Aye." Then the said curate did go with her unto the [baptismal] font, and, desiring the congregation with him to call upon God the Father through our Lord Jesus Christ that of His bounteous mercy He would grant to her that thing which by nature she could not have, that she might be baptized with water and the Holy Ghost and received into Christ's Holy Church and be made a lively member of the same, amen. Then the said curate using the rest of the words of the Queen's Majesty's Book [*the* Book of Common Prayer], until he did come unto the questions to be demanded, which questions he did demand of her. Unto which questions she answered as it is set down in the Queen's Majesty's Book, and the minister afterwards praying according to order, which, being done, he said unto the witnesses (whose names were William Benton, Margery Barrick, and Millicent Porter), saying unto them, "You shall name this child," who named her Mary Fillis of Morisco, the daughter to Fillis of Morisco, a blackamoor, being as she said in that country both a basket maker and a shovel maker. So that I do say that the said Mary Fillis, a blackamoor at this time dwelling with Millicent Porter a seamster of the liberty of East Smithfield, was christened on Friday being the third day of June Anno 1597.

4.9   Joan Butcher's Allegation of Slander in the Parish Church (1604)

From the Consistory Court of Bath and Wells Deposition Book, excerpted by Patricia Crawford and Laura Gowing (eds), *Women's Worlds in Seventeenth-Century England: A Sourcebook* (London: Routledge, 2000), 216–18.

The Church did not always succeed as a socializing mechanism. From fifteenth-century records come accounts of one woman smashing the paxbred circulated at Catholic mass because another woman had been allowed to kiss it first. In this later record, a neighborhood quarrel was carried into Protestant church pews. The complainant, Joan Butcher, was the twenty-eight-year-old wife of a Somerset blacksmith.

The above named Elizabeth Fontstone and this examinant being seat or pewmates in the parish church . . . and present in their seat hearing divine service, the said Elizabeth Fontstone fell out with [*quarreled with*] this examinant and brawled with her in the said seat, saying, "Dost thou pull thy daughter over my daughter's back, thou proud beggarly jade? Pride will have a fall, and thy pride is falling already, and I hope to live to see thee pulled lower yet. Go home, jade, and pluck down thy pride, for it is for no devotion that thou comest to the church, Mistress Turdpie."

4.10   Nehemiah Wallington's Dullness in Church (1630)

From "A Record of God's Mercies," GL Ms 204, 21–3.

Religion was central to the life of this London craftsman and strict Puritan. In more than fifty handwritten volumes of spiritual autobiography and religious observations, Wallington made lengthy reports of sermons he had heard. As he admitted in a volume he called "A Record of God's Mercies," though, even he suffered a familiar complaint which he called "dullness in the service of God."

There is another sin which reigns in me and grieves me very much, and that is irksomeness and tediousness and dullness in the service of God. . . . I have not gone with a love unto it [*i.e., to church*] but for some by-respect, as to please my father, or to be well thought of by others, or for fashion's sake, or custom's sake. I have wished many times, "When will the Sabbath be gone?" And I have thought long till the sermon was done and, looking on the hourglass, wishing it were run out. I have suffered mine eyes to gaze about in thine house, and my mind to wander on vain thoughts that will not profit, and I have many times slept at church hearing of God's word. . . .

When dullness begins to come upon me I then do think that now there is something that especially concerns me, because the devil so labors to lull me asleep. Whereupon I begin then to stir up myself and to give the more diligent heed unto the Word. And I say within myself, "Strike home, O Lord, strike home to my poor soul, that I may go home refreshed in my soul this day." . . .

The outward means that I used is this: when I found myself sleepy at church, I would prick my self with a pin. Sometime I would bite my tongue. Sometime I would pinch myself. . . . I would take with me to church some pepper or ginger or some cloves, and when I found myself sleepy, I would bite some of them. And so I have by the goodness of God got some victory over this sin.

4.11   Henry Goodcole, *The Wonderful Discovery of Elizabeth Sawyer, a Witch* (1621)

From STC 12014 (BL copy), C1^{r-v}, C2^v, C3^{r-v}, C4^v.

The history of religious change in England is told largely as a conflict between Roman Catholics and, in all their various degrees of conformity and radicalism, Protestants. But nothing entirely supplanted an alternate belief system involving the "white" magic of charms and spells. Black magic, a different matter, was vigorously prosecuted, especially during the reign of James VI and I. The Puritan minister Henry Goodcole interviewed many accused witches and murderers in London's Newgate prison. His report concerning Elizabeth Sawyer formed the basis of a stage play by John Dekker, John Ford, and William Rowley. The Witch of Edmonton *was surprisingly progressive in showing that Sawyer resorted to witchcraft when confronted by extreme poverty. Even Goodcole admits that it was "because her neighbors where she dwelt would not buy brooms of her" that she entertained thoughts of malicious "revenge."*

Question: By what means came you to have acquaintance with the Devil, and when was the first time that you saw him, and how did you know that it was the Devil?

Answer: The first time that the Devil came unto me was when I was cursing, swearing, and blaspheming; he then rushed in upon me, and never before that time did I see him, or he me. And when he, namely the Devil, came to me, the first words that he spake unto me were these: "Oh, have I now found you cursing, swearing, and blaspheming? Now you are mine."
. . .

Question: In what shape would the Devil come unto you?

Answer: Always in the shape of a dog, and of two colors, sometimes of black and sometimes of white.
. . .

Question: In what place of your body did the Devil suck of your blood, and whether did he choose the place or did you yourself appoint him the place? Tell the truth, I charge you, as [you] will answer unto the Almighty God, and tell the reason if that you can why he would suck your blood.

Answer: The place where the Devil sucked my blood was a little above my fundament [*anus*], and that place chosen by himself. And in that place by continual drawing there is a thing in the form of a teat at which the Devil would suck me. And I asked the Devil why he would suck my blood, and he said it was to nourish him.

Question: Whether did you pull up your coats or no when the Devil came to suck you?

Answer: No, I did not, but the Devil would put his head under my coats, and I did willingly suffer him to do what he would.

Question: How long would the time be, that the Devil would continue sucking of you, and whether did you endure any pain, the time that he was sucking of you?

Answer: He would be sucking of me the continuance of a quarter of an hour, and when he sucked me I then felt no pain at all.

Question: What was the meaning that the Devil, when he came unto you, would sometimes speak and sometimes bark?

Answer: It is thus: when the Devil spake to me, then he was ready to do for me what I would bid him to do. And when he came barking to me, he then had done the mischief that I did bid him to do for me. . . .

Question: Did the Devil at any time find you praying when he came unto you?

And did not the Devil forbid you to pray to Jesus Christ, but to him alone? And did not he bid you pray to him, the Devil, as he taught you?

Answer: Yes, he found me once praying, and he asked of me to whom I prayed. And I answered him, "To Jesus Christ." And he charged me then to pray no more to Jesus Christ, but to him the Devil, and he the Devil taught me this prayer: "*Santibicetur nomen tuum*. Amen."

Question: Were you ever taught these Latin words before by any person else? Or did you ever hear it before of anybody? Or can you say any more of it?

Answer: No, I was not taught it by anybody else but by the Devil alone. Neither do I understand the meaning of these words, nor can speak any more Latin words.

4.12 James VI and I, *The King's Majesty's Declaration to his Subjects Concerning Lawful Sports to be Used* (1618)

From STC 9238.9 (HL copy), A4^r–B1^r, B2^{r-v}.

James VI and I learned that his government needed to be as concerned with the strictness of Puritans as with continuing loyalties to Roman Catholicism. With "The Book of Sports" (as it was popularly known), he aimed to preserve a place for pleasure in public culture. In 1633 Charles I republished the "Book" and ordered it read from every parish pulpit. There was a fierce backlash, and in 1643 Puritans in Parliament required all copies to be burned.

It is true that at our first entry to this crown and kingdom we were informed, and that too truly, that our county of Lancashire abounded more in popish recusants than any county of England. And thus hath still continued since, to our great regret, with little amendment, save that now of late, in our last riding through our said county, we find both by the report of the judges and of the bishop of that diocese that there is some amendment now daily beginning which is no small contentment to us.

The report of this growing amendment amongst them made us the more sorry, when with our own ears we heard the general complaint of our people that they were barred from all lawful recreation and exercise upon the Sunday's afternoon after the ending of all divine service, which cannot but produce two evils. The one, the hindering of the conversion of many, whom their priests will take occasion hereby to vex, persuading them that no honest mirth or recreation is lawful or tolerable in our religion – which cannot but breed a great discontentment in our people's hearts, especially of such as are peradventure upon the point of turning. The other inconvenience is that this prohibition barreth the common and meaner sort of people from using such exercises as may make their bodies more able for war when we or our successors shall have occasion to use them. And, in place thereof, sets up filthy tipplings and drunkenness and breeds a number of idle and discontented speeches in their alehouses. For when shall the common people have leave to exercise, if not upon the Sundays and holy days, seeing they must apply their labor and win their living in all working days?

Our express pleasure therefore is . . . that after the end of divine service, our good people be not disturbed, letted [*prevented*], or discouraged from any lawful recreation such as dancing (either men or women), archery (for men), leaping, vaulting, or any other such harmless recreation, nor from having of May-games, Whitsun ales, and morris dances, and the setting up of maypoles and other sports therewith used, so as the same be had in due and convenient time, without impediment or neglect of divine service. And that women shall have leave to carry rushes to the church for the decoring [*adorning*] of it according to their old custom. But withal we do here account still as prohibited all unlawful games to be used upon Sundays only, as bear and bull baitings, interludes [*comic stage-plays*], and, at all times in the meaner sort of people by law prohibited, bowling.

5

Philosophy and Ideas

The concept of a "Renaissance" is not self-contained. To characterize this period as one of rebirth is, necessarily, to believe that there was a pre-existing period from which culture emerged renewed. Thus, there could not have been an idea of the Renaissance without a corollary conviction that the medieval years were "dark" ages.

Ironically, however, the impetus for the *philosophical* Renaissance was not the intellectual crudity of earlier thought. Instead, the problem for early modern thinkers was that the philosophy of the Middle Ages was over-sophisticated. Medieval scholasticism sought to reconcile Aristotelian (pre-Christian) and Catholic thought. Within its narrow frame of reference, it had developed into a highly self-referential discourse conducted in exhaustive exchanges of commentary on its small and selective canon of texts. It existed out of time, in the realm of lofty and abstract argument. The esoteric discussions and debates of medieval philosophy were confined to the most elite scholastic circles, generally monastic ones. In all its guises – as the Reformation, the Print Age, the Rise of Individualism, the Age of Exploration, the Scientific Revolution – the Renaissance inspired intellectual ferment that moved out of these restricted confines to inform public culture.

Humanist Philosophy

The most important development in sixteenth-century European thought was humanism. At base, this was a challenge to traditional religion, inasmuch as it focused on the concerns of this world and not those of the afterlife. Humanists were centrally persuaded of the dignity, ability, and worth of the individual. In Italy the first great humanist, Petrarch, issued the call "to reveal man to himself once more."

Petrarch's challenge was to involve many changes in the practice of philosophy, but six must be emphasized. First, humanists believed that their work should engage with human problems. No longer was philosophy valued for its impalpable remoteness from everyday life. Their revolutionary idea was that philosophy could be responsive to contemporary events and contributive to social development. Second, the phenomena encountered by early modern philosophy included the crisis of ecclesiastical schism, the rise of the European nation-state, the development of civic institutions and legal culture, a new economy of cash transactions and globalized commerce, and revolutionary medical and astronomical discoveries and inventions. To the humanists, the politics and ethics of these developments seemed of more urgent concern than metaphysics and theology. They addressed the importance of good counsel to a commonwealth, the meaning of art, and the purpose of scientific knowledge. Third, upward mobility in the period was intellectual as well as economic. Where learning had previously been confined to the nobility, the universities, and the church, it now catered to a less rarified demographic. This was especially true in England, following the Dissolution of the monasteries and the disbanding of their scholarly communities. Between 1558 and 1642, nearly three hundred grammar schools were founded. They embraced a mission to educate the citizenry about its public duty.

Fourth, humanists recognized that if philosophy was to be efficacious it must be expressed not in the specialized language of elite intellectuals but, rather, in widely accessible terms, and often in the vernacular rather than Latin. There was a pragmatic emphasis on the capacities of rhetoric for persuasion. Fifth, humanist scholarship was classical rather than biblical – indeed, the Renaissance would not have been figured as a *re*birth were not the "birth" of western culture understood to have been located in ancient Greece and Rome. But while sixteenth-century humanists still honored Aristotle, many developed an interest in Plato, and they also scoured monastic and university libraries across Europe and in Constantinople in search of neglected treatises by other classical authors. These were virgin texts, uncontaminated by centuries of exhaustive scholastic analysis. Thus the discourses of philosophy were invigorated by the infusion of previously unknown ideas. Sixth, Pyrrho, Sextus Empiricus, and other skeptics were among the rediscovered ancients. Their ideas were congruent with the prevailing mood to interrogate the work of medieval scholasticists. The questioning of any authority opened all authorities to challenge. Skepticism was as important for Renaissance philosophy as it was for the Scientific Revolution.

Order and Degree

In England, the philosophical beliefs that were most widely acculturated were those that were reinforced by the Crown and from the pulpit. The principal project of orthodox political theory was to justify inequitable distributions of power. For this, warrant was sought wherever it could be found, whether the appeal was to nature or to the Christian Bible. Thus, while English public ideology spoke to real-world issues of social organization, it diverted from humanism in having a more pronounced religious cast. Political arguments were routinely authenticated in citations from the Bible. Perhaps more surprisingly, religious belief was itself shaped by political thought. Stories of the fall of Lucifer from heaven and the fall of man in the Garden of Eden, for example, were politicized as admonitory lessons about the consequences of a subject disobeying his superior. By accepting his crucifixion, Jesus was believed to have redeemed the sins of Adam through a compensatory act of obedience to God.

A basic tenet of prevailing thought was that God had created a universe of analogous systems and that all systems were ordered hierarchically. Just as each planet occupied its designated place or "degree" in the hierarchy of planets, so, too, did each angel in heaven, each citizen of the commonwealth, each member of a family, and each part of the human body. The degree of humankind was located midway on what was known as the "Great Chain of Being," between angels and beasts. Man was inferior to one but superior to the other. Within this overall framework, humanity was then further differentiated. Rankings within the human sphere were established by power, social standing, birth order, and gender – all understood to be divinely ordained.

As integral elements of God's creation, the systems were believed to be mutually dependent. In a powerful incentive to observe degree, a violation in one sphere was said to jeopardize the order of the entire universe. This is why, when Macbeth kills his king to usurp a higher position than that in which he belongs, Shakespeare imagines chaos across the spheres. The planets are so disordered that it is dark at midday, and the Chain of Being so disrupted that horses attack men. Degree was also implicated in the foundational myth of the origin of evil. Lucifer was not only disobedient to God; he also challenged his own place in the hierarchy of angels.

For this act, Lucifer was cast out of heaven and became known by his fallen name, Satan. Man, too, was a fallen creature. Eating the forbidden fruit, Adam and Eve both defied God and challenged the limits of the knowledge designated to them. Despite being exiled from Paradise and made subject to sin, however, human beings remained capable of demonstrating virtue. In common culture, nature was seen as a mediator between the human and the divine, and nature was understood to have imprinted upon man's heart and mind an innate ability to recognize order and degree. The "law of nature" was expressed biblically in the Ten Commandments.

Public Ideology

No belief was more urgently defended in the early modern period than the necessity of government. Without political order, it was argued, such savagery would prevail that humans would descend on the Great Chain of Being to the level of beasts. Not long before, England had been a kingdom of mighty feudal magnates, each with his own stronghold and band of retainers. The political thought of the period was now occupied with rationalizing the monarchic form of government, with justifying the Tudor/Stuart consolidation of authority, and with exhorting obedience on the part of all subjects. History plays by

Shakespeare and others portrayed the civil unrest that had once followed from rivalries among leading noblemen. In this, dramatists participated in the early modern project of defending the Renaissance monarch's pre-eminence over the aristocracy.

By means of analogical thought, early modern thinkers argued for the divine sanction of monarchy. Every sphere demonstrated the principle: the cosmos was commanded by God, the Church by Christ, the body by its head, the family by a father. It was only "natural" that a kingdom should be ruled by a king. For the purposes of hegemonic ideology, however, it was awkward that the Ten Commandments, which mandated honor to God ("Thou shalt have no other gods before me," "Thou shalt not make unto thee any graven image," "Thou shalt not take the name of the Lord thy God in vain") and which issued social prohibitions ("Thou shalt not kill," "Thou shalt not commit adultery," "Thou shalt not steal," "Thou shalt not bear false witness against thy neighbor") were largely apolitical. Only the Fifth Commandment seemed susceptible of political interpretation, and it was inconveniently dualized: "Honor thy father and thy mother." One of the reasons that the primacy of the father in the family was so vehemently asserted in the early modern period was that it was essential to the analogical argument: if nothing could be as "natural" as that a father should head his family, neither could anything be so necessary as that a king should head the kingdom. Thus, in the interest of the monarchy and of social order, the Old Testament authorization of mothers was discreetly suppressed through emphasis on the New Testament patriarchalism of St. Paul: "Let women be subject to their husbands as to the Lord, for the husband is the head of the woman as Christ is head of the Church."

Because the system of correspondences was believed to have been created by God, it followed (or so it was said) that the king received his power from God. Thus, he did not require the consent of the people to govern; he was put in place by and accountable only to God. And if the Bible commanded that the father should be honored, so also the king should be obeyed. These were the beliefs argued by political theorists known as "absolutists," among whom were to be numbered James VI and I and his son Charles I. Many other power relationships – master over servant, teacher over student, priest over parishioner – were instantiated by the need of the monarchy to validate itself in the biblical sanction of the Fifth Commandment.

Resistance Theory

Natural law, concepts of order and degree, patriarchalism, the divine right of kings – all these ideas were aspects of public culture. While no early modern could escape the theories promulgated in the authorized *Homilies* that were read from the pulpit every Sunday, not all believed them or were guided by them. History throws up countless examples of wives behaving independently, children disobeying their parents, servants flouting their masters, subjects criticizing the king, and rebels plotting against the government. These actions were not necessarily grounded philosophically. However, amid the skeptical climate of humanist thought and the many crises of state religion and royal succession, there also developed alternative belief systems. Under the pressure of events and competing self-interests, some thinkers developed a formal, intellectualized discourse of political resistance. Ideas first articulated in the sixteenth century were to contribute to the philosophical underpinnings of the English Civil Wars in the seventeenth century and the American and French Revolutions in the eighteenth century.

For England, some of the most important theorists were from other countries in Europe. Indeed, the larger story of Renaissance philosophy should properly be told in terms of such great Continental thinkers as Francesco Petrarch, Leonardo Bruni, Poggio Bracciolini, Lorenzo Valla, Coluccio Salutati, Leon Battista Alberti, Marsilio Ficino, Giovanni Pico, and Nicholas of Cusa, among others. Here, however, the documentary readings tell the more focused story of ideas that circulated in the public culture of early modern England, whether they were naturalized from the works of men such as Niccolò Machiavelli, were authored by Elizabeth's counselors for pronouncement in parish churches, or were written oppositionally. These were the concepts that informed literary production and reception in England, as well as daily life.

5.1   William Shakespeare on Order and Degree (1602)

From STC 22332 (BL copy), B4^{r-v}.

The most famous statement of Elizabethan ideas of order is presented by a Greek general in the play Troilus and Cressida. *Without hierarchy, degree, the analogical organization of the world's different spheres, and obedience (Ulysses argues), the universe would fall into chaos. Shakespeare himself may no more have agreed with Ulysses than with another of his characters, Jack Cade (the rebel in* King John *who cries, "The first thing we do, let's kill all the lawyers!"). But the powerful and eloquent language he gives Ulysses represents how forceful these ideas were in Renaissance culture.*

> *Ulysses:*
> The heavens themselves, the planets, and this center[1]
> Observe degree, priority, and place,
> Infixture,[2] course, proportion, season, form,

---

1 *this center*: i.e., the earth.
2 *infixture*: fixity.

Office[3] and custom, in all line of order.
And therefore is the glorious planet Sol
In noble eminence enthroned and sphered
Amidst the other, whose med'cinable eye
Corrects the influence of evil planets
And posts like the commandment of a king,
Sans check, to good and bad. But when the planets
In evil mixture to disorder wander,
What plagues and what portents, what mutiny?
What raging of the sea, shaking of earth?
Commotion in the winds, frights, changes, horrors
Divert and crack, rend and deracinate
The unity and married calm of states
Quite from their fixture. O when degree is shaked
(Which is the ladder of all high designs),
The enterprise is sick. How could communities,
Degrees in schools, and brotherhoods in cities,
Peaceful commerce from dividable shores,
The primogenity[4] and due of birth,
Prerogative of age, crowns, scepters, laurels,
But by degree stand in authentic place?
Take but degree away, untune that string,
And hark what discord follows: each thing [meets]
In mere oppugnancy.[5] The bounded waters
Should lift their bosoms higher than the shores
And make a sop of all this solid globe;
Strength should be lord of imbecility;
And the rude son should strike his father dead.
Force should be right – or rather, right and wrong
(Between whose endless jar justice resides),
Should lose their names, and so should justice, too.
Then everything include itself in power,
Power into will, will into appetite;
And appetite (an universal wolf,
So doubly seconded with will and power),
Must make perforce an universal prey,
And, last, eat up himself.

---

3 *Office*: function.
4 *primogenity*: primogeniture, the condition of being a first-born child, especially a son; the term generally refers to the comprehensive rights of inheritance of a first-born son.
5 *oppugnancy*: opposition.

5.2 "An Homily against Disobedience and Willful Rebellion" (1570)

From STC 13679.2 (HL copy), A1^{r-v}, A2^{r-v}, A3^{v}–A4^{v}, B1^{r}.

Because literacy was not universal in early modern England, royal messages were disseminated orally in church – where attendance was expected to be universal. In 1547, under Edward VI, twelve homilies were read in rotation on successive Sundays. In 1563, under Elizabeth I, the collection grew to twenty-one. Then, in 1569, a group of powerful noblemen from northern England determined to make the country Catholic again. With no separation of church and state, religious resistance was a political threat; the earls meant to depose Elizabeth and replace her with Mary of Scotland. The "Northern Rebellion" was put down, but Pope Pius V excommunicated the English queen, declaring that her Catholic subjects owed her no allegiance. The measure of the perceived danger is indicated by the fact that the 1570 edition of authorized public sermons included not just one Sunday's worth on the subject of obedience, but four.

As God the creator and lord of all things appointed his angels and heavenly creatures in all obedience to serve and to honor his majesty, so was it his will that man, his chief creature upon the earth, should live under the obedience of him his creator and lord. And for that cause, God, as soon as he had created man, gave unto him a certain precept and law which he (being yet in the state of innocency and remaining in Paradise) should observe as a pledge and token of his due and bounden obedience, with denunciation of death if he did transgress and break the said law and commandment. And as God would have man to be his obedient subject, so did he make all earthly creatures subject unto man, who kept their due obedience unto man so long as man remained in his obedience unto God. In the which obedience if man had continued still, there had been no poverty, no diseases, no sickness, no death, nor other miseries wherewith mankind is now infinitely and most miserably afflicted and oppressed. So here appeareth the original kingdom of God over angels and man, and universally over all things, and of man over earthly creatures which God had made subject unto him, and withal the felicity and blessed state which angels, man, and all creatures had remained in had they continued in due obedience unto God their king. For as long as in this first kingdom the subjects continued in due obedience to God their king, so long did God embrace all his subjects with his love, favor, and grace, which to enjoy is perfect felicity.

Whereby it is evident that obedience is the principal virtue of all virtues, and indeed the very root of all virtues and the cause of all felicity. But as all felicity and blessedness should have continued with the continuance of obedience, so with the breach of obedience and breaking in of rebellion, all vices and miseries did withal break in and overwhelm the world. The first author of which rebellion, the root of all vices and mother of all mischiefs, was Lucifer, first God's most excellent creature and most bounden subject, who, by rebelling against the majesty of God, of the brightest and most glorious angel is become the blackest and most foulest fiend and devil, and from the height of heaven is fallen into the pit and bottom of hell. . . . Thus became rebellion, as you see, both the first and greatest, and the very root of all other sins, and the first and principal cause both of all worldly and bodily miseries (sorrows, diseases, sicknesses, and deaths), and, which is infinitely worse than all these, as is said, the very cause of death and damnation eternal also.

After this breach of obedience to God and rebellion against his majesty, all mischiefs and miseries breaking in therewith and overflowing the world, lest all things should come unto confusion and utter ruin, God forthwith, by laws given unto mankind, repaired again the rule and order of obedience thus by rebellion overthrown, and, besides the obedience due unto His Majesty, he not only ordained that in families and households the wife should be obedient unto her husband, the children unto their parents, the servants unto their masters, but also, when mankind increased and spread itself more largely over the world, he by his Holy Word did constitute and ordain in cities and countries several and special governors and rulers, unto whom the residue of his people should be obedient.

As in reading of the Holy Scriptures, we shall find in very many and almost infinite places, as well of the Old Testament as of the New, that kings and princes, as well the evil as the good, do reign by God's ordinance, and that subjects are bounden to obey them; that God doth give princes wisdom, great power, and authority; that God defendeth them against their enemies and destroyeth their enemies horribly; that the anger and displeasure of the prince is as the roaring of a lion and the very messenger of death; and that the subject that provoketh him to displeasure sinneth against his own soul. . . . It is most evident that kings, queens, and other princes (for he speaketh of authority and power, be it in men or women[6]) are ordained of God, are to be obeyed and honored of their subjects; that such subjects as are disobedient or rebellious against their princes disobey God and procure their own damnation; that the government of princes is a great blessing of God, given for the commonwealth, specially of the good and godly, for the comfort and cherishing of whom God giveth and setteth up princes; and, on the contrary part, to the fear and for the punishment of the evil and wicked. Finally, that if servants ought to obey their masters, not only being gentle but such as be froward [*hard to please*], as well and much more ought subjects to be obedient, not only to their good and courteous but also to their sharp and rigorous princes.

It cometh therefore neither of chance and fortune (as they term it), nor of the ambition of mortal men and women climbing up of their own accord to dominion, that there be kings, queens, princes, and other governors over men being their subjects. But all kings, queens, and other governors are specially appointed

---

6 *be it in men or women*: The homily allows for the possibility of a female ruler such as Elizabeth.

by the ordinance of God. And as God himself, being of an infinite majesty, power, and wisdom, ruleth and governeth all things in heaven and in earth, as the universal monarch and only king and emperor over all, as being only able to take and bear the charge of all, so hath he constitute[d], ordained, and set earthly princes over particular kingdoms and dominions in earth, both for the avoiding of all confusion, which else would be in the world if it should be without such governors, and for the great quiet and benefit of earthly men their subjects. And also that the princes themselves in authority, power, wisdom, providence, and righteousness in government of people and countries committed to their charge should resemble his heavenly governance as the majesty of heavenly things may by the baseness of earthly things be shadowed and resembled. And for that similitude that is between the heavenly monarchy and earthly kingdoms well governed, our savior Christ in sundry parables sayeth that the kingdom of heaven is resembled unto a man, a king, and as the name of the king is very often attributed and given unto God in the Holy Scriptures, so doth God himself in the same Scriptures sometime vouchsafe to communicate his name with earthly princes, terming them gods, doubtless for that similitude of government which they have or should have, not unlike unto God their king. . . .

What shall subjects do then? Shall they obey valiant, stout, wise, and good princes, and condemn, disobey, and rebel against children being their princes, or against indiscreet and evil governors? God forbid. For first, what a perilous thing were it to commit unto the subjects the judgment which prince is wise and godly and his government good, and which is otherwise. As though the foot must judge of the head: an enterprise very heinous, and must needs breed rebellion. For who else be they that are most inclined to rebellion but such haughty spirits? From whom springeth such foul ruin of realms? Is not rebellion the greatest of all mischiefs? And who are most ready to the greatest mischiefs but the worst men?

5.3 John Ponet, *A Short Treatise of Politic Power* (1556)

From STC 20178 (HL copy), B4ʳ, C2ʳ⁻ᵛ, C4ᵛ–C5ᵛ, F8ʳ⁻ᵛ, G5ʳ⁻ᵛ, G6ᵛ, H1ʳ.

Each Tudor and Stuart monarch faced uprisings: for Henry VII, the Yorkshire Rebellion and Cornish Rebellion; for Henry VIII, the Pilgrimage of Grace, Western Rebellion, and Kett's Rebellion; for Mary I, Wyatt's Rebellion; for Elizabeth I, the Rebellion of the Northern Earls, the Throckmorton Plot, Tyrone's Rebellion, and the Essex Rebellion; for James VI and I, the Bye Plot, the Main Plot, and the Gunpowder Plot; for Charles I, the Civil Wars which ended in his deposition. These are the most famous instances of unrest and sedition; there were many more. The religious upheavals of the sixteenth century, however, provoked something entirely new in political discourse: a learned defense of resistance as a moral duty. John Ponet was a Protestant ecclesiast who fled to Europe rather than submit to Mary I (to whom he refers directly, below, with reference to the monarch who will "bring the people under a foreign power" – in Mary's case, the Roman Pope, her Spanish husband, or both).

Whether kings, princes, and other governors have an absolute power and authority over their subjects?

Before magistrates were, God's laws were. Neither can it be proved that by God's word they have any authority to dispense or break them, but that they be still commanded to do right, to minister justice, and not to swerve neither on the right hand or on the left. Then must it needs follow that this absolute authority which they use must be maintained by man's reason or it must needs be an usurpation.

Whether kings, princes, and other politic governors be subject to God's laws and the positive laws of their countries?

The whole Decalogue [*the Ten Commandments*] and every part thereof is as well written to kings, princes, and other public persons as to private persons. A king may no more commit idolatry than a private man; he may not take the name of God in vain; he may not break the Sabbath no more than any private man. It is not lawful for him to disobey his parents, to kill any person contrary to the laws, to be an whoremonger, to steal, to lie and bear false witness, to desire and covet any man's house, wife, servant, maid, ox, ass, or any thing that is another's, more than any other private man. No, he is bounden and charged under greater pains to keep them than any other, because he is both a private man in respect of his own person and a public in respect of his office. . . .

Neither is that power and authority which kings, princes, and other ministers of justice exercise only called a power, but also the authority that parents have over their children and masters over their servants is also called a power. And neither be the parents nor masters the power itself, but they be ministers and executors of the power being given unto them by God. . . . And they being but executors of God's laws and men's just ordinances, be also not exempted from them but be bounden to be subject and obedient unto them. For good and just laws of man be God's power and ordinances, and they are but ministers of the laws and not the law's self. And if they were exempt from the laws, and so it were lawful for them to do what them lusteth, their authority being of God, it might be said that God allowed their tyranny, robbery of their subjects, killing them without law – and so God the author of evil, which were a great blasphemy. . . .

It is also a principle of all laws grounded on the law of nature that every man should use himself and be obedient to that law that he will others be bounden unto. For otherwise he taketh away that equality (for there is no difference between the head and foot, concerning the use and benefit of the laws) whereby commonwealths be maintained and kept up. What equality (I beseech you) should there be, where the subject should do to his ruler all the ruler would, and the ruler to the subject that the ruler lusted?

Whether all the subjects' goods be the kaiser's and king's own and that they may lawfully take them as their own?

As in a great man's house all things be said to be the steward's[7] because it is committed to his charge, to see that every man in the house behave himself honestly and do his duty, to see that all things be well kept and preserved, and may take nothing away from any man nor misspend or waste, and of his doings he must render accompt to his lord for all: so in a realm or other dominion. The realm and country are God's. He is the lord; the people are his servants; and the king or governor is but God's minister or steward, ordained not to misuse the servants (that is, the people), neither to spoil them of that they have, but to see the people do their duty to their Lord God, that the goods of this world be not abused but spent to God's glory, to the maintenance and defense of the commonwealth and not to the destruction of it. The prince's watch ought to defend the poor man's house; his labor, the subject's ease; his diligence, the subject's pleasure; his trouble, the subject's quietness. And as the sun never standeth still but continually goeth about the world doing his office, with his heat refreshing and comforting all natural things in the world, so ought a good prince to be continually occupied in his ministry, not seeking his own profit but the wealth of those that be committed to his charge.

Whether it be lawful to depose an evil governor and kill a tyrant?

The body of every state may (if it will), yea, and ought to redress and correct the vices and heads of their governors. And forasmuch as ye have already seen whereof politic power and government groweth, and the end whereunto it was ordained, and seeing it is before manifestly and sufficiently proved that kings and princes have not an absolute power over their subjects, that they are and ought to be subject to the law of God and the wholesome positive laws of their country, and that they may not lawfully take or use their subjects' goods at their pleasure, the reasons, arguments, and law that serve for the deposing and displacing of an evil governor will do as much for the proof that it is lawful to kill a tyrant if they may be indifferently heard. As God hath ordained magistrates to hear and determine private men's matters and to punish their vices, so also will he that the

---

7 *all things be said to be the steward's*: All domestic responsibilities, including procurement and staff supervision, are under the supervision of the steward.

magistrates' doings be called to accompt and reckoning and their vices corrected and punished by the body of the whole congregation or commonwealth. . . .

This law testifieth to every man's conscience that it is natural to cut away an incurable member which, being suffered, would destroy the whole body. Kings, princes, and other governors, albeit they are the heads of a politic body, yet they are not the whole body. And though they be the chief members, yet they are but members. Neither are the people ordained for them, but they are ordained for the people. . . .

If a prince rob and spoil his subjects, it is theft, and as a thief [he] ought to be punished. If he kill and murder them contrary or without the laws of his country, it is murder, and as a murderer he ought to be punished. If he commit adultery, he is an adulterer and ought to be punished with the same pains that others be. If he violently ravish men's wives, daughters, or maidens, the laws that are made against ravishers ought to be executed on him. If he go about to betray his country and to bring the people under a foreign power, he is a traitor and as a traitor he ought to suffer. And those that be judges in commonwealths ought (upon complaint) to summon and cite them to answer to their crimes, and so to proceed as they do with others.

5.4   John Knox, *The First Blast of the Trumpet against the Monstrous Regiment of Women* (1558)

From STC 15070 (HL copy), B1^r, B2^r, B2^v–B3^r, B4^r, E2^r, F7^{r-v}.

The Scot John Knox was chaplain to Edward VI. Like John Ponet, he left England when Mary I succeeded to the throne. From Geneva, Knox argued that female rule violates nature, God's order, classical tradition, and civil law. For Knox, though, misogyny was strategic; his real complaint against Mary was not her gender but her religion. He promised to publish Second *and* Third Blasts, *but completed just a few pages of the* Second *before being overtaken by events. Mary died within months of the* First Blast, *and Knox was not prepared to argue against her sister and successor, the queen who would restore Protestantism to England.*

To promote a woman to bear rule, superiority, dominion, or empire above any realm, nation, or city is repugnant to nature, contumely [*insolent*] to God, a thing most contrarious to his revealed will and approved ordinance, and, finally, it is the subversion of good order, of all equity and justice.

. . . Thus writeth Aristotle in the second of his *Politics*: "What difference shall we put," saith he, "whether that women bear authority or the husbands that obey the empire of their wives be appointed to be magistrates? For what ensueth the one must needs follow the other, to wit, injustice, confusion, and disorder." . . . What would this writer, I pray you, have said to that realm or nation where

Figure 7   Elizabeth I in Parliament, from Robert Glover's *Nobilitas Politica Vel Civilis* (1608). Courtesy of Pictorial Press Ltd/Alamy.

Elizabeth I, presiding from the throne and surrounded by her chief ministers, faces the Speaker of Parliament (in the foreground), members of the House of Lords (in rows), and scribes. With this image, John Knox's dismay that a woman should sit "crowned in Parliament amongst the midst of men" is realized. The engraving was published five years after the queen's death, in a book on the noble families of England.

a woman sitteth crowned in Parliament amongst the midst of men? Oh fearful and terrible are thy judgments, O Lord, which thus hast abased man for his iniquity! I am assuredly persuaded that if any of those men which (illuminated only by the light of nature) did see and pronounce causes sufficient why women ought not to bear rule nor authority, should this day live and see a woman sitting in judgment or riding from Parliament in the midst of men, having the royal crown upon her head, the sword and scepter borne before her in sign that the administration of justice was in her power – I am assuredly persuaded, I say, that such a sight should so astonish them that they should judge the whole world to be transformed into Amazons, and that such a metamorphosis and change was made of all the men of that country (as poets do feign was made of the companions of Ulysses), or at least that albeit the outward form of men remained, yet should they judge that their hearts were changed from the wisdom, understanding, and courage of men to the foolish fondness and cowardice of women. Yea, they further should pronounce that where women reign or be in authority that there must needs vanity be preferred to virtue, ambition and pride to temperancy and modesty, and, finally, that avarice, the mother of all mischief, must needs devour equity and justice. . . . And Aristotle, as before is touched, doth plainly affirm that wheresoever women bear dominion there must needs the people be disordered, living and abounding in all intemperancy, given to pride, excess, and vanity. And finally, in the end, that they must needs come to confusion and ruin. . . .

For this present, I say that the erecting of a woman to that honor is not only to invert the order which God hath established, but also it is to defile, pollute, and profane (so far as in man lieth) the throne and seat of God, which he hath sanctified and appointed for man only, in the course of this wretched life, to occupy and possess as his minister and lieutenant, secluding from the same all women, as before is expressed. . . . The question is not if women may not succeed to possession, substance, patrimony, or inheritance, such as fathers may leave to their children; for that I willingly grant. But the question is if women may succeed to their fathers in offices, and chiefly to that office the executor whereof doth occupy the place and throne of God. And that I absolutely deny, and fear not to say that to place a woman in authority above a realm is to pollute and profane the royal seat, the throne of justice which ought to be the throne of God, and that to maintain them in the same is nothing else but continually to rebel against God.

5.5 John Aylmer, *An Harbor for Faithful and True Subjects against the Late-Blown Blast Concerning the Government of Women* (1559)

From STC 1005 (HL copy), B1^r–B2^r, H3^v–H4^r.

John Aylmer wrote in direct response to John Knox, arguing that England could withstand female rulership because it had a "mixed" government, with the power of

Parliament limiting that of the monarch. Aylmer was, like Knox, a Protestant reformer.
Earlier in his career he had served as tutor to the Nine Days' Queen, Jane Grey. When
Jane I was deposed in favor of Mary I, Aylmer also fled to the Continent. He returned
when Elizabeth I came to the thone. She rewarded him for his loyalty by appointing him
first Archdeacon of Lincoln and then Bishop of London.

Happening therefore not long agone to read a little book strangely written by a
stranger,[8] to prove that the rule of women is out of rule and not in a commonwealth tolerable . . . I thought it more than necessary to lay before men's eyes
the untruth of the argument, the weakness of the proofs, and the absurdity of
the whole. . . .

So this author seeing the torments of martyrs, the murdering of good men,
the imprisonment of innocents, the racking of the guiltless, the banishing of
Christ, the receiving of Antichrist, the spoiling of subjects, the maintenance
of strangers, the moving of wars, the loss of England's honor, the purchasing of
hatred where we had love, the procuring of trouble where we had peace, the
spending of treasure where it was needless and, to be short, all out of joint: he
could not but mislike that regiment from whence such fruits did spring.[9] Only
in this he was not to be excused (unless he allege ignorance): that he swerved
from the . . . particular question to the general, as though all the government of
the whole sex were against nature, reason, right, and law, because that the
present state then through the fault of the person, and not of the sex, was un-
natural, unreasonable, unjust, and unlawful. . . .

It is not in England so dangerous a matter to have a woman ruler as men take
it to be. For, first, it is not she that ruleth but the laws, the executors whereof be
her judges (appointed by her), her justices of peace, and such other officers. But
she may err in choosing such. So may a king. And therefore they have their
Council at their elbow, which by travel abroad know men how fit or unfit they
be for such offices. 2. She maketh no statutes or laws, but the honorable Court
of Parliament; she breaketh none, but it must be she and they together or else
not. 3. If she should judge in capital crimes, what danger were there in her
womanish nature? None at all. For the verdict is the twelve men's which pass
upon life and death, and not hers. Only this belongeth to her ministry: that
when they have found treason, murder, or felony, she utter [*declare*] the pain
[*penalty*] limited in the law for that kind of trespass. Yea, but this she cannot do
because a woman is not learned in the laws; no more is your king. And therefore
have they their ministers which can skill [*know*] if they be cruel wicked hand-
makers[10] and bribers; it is their fault and not the prince's (unless he know them
to be such and wink at [*connive at*] it). What may she do alone wherein is peril?

---

8 *stranger*: Knox was a Scot.

9 *that regiment from whence such fruits did spring*: i.e., the reign of Mary I.

10 *hand-makers*: those who make financial gains fraudulently.

She may grant pardon to an offender – that is her prerogative – wherein if she err it is a tolerable and pitiful [*compassionate*] error to save life. She may misspend the revenues of the crown wantonly. So can kings do, too, and commonly do, and yet may they be kings.

If on the other part, the regiment were such as all hanged upon the king's or queen's will, and not upon the laws written; if she might decree and make laws alone, without her senate; if she judged offenses according to her wisdom and not by limitation of statutes and laws; if she might dispose alone of war and peace; if, to be short, she were a mere monarch, and not a mixed ruler:[11] you might peradventure make me to fear the matter the more and the less to defend the cause.

5.6   Edmund Plowden on the Monarch's Two Bodies (1571)

From *The Commentaries or Reports of Edmund Plowden . . . Originally Written in French* (London, 1761), 213.

Edmund Plowden articulated the philosophical underpinning for Mary of Scotland's claim to the English throne. He admitted that she was not native born, but he insisted that birth was an impediment to inheritance only in the common law, applicable to a "natural" person but not to the "political" entity of royalty. As a direct descendant of Henry VII, Mary possessed royal blood that eclipsed her human circumstances. The medieval concept of the monarch's "two bodies" arose also in Plowden's report, below, of a legal controversy concerning property in the Duchy of Lancaster. Edward VI had granted lands to a subject. Elizabeth I, who wished to give them to a follower of her own, argued that the earlier grant violated common law, which prohibited property transfers by a minor. But the decision went against her on the grounds that the "body politic" could not suffer the disability of underage. This brief passage is frequently cited as an explanation for the mystique of monarchy.

The king has in him two bodies, viz., a body natural and a body politic. His body natural (if it be considered in itself) is a body mortal, subject to all infirmities that come by nature or accident, to the imbecility of infancy or old age, and to the like defects that happen to the natural bodies of other people. But his body politic is a body that cannot be seen or handled, consisting of policy and government, and constituted for the direction of the people and the management of the public weal, and this body is utterly void of infancy and old age and other natural defects and imbecilities which the body natural is subject to. And for this cause, what the king does in his body politic cannot be invalidated or frustrated by any disability in his natural body.

---

11 *mixed ruler*: ruler of a "mixed" government, with power shared by monarch and Parliament.

5.7 Elizabeth I's Accession Address to her Lords (20 November 1558)

From SP 12/1: 7.

At the news of Elizabeth I's accession to the throne, a group of peers traveled to Hatfield House in Hertfordshire, where the princess resided, to offer her their allegiance. It was fitting that Elizabeth alluded to the monarch's two bodies in her first speech of political philosophy as queen, for the immortality and transferrability of the body politic was the rationale behind the common cry, "The king is dead. Long live the king": with the natural death of Mary, Elizabeth assumed the second body of sovereignty. But, as interested in the pragmatics of rule as in the theory, Elizabeth then moved quickly to a subject of immediate interest to her courtiers. Explaining why she would limit the size of her Privy Council, she anticipated a concern that was to preoccupy Sir Francis Bacon (in document 5.11).

My lords, the law of nature moves me to sorrow for my sister; the burden that is fallen upon me maketh me amazed; and yet, considering I am God's creature, ordained to obey his appointment, I will thereto yield, desiring from the bottom of my heart that I may have assistance of his grace to be the minister of his heavenly will in this office now committed to me. And as I am but one body naturally considered, though by his permission a body politic to govern, so I shall desire you all my Lords (chiefly you of the nobility, every one in his degree and power) to be assistant to me, that I with my ruling and you with your service may make a good account to Almighty God and leave some comfort to our posterity in earth. I mean to direct all my actions by good advice and counsel. And they which I shall not appoint, let them not think the same for any disability in them, but for that I do consider a multitude doth make rather discord and confusion than good counsel.

5.8 Richard Hooker, *Of the Laws of Ecclesiastical Polity* (1593–1604)

From Wing STC H2635A (CUL copy), T4^{r-v}, V1^{r-v}.

With Thomas Cranmer (see documents 4.3 and 4.5), Richard Hooker was the principal architect of Anglican theological thought. He made governance of the church as much a subject of philosophy as governance of the kingdom, and he demonstrated how one consequence of the Reformation was that there was no separation, in England, between church and state. Hooker subscribed fully to the supremacy of the king in religious matters, but he resisted the idea of royal divinity that, under the influence of James VI and I, increasingly shaped public culture. Hooker published the first four books of Ecclesiastical Polity *in 1593 and a fifth book in 1597. This excerpt is from Book 8, which was published posthumously.*

Wherefore to end this point I conclude. First, that under the dominions of infidels, the Church of Christ and their commonwealth were two societies independent. Secondly, that in those commonwealths where the Bishop of Rome beareth sway, one society is both the Church and the commonwealth. But the Bishop of Rome doth divide the body into two diverse bodies and doth not suffer the Church to depend upon the power of any civil prince and potentate. Thirdly, that within this realm of England the case is neither as in the one nor as in the other of the former two. But from the state of pagans we differ, in that with us one society is both the Church and commonwealth, which with them it was not. As also from the state of those nations which subjected themselves to the Bishop of Rome, in that our Church hath dependence from the chief in our commonwealth, which it hath not when he is suffered to rule. In a word, our state is according to the pattern of God's own ancient elect people, which people was not part of them the commonwealth and part of them the church of God, but the selfsame people whole and entire were both under one chief governor, on whose supreme authority they did all depend. . . .

Without order there is no living in public society, because the want thereof is the mother of confusion, whereupon division of necessity followeth and, out of division, destruction. . . . The whole world consisting of parts so many, so different, is by this only thing upheld: he which framed them hath set them in order. The very Deity itself both keepeth and requireth for ever this to be kept as a law, that wheresoever there is a coaugmentation [*joining*] of many, the lowest be knit unto the highest by that which being interjacent may cause each to cleave to the other, and so all to continue one.

This order of things and persons in public societies is the work of policy, and the proper instrument thereof in every degree [is] power, power being that ability which we have of ourselves or receive from others for performance of any action. If the action which we have to perform be conversant about matters of mere religion, the power of performing it is then spiritual. And if that power be such as hath not any other to overrule it, we term it dominion or power supreme, so far as the bounds thereof extend. When therefore Christian kings are said to have spiritual dominion or supreme power in ecclesiastical affairs and causes, the meaning is that within their own precincts and territories they have an authority and power to command even in matters of Christian religion, and that there is no higher nor greater that can in those cases over-command them, where they are placed to reign as kings.

5.9   James VI and I, *The True Law of Free Monarchies* (1598)

From STC 14409 (CUL copy), A3^r, A3^v–A4^r, B3^v–B5^r, C6^v–C7^r, C7^v–C8^r, C8^v–D1^v, D2^r.

James developed and recorded his belief in the divine rights of the monarch while King of Scotland. When he was named Elizabeth I's successor, this tract was quickly

republished in London. Thus his new subjects were introduced to a forceful articulation
of political patriarchalism, to defiance of such "seditious writers" as John Ponet, and
to arguments for the king's absolute prerogatives with respect to law, property, and
powers of life and death.

Accept, I pray you my dear countrymen, as thankfully this pamphlet that I offer
unto you, as lovingly it is written for your weal [*benefit*]. . . . The profit I would
wish you to make of it is as well so to frame all your actions according to these
grounds as may confirm you in the course of honest and obedient subjects to
your king in all times coming. As also when ye shall fall in purpose with any that
shall praise or excuse the by-past rebellions that brake forth either in this country or in any other, ye shall herewith be armed against their siren songs. . . .

In the coronation of our own kings (as well as of every Christian monarch),
they give their oath first to maintain the religion presently professed within
their country (according to their laws whereby it is established) and to punish all
those that should press to alter or disturb the profession thereof; and next to
maintain all the lowable [*sanctioned*] and good laws made by their predecessors,
to see them put in execution, and the breakers and violators thereof to be
punished according to the tenor of the same; and lastly to maintain the whole
country, and every state therein in all their ancient privileges and liberties, as
well against all foreign enemies as among themselves. And shortly to procure the
weal and flourishing of his people, not only in maintaining and putting to
execution the old lowable laws of the country and by establishing of new (as
necessity and evil manners will require), but by all other means possible to foresee and prevent all dangers that are likely to fall upon them, and to maintain
concord, wealth, and civility among them, as a loving father and careful watchman, caring for them more than for himself; knowing himself to be ordained for
them, and they not for him; and therefore countable to that great God who
placed him as his lieutenant over them, upon the peril of his soul to procure the
weal of both souls and bodies as far as in him lieth, of all them that are committed to his charge. And this oath in the coronation is the clearest civil and fundamental law, whereby the king's office is properly defined.

By the law of nature the king becomes a natural father to all his lieges at his
coronation. And as the father of his fatherly duty is bound to care for the nour-
ishing, education, and virtuous government of his children, even so is the king
bound to care for all his subjects. As all the toil and pain that the father can take
for his children will be thought light and well bestowed by him, so that the
effect thereof redound to their profit and weal, so ought the prince to do towards
his people. As the kindly father ought to foresee all inconveniences and dangers
that may arise towards his children, and though with the hazard of his own
person press to prevent the same, so ought the king towards his people. As the
father's wrath and correction upon any of his children that offendeth ought to
be by a fatherly chastisement seasoned with pity (as long as there is any hope of

amendment in them), so ought the king towards any of his lieges that offends in that measure. And shortly, as the father's chief joy ought to be in procuring his children's welfare, rejoicing at their weal, sorrowing and pitying at their evil, to hazard for their safety, travail for their rest, wake for their sleep, and, in a word, to think that his earthly felicity and life standeth and liveth more in them nor in himself: so ought a good prince think of his people. . . .

The truth is directly contrary in our state to the false affirmation of such seditious writers as would persuade us that the laws and state of our country were established before the admitting of a king, where by the contrary ye see it plainly proved: that a wise king coming in among barbar[ians] first established the estate and form of government, and thereafter made laws by himself, and his successors according thereto. The kings therefore in Scotland were [*existed*] before any estates or ranks of men within the same, before any Parliaments were holden, or laws made. And by them was the land distributed (which at the first was whole [*entirely*] theirs), states erected and discerned [*distinguished*], and forms of government devised and established. And so it follows of necessity that the kings were the authors and makers of the laws and not the laws of kings. . . .

And according to these fundamental laws already alleged, we daily see that in the Parliament (which is nothing else but the head court of the king and his vassals) the laws are but craved by his subjects and only made by him at their rogation [*request*] and with their advice. For albeit the king make daily statutes and ordinances, enjoining such pains thereto as he thinks meet, without any advice of Parliament or estates, yet it lies in the power of no Parliament to make any kind of law or statute without his scepter be put to it for giving it the force of a law. . . . And for conclusion of this point that the king is overlord over the whole lands, it is likewise daily proved by the law of our hoards, of want of heirs, and of bastardies. For if a hoard be found under the earth, because it is no more in the keeping or use of any person, it of the law pertains to the king. If a person, inheritor of any lands or goods, die without any sort of heirs, all his lands and goods return to the king. And if a bastard die unrehabiled [*unrestored*], without heirs of his body (which rehabling only lies in the king's hands), all that he hath likewise returns to the king.

And as ye see it manifest that the king is overlord of the whole land, so is he master over every person that inhabiteth the same, having power over the life and death of every one of them. For although a just prince will not take the life of any of his subjects without a clear law, yet the same laws whereby he taketh them are made by himself or his predecessors, and so the power flows always from himself. As by daily experience we see good and just princes will from time to time make new laws and statutes, adjoining the penalties to the breakers thereof, which, before the law was made, had been no crime to the subject to have committed. Not that I deny the old definition of a king and of a law, which makes the king to be a speaking law and the law a dumb king. For certainly a king that governs not by his law can neither be countable to God for his administration nor have a happy and established reign. For albeit it be true that I have at length proved that the king is above the law, as both the author and giver of strength thereto, yet a good king will not only delight to rule his subjects by the law, but even will conform himself in his own actions thereunto, always keeping that ground that the health of the commonwealth be his chief law. . . .

As I have already said, a good king, although he be above the law, will subject and frame his actions thereto, for example's sake to his subjects, and of his own free will, but not as subject or bound thereto. Since I have so clearly proved then (out of the fundamental laws and practice of this country) what right and power a king hath over his land and subjects, it is easy to be understood what allegiance and obedience his lieges owe unto him.

5.10   Niccolò Machiavelli, *The Prince* (1515)

From Wing STC M137 (1661; Illinois copy), 39–40, 66–7, 72–3, 75–7.

Even though the English translation of this Italian treatise was not printed until 1661, it was enormously influential, not only on political philosophy but also in common culture. Machiavelli's highly pragmatic, cynical observations about power and its uses informed the characterization of many stage villains by Shakespeare and other dramatists.

Concerning those who by wicked means have attained to a principality

In the laying hold of a state, the usurper thereof ought to run over and execute all his cruelties at once, that he be not forced often to return to them and that he may be able, by not renewing of them, to give men some security and gain their affections by doing them some courtesies. He that carries it otherwise, either for fearfulness or upon evil advice, is always constrained to hold his sword drawn in his hand. Nor ever can he rely upon his subjects, there being no possibility for them (because of his daily and continual injuries) to live in any safety. For his injuries should be done altogether that, being seldomer tested, they might less offend. His favors should be bestowed by little and little to the end they might keep their taste the better.

Of those things in respect whereof men, and especially princes, are praised or dispraised

That man who will profess honesty in all his actions must needs go to ruin among so many that are dishonest. Whereupon it is necessary for a prince desiring to preserve himself to be able to make use of that honesty and to lay it aside again, as need shall require. . . . Everyone will confess it were exceedingly praiseworthy for a prince to be adorned with all these . . . qualities that are good. But because this is [not] possible, nor do human conditions admit such perfection in virtue, it is necessary for him to be so discreet that he know how to avoid the infamy of those vices which would thrust him out of his state and, if it be possible, beware of those also which are not able to remove him thence. But where it cannot be, let them pass with less regard. And yet, let him not stand much upon it, though he incur the infamy of those vices without which he can very hardly save his state. For if all be thoroughly considered, some thing we shall find which will have the color and very face of virtue and, following them, they will lead thee to thy destruction. Whereas some others that shall as much seem vice, if we take the course they lead us, shall discover unto us the way to our safety and well-being.

Of cruelty and clemency, and whether it is better to be beloved or feared

A man would wish he might be the one and the other, but, because hardly can they subsist both together, it is much safer to be feared than be loved – being that one of the two must needs fail. For, touching [*concerning*] men, we may say this in general: they are unthankful, unconstant dissemblers. They avoid dangers and are covetous of gain. And whilst thou dost them good, they are wholly thine. Their blood, their fortunes, lives, and children are at thy service, as is said before, when the danger is remote; but when it approaches, they revolt. And that prince who wholly relies upon their words, unfurnished of all other preparations, goes to wrack. For the friendships that are gotten with rewards and not by the magnificence and worth of the mind are dearly bought indeed. But they will neither keep long nor serve well in time of need. And men do less regard to offend one that is supported by love than by fear. For love is held by a certainty of obligation which, because men are mischievous, is broken upon any occasion of their own profit. But fear restrains with a dread of punishment which never forsakes a man.

In what manner princes ought to keep their words

How commendable in a prince it is to keep his word and live with integrity (not making use of cunning and subtlety), everyone knows well. Yet we see by experience in these our days that those princes have effected great matters who have made small reckoning of keeping their words, and have known by their craft to turn and wind men about and, in the end, have overcome those who have grounded upon the truth. You must then know there are two kinds of combatting or fighting: the one by right of the laws, the other merely by force. That first way is proper to men; the other is also common to beasts. But because the first many times suffices not, there is a necessity to make recourse to the second. . . .

He had need then be a fox (that he may beware of the snares) and a lion (that he may scare the wolves). Those that stand wholly upon the lion understand not well themselves. And therefore a wise prince cannot nor ought not keep his faith given, when the observance thereof turns to disadvantage and the occasions that made him promise are past. For if men were all good, this rule would not be allowable. But, being they are full of mischief and would not make it good to thee, neither art thou tied to keep it with them. Nor shall a prince ever want lawful occasions to give color to this breach. Very many modern examples hereof might be alleged, wherein might be showed how many peaces concluded and how many promises made have been violated and broken by the infidelity of princes. And ordinarily things have best succeeded with him that hath been nearest the fox in condition. But it is necessary to understand how to set a good color upon this disposition and to be able to feign and dissemble thoroughly. And men are so simple and yield so much to the present necessities that he who hath a mind to deceive shall always find another that will be deceived. . . . Therefore is there no necessity for a prince to be endued with all [virtuous] qualities,[12] but it behooveth well that he seem to be so – or, rather, I will boldly say this – that, having these qualities and always regulating himself by them, they are hurtful. But seeming to have them, they are advantageous.

5.11   Sir Francis Bacon, *The Essays or Counsels Civil and Moral* (1625)

From STC 1148 (CUL copy), E1^v–E2^r, E3^v–E4^r, Q2^{r-v}, Q3^{r-v}, Q4^r–R1^r, R2^v.

The influential French author Michel de Montaigne mastered the short prose form called the "essay." Sir Francis Bacon imitated the new genre in a collection that, over the course of thirteen editions between 1597 and 1625, grew from ten essays to fifty-eight (another example is included as document 8.5). Despite his philosophical sophistication, however, Bacon fell afoul of real-world politics when accused of bribery and corruption. His petition to the king's "absolute power of pardon" was unavailing; in 1621 he was stripped of his Lord Chancellorship, deprived of all other public offices, and banned from court and Parliament.

Of Simulation and Dissimulation

If a man have that penetration of judgment as he can discern what things are to be laid open, and what to be secreted, and what to be showed at half lights, and to whom and when (which indeed are arts of state and arts of life, as Tacitus well calleth them), to him a habit of dissimulation is a hindrance and a poorness. But

---

12 *qualities*: Machiavelli mentions compassion, good faith, mildness of temper, piety, integrity.

if a man cannot obtain to that judgment, then it is left to him generally to be close and a dissembler. For where a man cannot choose or vary in particulars, there it is good to take the safest and wariest way in general, like the going softly by one that cannot well see. Certainly the ablest men that ever were have had all an openness and frankness of dealing and a name of certainty and veracity, but then they were like horses well managed, for they could tell passing well when to stop or turn. And at such times when they thought the case indeed required dissimulation, if then they used it, it came to pass that the former opinion spread abroad of their good faith and clearness of dealing made them almost invisible.

There be three degrees of this hiding and veiling of a man's self. The first, closeness, reservation, and secrecy: when a man leaveth himself without observation or without hold [*reservation*] to be taken what he is. The second, dissimulation, in the negative: when a man lets fall signs and arguments that he is not that he is. And the third, simulation, in the affirmative: when a man industriously and expressly feigns and pretends to be that he is not. . . .

The great advantages of simulation and dissimulation are three. First, to lay asleep opposition and to surprise. For where a man's intentions are published, it is an alarum to call up all that are against them. The second is to reserve to a man's self a fair retreat. For if a man engage himself by a manifest declaration, he must go through or take a fall. The third is the better to discover the mind of another. For to him that opens himself, men will hardly show themselves adverse but will fair let him go on, and turn their freedom of speech to freedom of thought. And therefore it is a good shrewd proverb of the Spaniard, "Tell a lie and find a troth" [*truth*] – as if there were no way of discovery but by simulation. There be also three disadvantages, to set it even. The first, that simulation and dissimulation commonly carry with them a show of fearfulness, which in any business doth spoil the feathers of round flying up to the mark.[13] The second, that it puzzleth and perplexeth the conceits of many that perhaps would otherwise cooperate with him, and makes a man walk almost alone to his own ends. The third and greatest is that it depriveth a man of one of the most principal instruments for action, which is trust and belief. The best composition and temperature is to have openness in fame and opinion; secrecy in habit; dissimulation in seasonable [*opportune*] use; and a power to feign, if there be no remedy.

Of Counsel

The wisest princes need not think it any diminution to their greatness or derogation to their sufficiency to rely upon counsel. God himself is not without, but hath made it one of the great names of his blessed son, "the Counselor" [*Isaiah*

---

13 *feathers of round flying up to the mark*: feathered arrows reaching their target.

9:6]. Solomon hath pronounced that "in counsel is stability" [*Proverbs 20:18*]. Things will have their first or second agitation: if they be not tossed upon the arguments of counsel, they will be tossed upon the waves of fortune and be full of inconstancy, doing and undoing like the reeling of a drunken man. . . .

Let us now speak of the inconveniences of counsel, and of the remedies. The inconveniences that have been noted in calling and using counsel are three. First, the revealing of affairs, whereby they become less secret. Secondly, the weakening of the authority of princes, as if they were less of themselves. Thirdly, the danger of being unfaithfully counseled, and more for the good of them that counsel than of him that is counseled. For which inconveniences, the doctrine of Italy and practice of France, in some kings' times, hath introduced cabinet counsels,[14] a remedy worse than the disease.

As to secrecy, princes are not bound to communicate all matters with all counselors, but may extract and select. Neither is it necessary that he that consulteth what he should do should declare what he will do. But let princes beware that the unsecreting of their affairs comes not from themselves. . . . For weakening of authority, the fable showeth the remedy. Nay, the majesty of kings is rather exalted than diminished when they are in the chair of counsel. Neither was there ever prince bereaved of his dependences by his counsel, except where there hath been either an overgreatness in one counselor or an overstrict combination in diverse, which are things soon found and holpen [*helped*]. For the last inconvenience, that men will counsel with an eye to themselves . . . there be that are in nature faithful and sincere and plain and direct, not crafty and involved; let princes, above all, draw to themselves such natures. Besides, counselors are not commonly so united but that one counselor keepeth sentinel over another, so that if any do counsel out of faction, or private ends, it commonly comes to the king's ear. But the best remedy is if princes know their counselors as well as their counselors know them: *Principis est Virtus maxima nosse suos* [*A prince's greatest virtue is to know his own people*]. And on the other side, counselors should not be too speculative into their sovereign's person. The true composition of a counselor is rather to be skillful in their master's business than in his nature, for then he is like to advise him and not to feed his humor. It is of singular use to princes if they take the opinions of their counsel both separately and together. For private opinion is more free, but opinion before others is more reverend. In private, men are more bold in their own humors; and in consort, men are more obnoxious to others' humors. Therefore it is good to take both, and of the inferior sort, rather in private, to preserve freedom; of the greater, rather in consort, to preserve respect. It is in vain for princes to take counsel concerning matters, if they take no counsel likewise concerning persons, for all matters are as dead

---

14 *cabinet counsels*: Elizabeth's Privy Council never had more than eighteen members and sometimes had twelve; that of James had as many as thirty-five. With so large a group, James relied on a subset of favorites consulted in his cabinet, or private room – a practice of which Bacon disapproves. See also Elizabeth's remarks on the matter in 5.7.

images, and the life of the execution of affairs resteth in the good choice of persons. . . . A king, when he presides in counsel, let him beware how he opens his own inclination too much, in that which he propoundeth. For else counselors will but take the wind of him, and instead of giving free counsel sing him a song of *Placebo*.[15]

---

15 *Placebo*: "I shall please." Bacon's point is that a good counselor cannot be a yes-man.

6

High Culture

What did it mean to be a "Renaissance man"? In 1528, Baldassare Castiglione created the prototype in *Il Cortegiano*, a dialogue based on his own real-life experiences at the glittering court of Urbino in Italy. Ideally, a prince's attendants were to be men of accomplishment in political, military, and cultural fields. They were also to display *sprezzatura*, that touch of nonchalance which lent their most impressive deeds an appearance of ease. Today it is sometimes forgotten that Castiglione described the skills of the exemplary female courtier, as well. More important than any of his specific recommendations, however, were the ideas that the social self could be – and should be – a matter of conscious construction.

Il Cortegiano, translated as *The Book of the Courtier* in 1561, indelibly informed English ideas of aristocratic pursuits, behaviors, and self-presentations. This was just one of many ways in which England was inspired by the Renaissance of Italy and France. While high culture might therefore be described, first, as strongly influenced by Continental trends and tastes, it should at the same time be understood, secondly, to have been London-based. The upper classes were composed of landed people whose estates were scattered across the countryside. They traveled to London frequently, however, and in the capital city they shared interests and experiences that transcended the regional differences of their locations. London was the home of the royal court, of Parliament, and of the law courts. There, members of the elite cultivated the sovereign's favor, mingled with their social peers, conducted business, enjoyed urban amusements and pleasures, kept abreast of vogues in apparel and furnishings, and purchased fine imported goods to send back to their country houses.

A third characteristic of Renaissance high culture was that creative and intellectual pursuits were not yet thoroughly professionalized. In the late sixteenth century, there were a handful of craftsmen who were newly referred to as "architectors," for example, but many gentlemen were themselves designers of the magnificent stately homes of the period. Castiglione recommended the study of painting, musicianship, and dancing because, while rulers had highly skilled artists and entertainers in their employ, there was still room for these arts to be practiced by members of the court. England's cultural history was shaped by the noble and gentle men and women who possessed the leisure to write poetry, read philosophy, and conduct experiments: in literature, Henry Howard, Earl of

Surrey, Sir Thomas Wyatt, and Lady Mary Wroth; in building, Sir John Thynne, Elizabeth, Countess of Shrewsbury (see below), and Sir Thomas Tresham; in science and philosophy, Sir Francis Bacon (see documents 5.11, 8.5, and 10.2).

Sir Philip Sidney is often described as the English exemplar of a Renaissance man: educated at Oxford and widely traveled on the Continent; a courtier; patron to the poet Edmund Spenser; himself author of a long prose romance (*The Arcadia*), a sonnet sequence (*Astrophil and Stella*), and an *Apology for Poetry* (see document 8.8); and a military hero who died in 1586, aiding Dutch Protestants in a skirmish with Spanish forces. Wounded on the battlefield, Sidney reportedly passed his water bottle to another injured soldier, saying, "Thy need is greater than mine." Whether or not it was true, the story conferred upon his legend the quality of *sprezzatura*.

Culture and the Crown

No discussion of Renaissance culture should overlook Henry VIII, who aspired to be as great a monarch as the kings of France and Spain. When he came to the throne in 1509, Henry inherited thirteen royal houses; at the time of his death thirty-eight years later, he owned fifty-five. His favorites were Greenwich, Hampton Court, and Whitehall, but he was proudest of the building he designed himself, the fabulous Nonsuch. Henry hired an artificer from Modena to ornament the Nonsuch façade with stucco panels set in frames of carved and gilded slate, the panels illustrating classical fables. Remodeling Hampton Court, Henry employed German, Italian, French, and Dutch artisans to install wainscotting, painted decorations, and window glass. At Whitehall he commissioned grand-scale paintings with scenes from his own life. Henry's court was also the setting for lavishly costumed entertainments and for jousts, tilts, and concerts. The inventory of personal possessions at his death was more than 20,000 items long. It included jewels, watches, portrait miniatures, medals, over 1,500 books and manuscripts (many from dissolved monastic libraries), and more than 300 musical instruments (which he played himself). Thirty-three musical compositions survive in Henry's name, though most were his arrangements of Continental pieces.

Elizabeth I was another notable collector, especially of apparel and jewelry, but she was not a builder and made few improvements to her palaces. Instead, she encouraged her nobility and gentry to construct great country houses and then went "on progress" among them, being extravagantly feted at one after another. Court entertainments grew more splendid under the patronage of James VI and I and his cultivated queen, Anna of Denmark. But the monarch who outmatched Henry VIII for magnificence was Charles I. The ill-fated Stuart king was the greatest of the Renaissance royal collectors. He acquired works by Titian and Raphael as well as rare books, sculptures, and antique medals. He

Figure 8   Nonsuch Palace, after John Speed's *Theatrum Imperii Magnae Britanniae* (1616). Courtesy of Mary Evans Picture Library.

Henry VIII destroyed the village, manor house, and church of Cuddington in order to build on their site a Renaissance palace. The project took nine years and cost the enormous sum, for the time, of nearly £25,000. This most famous image of Nonsuch is a detail from John Speed's map of Surrey. It shows the south elevation, with an outer courtyard leading, by means of an inner central gatehouse, to an inner court-yard. At each corner of the outer courtyard was an eight-sided turret, and both inner and outer walls were covered with stucco and slate decorations that celebrated the birth of Henry's long-awaited son Edward with illustrations of royal duties and royal magnificence. Much later, Charles II gave Nonsuch to his mistress Barbara Villiers. In 1683, to pay her gambling debts, she demolished the palace and sold off its lands and building materials.

commissioned ceiling paintings by Rubens, portraits by Van Dyck, sculptures by Bernini, and entertainments by Inigo Jones. In the best participatory tradition of the time, Charles was himself an inventor. He helped create a process for enameling miniature portraits on gold.

Magnificence

In 1577 the social historian William Harrison wrote proudly that there were no fortified castles remaining in England, except on the sea coasts. In other words, England continued to protect itself from foreign invaders but no longer experienced the threat of feudal lords who challenged the king for power. In more peaceable times, the emphasis could be on building for show rather than security. "If ever curious building did flourish in England," Harrison boasted, "it is in these our years, wherein our workmen excel, and are in manner comparable in skill with old Vitruvius." The comparison to the leading classical authority on architecture was exaggerated, as was the description of civil tranquility. But it is true that in the sixteenth and seventeenth centuries England's most impressive achievements in the visual arts were architectural. In this field, too, Continental writers were influential. Under the influence of Leon Battista Alberti's *Ten Books on Architecture* (1452), people learned to think about reshaping their material world as well as their social behaviors.

Because it was easier to redecorate buildings than to rethink them, the first Renaissance elements to appear in England were ornamental. When stained glass windows, embroidered priestly vestments, and crucifixion scenes were removed from Protestant churches, color and imagery seemed to burst out in private homes instead. There were carved paneling on the walls, molded plaster designs on the ceilings, elaborately ornamental fire surrounds and door frames, vibrant tapestries and painted cloths, and needleworked table coverings and cushions. Especially popular were the Doric, Ionic, and Corinthian capitals of the rediscovered classical orders. The medieval castle had one room of importance, the great hall, but in Tudor and Stuart years there were more rooms designed to impress: parlors, dining chambers, bedchambers, and long galleries. The last was another idea imported from the Continent, an enormous space used for walking in inclement weather. England's new language of privilege was a conspicuous display of wealth rather than a show of feudal manpower.

Status housing in the medieval years had translated power relations differently. In the great hall the lord's retainers ate, slept, and constituted a ready army. He himself dined at a head table placed on a slightly raised dais, as far as possible from the entrance, with all his men between him and the door, and with his own view out through a projecting window. The great hall might be located centrally in the building, but the lord's window always appeared to one side of the façade; the building was asymmetrical because power is asymmetrical. On the Continent, however, Andrea Palladio developed a more regular plan.

William Harrison described the slow and expensive process of adapting England's traditional structures to Europe's new, regularized elevations: "in the proceeding also of their works, how they set up, how they pull down, how they enlarge, how they restrain, how they add to, how they take from, whereby their heads are never idle, their purses never shut, nor their books of account never made perfect." One of the first to subordinate the native great hall to a Renaissance concept was Elizabeth, Countess of Shrewsbury (known as "Bess of Hardwick"), working in collaboration with the earliest architect of name, Robert Smythson. At Hardwick Hall, Bess and Smythson created a strictly symmetrical façade in the 1590s. In the first part of the seventeenth century, Inigo Jones executed royal commissions in which he displayed a revolutionary ability to synthesize form and function. Where Tudor architecture had been an exuberant and eccentric meld of old forms and new ideas, Stuart architecture became formal and disciplined.

Henry VIII's collections were symptomatic of the exploding consumer culture that would fill out the new spaces. On cupboards, people displayed their silver plate; in chests, they stocked quantities of household linen. These highly liquid commodities, not banks, were places in which to store surplus wealth. Some early moderns treasured such curiosities as exotic animal horn and cups made of coconuts mounted in precious metal; others collected portraits of monarchs, heroes, and family members; a few imported classical sculptures and other antiquities. Arguably the most expensive category of luxury goods in the period, however, was clothing. Upper-class men and women wore velvet and satin garments that were embellished with lace, ribbons, gems, and embroidery. Elizabeth I was notorious for her extravagant garments and jewels, but James VI and I was far from frugal. Records from the middle years of his reign show him buying a cloak, a waistcoat, three suits of hose and doublet, six or seven pairs of stockings, and thirty pairs of gloves every month (gloves were frequent gifts). The early moderns who commissioned their own portraits seem to have been less concerned with good likenesses than with detailed displays of their magnificence in dress.

The Court Masque

The court's most elaborate activity was the masque, an entertainment involving music, dance, spectacle, costume, and poetry. Professional actors were recruited to speak at the outset, in the antimasque, but then members of the court themselves took the floor wearing disguises. Often, they assumed allegorical or mythological roles. Sometimes their entrances were effected by trapdoors and "turning machines." Painted partitions set in grooves in the floor could be pulled back, one pair after another, to reveal visually stunning changes of scene. Lighting effects were created with candles, colored lamps, mirrors, and metallic or spangled costumes. A single masque, performed once or perhaps twice for at most 1,000 people, would cost the astonishing sum of £3,000, in an age when skilled craftsmen might earn £5 a year.

Generally, the evening's entertainment ended with the audience invited to join the principals in dancing. With these revels, everyone was incorporated into the idealized courtly vision that was the object of the event. As a participatory art form, with its emphasis on role-playing and self-display, and in its conspicuous consumption, the masque exemplified Renaissance high culture.

6.1   Baldassare Castiglione, *The Book of the Courtier* (1528)

From *The Courtier of Count Baldassare Castilio . . . done into English by Thomas Hoby* (1561), STC 4778 (HL copy), Yy4^r–Zz4^v.

Sir Thomas Hoby translated Castiglione's Il Cortegiano *while in voluntary exile from England during the reign of Mary I. He first published* The Book of the Courtier *in Paris. When Elizabeth I succeeded to the throne, Hoby returned home and, in 1561, brought out another English edition of this classic text on Renaissance protocols and behaviors.*

A Brief Rehearsal of the Chief Conditions and Qualities in a Courtier

To be well born and of a good stock [*family*].

To be of a mean [*middling*] stature, rather with the least than too high, and well made to his proportion.

To be portly [*dignified*] and amiable in countenance unto whoso beholdeth him.

Not to be womanish in his sayings or doings.

Not to praise himself unshamefully and out of reason.

Not to crake [*brag*] and boast of his acts and good qualities.

To shun affectation or curiosity [*fastidiousness*] above all thing in all things.

To do his feats with a slight [*carelessly*], as though they were rather naturally in him than learned with study, and use a recklessness to cover art, without minding [*caring*] greatly what he hath in hand, to a man's seeming.

Not to carry about tales and trifling news.

Not to be overseen in speaking words otherwhile [*occasionally*] that may offend where he meant it not.

Not to be stubborn, willful, nor full of contention, nor too contrary, and overthwart [*contentious with*] men after a spiteful sort.

Not to be a babbler, brawler, or chatter[er], nor lavish of his tongue.

Not to be given to vanity and lightness, nor to have a fantastical [*fanciful*] head.

No liar.

No fond [*foolish*] flatterer.

To be well spoken and fair languaged.

To be wise and well seen [*well-versed*] in discourses upon states.

To have a judgment to frame himself to the manners of the country wherever he cometh.

To be able to allege good and probable reasons upon every matter.

To be seen in tongues, and specially in Italian, French, and Spanish.

To direct all things to a good end.

To procure wherever he goeth that men may first conceive a good opinion of him before he cometh there.

To fellowship himself for the most part with men of the best sort and of most estimation, and with his equals, so he be also beloved of his inferiors.

To play for his pastime at dice and cards, not wholly for money's sake, nor fume and chafe in his loss.

To be meanly seen in the play at chests [*chess*] and not over-cunning.

To be pleasantly disposed in common matters and in good company.

To speak and write the language that is most in use among the common people, without inventing new words, inkhorn [*bookish*] terms, or strange phrases, and such as be grown out of use by long time.

To be handsome [*seemly*] and cleanly in his apparel.

To make his garments after the fashion of the most, and those to be black or of some darkish and sad [*dull*] color, not garish.

To get him an especial and hearty friend to company withal.

Not to be ill-tongued, especially against his betters.

Not to use any fond sauciness [*impertinence*] or presumption.

To be no envious or malicious person.

To be an honest, a fair conditioned man, and of an upright conscience.

To have the virtues of the mind, as justice, manliness, wisdom, temperance, staidness [*constancy*], noble courage, sober mood, etc.

To be more than indifferently well seen in learning in the Latin and Greek tongues.

Not to be rash nor persuade himself to know the thing that he knoweth not.

To confess his ignorance when he seeth time and place thereto, in such qualities as he knoweth himself to have no manner [of] skill in.

To be brought to show his feats and qualities at the desire and request of others, and not rashly press to it of himself.

To speak always of matters likely, lest he be counted a liar in reporting of wonders and strange miracles.

To have the feat of drawing and painting.

To dance well without over-nimble footings or too-busy tricks.

To sing well upon the book.

To play upon the lute and sing to it with the ditty.

To play upon the viol and all other instruments with frets.

To delight and refresh the hearers' minds in being pleasant, feat [*proper*], conceited [*witty*], and a merry talker, applied to time and place.

Not to use sluttish [*despicable*] and ruffian-like pranks with any man.

Not to become a jester or scoffer to put any man out of countenance.

To consider whom he doth taunt and where, for he ought not to mock poor seely [*miserable*] souls, nor men of authority, nor common ribalds [*rascals*] and persons given to mischief, which deserve punishment.

To be skillful in all kind of martial feats both on horseback and afoot, and well practiced in them, which is his chief profession (though his understanding be the less in all other things).

To play well at fence upon all kind of weapons.

To be nimble and quick at the play at tennis.

To hunt and hawk.

To ride and manage well his horse.

To be a good horseman for every saddle.

Seldom in open sight of the people but privily with himself alone, or among his friends and familiars: To swim well, to leap well, to run well, to vault well, to wrestle well, to cast the stone well, to cast the bar well.

These things in open sight to delight the common people withal: to run well at tilt and at ring, to tourney [*contend at chivalric sports*], to fight at barriers [*martial exercises*], to keep [*defend*] a passage or street, to play at Jogo di Canne [*stick fencing*], to run at bull, to fling a spear or dart.

Not to run, wrestle, leap, nor cast the stone or bar with men of the country, except he be sure to get the victory.

To set out himself in feats of chivalry in open shows well provided of horse and harness, well trapped, and armed, so that he may show himself nimble on horseback.

Never to be of the last that appear in the lists [*arena*] at jousts or in any open shows.

To have in triumphs comely armor, bases [*skirts*], scarves, trappings, liveries, and such other things of sightly and merry colors, and rich to behold, with witty poesies and pleasant devices, to allure unto him chiefly the eyes of the people.

To disguise himself in masquery either on horseback or afoot, and to take the shape upon him that shall be contrary to the feat that he mindeth to work.

To undertake his bold feats and courageous enterprises in war out of company and in the sight of the most noble personages in the camp and (if it be possible) before his prince's eyes.

Not to hazard himself in foraging and spoiling or in enterprises of great danger and small estimation, though he be sure to gain by it.

Not to wait upon or serve a wicked and naughty person.

Not to seek to come up by any naughty or subtle practice.

Not to commit any mischievous or wicked fact at the will and commandment of his lord or prince.

Not to follow his own fancy or alter the express words in any point of his commission from his prince or lord, unless he be assured that the profit will be more (in case it have good success) than the damage (if it succeed ill).

To use evermore toward his prince or lord the respect that becometh the servant toward his master.

To endeavor himself to love, please, and obey his prince in honesty.

Not to covet to press into the chamber or other secret part where his prince is withdrawn at any time.

Never to be sad, melancholy, or solemn before his prince.

Seldom or never to sue [*petition*] to his lord for anything for himself.

His suit to be honest and reasonable when he sueth for others.

To reason of pleasant and merry matters when he is withdrawn with him into private and secret places, always doing [*giving*] him to understand the truth without dissimulation or flattery.

Not to love promotions [*advancement*] so that a man should think he could not live without them, nor unshamefastly to beg any office.

To refuse them after such a comely sort that the prince offering him them may have a cause to offer them with a more instance [*insistance*].

Not to press to his prince wherever he be, to hold him with a vain talk, that [*so that*] others should think him in favor with him.

To consider well what it is that he doth or speaketh: where, in presence of whom, what time, why, his age, his profession, the end, and the means.

The final end of a courtier, whereto all his good conditions and honest qualities tend, is to become an instructor and teacher of his prince or lord, inclining him to virtuous practices, and to be frank and free with him, after he is once in favor in matters touching his honor and estimation, always putting him in mind to follow virtue and to flee vice, opening unto him the commodities [*benefits*] of the one and inconveniences of the other, and to shut his ears against flatterers, which are the first beginning of self-liking and all ignorance.

His conversation with women to be always gentle, sober, meek, lowly [*humble*], modest, serviceable, comely [*decorous*], merry, not biting [*speaking sharply*] or slandering with jests, nips [*reproofs*], frumps [*mockings*], or railings [*abuses*] the honesty of any.

His love toward women not to be sensual or fleshly but honest and godly, and more ruled with reason than appetite, and to love better the beauty of the mind than of the body.

Not to withdraw his mistress' good will from his fellow lover with reviling or railing at him, but with virtuous deeds and honest conditions and with deserving more than he, at her hands for honest affection's sake.

Of the Chief Conditions and Qualities in a Waiting Gentlewoman

To be well born and of a good house.

To flee affectation or curiosity.

To have a good grace in all her doings.

To be of good conditions and well brought up.

To be witty and foreseeing, not heady [*impetuous*] and of a running [*volatile*] wit.

Not to be haughty, envious, ill-tongued, light, contentious, nor untowardly [*ill-disposed*].

To win and keep her in her lady's favor and all others.

To do the exercises meet for women, comely and with a good grace.

To take heed that she give none occasion to be ill reported of.

To commit no vice, nor yet to be had in suspicion of any vice.

To have the virtues of the mind, as wisdom, justice, nobleness of courage, temperance, strength of the mind, continency, sober mood, etc.

To be good and discreet.

To have the understanding, being married, how to order her husband's substance, her house and children, and to play the good housewife.

To have a sweetness in language and a good utterance to entertain all kind of men with communication worth the hearing, honest, applied to time and place and to the degree and disposition of the person – which is her principal profession.

To accompany sober and quiet manners and honesty with a lively quickness of wit.

To be esteemed no less chaste, wise, and courteous than pleasant, feat, conceited, and sober.

Not to make wise to abhor company and talk, though somewhat of the wantonnest [*least disciplined*]; to arise and forsake them for it.

To give the hearing of such kind of talk with blushing and bashfulness.

Not to speak words of dishonesty and bawdry; to show herself pleasant, free, and a good fellow [*companion*].

Not to use overmuch familiarity without measure and bridle [*restraint*].

Not willingly to give ear to such as report ill of other women.

To be heedful in her talk that she offend not where she meant it not.

To beware of praising herself undiscreetly and of being too tedious and noisome [*annoying*] in her talk.

Not to mingle with grave and sad matters, merry jests and laughing matters; nor with mirth, matters of gravity.

To be circumspect that she offend no man in her jesting and taunting to appear thereby of a ready wit.

Not to make wise to know the thing that she knoweth not, but with soberness get her estimation with that she knoweth.

Not to come on loft [*acrobatically*] nor use too swift measures in her dancing.

Not to use in singing or playing upon instruments too much division and busy points, that declare more cunning than sweetness.

To come to dance or to show her music with suffering herself to be first prayed somewhat and drawn to it.

To apparel herself so that she seem not fond and fantastical.

To set out her beauty and disposition of person with meet garments that shall best become her, but as feigningly as she can, making semblant to bestow no labor about it, nor yet to mind it.

To have an understanding in all things belonging to the courtier, that she may give her judgment to commend and to make of gentlemen according to their worthiness and deserts.

To be learned.

To be seen in the most necessary languages.

To draw and paint.

To dance.

To devise sports and pastimes.

Not to be light of credit that she is beloved, though a man commune familiarly with her of love.

To shape him that is oversaucy with her, or that hath small respect in his talk, such an answer that he may well understand she is offended with him.

To take the loving communication of a sober gentleman in another signification, seeking to stray from that purpose.

To acknowledge the praises which he giveth her at the gentleman's courtesy, in case she cannot dissemble the understanding of them, debasing her own deserts.

To be heedful and remember that men may with less jeopardy show to be in love than women.

To give her lover nothing but her mind, when either the hatred of her husband or the love that he beareth to others inclineth her to love.

To love one that she may marry withal, being a maiden and minding to love.

To show such a one all signs and tokens of love, saving such as may put him in any dishonest hope.

To use a somewhat more familiar conversation with men well grown in years than with young men.

To make her self beloved for her deserts, amiableness, and good grace, not with any uncomely or dishonest behavior, or flickering enticement with wanton looks, but with virtue and honest conditions.

The final end whereto the courtier applieth all his good conditions, properties, feats, and qualities serveth also for a waiting gentlewoman: to grow in favor with her lady and by that means so to instruct her and train her to virtue that she may both refrain from vice and from committing any dishonest matter, and also [to] abhor flatterers, and give herself to understand the full truth in everything without entering into self-liking and ignorance either of other outward things or yet of her own self.

6.2 Henry Peacham, *The Complete Gentleman* (1622)

From STC 19502 (HL copy), O3^r–O4^r, P2^r, P3$^{r–v}$, Cc4^v–Dd1^v.

Henry Peacham's manual for refined behavior and activities demonstrates how widely the message of The Courtier *spread: to "mere" gentlemen and the aspirational.*

Peacham, the son of a minister, succeeded in gaining the patronage of Prince Henry by presenting him with a hand-illustrated tribute volume to the Basilicon Doron, *a book of royal advice written by Henry's father the king. With his hopes for further advancement derailed by Henry's untimely death, Peacham left England for the Continent, where he became convinced that education, especially in the arts, was superior to that of England. His* Complete Gentleman *was written for those just like himself: ambitious, upwardly mobile men who may not have been born into the highest registers but who sought to take advantage of new opportunities for social advancement by equipping themselves with all the outward appearances of learning and civility.*

Of Music

The physicians will tell you that the exercise of music is a great lengthener of the life by stirring and reviving of the spirits, holding a secret sympathy with them. Besides, the exercise of singing openeth the breast and pipes. It is an enemy to melancholy and dejection of the mind. . . . It is a most ready help for a bad pronunciation and distinct speaking, which I have heard confirmed by many great divines. Yea, I myself have known many children to have been holpen of their stammering in speech only by it.[1] Plato calleth it "a divine and heavenly practice," profitable for the seeking out of that which is good and honest. . . .

I might run into an infinite sea of the praise and use of so excellent an art, but I only show it you with the finger because I desire not that any noble or gentleman should, save [during] his private recreation at leisurable hours, prove a master in the same or neglect his more weighty employments – though I avouch it a skill worthy the knowledge and exercise of the greatest prince. . . . Infinite is the sweet variety that the theoric of music exerciseth the mind withal, as the contemplation of proportion, of concords and discords, diversity of moods and tones, infiniteness of invention, etc. But I dare affirm there is no one science in the world that so affecteth the free and generous spirit with a more delightful and inoffensive recreation, or better disposeth the mind to what is commendable and virtuous.

Of Drawing, Limning, and Painting

In all mathematical demonstrations nothing is more required in our travel in foreign regions. It bringeth home with us from the farthest part of the world in our bosoms whatsoever is rare and worthy of observance, as the general map of the country; the rivers, harbors, havens, promontories, etc. within the landscape; of fair hills, fruitful valleys; the forms and colors of all fruits; several beau-

---

1 *only by it*: by it alone.

ties of their flowers; of medicinable simples[2] never before seen or heard of; the orient colors and lively pictures of their birds; the shape of their beasts, fishes, worms, flies, etc. It presents our eyes with the complexion, manner, and their attire. It shows us the rites of their religion, their houses, their weapons, and manner of war. Besides, it preserveth the memory of a dearest friend or fairest mistress. . . . And that you should not esteem basely of the practice thereof, let me tell you that in ancient times painting was admitted into the first place among the liberal arts, and throughout all Greece taught only to the children of noblemen in the schools, and altogether forbidden to be taught to servants or slaves.

Of Travel

I will conclude with travel. . . . For if it be the common law of nature that the learned should have rule over and instruct the ignorant, the experienced the unexperienced, what concerneth more nobility, taking place above other, than to be learned and wise? And where may wisdom be had but from many men and in many places? Hereupon we find the most eminent and wise men of the world to have been the greatest travelers. . . . But before you travel into a strange country, I wish you, as I have heretofore said, to be well acquainted with your own. For I know it by experience that many of our young gallants have gone over with an intent to pass by nothing unseen or what might be known in other places, when they have been most ignorant here in their own native country, and strangers, to their just reproof, could discourse and say more of England than they.

6.3 "The House of an Earl" (1630s)

From *Some Rules and Orders for the Government of the House of an Earl Set Down by R. B.* (London: 1821), 3–4, 6–11, 17, 20–1, 27–8, 31–2, 39–40, 45.

Describing the qualities to be desired in an earl's servants, R. B. also provides an overview of the many offices and functions of a great country house. Earls were second only to dukes among the nobility and thus possessors of great power as well as wealth. Except for the members of the principal family and women charged with laundry and childcare, theirs were primarily male establishments. R. B., often presumed to be the prolific author Richard Brathwait, laments the decline of "hospitality," the tradition of offering drink, leftover food, and temporary lodging to the poor. Like other writers of the day, he believed that the wealthy now neglected charity for their own comforts and luxuries.

---

2 *simples*: medical preparations composed of a single ingredient.

What officers and servants the state of an earl requireth to have (which may be added unto or diminished as pleaseth his lordship)

First, a steward, a treasurer, and comptroller, which three are to be called the chief officers. He may have an auditor and a receiver, but these are extraordinary, and two of the chief officers, being men of experience, may supply those places, the one in taking accompt, the other in receiving rents and profits (and thereby free the earl from fees that belong to those officers). He may have a clerk comptroller, but that needeth not if the chief officers be painful [*diligent*] in their places. He is to have two gentlemen ushers [*door-keepers*]; a preacher or chaplain in ordinary [*in regular attendance*], besides as many extraordinary as he pleaseth; a gentleman of the horse; a secretary; ten gentlemen waiters; two gentlemen pages; a clerk of the kitchen; an yeoman usher and groom of the great chamber; two yeomen of the wardrobe of apparel for the earl and lady; two grooms for their bedchamber; one yeoman and groom for the wardrobe of beds; an yeoman usher and groom for the hall; an yeoman and groom for the cellar [*for storage of beer, wine, and coal*]; an yeoman and groom for the pantry [*for dry provisions*], an yeoman and groom for the buttery [*for liquid provisions*]; an yeoman for the ewery [*for table linens*]; an yeoman of the horse; an yeoman rider; five musicians; six yeomen waiters; two footmen; an yeoman purveyor; a master cook; under-cooks and pastrymen three; an yeoman and groom in the scullery [*for tableware*]; one to be in the larder [*for meat storage*] and slaughterhouse; an achatour [*purchaser*]; conducts [*hirelings*] and kitchen boys three; two in the woodyard; in the bakehouse, brewhouse, and granary five; a trumpeter, a drum; an yeoman and groom in the armory; an yeoman and groom for the garden; a coachman, a wagoner; six grooms for the stable; a groom for the laundry; two yeomen porters [*gatekeepers*]; gentlewomen, chambermaids, and launderers (the number to be set down by the earl and his lady). . . .

I think it fit that the earl call before himself in place convenient all or the greatest part of the officers and servants and either by himself or by such other person as pleaseth him to appoint thereto, to let them understand that in respect of the service he is to do his king and country and [of] his other affairs, he cannot himself oversee the government and order of his family and therefore hath made choice of [two or three of them] to be his chief officers. . . .

What men they are to be, which are fit to serve the earl for his chief officers, and what doth appertain to their place

The chief officers should be men not only well born and of good livings, but also grave and experienced, not proud and haughty, neither too affable and easy, gentle and courteous in matters concerning themselves but severe and sharp if offenses be committed against God or their lord. They are not only to be experienced in household matters but also skillful in foreign affairs, to be able to survey and measure lands, to view and value woods, to know the worth of demesne [*estate*] lands and tenements. . . . They should not be ignorant how to follow suits in law for, albeit the earl have a solicitor, yet if a chief officer that is known to be in credit with his lord come with him either to sergeant or counselor his chamber, he will be the better regarded and sooner dispatched, especially if the earl be not in London. They are also to be skillful in the buying of cloths of gold and silver, velvets and all kinds of silks; household furnitures as plate, hangings, damask and diaper [*patterned linen*] napery, and linen cloths; broadcloths [*black fabrics*] and friezes [*coarse woolens*]; and all other both ordinary and extraordinary necessaries. They must be able to judge not only of the prices but also of the goodness of all kinds of corn [*grains*], cattle, and other household provisions and, the better to enable themselves thereto, are oftentimes to ride to fairs and great markets and there to have conference with graziers and purveyors (being men of wit and experience) and of them to learn what places are fittest to make provisions at and where best to put off. . . .

They must daily go into every office of household to see that every officer do his duty. . . . They are often to look into the larders, to see the powdered meats and salt store be well ordered and kept. They must go into the slaughterhouse to see what beefs, veals, and muttons are killed and that the hides, fells [*skins*], and tallow be orderly and safe kept. They must go into the bakehouse to see the manchet [*fine wheat*] and cheat [*inferior wheat*] bread made according to the weight and size by them set down, and that it be well seasoned and baked, and to look that the bakers bolt [*sift*] their flour and meal as they ought to do. From thence into the brewhouse to see the brewers make, at every brewing, the full number of hogsheads of beer and ale, to be of that proportionable goodness which they are rated to make, and that their vessels and hogsheads be sweet and well kept. Also into the granary, to see how all kind of grain is there kept and ordered. From thence they are to go into the cellar, buttery, pantry, and ewery; in the last two offices they must be vigilant to see the officers make not their fees otherwise than they should do, that they put not broken bread amongst their chipping [*crusts*], nor with the paring of the tallow lights to cut off the great ends of them to make their fees the more. They must in every of these offices oversee that all things appertaining unto them be kept in orderly and decent manner, that all wasteful expenses in every of them may be avoided. They must go into the woodyard to see the wood and coal be orderly placed and not wastefully expended. Also into the armory and garden at times convenient, to see how all things are ordered and used, and sometimes into the wardrobe of beds and strangers' lodging, albeit the gentlemen ushers are to oversee them. Often they are to go into the porter's lodge, to see it be not the place for the receipt of the unthriftiness of the house nor the harbor of drinking companions. . . . I do know there are some persons that upon a little knowledge think themselves as able to take upon them offices in noble houses as they are that be best experienced and of most understanding – but time will try [*test*] them and show them to be foully deceived.

What kind of men the gentlemen ushers should be, and their office

In former times gentlemen that were of years, and long-trained and experienced in that kind of service, were chosen to this place. But of later years earls and ladies have better liked young gentlemen that were neat and fine in their apparel to serve them in that room [*position*]. . . . The better to furnish themselves with knowledge, they are to make means that they be in the presence chamber not only at ordinary times but also when the King's Majesty feasteth and entertaineth great strangers and ambassadors.

The secretary his place

He should be a man brought up in the universities, having studied both logic and rhetoric. He is to understand the Latin and Greek tongues, also the Italian, French, and Spanish, with other languages. And not only to understand those tongues but also to speak and write well in them; thereby he shall be the better able to discourse with other noblemen's men and strangers. But as he carrieth the name of a secretary, so ought he to be very secret, and not to make show of his knowledge and credit by blabbing abroad that which he should keep secret and unrevealed. He is to have a closet with cupboards of drawing boxes and shelves, therein and upon to place in due order all letters received from the King's Majesty, from the lords of the Privy Council, and from other noblemen and gentlemen. Likewise all copies of letters written by his lord to His Majesty, or any of the rest above written, he having written upon every of them briefly part of their contents, with their dates, that he may readily find them when he hath occasion.

The marshal of the hall

If the earl be to receive and entertain the King's Majesty, Queen, or our Lord the Prince, for that time he is to make choice of such a gentleman (either of his ordinary household or of his retainers) as his lordship shall think fittest to supply that place, who should be a man well experienced, courteous, and well spoken. He is to carry in his hand a white rod and to appoint the yeomen ushers to place all strangers according to their degrees as he shall direct them. He must be allowed out of the household offices to have such meat, bread, and beer as he will send unto them for. For it is not sufficient that the King's Majesty and such nobles as attend be royally feasted and entertained, if servingmen and such meaner personages be not liberally and bountifully served. Nor shall the feast carry any great fame if the hall and such places wherein servingmen and their like are, be straited and scanted. . . . The greatest state that ever I did hear of in an earl's house (the late queen being there) was at Killingworth, where she was sundry times with the Earl of Leicester, and at New Hall in Essex with the Earl of Sussex, then Lord Chamberlain. But as I do well like that bounty and liberality should be at such times, so were it to be wished that there were more moderation and temperance not only in noblemen's houses but also in men of meaner sort. . . . Yea, in my time, I have seen an earl keeping his house in the Christmas time with great state, having many strangers, and, as the use hath been upon Twelfth Day at night, to have a banquet only of some ordinary fruits and comfits [*sweetmeats*], with some banqueting dishes made by his own cook, the charge of all not being very great. But since, I have known that the finest confectionary shop in all Bearbinder Lane and the Blackfriars[3] must be sought into for all kinds of conserved, preserved, and candied fruits and flowers – the charge of a banquet arising to as great a sum of money as would have kept a good house all Christmas, wherein should have been great dishes filled with great pieces of beef, veal, swan, venison, capons, and such like English meats. Of the which there would have been great plenty left for the relief of the poor, a matter in these days too little regarded. And therefore there is now just cause of complaint against needless prodigality and want of orderly frugality, which is the cause that many of our nobility, having spent in a week or a month that which might well have served them the most part of an year, do then break up their houses, turn away some of their servants to steal or beg, and least of all do they regard the want of relief which the poor in their countries by their means are driven unto.

The grooms of the bed chamber

They should be men brought up at tailor's occupation, that if there be anything amiss in the earl or lady's garments they may be able to mend the same, skillful to brush and rub over not only garments of cloth, velvet, and silks, but also cloth of gold and silver, and also in what sort to fold and lay up the same. They are to have a chimney in their wardrobe for airing of apparel. Their wardrobe must be furnished with standards [*large chests*], trunks, presses [*linen cupboards*]; brushing tables; linen cloths, buckrams, and pieces of sarcenet [*fine silk*] to cover and carry garments in – which wardrobe they must be passing careful to keep very clean and see that all things therein be placed in decent order. They are to have a book wherein is to be recorded all the apparel both of the earl and his lady and also all necessaries within their office. And what apparel or necessaries soever are bought in every month are to be entered into that book and likewise what apparel is given away and worn out.

The office of the kitchen

The master cook should be a man of years, well experienced, whereby the younger cooks will be drawn the better to obey his directions. In ancient times,

---

3 *Bearbinder Lane and the Blackfriars*: areas in London known for their confectionery shops.

noblemen contented themselves to be served with such as had been bred in their own houses. But of later times, none could please some except Italians and Frenchmen or, at the least, brought up in the court or under London cooks. Nor would the old manner of baking, boiling, or roasting please them, but the boiled meats must be after the French fashion, the dishes garnished about with sugar and preserved plums, the meat covered over with orangeade, preserved lemons, and with diverse other preserved and conversed stuff fetched from the confectioneries – more honey and sugar spent in boiling fish to serve at one meal than might well serve the whole expense for the house in a day. The baked meats must be set out with arms and crests, flourished and gilded, more fit for monuments[4] in churches (where they might have continuance) than to be set upon tables where they are little sooner seen than consumed. The roast meats, without their sundry kinds of new devised sauces little esteemed of, they must have most kinds not only of flesh but also of fish cold and sauced, all of these being more delightful to the sight and pleasing to the taste than needful or wholesome to the stomach and body.

The garden

The gardeners should not only be diligent and painful but also experienced and skillful, at the least the one of them to have seen the fine gardens about London and in Kent. To be able to cast out the quarters of the garden as may be most convenient, that the walks and alleys[5] may be long and large, to cast up mounts[6] and make fine arbors, to set hedges and finely to cut them, to tread out knots in the quarters of arms and fine devices, to set and sow in them sweet-smelling flowers and strewing herbs. To have in the fittest parts of the garden artichokes, pompions [pumpkins], melons, cucumbers, and such like; in other places convenient, radishes . . . carrots, and other roots, with store of all kind of herbs for the kitchen and apothecary. . . . To make fair bowling alleys, well banked and soaled[7] . . . the garden being a place not only pleasant but also profitable if the earl and lady often go into it, and, finding things well, he will commend the gardeners, and sometimes giving them money will encourage them to more pains.

The laundry

For that the countess is to appoint such an ancient gentlewoman or other as pleaseth her to have the oversight both of laundry and nursery, I will not set

---

4 *monuments*: sculptural tombs.
5 *alleys*: from the French *allée*, for a garden path bordered with trees or bushes.
6 *mounts*: artificial mounds of earth or stone.
7 *soaled*: prepared for the throw of the bowling ball.

down any directions for those places, wholly referring them to her honor's pleasure.

6.4 Letter from Robert Dudley, Earl of Leicester, to Dr. Jean Hotman (23 January ?1588)

FSL Ms V.b.282.

This letter from an earl to one of his officers pre-dates R. B.'s "Rules and Orders," but it demonstrates the determination to live in a Continental manner of which R. B. was to complain. Dudley, Elizabeth I's great favorite, embraced a courtly fad for white wines and may have initiated one for salads. In 1582 he engaged as his secretary Jean Hotman, a French marquis who had received a law degree from Oxford University. After service in the Netherlands as Elizabeth's Governor-General from 1586 to 1588, Dudley returned to England, leaving Hotman as his agent in Utrecht. Dudley died in September 1588.

I am very glad to hear that you have provided me of a gardener. I doubt not but he shall be used to his contentation [*contentment*].

Touching the wines: you may forbear to send any, for I find the Rhenish wines very good this year.

If you can get a good young cook and a Protestant, I will thank you for him, and you shall deliver him to my servant Arden, whom I have licensed to wait upon th'Earl of Derby this journey.

I have also sent a young man, an Englishman, brought up in my kitchen and prettily entered [*skillfully begun*] already, to spend a year or two there with some good principal cook in Paris, such as do use to serve the most of the noblemen, and is most frequented and set on work. I pray you travail with some of your acquaintance to place him. And look what allowance he will ask for his teaching, and his board shall be quarterly sent over for him to such as you shall nominate. And do pray you to give very earnest charge for his well teaching, as also to have him kept under for rioting [*carousing*] abroad. And as hitherto he hath been of good honest disposition, so being young and lacking some to keep in awe, he may stray now abroad. But let him know that you have given order that there shall be watch over his behavior and that I have written to you earnestly to advertise [*notify*] me how he shall behave himself. And give charge to his master to keep him under and from liberty, but to set him to work enough. And whilst you remain there, I pray you have an eye to him and, as near as you can, let none of our papists know that I have any such cook there, for I would not have him known to them. And let him come to hear preaching and service at the Amba[ssador's], but no way to charge him.

I do send you by Arden a letter to the party for a hundred crowns for you.

Arden shall also deliver you money to send the gardener away to me with speed. Willing you to take care and Arden together, to have somebody come over with him to bring him to me with your letters.

I pray you let him bring with him all manner of seeds, the best you can procure there among the Italians, as well for herbs and salads as for all kind of rare flowers, beside seeds for melons, cauliflower and such like, asparagus, and all sorts of radish.

6.5   Elizabeth Hardwick's New Year's Gift to the Queen (1576)

From FSL Mss X.d.428 (129), (127), (128), (130).

The great builder known as "Bess of Hardwick," born Elizabeth Hardwick, wed successively Robert Barlow, Sir William Cavendish, Sir William St. Loe, and George Talbot, sixth Earl of Shrewsbury – each time marrying up and acquiring new properties to develop. She was a gentlewoman of the Privy Chamber until 1561, when Elizabeth I discovered that Hardwick knew of the unauthorized union of Katherine Grey and Edward Seymour, Earl of Hertford. (It was treason for anyone with royal blood to wed without the approval of the monarch, and Grey was great-granddaughter to Henry VII.) These letters suggest how Hardwick worked her way back into the queen's favor by relying on kin and friends to send word to her in Derbyshire of the best London fashions. Anthony Wingfield earnestly reported conflicting advice; Elizabeth Wingfield perhaps inflated reports of their strategic success on Hardwick's behalf. Court records document the extravagant gifts that Elizabeth received from her courtiers for each new year.

Elizabeth Wingfield to her sister Elizabeth, Countess of Shrewsbury, 21 October 1568

May it please you to understand that Master Wingfield hath delivered your venison to the Queen's Majesty with my lord's [*the Earl of Shrewsbury's*] most humble commendations and [those of] your lady[ship], with humble thank[s] from both your honors for Her Highness's great goodness. I assure your ladyship of my faith. Her Majesty did talk one long hour with Master Wingfield of my lord and you so carefully that, as God is my judge, I think your honors have no friend living that could have deeper consideration nor more show love and great affection. In the end she asked when my lord meant to come to the Court. He answered he knew not. Then said she, "I am assured if she might have her own will she would not be long before she would see me." Then said she, "I have been glad to see my Lady St. Loe, but now more desirous to see my Lady Shrewsbury.[8]

---

8   *my Lady St. Loe . . . my Lady Shrewsbury*: Elizabeth refers to Hardwick's change of husband (and name) since last she saw her.

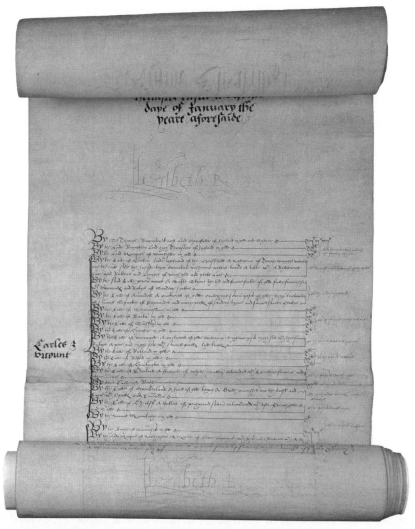

Figure 9 Elizabeth I's New Year's Gift Roll, 1585. Courtesy of the Folger Shakespeare Library.

At court, a list was prepared annually of gifts given to the Queen for the new year. The 1585 log is unrolled to show presents from "Earls and Viscounts," mostly of gold, plate, furs, and jewels. The Earl of Arundel and the Earl of Warwick both offered pieces of fine cloth studded with such ornaments as gold, diamonds, rubies, and pearls; the Earl of Pembroke gave "a forepart [*an upper-body garment*] of white satin embranded with gentian flowers and other leaves"; and the Earl of Hertford presented "a doublet of peach-colored satin embroidered with roses of venus [*crystal*], gold, and silk." Elizabeth's signature is seen twice on the roll.

I hope," said she, "my lady hath known my good opinion of her. And thus much I assure you: there is no lady [in] this land that I better love and like." Master Bateman can more at large declare unto your honor, and so with most humble commendations to my very good lord, I wish to you both as the Queen's Majesty doth desire.

Anthony Wingfield to his wife Elizabeth Wingfield, 13 October 1575

I have dealt with my Lady of Sussex and my Lady Cobham for my lady's [*the Countess of Shrewsbury's*] gift unto the queen. And my Lady of Sussex's opinion was that my lady should have given the fair bed that my lady makes to her hangings, and my Lady Cobham would in no wise that it should be so but would have my lady give forty pound[s] in money or a cup of gold about that value. But in any wise my Lady of Sussex would have my lady give a safeguard⁹ and a cloak of some watchet [*light blue*] satin or peach color and embroidered with some pretty flowers and leaves with sundry colors made with gold spangles and silk. These fantastical things will be more accepted than cup or jewel. And my Lady of Sussex would have Walter Fish [*a trusted London tailor*] to have the doing of it. . . . I have to write unto you that my Lady of Sussex hath so handled the cause in my lady's behalf that she finds that if my lady would come up to see the queen she might make her way as she would.

Anthony Wingfield to his wife Elizabeth Wingfield, 13 December 1575

I could not speak with my Lady of Sussex till yesterday at night. . . . Then I dealt with her for her judgment for the New Year's gift, and this is her mind: that she would have the color to be of a light wachet satin and guarded [*bordered*] with small gorgets [*ornaments*] of carnation velvet, and upon the guard embroidered with pansies of all fashions so that in them be all manner of colors, and to be trimmed with glistering gold and silver to the best show, and not with great pearl but to the best show of small pearl, the guard to be a good inch broad and not above. For in a narrow guard the pansy flowers will show best, because that small flower and leaf will show best in a small guard. That is my Lady of Sussex's opinion, and, as she says, the queen likes best of that flower, and to have the satin a light watchet because she hath no garment of that color already. . . . And thus I have sent my Lady's mind in this matter.

---

9 *safeguard*: an outer skirt designed to protect a lady's dress when riding, here a decorative garment in its own right.

Elizabeth Wingfield to her sister Elizabeth, Countess of Shrewsbury, 2 January 1576

Your honor shall know that after my cousin William and my careful toil[10] (by reason of the short time), we have reaped such recompense as could not desire better. First Her Majesty never liked anything you gave her so well; the color and strange trimming of the garments with the rich and great cost bestowed upon it hath caused her to give out such good speeches of my lord and your ladyship as I never heard of better. She told my Lord of Leicester and my Lord Chamberlain that you had given her such garments this year as she never had any so well liked her. And said, "That good noble couple! This show[s] in all things what love they bear me. And surely, my Lord, I will not be found unthankful." If my lord and your ladyship had given five hundred pound[s], in my opinion it would not have been so well taken. And for your other thing my cousins William and Charles will give your honor a full advertisement [*report*]. But surely in general all was so well and thankfully taken as is possible, with Master Attorney and his wife's most humble duty.

And now I humbly pray your honor that I may receive the rest of the money. I have received £50 and have promised payment for the rest with speed. And so I beseech the Almighty to make the rest of my very good lord and your ladyship's years as prosperous as this beginning. So with my humble prayer to God for you and all yours, I end with my humble duty this 2 January.

6.6   The Queen's Sumptuary Laws (1574)

From STC 8066 (Bodleian copy).

Increasing lavishness in dress prompted Elizabeth I to revive the sumptuary legislation enacted by both her father Henry VIII and her sister Mary I. The regulations aimed to reinforce social hierarchies by preserving privilege and also to restrain extravagant spending among the upwardly mobile. There was one list of fabrics and colors prohibited in men's apparel (with exceptions given for those of certain designated ranks) and another for women's apparel; that for men is reproduced here.

The excess of apparel and the superfluity of unnecessary foreign wares thereto belonging now of late years is grown [to cause] the wasting and undoing of a great number of young gentlemen otherwise serviceable, and others seeking by show of apparel to be esteemed as gentlemen, who, allured by the vain show of

---

10 *my cousin William and my careful toil*: that is, the hard work of Elizabeth Wingfield and her cousin Charles Cavendish (Hardwick's son).

those things, do not only consume themselves, their goods, and lands which their parents have left unto them, but also run into such debts and shifts as they cannot live out of danger of laws without attempting of unlawful acts, whereby they are not any ways serviceable to their country as otherwise they might be. Which great abuses tending both to so manifest a decay of the wealth of the realm and to the ruin of a multitude of serviceable young men and gentlemen and of many good families, the Queen's Majesty hath of her own princely wisdom so considered as she hath of late with great charge to her Council commanded the same to be presently and speedily remedied both in her own court and in all other places of her realm, according to sundry good laws heretofore provided. . . .

Prohibited Men's Apparel

Silk of the color of purpure,[11] cloth of gold tissued [*woven with gold or silver thread*], nor fur of sables *BUT ONLY* the king; queen; king's mother, children, brethren and sisters, uncles and aunts *AND EXCEPT* dukes, marquesses, and earls, who may wear the same in doublets, jerkins [*jackets*], linings of cloaks, gowns, and hose. And those of the Garter,[12] purple in mantles only.

Cloth of gold, silver, tinseled satin; silk or cloth mixed or embroidered with any gold or silver *EXCEPT* all degrees above viscounts; and viscounts, barons, and other persons of like degrees; in doublets, jerkins, linings of cloaks, gowns, and hose.

Woolen cloth made out of the realm, but in caps only; velvet, crimson or scarlet; furs, black jennets [*horses*] [or] lucerns [*lynxes*]; embroidery or tailor's work having gold or silver or pearl therein *EXCEPT* dukes, marquesses, earls, and their children; viscounts, barons, and knights being companions of the Garter; or any person being of the Privy Council.

Velvet in gowns, coats, or other outermost garments; fur of libards [*leopards*]; embroidery with any silk *EXCEPT* men of the degrees above mentioned, barons' sons, knights, and gentlemen in ordinary office attendant upon Her Majesty's person, and such as have been employed in embassages to foreign princes.

Caps, hats, hatbands, capbands, garters, boothose trimmed with gold or silver or pearl; silk netherstocks; enameled chains, buttons, aglets [*metal tips on laces*] *EXCEPT* men of the degrees above mentioned, the gentlemen attending upon the queen's person in Her Highness's Privy Chamber or in the office of Cupbearer, Carver, Sewer,[13] Esquire for the Body, gentlemen ushers, or esquires of the Stable.

Satin, damask, silk camlet [*silk and angora*], or taffeta in gown, coat, hose, or

---

11 *purpure*: purple color associated with royal rank.
12 *those of the Garter*: members of the highest order of knighthood.
13 *Sewer*: attendant who supervised state meals.

uppermost garments; fur whereof the kind groweth not within the queen's dominions, except foins [*martens*], gray jennets, and budge [*lambskin*] EXCEPT the degrees and persons above mentioned and men that may dispend £100 by the year (and so valued in the subsidy book).

Hat, bonnet, girdle; scabbards of swords, daggers, etc.; shoes and pantophles [*slippers*] of velvet EXCEPT the degrees and persons above named and the son and heir apparent of a knight.

Silk other than satin, damask, taffeta, camlet in doublets; and sarcenet, camlet, or taffeta in facing of gowns and cloaks; and in coats, jackets, jerkins, coifs [*caps*], purses being not of color scarlet, crimson, or blue; fur of foins, gray jennets, or other, as the like groweth not in the queen's dominions EXCEPT men of the degrees and persons above mentioned, son of a knight, or son and heir apparent of a man of 300 marks land by year (so valued in the subsidy books), and men that may dispend £40 by the year (so valued *ut supra* [*as above*]).

Spurs, swords, rapiers, daggers, skenes [*knives*], woodknives, or hangers [*loops on sword belts*]; buckles of girdles gilt, silvered, or damasked [*richly engraved*] EXCEPT knights' and barons' sons; and other of higher degree or place; and gentlemen in ordinary office attendant upon the Queen's Majesty's person, which gentlemen so attendant may wear all the premises [*foregoing*] saving gilt, silvered, or damasked spurs. . . .

Note that Her Majesty's meaning is not, by this order, to forbid in any person the wearing of silk buttons; the facing of coats, cloaks, hats, and caps for comeliness only with taffeta, grosgrain, velvet, or other silk as is commonly used.

6.7 Frederic Gerschow's Travel Diary (1605)

From "Diary of the Journey of Philip Julius, Duke of Stettin-Pomerania, through England in the Year 1602," ed. Gottfried von Bülow with Wilfred Powell, *Transactions of the Royal Historical Society*, 2nd ser. 6 (1892), 25–33, 51–5.

The Prussian duke Philip Julius was eighteen when he embarked on a grand tour of Europe with an entourage of sixteen attendants, including his tutor Frederic Gerschow. In England from 10 September till 3 October 1602, the group visited not only London and some nearby great houses but also the two university towns of Cambridge and Oxford. Gerschow kept a travel diary for the duke, which he completed in 1605. This is a translation from the German.

18 September

On the 18th, His Princely Grace having heard of a museum arranged by a gentleman, Master Kopf, we drove there and found a great many wonderful objects, as various arms and weapons used in India Orientali; some crowns worn by the queen in America; a number of shields and swords. A dagger entirely made of steel had a scabbard made wholly of black lac or Spanish wax. Further, two teeth of the sea-horse. The horn of a rhinoceros was not long but bent upwards; also the tail with very coarse hair. Many strange worms, birds, and fishes; a salamander scolopendra;[14] a little Indian bird phosphorescent by night. The celebrated little fish remoram had scales almost square like a stone perch, a head like an eel-pout; also a cauda Delphini [*tail of a dolphin*] and a mummy. We further saw many Indian manuscripts and books; a passport given by the King of Peru to the English, neatly written on wood; various strange cucumber plants. The musical instrument celebrated in ancient times, and called *cymbalum*, was round like a globe of brass or steel; when touched it gave forth a sound like a triangle, but it is not now known how it was used in early times. . . .

Thence we went to the children's *Comediam*. . . . The queen keeps a number of young boys who have to apply themselves zealously to the art of singing and to learn all the various musical instruments and to pursue their studies at the same time. . . . And in order that they may acquire courteous manners, they are required to act a play once a week. . . . They do all their plays by [artificial] light, which produces a great effect. For a whole hour before, a delightful performance of *musicam instrumentalem* is given on organs, lutes, pandores, mandolins, violins, and flutes; and a boy's singing *cum voce tremula* in a double-bass so tunefully that we have not heard the like of it on the whole journey, except perhaps the nuns in Milan did it better.

20 September

We started today from London (which lies in Middlesex) for Theobalds in the county of Hertford, three miles off, erected by William Cecil, Lord of Burleigh, whose son, the Lord Secretary, possesses it at present. . . . Especially noteworthy were the three galleries. In the first were representations of the principal emperors and knights of the Golden Fleece, with the most splendid cities in the world and their garments and fashions. In the next, the coats-of-arms of all the noble families of England, twenty in number; also all the viscounts and barons, about forty-two; the labors [of] Hercules; and the game called billiards, on a long cloth-covered table. In the third, all England, represented by fifty-two trees, each tree representing one province. On the branches and leaves were pictured the coats-of-arms of all the dukes, earls, knights, and noblemen residing in the country and, between the trees, the towns and boroughs together with the principal mountains and rivers. . . . We were told that some big stags in the deer park, close to the pleasure garden, had been brought to Theobalds from a large forest

---

14 *scolopendra*: a fish allegedly able to vomit its intestines to expel a fishhook.

more than fifty German miles off by some peasants marching before them with flutes and other [musical instruments], the stags following the sounds . . . but I reserve my opinion.

26 September

On the 26th His Princely Grace arrived at Oatlands. . . . [In] the garden close to the palace . . . Her Majesty also gave him to understand that she would like to see His Princely Grace, according to the English fashion, kiss her hands, which, however, his Grace, for various weighty reasons, politely declined to do. At last the queen, to show her royal rank, ordered some of the noble lords and coun-selors to approach and they, in their stately dress, were obliged to remain on their knees all the time the queen addressed them. Meanwhile, the queen uncov-ered herself down to the breasts, showing her snow-white skin. To judge from portraits showing Her Majesty in her thirtieth year, there cannot have lived many finer women at the time; even in her old age she did not look ugly when seen from a distance. . . .

We traveled today as far as Hampton Court, three miles. . . . In the queen's cabinet stood a virginal or instrument of glass, artistically made as if it were set with pearls and precious stones. Also a beautiful bed-curtain worked by Anne Boleyn in gold, with her own hands. Also a large and high bedstead that Henry VIII used to take with him into camp, everything thereon being embroidered in gold. Another large bed in which Edward VI had been cut alive from his mother's womb. . . . At last we reached the Paradise Chamber, the most magnif-icent and most splendid room in the whole mansion, perhaps even in the whole realm. The tapestry was of Persian workmanship. On the table that was twenty-eight feet long lay a velvet coverlet reaching down to the ground, thickly set with pearls as large as peas. The throne was of brown velvet worked magnifi-cently with gold and set with pearls and precious stones. Especially brilliant were three large diamonds worth a mighty sum of money, a table of Brazilian wood inlaid with silver. Upon it lay a cushion with a mirror and many turquoises thereon, a draught-board of ebony, a chessboard of ivory, and then, on a little table, seven ivory fifes mounted with gold.

6.8 John Manningham's London Diary (1602–3)

From BL Ms Harleian 5353, 29^{r-v}, 110^v, 112^r.

John Manningham, born in Cambridgeshire, was adopted by his childless uncle, a London mercer. As a law student, Manningham kept a notebook recording gossip, proverbs, sermons, amusing stories, and general observations. He witnessed the common culture of the capital city.

June 1601

In times past men were afeared to commit sin but ready to make confession. Now the world is changed, for now everyone dares commit any sin but is ashamed to make confession.

20 June 1601

Master Foster of Lincoln's Inn told these jests of Sir Thomas More as we went to Westminster: One which had been a familiar acquaintance of Sir Thomas More's in his meaner fortunes came to visit him when he was in the height of his prosperity. Sir Thomas amongst other parts of entertainment showed him a gallery which he had furnished with good variety of excellent pictures, and desired his friend's judgment which he liked best. But he making difficulty to prefer any, Sir Thomas showed him the picture of a death's head with the word *Memento morieris* [*remember death*], which he commended as most excellent for the device and conceit. The gentleman being desirous to know what he conceived extraordinary in so common a sentence, he told him, "Sir, you remember sometimes you borrowed some money of me, but I cannot remember you have remembered to repay it. It is not much, and though I be Chancellor I have use for as little, and now methinks this picture speaks unto you *Memento Mori aeris*: Remember to pay More his money."

13 March 1602

Upon a time when Burbage played Richard III, there was a citizen grown so far in liking with him that before she went from the play she appointed him to come that night unto her by the name of Richard the Third. Shakespeare, overhearing their conclusion, went before, was entertained and at his game ere Burbage came. Then message being brought that Richard the Third was at the door, Shakespeare caused return to be made that William the Conqueror was before Richard the Third. Shakespeare's name "William."

24 March 1603

This morning about three at clock Her Majesty departed this life mildly like a lamb, easily like a ripe apple from the tree. . . . I doubt not but she is amongst the royal saints in heaven in eternal joys. About ten at clock the Council and diverse noblemen, having been a while in consultation, proclaimed James the Sixth, King of Scots, [to be] the King of England, France, and Ireland, beginning at Whitehall gates, where Sir Robert Cecil read the proclamation, which he carried in his hand and after read again in Cheapside. . . . No tumult, no contradiction, no disorder in the city; every man went about his business as readily, as peaceably, as securely, as though there had been no change, nor any news ever heard of competitors. God be thanked, our king hath his right.

6.9 Dudley Carleton's Letter from the Court of King James (15 January 1604)

From SP 14/6: 21.

Dudley Carlton, Viscount Dorchester, born into a family of "lesser" Oxfordshire gentry, spent many years in London and France in search of a career or a patron. At first (falsely) implicated in the Gunpowder Plot, he finally earned the trust of James VI and I. He was made Secretary of State in 1628. In his earlier years he wrote regularly to the diplomat John Chamberlain, describing such occasions as James's first Christmas at Hampton Court.

We have had here a merry Christmas and nothing to disquiet us save brabbles amongst our ambassadors and one or two poor companions that died of the plague. The first holy days, we had every night a public play[15] in the great hall, at which the king was ever present and liked or disliked as he saw cause – but it seems he takes no extraordinary pleasure in them. The queen and prince were more the players' friends, for on other nights they had them privately and have since taken them to their protection. On New Year's night we had a play of Robin Goodfellow and a masque brought in by a magician of China. There was a heaven built at the lower end of the hall out of which our magician came down and after he had made a long sleepy[16] speech to the king of the nature of the country from whence he came . . . he said he had brought in clouds certain Indian and China knights to see the magnificency of this court. . . .

The Sunday following was the great day of [the] queen's masque, at which was present the Spanish and Polack ambassadors with their whole trains and the most part of the Florentines and Savoyards (but not the ambassadors themselves), who were in so strong competition for place and precedence that to displease neither it was thought best to let both alone. The like dispute was betwixt the French and the Spanish ambassadors. . . . The one end [of the hall] was made into a rock, and in several places the waits [*singers*] placed in attire like savages; through the midst from the top came a winding stair of breadth for three to march, and so descended the masquers by three and three, which being all seen on the stairs at once was the best presentation I have at any time seen. Their attire was alike, loose mantles [*sleeveless cloaks*] and petticoats[17] but of

---

15 *public play*: performance for all at court (not in a public theater such as the Globe).

16 *sleepy*: soporific – that is (to Carleton), boring.

17 *petticoats*: as with *gowns*, below, these were gender-neutral upper garments.

different colors, the stuffs embroidered satins and cloth of gold and silver, for which they were beholding to Queen Elizabeth's wardrobe. Their heads by their dressing did only distinguish the difference of the goddesses they did represent. Only Pallas [*Athena*] had a trick by herself, for her clothes were not so much below the knee but that we might see a woman had both feet and legs, which I never knew before. She had a pair of buskins [*boots*] set with rich stones, a helmet full of jewels, and her whole attire embossed with jewels of several fashions. Their torchbearers were pages in white satin loose gowns, set with stars of gold, and their torches of white virgin wax gilded. Their démarche [*walk*] was slow and orderly, and first they made their offerings at an altar in a temple which was built on the left side of the hall towards the upper end; the songs and speeches that were there used I send you here enclosed. . . . They retired themselves towards midnight in order as they came and quickly returned unmasked but in their masquing attire. From thence they went with the king and the ambassadors to a banquet provided in the Presence [Chamber], which was dispatched with the accustomed confusion. . . .

The valuation of the king's presents which he hath made to ambassadors since his coming into England comes to £25,000.

7

Everyday Life and Popular Culture

We assume that modern lives are far more complicated than those of the past, and in some ways this is so. But, reading of disputed betrothals and neighborhood conflicts in the early modern church courts, we discover that human relationships were as complex and as vexed then as they are now. Records from the realm of high politics show the Tudor and Stuart years to have involved as many intrigues and betrayals as anything we see today.

Everyday life, meanwhile, was certainly more difficult, with lighting provided only by candles and lanterns, land transit primarily on foot or horseback, and no refrigeration. In London the very rich could get water piped to their houses, but others had to fetch it at city conduits, and in the country people carried buckets from wells and springs. The only sources of heat were wood, coal, and peat burned in open fires, and there was always the threat of chimneys themselves catching fire and collapsing. With poorer nutrition, with no dental care, with none of the preventive medicine we associate with vaccines, and with visual examination of urine as the principal diagnostic tool, ill health and physical pain were common experiences. Almost everyone would have witnessed death directly, usually in the immediate family. Children were less protected from the harsher realities of life, and some were as young as ten and eleven when they were required to begin service or apprenticeship. Amid all these challenges, people needed both a wide range of skills and good fortune to survive and cope. Many did not.

And yet, some thrived, in the vast redistribution of wealth that over the course of the sixteenth and seventeenth centuries was to empower a rising middle class.

The Great Rebuilding

The housing revolution among the nobility and gentry exposed many others to new ways of living in comfort and style. Building their great houses, members of the privileged classes hired stoneworkers, brickmakers, masons, carters, carpenters, turners, joiners, plasterworkers, painters, glaziers, and day laborers. Also in their employ were household staff for cooking, brewing, dairying, cleaning, laundering, repairing, and serving. Many had secretaries for their business activities, stewards for estate management, and tutors for their children. Visitors included migrants in search of seasonal agricultural work, itinerant tinkers (who mended pots and pans), local housewives selling produce and handicrafts, wandering actors and musicians, and travelers in search of a mug of beer, food scraps, and sometimes a roof for the night.

For those in the middle ranks, early modern England was an aspirational culture. If they could not build on a grand scale, nonetheless they could *re*build, remaking medieval houses to new standards. In unprecedented numbers, they added rooms, chimneys, storage space, and other improvements.

Even peasant life changed. At the beginning of the sixteenth century, some poor country families still lived in "longhouses," small buildings that sheltered both the family and its farm animals. One side of the structure had the pens or stables, with a wide door to allow the passage of large beasts and with ground-level openings to flush animal waste. The byre also provided storage space for feed and firewood. The other side of the building, with a separate entrance, was the hall in which the family lived, worked, cooked, and slept. The main feature of the residential area was an open hearth in the middle of the floor. Spare as these houses were, they were nonetheless taller than was strictly necessary, to allow room for smoke to gather in the rafters before it was vented through a hole in the roof.

The transformation of the longhouse began when the hearth was replaced by a chimney, eliminating the need for open space overhead. At this point a shallow second story might be created for the storage of dry provisions accessible by ladder. Eventually a staircase replaced the ladder and an upper-level opening was created in the chimney stack: thus, the storage area was transformed into a heated sleeping loft. A high gable window, allowing for natural light, completed the conversion to a fully functional upper bedchamber. Often, the next step was for animals to be moved into a separate building, so that the byre could be recuperated as two-storied domestic space. In this way a family that had once shared one open hall now had four rooms. A similar process occurred in more middle-class houses: chimneys were constructed and upper levels were inserted to double the living area.

People needed larger houses because all but the poorest possessed more goods than ever before: more cooking utensils, more bed and table linens, more dinnerware. Most household furnishings were available in a range of qualities and costs. Only the wealthiest early moderns could afford tapestries, for example. These were imported from the Continent. But nearly everyone could hang painted cloths on their walls. Itinerant artists, many of them from Europe, created hunting scenes, landscapes, Biblical images, and floral designs that added color and imagery even in the homes of husbandmen and laborers. Window glass was also becoming more common. In both fixed frames and casements, it replaced the old combination of shutters (for warmth and security), thin sheets of animal horn or paper (which admitted light), and lattices (open to the air).

In one-room houses, the hall sheltered all household functions. Newer rooms, however, were more specialized. People at many different social levels came to have kitchens, parlors, and bedchambers. Purpose-specific spaces helped people think about their lives less as the undifferentiated pursuit of survival and more as a collection of different activities conducing to leisure as well as labor. Each room that was associated with a distinct activity seemed also to mandate a distinct behavior. Thus changes in the built world caused changes in social personality, as well. It was what has sometimes been called a "civilizing" process.

Food and Drink

Although cookery was a topic of early modern self-help books, these dealt mostly with fine foods, fancy sweets, and exotic ingredients. There was no need to write down recipes that everyone knew, for such staples as pottage and bread. Like many matters of everyday life, ordinary food has a largely unrecorded history. Skills were generally passed through direct demonstration, from parent to child and mistress to maidservant.

The main meal was taken at midday. Pottage, based in oats or barley, was similar to modern porridge but took on a wide variety of tastes, depending on the mix of vegetables, meats, and herbs that were added. Long cook times meant that women could set pottage ingredients in a cauldron over the fire and leave it unattended, except for the occasional stir, while minding children, spinning wool, or doing other housekeeping and manufacturing tasks. Much summer labor involved putting up produce for winter. When dried, peas were the primary ingredient for a rough peasant bread. Milk was preserved in the form of cheese and butter. Pigs were slaughtered in the autumn, before they required winter feed, and their flesh was preserved with brine or salt. Even after the Reformation, everyone was required to eat meatless meals twice a week. Some had access to fresh fish, but others ate imported fish from Scandinavia that had been dried and salted and that required prolonged soaking and hammering to become edible.

Many households brewed their own ale and beer, which were drunk in great quantities. Both were made from a grain such as barley, which was germinated, roasted, boiled, and then stored in a barrel with yeast. Ale was flavored with herbs or spices; for beer, hops were added. Brewers got three boilings out of each measure of malt. The first produced strong beer, which the housewife might sell for extra income. By the third boil the drink was so weak that it was called "small" beer, suitable even for very young children.

Cleaning and Sanitation

It is not surprising that the people of the Renaissance bathed infrequently; water had to be hauled to the tub by the bucketful and was frigid unless boiled.

However, washing in basins and bowls was far more common than is sometimes imagined. And while the wool of most clothing could not be laundered – it was brushed down periodically and spot-cleaned – the long linen shirts worn as undergarments by both men and women were regularly washed and bleached. Because water was so difficult to transport, laundry was often done at the site of a spring, river, or conduit, especially for such heavy cloths as sheets. To dry, they were spread on the ground or draped over hedges.

In the late sixteenth century, Sir John Harington wrote a mock epic narrative about a new invention, the watercloset. But too few houses had the piped-in water required for this prototype of the modern toilet. Instead, people used privies and chamberpots. The close stool, a box with a chamber pot inside it, allowed the user to sit rather than squat. There are many reports of men "making water" against walls or into chimneys (to douse the fire), but there were social prohibitions against public urination, too. When away from home to run errands or do their marketing, women were known to carry sponges into which they could urinate when no facilities were available. There were various other alternatives for modern implements: silver earpickers, twig toothbrushers, fine-toothed combs for lice, the horsetail plant to scour dishes, an almond paste for hand cream, and, as John Gerard advised in his *Herbal*,[1] a concoction of thistles to prevent "the filthy smell of the armholes."

Common Culture

In the sixteenth and seventeenth centuries, England was a country of strong regional difference in terms of dialects, customs, agricultural produce, manufacturing specializations, and local legends. Together, however, church and state worked to effect a common culture through the homilies that were read regularly from the Reformed pulpit. The print industry also crossed local borders. Crudely illustrated ballads were the tabloid journalism of the day, printed on just one side of a large sheet of paper so that they could be posted publicly. In poems set to popular tunes, they attempted to legitimate their reports of sensational crimes and freaks of nature with long descriptions of repentance and pathos, all supposedly to preach conventional morals. Royal and Biblical legends were also frequent subjects.

There was an extensive pamphlet literature concerned with notorious murders, maleficent witches, and an imaginary criminal underworld with its own complex social organization and private jargon. Plays by Shakespeare and other dramatists also contributed to the development of a national reference-base of heroes and anti-heroes, such as the martyr Sir Thomas More, the magician Merlin, the rebel Jack Cade, and royal mistress Jane Shore. At the same time,

---

1 *as John Gerard advised in his* Herbal: See document 10.4.

the public theater created its own celebrities. As shown in the diary of the law student John Manningham (see document 6.8), Shakespeare was among them. The famous comedic actor Will Kemp capitalized on his stage fame in undertaking to dance a hundred miles from London to Norwich. He called the stunt a "Nine Days Wonder."

Much of the shared experience of early modern England was associated with the Christian calendar of feast and holy days: New Year's Day, Plough Sunday, Plough Monday, Shrove Tuesday, Mid-Lent Sunday, All Fool's Day, Easter, Hock Monday, Hock Tuesday, Rogantide, May Day, Whitsuntide, Midsummer Day, All Soul's Day, and the Twelve Days of Christmas. The celebration of May Day, Whitsuntide, and Midsummer Day involved carnivalesque inversions of class and gender hierarchies, with the world turned briefly upside down during traditional folk rituals. Calendar, climate, and cosmological forces were the subject of almanacs, to which nearly everyone had access. Another symptom of commonality was folk and proverbial knowledge: "Possession is eleven points of the law"; "Love thy neighbor, yet pull not down thy hedge"; and, in a warning against unseemly ambition in a culture of new opportunities, "Look high and fall into a cow-turd."

7.1   William Harrison, "The Description of England" (1587)

From *The First and Second Volumes of Chronicles . . . first collected and published by Raphael Holinshed, William Harrison, and others, now newly augmented and continued*, STC 13569 (HL copy), R3^v–R4^r.

In his preface to Raphael Holinshed's chronicle history of England, William Harrison remarked that standards of living were so greatly improved in the sixteenth century that "every man almost is a builder." He also observed the "trickle-down" factor, that even middling income men and women were experiencing a consumer revolution. Between the first edition of 1577 and this second edition of 1587 he documented a continued increase in household goods, luxury possessions, and personal comforts.

The furniture of our houses also exceedeth and is grown in manner even to passing delicacy [*luxury*]. And herein I do not speak of the nobility and gentry only, but likewise of the lowest sort in most places of our south country that have anything at all to take to. . . . In time past the costly furniture stayed there, whereas now it is descended yet lower, even unto the inferior artificers and many farmers, who, by virtue of their old and not of their new leases,[2] have for

---

2 *of their old and not of their new leases*: a reference to those with discretionary income; they were still paying rental rates set years before and not adjusted upward for inflation (as new rates were by a factor of ten or more).

the most part learned also to garnish their cupboards with plate, their joint beds with tapestry and silk hangings, and their tables with carpets and fine napery, whereby the wealth of our country (God be praised therefore and give us grace to employ it well) doth infinitely appear. . . .

There are old men yet dwelling in the village where I remain which have noted three things to be marvelously altered in England within their sound remembrance. . . . One is the multitude of chimneys lately erected, whereas in their young days there were not above two or three, if so many, in most uplandish towns of the realm (the religious houses and manor places of their lords always excepted, and peradventure some great personages). But each one made his fire against a reredos[3] in the hall, where he dined and dressed his meat.

The second is the great (although not general) amendment [*improvement*] of lodging [*bed furnishings*], for (said they) our fathers, yea, and we ourselves also, have lain full oft upon straw pallets, on rough mats covered only with a sheet, under coverlets made of dagswain or hap-harlots[4] (I use their own terms), and a good round log under their heads instead of a bolster or pillow. If it were so that our fathers or the goodman of the house had within seven years after his marriage purchased a mattress or flock-bed, and thereto a sack of chaff [*straw or husks*] to rest his head upon, he thought himself to be as well lodged as the lord of the town, that peradventure lay seldom in a bed of down or whole feathers, so well were they contented and with such base kind of furniture (which also is not very much amended as yet in some parts of Bedfordshire and elsewhere further off from our southern parts). Pillows, said they, were thought meet only for women in childbed. As for servants, if they had any sheet above them it was well, for seldom had they any under their bodies to keep them from the pricking straws that ran oft through the canvas of the pallet and razed [*cut*] their hardened hides.

The third thing they tell of is the exchange of vessel, as of treen [*wooden*] platters into pewter, and wooden spoons into silver or tin. For so common were all sorts of treen stuff in old time that a man should hardly find four pieces of pewter (of which one was peradventure a salt [*salt-cellar*]) in a good farmer's house. And yet for all this frugality (if it may so be justly called) they were scarce able to live and pay their rents at their days without selling of a cow or an horse or more, although they paid but four pounds at the uttermost by the year. Such also was their poverty that if some one odd farmer or husbandman had been at the alehouse (a thing greatly used in those days, amongst six or seven of his neighbors) and there, in a bravery to show what store he had, did cast down his purse, and therein a noble or six shillings in silver, unto them (for few such men then cared for gold because it was not so ready payment, and they were oft enforced to give a penny for the exchange of an angel[5]), it was very likely that

---

3 *reredos*: a low barrier against which a fire was built in a central hearth.

4 *dagswain or hap-harlots*: rough, coarse, and shaggy fabrics.

5 *angel*: a gold coin with the image of the archangel Michael piercing the dragon, worth 6s. 8d. when first struck in 1465, 8s. at the end of Henry VIII's reign, and 10s. during the reign of Edward VI.

all the rest could not lay down so much against it; whereas in my time, although peradventure four pounds of old rent be improved to forty, fifty, or an hundred pounds, yet will the farmer, as another palm or date tree, think his gains very small toward the end of his term if he have not six or seven years' rent lying by him [*in reserve*], therewith to purchase a new lease, beside a fair garnish of pewter [*set of pewter dishes*] on his cupboard, with so much more in odd vessel going about the house, three or four feather beds, so many coverlets and carpets of tapestry, a silver salt, a bowl for wine (if not an whole nest), and a dozen of spoons to furnish up the suit.

7.2   Elizabeth Morgan's Almshouse Ordinances (6 February 1592)

From PROB 11/81, 294^{v}–295^{v}.

Following the Dissolution of the monasteries, private citizens took up the challenge of poor relief. Elizabeth Morgan of Pentrebach in South Wales was one of many who established almshouses. Her will dictated that rents from land she owned (producing £10 annually) should endow free lodgings for ten poor widows in nearby Carleon. Charity was often tied to good behavior in the period, and Morgan's directions set out a map for the daily life of those who were to benefit from "my good work."

First, I will that there shall be such widows as shall be given to serve God before all other exercises and such as have lived in good name and fame and so doth continue: no swearers; no cursers; no recusants; no drunkards; no scolds; no breakers of hedges or annoyers of their neighbors; but of good and godly conversation, to the better examples of others. They shall be of the age of threescore years – or of six and fifty at the least – before they shall be admitted to dwell in the said House. And if any of them shall fortune to marry, they shall depart the said House and not to be admitted thereunto again.

Secondly, I will that they and every of them shall usually resort to the parish church of Carleon, especially upon the Sabbath Day, Wednesdays, and Fridays every week (at which days there is service said in the same church). And if they or any of them shall be absent from the said church at service-time, not being hindered by sickness, they so offending shall pay twopence at every time, which shall be put into the poor-mens' box[6] in the said parish church.

Thirdly, they nor any of them shall not lodge nor suffer to be lodged or harbored by day nor yet by night any manner of person, neither man nor woman nor child, within any of their lodgings, but only themselves – without it

---

6 *poor-mens' box*: Many institutions had such collection boxes. Fines for petty infractions were redistributed to poor persons as charity.

be in some great extremity of sickness, whereas of necessity some ancient woman keeper [*nurse*] may watch with any of them for a night or two upon great necessity. Or else not to lodge, harbor, keep or maintain, or suffer to be lodged, harbored, kept or maintained, neither by day nor yet by night, any manner of person, although they be never so near of their blood or kindred – unless it be a girl of their kindred to attend them under thirteen years of age. But if any of them shall so do, she or they shall presently avoid [*depart*] out of her or their lodgings within twenty days next after any such offense committed, and never to be admitted to dwell in any of the said lodgings again. My meaning is not but that they may come the one to the other's lodgings or their friends' to be merry together when they shall think meet, lovingly as honest neighbors use to do, at hours convenient, and so to depart in good order.

Fourthly, they shall be no keepers of sick persons in other houses which shall be sick of the plague or any infectious diseases, for fear of bringing infection among themselves.

Fifthly, they shall not, whiles they have health and strength, live idly, nor suffer such girls as are with them of their kindred to live in idleness, but shall work and labor to their power and ability for their better maintenance and relief.

Sixthly, they shall have care that neither they nor their maids do break hedges or enclosures or do any damage or annoyance unto any.

Seventhly, they shall make no ale to sell nor sell any kind of victual, nor set up alestake[7] nor shop in their house.

Eighthly, it shall be lawful for them to set up an alms box at the door of their house, to receive the charitable devotion of such as shall be disposed to give aught for their relief. But they shall not beg any alms neither at their door of their house, nor in the street, nor in any other place.

Ninthly and lastly, if any of them be found to have offended against any of these articles or if any of the said widows do or shall know that any of them have offended the articles aforesaid and do not show the same to such persons as shall have authority to correct and amend it, they, so offending, shall be put out of the same House and not to be admitted any more thereunto.

7.3   A Proclamation Pricing Victuals (7 August 1588)

From STC 8173 (Bodleian copy).

In August 1588 England was on a war footing, under threat by the Spanish Armada. The day before she delivered her famous speech at Tilbury (see document 1.9), Elizabeth I released this price-setting proclamation, to prevent opportunistic merchants from overcharging her soldiers for basic expenses. Her regulations show that, as with all

---

7 *alestake*: post set up as the sign of an alehouse.

consumer goods, provisions were available in a range of qualities and costs. The mone-
tary system of the time was based in pounds, shillings, and pence, with twelve pennies
to the shilling and twenty shillings to the pound. Abbreviations used here include s. *for*
shilling *(from the Latin* solidus*),* d. *for* penny *(denarius),* ob. *for* halfpenny
(obolus), and q. *for* quarter-penny *or* farthing *(quarta).*

A limitation of such rates and prices of grain, victuals, horse meat, lodgings, and
other things, as by virtue of this proclamation here above expressed are to be
sold and uttered [*marketed*], as well within all manner of liberties[8] as without.

First, a quarter [*8 bushels*] best wheat, clean and sweet,
   in the market   20s.
And a quarter second wheat in the market   16s.
Item, a quarter third wheat or best rye in the market   12s.
And a quarter second rye in the market   10s.   8d.
Item, a quarter best barley in the market   10s.   8d.
And a quarter second barley in the market   9s.   4d.
Item, a quarter best malt, clean and sweet, in the market   11s.   4d.
And a quarter second malt in the market   10s.
Item, a quarter beans or peas in the market   12s.
Item, a quarter best oats in the market   6s.   8d.
Item, a bushel of the same oats within every house   13d.
Item, a bushel best wheatmeal in the market   2s.   8d.
And a bushel second wheatmeal in the market   2s.   6d.
Item, a bushel best maslin [*mixed grains*] meal in the market   21d.
And a bushel second maslin meal in the market   18d.
Item, a bushel best great oatmeal in the market   2s.   4d.
And a bushel small oatmeal in the market   16d.
Item, a kilderkin [*cask*] of the best ale or beer at the brewers,
   with carriage   3s.
And a kilderkin single ale or beer at the brewers, with carriage   20d.
Item, a thirdendeal[9] of the best ale or beer within and without
   every house   1d.
And a full quart of good single ale or beer within and without
   every house   ob.
Item, a pound of butter, sweet and new, the best in the market   3d.
And a pound of barrel or salt butter in shop or in market   2d. ob. q.
Item, a pound of good Essex cheese in the shop or in market   1d. ob.
And a pound of good Suffolk cheese in shop or in market   1d. ob. q.

---

8 *liberties*: a district outside the jurisdiction of a sheriff, with its own peace officers.
9 *thirdendeal*: a third of a tun, or 252 gallons; thus, 84 gallons.

Item, seven eggs, the best in the market		2d.
And three of the same eggs within every house		1d.
Item, a stone[10] best beef at the butchers' weighing 8 pound		12d.
And a stone second beef at the butchers'		11d.
Item, a quarter best veal at the butchers'	2s.	2d.
And a quarter second veal at the butchers'		20d.
Item, a quarter best wether mutton[11] at the butchers'	2s.	4d.
And a quarter second mutton at the butchers'		20d.
Item, a quarter best lamb in the market		12d.
And a quarter second lamb in the market		9d.
Item, a fat pig, the best in the market		14d.
And a lean or second pig in the market		8d.
Item, a couple capons [*castrated cocks*], the best in the market		20d.
And a couple second capons in the market		16d.
Item, a couple of chickens or rabbits, the best in the market		8d.
And a couple second chickens or rabbits in the market		6d.
Item, a dozen pigeons, the best in the market		18d.

. . .

Item, a pound of tallow candles made of wick		3d. ob.
Item, a featherbed for one man one night and so depart		1d.
Item, a featherbed with necessary apparel thereunto for one man alone by the week		6d.
And the like featherbed and furniture by the week for two lying together		8d.
Item, a mattress or flockbed for one or two together by the week		4d.

. . .

Item, a vacant or empty room, either chamber room or stable, by the whole week		4d.

7.4   Elizabeth Forde's Protest against Price Fixing (21 July 1573)

From CLRO Repertories of the London Court of Aldermen 18, 48ʳ.

In London, prices were also mandated by the mayor and aldermen, who were responsible for monitoring food supplies in the city. Here, a shop assistant is reported to have protested rates set artificially low. Sent for punishment to Christ's Hospital, the city orphanage, rather than to the Bridewell, its house of correction, Elizabeth Forde was undoubtedly a minor.

---

10 *stone*: now commonly 14 pounds avoirdupois; in the sixteenth century, between 8 and 24 pounds, depending on the commodity being weighed.

11 *wether mutton*: meat from a male sheep, especially a castrated ram.

This day it was ordered that Elizabeth Forde, servant with John Stapulford, poulterer, for that she spake very lewd [*naughty*] words of my Lord Mayor, saying that when a man came to her mistress's shop to buy a rabbit and offered my Lord Mayor's price for the same, she in discorne [*contempt*] did answer that he should go to my Lord Mayor and bid him saddle a cat and ride into the country to buy rabbits himself. Which words were proved to be spoken that she shall be committed to Christ's Hospital and there to beat her with a rod for her lewd speech and so delivered [*set free*].

7.5 A New Almanac and Prognostication . . . Made by Thomas Buckminster (1590)

From STC 423.5 (FSL copy), C2ᵛ–C5ʳ.

Each year, enough almanacs were printed for one in every fourteen men, women, and children. Most included an illustration of the "anatomical man," showing how the signs of the zodiac influenced the human body. There were also a calendar; a chart of the phases of the moon; advice for planting; "prognostications" (prophecies) involving weather, eclipses, comets, and other astronomical and astrological phenomena; as well as such recommendations as these for the treatment and prevention of disease.

Some short notes to be considered in letting of blood,[12] purging, bathing, and sweating

Let just cause make thee to be let blood, and that with the counsel and advice of the learned physician, who by his knowledge and good discretion can consider of these or such like observations. First, to whom or for whom bloodletting is meet and necessary. Secondly, what is to be observed before bloodletting. Thirdly, what in the time or what after. Fourthly, in what time of the sickness it is to be used. Fifthly, what vein is to be opened. Sixthly, the measure and quantity to be let out, etc.

The general and usual signs for choleric complexions[13] to be let blood in are Cancer, Scorpio, and Pisces. For the phlegmatic, Aries and Sagittarius. For the melancholy, Libra, Aquarius, and Pisces. For the sanguine complexion, any of these will serve and may be used.

---

12 *letting of blood*: opening a vein in order to let blood flow.
13 *choleric complexions*: For more on the bodily "humors," see document 10.7.

Of purging

In purging, these things ought to be known and kept: 1. The humor which aboundeth. 2. The way best to avoid it. 3. The strength of the person. 4. The manner of the sickness. 5. The force and nature of the medicine. For where these things are not considered and observed, many perilous accidents may follow and greatly grieve the body.

Good signs for purging generally are Cancer, Scorpio, and Pisces. Particularly as with potions and drinks, purge when the moon hath her course in Scorpio. With electuaries,[14] when she is in Cancer. With pills, when she is in Pisces. Take vomits when she is in Aries, Taurus, and Capricorn. Take gargarisms [*gargles*] in Aries and Cancer. Take preparatives in Gemini, Libra, and Aquarius. Take clysters [*enemas*] when the moon is in Libra and Scorpio. Stop fluxes [*dysentery*], rheums, and lasks [*diarrhea*] when the moon is in Taurus, Virgo, and Capricorn. For using ointments and plasters [*emollients*], let the moon be in that sign which governeth the member or part of the body that is to be anointed or plastered.

Of bathing

Bathings are commonly used rather for pleasure than profit, especially where hothouses are over much haunted [*frequented*]. But I mind not to speak of them in this place, otherwise than to advertise those that tender their own health to be wary and circumspect in resorting unto them without just cause, and immediately after or with such persons as be unclean.

Know that it is not good to bathe when the moon is in the earthy signs, as in Taurus, Virgo, and Capricorn. The reason is because they are of cold and dry nature, and the nature of cold is to restrain and bind. And so the moon being in these signs, the pores of the body are closed and shut, so that there can be no resolution of humors and superfluities, which by bathing ought to be avoided.

But in the fiery signs, as when the moon is in Aries, Leo, and Sagittarius, then is it a good time for bathing. For then the body is apt to resolution, for it is the nature of heat to open and resolve.

It is best to bathe two or three days after the change [*new moon*] and at the full moon, for then the superfluities are ripe and ready to avoid [*empty*], and disposed to flow out and issue – which indeed is the very end and use of bathing. If any will enter into bath only for cleanliness' sake, let the moon be in Libra or Pisces. Further, if bathing be used for health, let the party grieved learn of the wise physician whether his sickness hath need of moistening or drying. For if it do require moistening, as in pthisis [*tuberculosis*] and such like, then let him bathe in watery signs having good aspects of Jupiter and Venus. But if the sick-

---

14 *electuaries*: medicinal compounds of powder mixed with honey or preserves.

ness require drying, as in paralysis and the like, then let him bathe, the moon being in fiery signs, having good aspects of Mars and Sol.

Also before ye enter into any bath, your body must be purged, for if a man go in unprepared and unpurged, peradventure he may be worse after than before.

The best time of the year to bathe in is in the spring and harvest, and in them the months of May and September. The best time of the day to go into the bath is an hour after the sun rising at the least, always provided that ye must walk either an hour or half an hour before, and have a stool [*bowel movement*], either by nature or by art. Ye must cover your head well so long as ye be in the bath, and beware that ye drink no cold drink though ye be very thirsty. But forbear all things that are cold, lest when ye are hot within, the cold strike suddenly into some principal member, and so hurt you.

The time of tarrying in the bath is commonly one hour, but it may be more or less according to the nature of the bath or sickness of the party, at the discretion of the good physician.

Of sweatings

Sweatings, as they are of two sorts (that is to say, natural and artificial), so they are used for two ends and purposes.

The natural sweat, if good heed be taken in opening the pores, will dissolve gross and thick humors, will cleanse the blood, will comfort the spirits, will put away cold, will consume raw humors, qualify and quench raging fevers, will help runs and the drunk.

The artificial sweat will cleanse scabs, put away the itch, amend the dullness in hearing, ease the stone, resolve congealed and cold melancholy blood and humors, etc. But for the better performing and effectual working in these cases, the counsel of the learned physician is to be desired and used.

The signs best to sweat in are Aries, Leo, and Sagittarius.

7.6   Sanitation Problems in London (1563–88)

From the Court Minutes of the Governors of St. Thomas's Hospital, LMA H01/ST/A/001/001, 74^v; H01/ST/A/001/002, 3^r; H01/ST/A/001/003, 65^v, 81^v. Repertories of the Court of Aldermen 16, CLRO X109/141, 530^v–531^r. Journals of the Common Council 19, CLRO COL/CC/01, 255^r. Repertories of the Court of Aldermen 17, CLRO X109/142, 145^v; 18, 54^r. Renters' Accounts of the London Drapers' Company, 1582–3, 11^r. Memoranda Books of St. Botolph Aldgate, GL Ms 9234/2, 5^v–6^r.

Early modern accommodations for human waste included chamber pots and privies (also called "houses of office," "houses of easement," and "withdraughts"). It was

*sufficiently troublesome and expensive to dig out privy reservoirs, as was required peri-
odically, that some Londoners preferred to use the city's common privies rather their
own. Nor were there always good options for emptying chamber pots in crowded living
quarters. Sanitation became a public concern as the city's population boomed.*

The Governors of St. Thomas's Hospital review tenants' complaints, 1563–72

17 May 1563: At this court Henry Twille's wife complained of William Cuer for
coming by her door unto a privy there, which did greatly annoy her and also her
neighbors. And it was agreed upon that Coxxon should nail up the door where
the said Cuer commonly useth to go the said privy.

25 September 1564: It was ordered at this court that whereas Master Cuer the
queen's saddler complained how that he was annoyed with a privy which was
joining to his house wherein he wrought [*manufactured objects*] for the Queen's
Majesty, that the said privy should be stopped and dammed up so that it should
not annoy the said Cuer. And in consideration thereof the said Cuer promised
to make a new privy and to set it up in the churchyard amongst others, at his
own proper [*personal*] costs and charges.

22 October 1571: That Master Raynoldes and Master Warre shall view [*inspect*] a
house next to Master Cuer's on the backside of Widow Penton's and Ellys
Williams's and to make report thereof at the next court that order may be taken
for the removing of the privy being noisome [*annoying*] to the said Master Cuer.

21 July 1572: At this court Master Ware reported that it is not meet [*proper*] a
privy to be made by Master Wyseman over the ditch or common sewer, for that
it is thought to be an annoyance to the inhabitants thereabouts.

The queen expresses concern about public health in London, 14 February 1570

The letters of the Queen's Majesty's most honorable Privy Council written unto
my Lord Mayor and my Masters the Aldermen . . . were read. . . . For the good
setting forward and accomplishment of the contents of the said letters, [a delega-
tion of city officials] were forthwith named and appointed by the court here to
travail and earnestly to take pains to search out and try and understand as nigh
as they can what number of mansion houses[15] are at this present surcharged or

---

15 *mansion houses*: large houses, but not as impressive as the term implies today.

pestered with a greater or more number of people than they ought commonly or reasonably to be. And also to make the like search for all such cottages and small tenements [*dwellings*] as are builded, erected, or made within any alleys or other place or places within this city or the liberties thereof, not having convenient houses of easement or withdraughts within the same. And to certify this court of the certainty thereof in writing with convenient speed, that some good and speedy reformation may here be taken and provided for the same.

The London Court of Common Council takes action, 13 June 1570

It is thought very expedient and needful that in all such tenements and houses as were and are in ancient alleys within this City of London which were alleys before ten years past that have no chimneys whereon to make their fire but reredoses and such like, to the great danger and peril not only of the inhabitants there within resident but also of others their neighbors adjoining; and also all tenements within such alleys as have not several houses of easement but one only common house of office for the service and use of the whole alley, to the great annoyance and decay of health of the said inhabitants; and also in every other tenement or house situated as well within lanes as in open streets or otherwise within this city and precincts of the same: there shall betwixt this and the last day of September next be erected in every tenement and dwelling house one convenient chimney and sufficient houses of office or privies such and so many as the alderman and common councillor of that ward (or the most part of them) shall think meet, requisite, and convenient. As also necessary gutters for the conveyance away of their noisome [*dirty and foul-smelling*] waters. Or else where such default shall be found and not reformed before the said last day of September next, the owner, lessee, or occupier of such house or houses, tenement or tenements at the choice and by the discretion of the Lord Mayor and Court of Aldermen of the said city shall be counted to prison, there to remain until sufficient bonds be made to the Chamberlain of London according to his discretion with sureties sufficient to reform the same[16] within time convenient.

The London Aldermen police the privies of the city, 1571–3

8 May 1571: It is ordered that Master Ducket and Master Bond, aldermen, shall confer with Sir Thomas Gresham, knight, for the making of some convenient place at the Royal Exchange[17] to make water in for the ease of people resorting to the same.

16 *sureties sufficient to reform the same*: guarantees that the problems will be remedied.
17 *Royal Exchange*: the trading center of London, a magnificent arcaded building erected in 1565.

11 August 1573: This day John Wood, brewer, was commanded either to provide and make privies in his tenements in Long Lane or else to take order that his tenements be put to other uses so that the neighbors and passers-by be not annoyed with the ordure and filth cast out of the same in pots, as hath been used.

The Wardens of the Drapers' Company invest in prevention, 1582–3

Paid for five lantern horns,[18] 4*d*. Paid for a proclamation,[19] 2*d*. The which horns were nailed over certain writings on the walls going into the garden by which writings persuasion was used for men to pass by without making of water against the said walls.

Eight Vestrymen of the Parish of St. Botolph Aldgate survey housing for the poor, 17 December 1588

By these viewers [*inspectors*] it is thought good that the common privy should be cleansed. . . .

It is thought good that Robert Tomkins shall take a lease of his new house and to make a privy to the same and so to be bound to make it tenantable. . . .

It was found that John Balderstone his house, Robert Sharp his house, and the widow Thomson her house have privies to them. Wherefore it is thought good that commandment be given them not to go to the common privy. . . .

It is thought good that all such as have garden plots to their houses should make privies within themselves to their houses. . . .

It is thought good that William Leeke, Thomas Pilkinton, and Robert Tomkins should make a privy betwixt them three to serve their houses. . . .

7.7   A Closet for Ladies [with] Diverse Sovereign Medicines and Salves for Sundry Diseases (1608)

From STC 5434 (BL copy), E7^v, F1^r, G8^v, K1^v–K2^v.

Until the seventeenth century, when medicine became an increasingly professionalized (and thus male-dominated) profession, most practical treatment was performed by women (especially outside London). Female practices, however, have a largely unrecorded history – except for notebooks in which literate women collected fancy recipes as well as medical concoctions. This Closet *compilation shares many charac-*

---

18 *lantern horns*: a thin sheet of animal horn used as a waterproof, translucent cover.
19 *proclamation*: public notice, sign.

teristics with the manuscript miscellanies, including its redundancies of therapy. It went into ten editions.

For the worms

Take a handful of basil-mints, a handful of lavender cotton, as much of wormwood, peach leaves as much, featherfew a handful, of unset leeks a handful; and boil them together in three spoonfuls of wine vinegar, and of his own water [urine] as much, and quilt them in a bag, and so lay it warm between his navel and his stomach.

For the worms

Take mare's milk and drink it as hot as you can have it from the mare, in the morning, fasting.

To know whether a child hath the worms or no

Take a piece of white leather and peck it full of holes with your knife, and rub it with wormwood, and spread honey on it, and strew the powder of alesackatrina, and lay it on the child's navel when he goeth to bed. And if he have the worms, the plaster will stick fast; and if he have them not, it will fall off.

For the worms

The powder of coralline to the weight of three pence in silver, given in the water of couchgrass.

Two remedies very good against worms in little children

Take flour of wheat well bolted [sifted], as much as will lie upon three crowns of gold. And put it in a glass and pour into it well-water, so much as will steep [soak] the said flour, and make it look as if it were milk and no thinner. Then give the child drink of it, and you shall see with his excrements the worms come forth dead, which is a very good remedy.

The second remedy against worms

For children that be so little that the medicine cannot be ministered at the mouth, you must take very good aqua vita, wherewith you must wash or wet the stomach or breast of the child. Then pour it upon the said place with the powder of fine myrrh and lay the child down a little while with his breast upward. And you shall see incontinently [*immediately*] the worms, with the child's dung, come forth dead.

To heal children of the lunatic disease, which happeneth unto them by reason of a worm with two heads that breedeth in their bodies, the which worm, coming to the heart, causeth such a passion in the child that oft times it killeth them

Take the tender stalks of a wilding-tree and dry them in the shadow, then stamp them well and sift them. And take of the said powder and roots of gentian and of long peony, of each of them a quarter of an ounce, and a quarter of an ounce of myrrh. All these well beaten to powder you must put in a dish or in some other vessel, and moist them with a little water. Then take of it with your two fingers and wet the lips and mouth of the child. Do this three or four times, and you shall see the worm come forth dead with the excrements.

7.8   Henry Best's Farming Account Books (1641)

From *Rural Economy in Yorkshire in 1641, Being the Farming and Account Books of Henry Best*, ed. Charles Best Robinson, Surtees Society, 33 (1857), 56–7, 93.

One of the great divides in Renaissance culture was that between city life and country life. The agricultural year had its own rhythms and rituals, as described by this Yorkshire landowner. Henry Best recorded farming methods and rural traditions as a guide for his son and heir. In these extracts he refers to the pea plant.

We began to pull pease this 16th of September being Thursday, being the same day that we got all mown barley. . . . We employ about this labor our mowers, binders, and only some of the ablest outliggers [*reapers*], where we think good. The men have eightpence a day and the women sixpence a day. . . . The best time for pulling of pease is in wet weather and dewy mornings, for that may be done best at such times when the ground is the wettest and softest. Then do they come up by the roots with most ease; again, they pull the best when they are the most feltered [*matted*] together. Pease pullers always lie one of their hands (viz., their uppermost hand) just on the end of the shaft, holding it something under the shaft, and their nethermost hand they always lie above the shaft, and so strike they with their hook near unto the roots of the pease. And so striking, they either break the stalks, cut the stalks, or else pull them up by the roots. And then ever as they strike they roll them on forwards, tumbling them over and over till

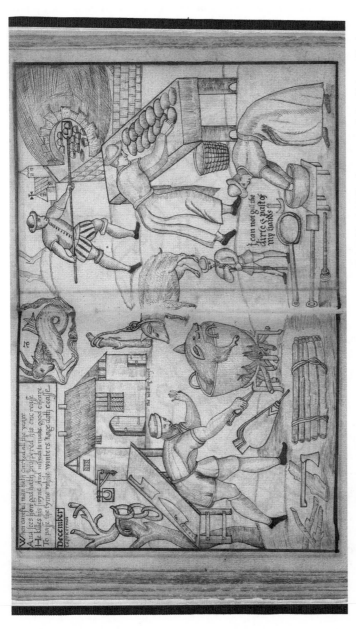

Figure 10 "December," from Thomas Fella's "A Book of Diverse Devises" (1585–1622). Courtesy of the Folger Shakespeare Library. This scene of country occupations in December shows a man who, near a "victualling house" or inn, "kills his swine . . . to make good cheer" in winter. The man has slaughtered a pig, chopped wood, used a bellows to build a fire, and now roasts one animal while another awaits its fate. Nearby, a woman shapes loaves of bread and a second man attends the bake oven. In the foreground, a woman complains that "I cannot get the dirt and paste off my hands" – the reference to "paste," a compound of flour and water, probably indicating that she should be understood to have kneaded the bread dough.

they be as many as they think sufficient for a reap [*sheaf*], and then do they part them and throw by the reap. Pease pullers are to be admonished that in making of their reaps they always observe to tumble them well over and wrap them up round, that they lie not flat towards the ground, for then do they drink up rain and keep long wet and moist. . . .

We use means always to get either eighteen or else twenty-four pease pullers, which we set always six on a land: viz., a woman and a man, a woman and a man, a woman or boy and a man, etc. – the weakest couple in the fore furrow, the next weakest in the hinder furrow, and the strongest on the rig [*ridge*], which should always come hindermost. We furnish all or most of them with pease-hooks (excepting one or two), and these we call for and see carried to the place where they used to lie so soon as that labor is done that our workfolks be come home.

It is usual in most places after they get all pease pulled or the last grain down to invite all the workfolks and their wives (that helped them that harvest) to supper, and then have they puddings,[20] bacon or boiled beef, flesh [*meat*] or apple pies, and then cream brought in platters, and everyone a spoon. Then after all they have hot cakes and ale; for they bake cakes and send for ale against that time. Some will cut their cake and put into the cream, and this feast is called the cream-pot or cream kit [*pail*]. For on the morning that they get all done, the workfolks will ask their dames if they have "good store of cream," and say that they "must have the cream kit anon."

7.9   Henry Bourne, *Antiquitates Vulgares: Or, the Antiquities of the Common People* (1725)

From pages 142, 145–6, 147–8, 151, 152–3, 157, 200–2, 210–11.

Henry Bourne was in training with a tailor until he was allowed to cancel his appren-ticeship indentures in order to continue his education. He received a Master's degree from the University of Cambridge in 1724 and was made a curate in Newcastle-upon-Tyne. The next year he published Antiquitates Vulgares. *Although his nominal purpose was to identify which traditional customs should be permitted and which should be abolished, he is often thought of as an early folk historian, here capturing practices that were centuries old.*

Of New Year's Day's Ceremonies

As the vulgar are always very careful to end the old year well, so they are also careful of beginning well the new one: as they end the former with a hearty

---

20 *puddings*: boiled, steamed, or baked dishes made with milk, eggs, and flour that could be either sweet or savory.

compotation [*drinking*], so they begin the latter with the sending of presents, which are termed New Year's gifts, to their friends and acquaintances. . . . Another old custom at this time is the wishing of a good New Year, either when a New Year's gift is presented, or when friends meet, or when a New Year's song is sung at the door, the burden of which is, *"we wish you a happy New Year."* . . . There is another custom observed at this time, which is called among us *mumming*, which is a changing of clothes between men and women, who, when dressed in each others' habits, go from neighbor's house to another and partake of their Christmas cheer and make merry with them in disguise, by dancing and singing and such-like merriments.

Of the Twelfth Day

In the Epiphany or manifestation of Christ to the gentiles, commonly called the Twelfth Day, the Eastern Magi were guided by the Star to pay their homage to their savior; and because they came that day, which is the twelfth after the day of the Nativity, it is therefore called Twelfth Day. The Twelfth Day itself is one of the greatest of the Twelve, and of more jovial observation than the others, for the visiting of friends and Christmas gambols [*frolics*]. . . . Not many years ago, this was a common Christmas gambol in both our universities, and it is still usual in other places of our land to give the name of king or queen to that person whose extraordinary luck hits upon that part of the divided cake which is honored above the others with a bean in it. . . . With some, Christmas ends with the Twelve Days, but with the generality of the vulgar, not till Candlemas [*2 February*]. Till then they continue feasting, and are ambitious of keeping some of their Christmas cheer, and then are as fond of getting quit of it. . . . The lengthening of the time from twelve to forty days seems to have been done out of honor to the Virgin Mary's lying-in. Under the old law, the time of Purification was forty days, which was to women then what the month is to women now. And as during that time the friends and relations of the women pay them visits and do them abundance of honor, so this time seems to have been calculated to do honor to the Virgin's lying-in.

Of May Day

On the calends, or the first day of May, commonly called May Day, the juvenile part of both sexes are wont to rise a little after midnight and walk to some neighboring wood accompanied with music and the blowing of horns, where they break down branches from the trees and adorn them with nosegays and crowns of flowers. When this is done they return with their booty homewards about the rising of the sun, and make their doors and windows to triumph in the flowery spoil. The afterpart of the day is chiefly spent in dancing round a tall pole which is called a May Pole, which, being placed in a convenient part of the village, stands there as it were consecrated to the goddess of flowers without the least violation offered it in the whole circle of the year. . . . This is the relic of an ancient custom among the heathen, who observed the four last days of April and the first of May in honor of the goddess Flora, who was imagined the deity presiding over the fruit and flowers. It was observed with all manner of obscenity and lewdness, and the undecent sports and postures of naked women who were called together with the noise of trumpets and danced before the spectators. . . . Many country people are of opinion that the observation of this ceremony is a good omen and a procurer of the success of the fruits of the earth.

Of Midsummer Eve

On the Eve of St. John Baptist, commonly called Midsummer Eve, it is usual in the most of country places and also here and there in towns and cities for both old and young to meet together and be merry over a large fire which is made in the open street. Over this they frequently leap and play at various games, such as running, wrestling, dancing, etc. But this is generally the exercise of the younger sort, for the old ones for the most part sit by as spectators and enjoy themselves and their bottle. And thus they spend the time till midnight, and sometimes till cock-crow. . . .

7.10   Hugh Plat, *The Jewel House of Art and Nature* (1594)

From STC 19991 (HL copy), C3^v–C4^r, E3^v–E4^r, F1^v–F2^r, G3^v, H2^{r-v}, H3^r, K2^{r-v}, K3^v, M1^{r-v}, M2^v–M3^r.

The full title of Hugh Plat's Jewel House *indicates that the volume contains "diverse rare and profitable inventions, together with sundry new experiments in the art of husbandry, distillation, and molding, faithfully and familiarly set down according to the author's own experience." His recipes, inventions, and hints were an eclectic mix of the useful and the fantastic. In 1605 James VI and I knighted Plat for such discoveries as a method for turning five cooking spits at once.*

A perspective ring that will discover all the cards that are near him that weareth it on his finger

A crystal stone or glass of the bigness of a twopenny piece of silver or thereabout, being the just half of a round ball or globe and cut hollow within, having a good foil[21] sweetly conveyed within the concave superficies thereof, and the

---

21 *foil:* a thin leaf of metal which was sometimes placed under a transparent substance to give it the appearance of a precious stone; also, metal placed under a precious stone to increase its brilliance.

stone itself neatly polished within and without, will give a lively representation to the eye of him that weareth it of all such cards as his companions which are next him do hold in their hands, especially if the owner thereof do take the upper end of the table for his place and, leaning now and then on his elbow or stretching out his arm, do apply his ring aptly for the purpose. I have discovered [*revealed*] this secret rather to discourage young novices from cardplay, who by one experiment may easily guess how many sleights [*trickeries*] and cozenages [*deceptions*] are daily practiced in our dicing and gaming houses, not doubting but that the general publication thereof will make the same so familiar with all men, as that I shall not justly be charged of any to have taught old knaves new school points. This secret is as yet merely French, but it had been long since either denizened or made English, if there could have been found any sufficient workman amongst us that could have foiled the stone so artificially [*skillfully*] as it ought to be. There be some English knights that can sufficiently testify the truth hereof by that which they have seen amongst the French gamesters.

To help venison that is tainted

If it be much tainted, cut away all the flesh that is green and cut out all the bones and bury it in a thin old coarse cloth a yard deep in the ground for twelve or twenty hours' space, and it will be sweet enough to be eaten, as I am informed by a gentlewoman of good credit [*reputation*] and upon her own practice.

A cheap lantern wherein a burning candle may be carried in any stormy or windy weather without any horn, glass, paper, or other defensative before it

Make a four-square box of six or seven inches every way, and seventeen or eighteen inches in length, with a socket in the bottom thereof. Close the sides well either with dovetails or cement, so as they take no air. Leave in the middest of one of the sides a slit or open door to put in the candle, which from the bottom to the top thereof may contain six or seven inches in length and two-and-a-half in breadth. Place your candle in the socket and, though it stand open and naked to the air without any defense, yet the wind will have no power to extinguish the same. The reason seemeth to be because the box is already full of air, whereby there is no room or place to contain any more. Neither can the air find any through-passage, by reason of the closeness thereof. The socket would be made to screw in and out at the bottom and then you may put in your candle before you fasten the socket. This is borrowed of one of the rarest mathematicians of our age.

To keep ink from freezing and molding

Put a few drops of aqua vitae[22] therein, and then it will not freeze in the hardest winter that can happen. And in summertime if you put salt therein it will not wax moldy, as I have been credibly informed.

How to speak by signs only, without the uttering of any word

Devise twenty-four signs, whereof every one may represent some one of the twenty-four letters.[23] But place your vowels for the more readiness in this manner: first, A upon the tip of your thumb on the left hand; E, upon the tip of your forefinger on the same hand; and so of the rest, so as when you lay the index or forefinger of your right hand on the tip of your thumb on the left hand, the party with whom you shall confer in this manner may always note the same for an A. The rest of the letters, which be consonants, may be understood by touching of several parts of your body or several gestures, countenances, or actions, as an hem for a B, a cross made on the forehead for a C, a fillip[24] for a D, and so of the rest. I have seen a gentleman together with a gentlewoman that were very ready in their conceited [*ingenious*] alphabet to deliver their minds each to other in this manner, whenas not any of the standers-by understood either word or letter of their meaning. And I hold the same a necessary art to be practiced of such as do naturally lack their speech, whereby they may be understood of others which otherwise could have no mutual conference with them.

A ready way for children to learn their ABC

Cause four large dice of bone or wood to be made, and upon every square one of the small letters of the cross-row [*alphabet*] to be graven, but in some bigger shape. And the child, using to play much with them and being always told what letter chanceth, will soon gain his alphabet, as it were by the way of sport or pastime. I have heard of a pair of cards whereon most of the principal grammar rules have been printed, and the schoolmaster hath found good sport thereat with his scholars.

---

22 *aqua vitae*: a common distilled spirit or unrectified alcohol.
23 *the twenty-four letters*: Because *i* and *j* were used interchangeably to signify the same letter, as were *u* and *v*, the Elizabethan alphabet had just twenty-four letters.
24 *fillip*: a gesture involving bending the top joint of a finger against the thumb and releasing it sharply.

To help a chimney that is on fire, presently

When you see the chimney on fire, forthwith get a large thick blanket or coverlet and, with the help of two or three persons, let the same be held close both above and below unto the mouth of the chimney, so as no air may enter. And if you can come easily to the top of the chimney, cover the same close also, either with a fit board or else with wet woolen cloths. And so the fire wanting air will presently go out and be smothered.

How to prevent drunkenness

Drink first a good large draft of salad oil, for that will float upon the wine which you shall drink and suppress the spirits from ascending into the brain. Also what quantity soever of new milk you drink first, you may well drink thrice as much wine after without danger of being drunk. But how sick you shall be with this prevention, I will not here determine. Neither would I have set down this experiment but only for the help of such modest drinkers as sometimes in company are drawn or rather forced to pledge in full bowls such quaffing [drinking] companions as they would be loath to offend, and will require reason at their hands (as they term it).

To kill rats in a garner

Be sure there be no holes in the bottom or sides of your garner [storehouse for corn and grains] or anywhere else, saving above the boards, which you must place shelving wise or in the manner of a penthouse [sloping roof] throughout the garner, about half a yard or two foot from the corn, so as when the rats have leaped down into the bulk of corn, they shall not be able to rise or bolt up again before you have sped [killed] them.

How to take away the offense of noisome vaults[25]

Make the vent thereof upward as large or larger than the tunnel downward and carry the same up to a convenient height. For so the offensive air as fast as it riseth hath issue [exits] and stayeth not in the passage.

To make parchment clear and transparent, to serve for diverse purposes

Make choice of the finest and thinnest parchment you can get, scrape the same over with a knife till it become very thin (but first you must wet it well in water),

---

25 *noisome vaults*: foul-smelling privies.

then strain it upon a frame and fasten it well. And when it is dry, oil it all over
with a pencil [*fine brush*], with the oil of sweet almonds, oil of turpentine, or oil
of spike [*French lavender*]; some content themselves with linseed oil. And when
it is thorough dry it will show very clear and serve in windows instead of glass,
especially in such rooms as are subject to overseers [*others looking in*]. You may
draw any personage, beast, tree, flower, or coat-armor [*heraldic insignia*] upon the
parchment before it be oiled, and then cutting your parchment into square
panes and making slight frames for them, they will make a pretty show in your
windows and keep the room very warm. This I commend before oiled paper
because it is more lasting, and will endure the blustering and stormy weather
much better than paper.

7.11   Thomas Hill, *The Most Pleasant Art of the Interpretation of Dreams* (1576)

From STC 13498 (FSL copy), A6^{r-v}, F7^{v}, G2^{v}–G3^{r}, G6^{r-v}, I4^{r}.

*Thomas Hill was known as an "honest and learned" compiler of almanacs; he was the
first to include blank pages to allow for personal notes. Many of his books on science
and the supernatural were translated from Latin and Italian, including two which
introduced the work of Paracelsus to a wider audience. Hill specialized in gardening,
physiognomy (the art of discerning character from facial features), and the interpretation of such presumed portents as comets, rainbows, earthquakes, and dreams.*

What hazard of life? What loss of substance? Or what danger of limb can a
dream put the dreamer unto? Even so much as when he awaketh, he wondreth
how such imagination or fancy crept into his mind. Be his dream never so terrible or fearful – as falling into the hands of thieves, were wounded by them,
fighting in bloody battles, or on every side beset with enemies, in such manner
as it would make a stout man to quake – yet when he awaketh no skin is broken,
he hath no ache in his bones, he is still in his quiet bed, as whole and as safe
as when he went to rest: nothing so nor so; it was only a dream. If now he have
his knowledge of divination, what a comfort will it be to him that, examining
the circumstances in their due time and order, shall prognosticate what such
things portend. And thereby may solace himself with good haps [*fortune*], and
labor to prevent or hinder the imminent misfortune, or at the least arm himself
so strongly with patience as quietly to bear them. For a mischief known of
before and diligently looked for is not so grievous as when it cometh on a
sudden. It is a wonderful thing and almost incredible that dreams should have
such virtue in them, were it not that God hath revealed it unto us when he
himself, as a mean, often used them to open unto his people of Israel his secret
will and pleasure. . . .

One dreamed that he went from home into a strange country and lost the key of his house, and when he came home again, he found his daughter to have lost her maidenhead. Which dream declared to him that all things at home could not be in safety when the key so lost was ready for another to take up. For either it signified, as it is thought, the misusage of his family; or else that his wife, daughters, or maidens were enticed to folly in his house; or else otherwise that his servants bribed and pilfered away from him. . . .

A certain woman dreamed that she thought she had her husband's privities cut from the rest of the body in her hands and that she took great care and much foresight how to keep them: who after bare her husband a son which she brought up herself. For the husband's privities signified the son which was got by him. And that it was taken or cut away from the rest of the body signified her bringing up of her son. But her husband was after bereft of life by death. . . .

And one thought in his dream to find in his jacket or coat very many and great stinking worms and to abhor them, and that also would shake them off, but could not. Who the next day following learned or understood that his wife had her accustomed fellowship carnally with another man, and understanding the same became very pensive and perplexed of mind, insomuch that he would have departed from her, but did not because he was otherwise prohibited or stayed by a certain letter. For the jacket or coat signified the wife girt or wrapped about him; and the stinking worms, her pollution. And whereas he could not pluck and cast them away at his will signified that he could neither after his desire and purpose depart from his wife.

And one thought in his sleep that he saw his house on fire, who after received letters that his brother lay grievously sick, and whiles he prepared himself to journey, a messenger came declaring him to be dead. Who after counted the time from that hour [in] which he saw the dream, conceived that his brother then died. But commonly this dream doth threaten death either to the dreamer or some principal of the house.

7.12   Simon Forman's Dream of the Queen (23 January 1597)

From Simon Forman's Journal, Ashmole Ms 208: 226, transcribed by A. L. Rowse in *Simon Forman: Sex and Society in Shakespeare's Age* (London: Weidenfeld and Nicolson, 1974), 20.

Dreams about leaders have long been a common phenomenon; they show the extent to which much common culture can be located in the person of the monarch. Simon Forman was a practicing physician with legitimate medical knowledge; he developed his own successful cure for the plague, for example, and argued that disease could not be diagnosed simply by examining urine. At the same time, more notoriously, he was an astrologer, alchemist, and necromancer.

Dreamt that I was with the queen and that she was a little elderly woman in a coarse white petticoat all unready.[26] She and I walked up and down through lanes and closes [*enclosed fields*], talking and reasoning. At last we came over a great close where were many people, and there were two men at hard words. One of them was a weaver, a tall man with a reddish beard, distract of his wits. She talked to him and he spoke very merrily unto her, and at last did take her and kiss her. So I took her by the arm and did put her away, and told her the fellow was frantic [*lunatic*]. So we went from him and I led her by the arm still, and then we went through a dirty lane. She had a long white smock very clean and fair, and it trailed in the dirt and her coat behind. I took her coat and did carry it up a good way, and then it hung too low before. I told her she should do me a favor to let me wait on her, and she said I should. Then said I, "I mean to wait upon you and not under you, that I might make this belly a little bigger[27] to carry up this smock and coat out of the dirt." And so we talked merrily. Then she began to lean upon me, when we were past the dirt, and to be very familiar with me, and methought she began to love me. When we were alone, out of sight, methought she would have kissed me.

7.13   *The Lamentation of Master Page's Wife of Plymouth, who, being enforced by her parents to wed him against her will, did most wickedly consent to his murder, for the love of George Strangwidge. For which fact she suffered death at Barnstaple in Devonshire. Written with her own hand a little before her death. [Sung] to the tune of "Fortune my Foe"* (1635)

From STC 6557.4 (BL copy).

Ballads and illustrated broadsides were a principal medium of common culture, often printed on just one side so they could be posted publicly. A favorite theme of the sensational press was domestic violence, especially when women featured not as victims but instead as spousal murderers. This ballad purports to convey the homicide Mistress Page's own words of repentance. A pamphlet version of the same case emphasized instead the way in which the crime was solved. The tale was also represented on stage by Ben Jonson and Thomas Dekker. Because the play is lost, there is no knowing whether it was a moral fable (like the ballad), a detective story (like the pamphlet), or, as seems likely from these authors, a black comedy of city life.

---

26 *petticoat all unready*: The petticoat was an upper-body undergarment, a tight-fitting coat or tunic; if it was revealed, its wearer was "unready," or in dishabille.

27 *make this belly a little bigger*: make her pregnant.

Unhappy she (whom fortune hath, forlorn,
Despis'd of grace), that proferred grace did scorn.
My lawless love that, luckless, wrought my woe.
My discontent, content did overthrow.

My loathèd life, too late, I do lament.
My hateful deed with heart I do repent.
A wife I was that willful went awry,
And for that fault am here prepared to die.

In blooming years, my father's greedy mind
Against my will a match for me did find.
Great wealth there was, yea, gold and money store.
But yet my heart had chosen long before.

My eye mislik'd my father's liking quite.
My heart did loath my parents' fond delight.
My grievèd mind and fancy told to me
That with his age my youth could not agree.

On knees I crav'd they would not me constrain.
With tears I cried their purpose to refrain.
With sighs and sobs I did them often move,
I might not wed whereas I could not love.

But all in vain my speeches still I spent.
My father's will my wishes did prevent.
Though wealthy Page possessed my outward part,
George Strangwidge still was lodgèd in my heart.

I wedded was but wrappèd in all woe.
Great discontents within my heart did grow.
I loath'd to live, yet liv'd in deadly strife,
Because perforce I was made Page's wife.

My chosen eyes could not his sight abide.
My tender youth did scorn his aged side.
Scant could I taste the meat whereon he fed,
My legs did loathe to lodge within his bed.

Cause knew I none I should despise him so,
That such disdain within my mind did grow –
Save only this, that fancy did me move
And told me still George Strangwidge was my love.

But here began my downfall and decay.
In mind I mus'd to make him straight away.
I that became his discontented wife,
Contented was he should be rid of life.

Methinks that heaven calls vengeance for my fact.
Methinks the world condemns my monstrous act.
Methinks within, my conscience tells me true,
That for that deed hell fire is my due.

My pensive life doth sorrow for my sin.
For this offense my soul doth bleed within.
Yet mercy, Lord, for mercy do I cry,
Save thou my soul and let my body die.

8

Literary Production and Reception

Perhaps Edmund Spenser, William Shakespeare, John Donne, and John Milton would have been literary geniuses in any time or place. But the poets as we know them emerged out of the uniquely nurturing conditions of the Renaissance. Humanist scholars were rediscovering a treasure trove of classical texts and translating them into the vernaculars of Europe. The English language was especially full of possibility, with its richly reduplicative vocabularies from Anglo-Saxon and Latinate sources, its distinctive regional variations, its archaisms and neologisms, and its specialized idioms from the worlds of law and religion. English authors were also aware of lively experiments in prosody on the Continent; they undertook their own versions of heroic couplets, ottava rima, terza rima, poulter's measure, septenaries, rime royal, hexameters, dizains, douzains, and, above all, the sonnet. Writing was a vibrant, collective art, with works circulating in manuscript at the royal court, between noble households, at the universities of Oxford and Cambridge, and at London's training centers for lawyers, the Inns of Court.

Textual encounters were not reserved to the privileged and the highly educated, however, in part because learned argument was now conducted in English as well as Latin. The revolutionary technology of movable type made mass-produced books available to the public at large. Literacy was encouraged by Reformation doctrine as a tool for devotional thought, but it came also to be thought of in terms of social utility. The aim was to develop a responsible and conforming citizenry. As the authorities recognized that the wider transmission of ideas was a double-edged sword, they moved to control publication through a program of licensing and censorship. Ben Jonson, for example, was imprisoned briefly for the dangerous ideas in his play *The Isle of Dogs*.

In general, authors had few rights of intellectual property in this period. But the cult of celebrity that attached to some Renaissance writers – Jonson among them – would eventually pave the way for a notion of literary creativity that has predominated ever since.

Textual Technologies

Until the mid-fifteenth century, texts existed exclusively in manuscript – that is, they were handwritten with quill and ink. Copies were made, one by one, by monks and professional scribes. Johannes Gutenberg is generally credited with having invented the movable-type printing press in Germany in the late 1440s. In 1455, in a matter of days, he was able to produce as many as 200 copies of the Bible, 150 on paper and another fifty on vellum, or treated animal skin (estimates of his first print run vary). Each of Gutenberg's letters was shaped in metal in a reversed form and attached to an individual wooden block. Blocks were placed in wooden trays in the order necessary to reproduce lines of text. The raised metal surfaces were then coated with an oil-based ink, a piece of paper was laid across them, and a heavy press caused the paper to be imprinted. For each sheet, the sequence of inking and compression was followed by drying. A sheet folded once, to create four large pages, was used for a volume called a *folio*; a sheet folded twice and trimmed, to create eight smaller pages, was used for a *quarto*. Paper, made from cotton rags in a process that had been invented in China in about 1100, took ink better than vellum did. It was the most expensive element of production – more than labor and ink combined.

All books printed before 1500 are called *incunables*, because they represent the cradle or infancy of printing. They were designed to imitate manuscripts with a continuous, unbroken style, typefaces that looked like handwriting, and ornamentation added manually with colored inks. In time, though, printed books developed their own, more reader-friendly form, with punctuation, indentation, and page breaks to create sentences, paragraphs, and chapters. Page numbers and indices were also added. A book was generally sold without a binding, as a collection of pages, which left the outer sheets vulnerable to dirt and damage. The title page was a practical invention that served as a protective wrapper and soon was exploited for its useful advertising function, describing the contents in ways designed to appeal to the consumer.

The democratization of knowledge was a revolution that did not go unnoticed in its own time. In 1620 Sir Francis Bacon wrote that "We should note the force, effect, and consequences of inventions which are nowhere more conspicuous than in those three which were unknown to the ancients, namely printing, gunpowder, and the compass. For these three have changed the appearance and state of the whole world."

The Book Trade in England

The first English printing press was operated by William Caxton in 1476. Printing would never be as fine an art in England as it was in the rest of Europe. Germany continued to be the capital of the western print trade, with an international book fair held in Frankfurt twice yearly. For England's industry, any day in London was a local book fair, because the open yard around St. Paul's Cathedral was crowded with bookstalls. St. Paul's was a popular meeting place for people who conducted their business as they walked up and down its aisles. Thus, books and broadsheets were at the center of urban life.

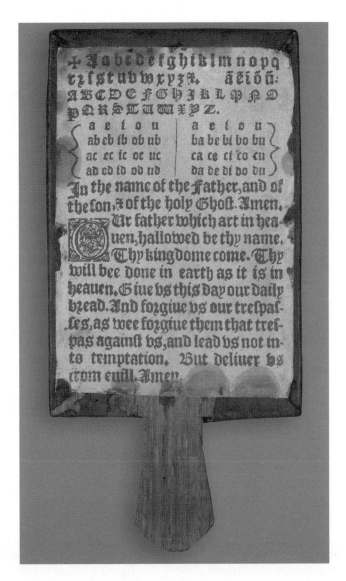

Figure 11 Hornbook. Courtesy of the Folger Shakespeare Library.

Children learned to read with small, hand-held paddles of wood to which were pasted sheets printed in "black-letter" type. Variations on the alphabet and common letter-combinations were followed by words familiar from the ceremony of baptism ("In the name of the Father, and of the son, and of the Holy Ghost. Amen") and by the Paternoster, or Lord's Prayer. This surviving example of a hornbook lacks the transparent layer of animal horn that would have been applied to protect the text (and for which it was named).

The process by which learning passed out of the monasteries, with their scriptoria and manuscript collections, and into secular universities, with their printing presses and libraries, was accelerated in England by the Dissolution engineered by Henry VIII. Those who were serious about ideas read texts in Latin, French, Italian, and other Continental languages. In 1602, however, Sir Thomas Bodley included English-language volumes in the collections of Oxford University. He arranged that a copy of every book registered with the London Company of Stationers was deposited in his Bodleian Library.

Literacy

Just how many people were able to read? Literacy rates were once estimated by sampling legal documents and comparing the number of signatures with the number of personal "marks," symbols that substituted for signatures. However, because some people who used marks in one situation showed their ability to sign in another, this is not a reliable standard of measure. And just because people could not write, it did not mean they could not read; these were skills taught separately. Numeracy was yet another learned ability, and a particularly useful one for most kinds of work. Scholars now estimate that in 1550 all members of the gentry were literate, along with 40 percent of the yeomanry and 20 percent of laborers. In total, this was perhaps 20 percent of men and 5 percent of women.

Statistics such as these, however, misrepresent the nature of reading in the period. It was not always a solitary activity, or a silent one. Often, it was a communal experience. The member of the household who was most skilled read aloud to others, especially from the Bible, of which there were many copies in private households. In this way, the common culture that was created by print had a broader reach than skills levels alone can indicate. Remarkably enough, there were 400,000 almanacs sold annually in England, one for every twelve members of the population, children as well as adults.

One of the ways in which print and manuscript co-existed throughout the sixteenth and seventeenth centuries was that individuals copied selected passages from printed books into their own notebooks. This practice, known as "commonplacing," meant that books had a larger circulation than their print run would indicate. As a way of creating a personal library of favorite quotations, it was a sign of how deeply people engaged with texts and of the incalculable effects of print culture upon intellectual life.

Literary Landmarks

One of the most famous printing initiatives of Tudor England was an anthology of poetry: *Songs and Sonnets Written by the Right Honorable Lord Henry Howard Late*

Earl of Surrey and Other. The collection, known as "Tottel's Miscellany" for its printer, Richard Tottel, was like a commonplace book in print, or a great-house exchange made public. First issued on 5 June 1557, it proved so popular that it was reprinted that same year, twice more in 1559, and then again in 1565, 1567, 1574, 1585, and 1587. The first edition had 271 poems, forty of them by Surrey and ninety-seven by Sir Thomas Wyatt; more were added later. Other poetry collections followed: *A Paradise of Dainty Devices* (ten editions between 1576 and 1606), *The Court of Virtue* (1565), *A Gorgeous Gallery of Gallant Inventions* (1577), and *A Handful of Pleasant Delights* (1584). The pastoral poem "The Passionate Shepherd's Song," from Shakespeare's *Love's Labor's Lost*, was reprinted first in an anthology called *The Passionate Pilgrim* (1599) and then in *England's Helicon* (1600).

Some of the most important literary efforts of the period were devoted to making Greek, Latin, Italian, and French texts available in English. There were notable translations of Virgil's *Aeneid*, by Henry Howard (Earl of Surrey), Thomas Phaer, and Richard Stanyhurst (1554, 1558, and 1582, respectively); Castiglione's *The Courtier*, by Sir Thomas Hoby (1561; see document 6.1); Ovid's *Metamorphoses*, by Arthur Golding (1567); Ovid's *Elegies*, by Christopher Marlowe (published posthumously, *c.*1640); Plutarch's *Parallel Lives*, by Sir Thomas North (1579; see below); Ariosto's *Orlando Furioso*, by Sir John Harington (1591); Plutarch's *Morals*, by Philemon Holland (1603); Montaigne's *Essays*, by John Florio (1603); and Homer's *Iliad* and *Odyssey*, by George Chapman (1616).

The nation also defined itself through chronicle histories: Edward Hall's *The Union of the Two Noble and Illustrate Families of Lancaster and York* (a celebration of the Tudor line and Tudor policies, published in 1548; see document 1.2), Raphael Holinshed's *Chronicles of England, Scotland, and Ireland* (1577, with a great social-history preface by William Harrison, "The Description of England," excerpted in 7.1); John Stow's *A Survey of London* (a street-by-street description of the capital city in 1598); and William Camden's *Annales rerum Anglicarum et Hibernicarum regnante Elizabetha* (a 1615 account of Elizabeth's reign soon translated into English; see document 1.7). In 1555, another revolutionary genre was introduced with the publication of *A Mirror for Magistrates*. This was a history anthology, but with history shaped into a sequence of individual tragedies such as that of Jane Shore, the mistress of Edward IV. Like the narrative chronicles, it was a goldmine of story lines for playwrights. If poetic anthologies had multiple authors, so, too, did these historical works. Edward Hall and Raphael Holinshed, for example, were lead names for larger teams.

The Birth of the Author

Collaborative and anonymous authorship were also common features of play-writing. Shakespeare, for example, contributed one scene to the play *Sir Thomas*

More, and his co-author for the late plays *Henry VIII* and *The Two Noble Kinsmen* was John Fletcher. At the start of his career some of his plays were published in quarto without attribution. When his name began to appear on title pages, this was a sign that it had become viable as a market commodity.

There was a literary sensation when Ben Jonson assembled a collection of his own poems, court masques, civic entertainments, and stage plays, printed them in folio size, and called them his *Works*. To represent the drama of the public theater as a serious literary activity was audacious; had he forgotten, some asked, the difference between work and play? But Jonson's folio of 1616 may have provided the inspiration for (arguably) the most important book of the Tudor–Stuart period, *Master William Shakespeare's Comedies, Histories, & Tragedies*, generally known as "The First Folio" of 1623 (there were to be three more editions of Shakespeare's plays before the end of the century).

In the 1590s Shakespeare had published a sequence of sonnets and two narrative poems, but most scholars have concluded that he was otherwise uninterested in cultivating a print readership. He grew wealthy not as an author but as a shareholder in the new commercial industry of the public theater – that is, he shared in the profits from admission fees taken at the door. Eighteen of the plays in the Folio had been printed before, in quarto, but eighteen had not. Plays such as *Antony and Cleopatra*, *As You Like It*, *Julius Caesar*, *Macbeth*, *The Tempest*, and *Twelfth Night* would have been lost forever were it not for the initiative of Shakespeare's friends and business partners John Heminges and Henry Condell. They undertook the difficult business of finding texts and securing rights *after* Shakespeare's death in 1616. The fact that rights were held not by Shakespeare's heirs or by his colleagues, but instead by previous publishers, made it a difficult project.

Attitudes towards intellectual property would change in succeeding years, in no small part because of Shakespeare himself. The Folio gives evidence of the market value that could be attached to an authorial name, and with value eventually came power. Where the fifteenth century saw the infancy of printing, the sixteenth and seventeenth centuries saw the birth of the idea of the Author.

8.1   Thomas Wilson, *The Art of Rhetoric* (1553)

From STC 25799 (HL copy), a1^v–a3^r.

Grammar-school education was organized around the "trivium" – grammar, rhetoric, and logic – and the "quadrivium" – arithmetic, music, geometry, and astronomy. Although Wilson's was not the first English-language treatise on rhetoric (a textbook by Leonard Cox was published as early as 1524), it was especially important as a humanist document, domesticating the Latin works of Quintilian and Cicero for writers in English. A revised edition came out in 1560, and there were reissues of this popular text in 1562, 1563, 1567, 1580, 1584, and 1585. Wilson was concerned not with the matter or subject of writing, but with its style of presentation.

The end [purpose] of rhetoric

Three things are required of an orator: to teach, to delight, and to persuade.

First, therefore, an orator must labor to tell his tale that the hearers may well know what he meaneth and understand him wholly, the which he shall with ease do if he utter his mind in plain words such as are usually received, and tell it orderly without going about the bush. That if he do not this, he shall never do the other. For what man can be delighted, or yet be persuaded, with the only hearing of those things which he knoweth not what they mean? The tongue is ordained to express the mind that one might understand another's meaning. Now what availeth to speak when none can tell what the speaker meaneth? Therefore, Phavorinus, the philosopher, as Gellius telleth the tale, did hit a young man over the thumbs very handsomely for using over-old and over-strange words.[1] . . . And remember that which Caesar sayeth: "Beware, as long as thou livest, of strange words, as thou wouldest take heed and eschew great rocks in the sea."

The next part that he hath to play is to cheer his guests and to make them take pleasure with hearing of things wittily devised and pleasantly set forth. Therefore, every orator should earnestly labor to file [*smooth*] his tongue, that his words may slide with ease and that in his deliverance he may have such grace as the sound of a lute or any such instrument doth give. Then his sentences must be well-framed and his words aptly used throughout the whole discourse of his oration.

Thirdly, such quickness of wit must be showed, and such pleasant saws [*adages*] so well applied, that the ears may find much delight – whereof I will speak largely when I shall entreat of moving laughter. And, assuredly, nothing is more needful than to quicken these heavy-loaden wits of ours and much to cherish these our lumpish [*sluggish*] and unwieldy natures. For except men find delight, they will not long abide. Delight them and win them; weary them, and you lose them forever. And that is the reason that men commonly tarry the end of a merry play and cannot abide the half-hearing of a sour, checking [*reproving*] sermon. Therefore even these ancient preachers must now and then play the fools in the pulpit, to serve the tickle [*credulous*] ears of their fleeting audience, or else they are like [*likely*] sometimes to preach to the bare walls. For though the spirit be apt and our will prone [*willing*], yet our flesh is so heavy, and humors[2] so overwhelm us, that we cannot, without refreshing, long abide to hear any one thing. Thus we see that to delight is needful, without the which weightier matters will not be heard at all.

---

1 *as Gellius telleth the tale*: Aulus Gellius's *Noctus Atticae* was effectively a commonplace book. One story involved Phavorinus, a Roman philosopher known for his eloquence (although few of his works survive).

2 *humors*: constitutional tendencies or temperaments believed to have been determined by the relative proportions of four fluids in the body: black bile, yellow bile, phlegm, and blood (for more, see document 10.7).

By what means eloquence is attained

First, needful it is that he which desireth to excel in this gift of oratory and longeth to prove an eloquent man must naturally have a wit and an aptness thereunto. Then must he to his book and learn to be well-stored with knowledge, that he may be able to minister matter for all causes necessary. The which when he hath got plentifully, he must use much exercise, both in writing and also in speaking. For though he have a wit and learning together, yet shall they both little avail without much practice. What maketh the lawyer to have such utterance? Practice. What maketh the preacher to speak so roundly [*fluently*]? Practice. Yea, what maketh women go so fast away with their words? Marry, practice, I warrant you.

8.2   *Injunctions Given by the Queen's Majesty* (1559)

From STC 10099.5 (BL copy), D1^{r-v}.

In recognition of the persuasiveness of rhetoric, the Crown was concerned to monitor all publishing activity. These 1559 provisions for the licensing of printed materials were issued with the Book of Common Prayer *and then updated on a near-annual basis. The* Injunctions *authorized government censorship and also promoted self-censorship. The licensing register had the further, unintended function of preserving information about books for which no copies survive today. We would not know they had existed were it not for the lists that the London Company of Stationers was required to maintain to satisfy the royal* Injunctions.

Because there is a great abuse in the printers of books (which for covetousness chiefly regard not what they print so they may have gain), whereby ariseth great disorder by publication of unfruitful, vain, and infamous books and papers, the Queen's Majesty straightly chargeth and commandeth that no manner of person shall print any manner of book or paper of what sort, nature, or in what language soever it be, except the same be first licensed by Her Majesty by express words in writing, or by six of her Privy Council, or be perused and licensed by the Archbishops of Canterbury and York, the Bishop of London, the Chancellors of both Universities, the Bishop being Ordinary,[3] and the Archdeacon also of the place where any such shall be printed, or by two of them, whereof the Ordinary of the place to be always one. And that the names of such as shall allow the same to be added in the end of every such work for a testimony of the allowance thereof. And because many pamphlets, plays, and ballads be oftentimes printed

---

3 *Bishop being Ordinary*: the ecclesiast who has jurisdiction in a diocese in his own right.

wherein regard would be had that nothing therein should be either heretical, seditious, or unseemly for Christian ears, Her Majesty likewise commandeth that no manner of person shall enterprise to print any such except the same be licensed by such Her Majesty's commissioners, or three of them, as be appointed in the City of London to hear and determine diverse causes ecclesiastical tending to the execution of certain statutes made the last Parliament for uniformity of order in religion. And if any shall sell or utter [*vend*] any manner of books or papers being not licensed, as is above said, that the same party shall be punished by order of the said commissioners as to the quality of the fault shall be thought meet. And touching all other books of matters of religion or policy or governance that hath been printed either on this side the seas or on the other side, because the diversity of them is great and that there needeth good consideration to be had of the particularities thereof, Her Majesty referreth the prohibition or permission thereof to the order which her said commissioners within the City of London shall take and notify. According to the which, Her Majesty straightly commandeth all manner her subjects and specially the wardens and Company of Stationers to be obedient – provided that these orders do not extend to any profane authors and works in any language that hath been heretofore commonly received or allowed in any the universities or schools, but the same may be printed and used as by good order they were accustomed.

8.3 Sir Thomas North, Preface to *The Lives of the Noble Grecians and Romans Compared Together by that Grave Learned Philosopher and Historiographer Plutarch of Chaeronea, Translated out of Greek into French by James Amyot . . . and out of French into English by Thomas North* (1579)

From STC 20065 (HL copy), *2^{r-v}.

To produce an English-language Plutarch, North worked primarily from a French translation, though he made corrections that suggest he also consulted Greek and Latin versions. Plutarch paired Greek and Roman lives (for example, Theseus and Romulus) and is best known as a source for many of Shakespeare's plays (Antony and Cleopatra, Coriolanus, *and* Julius Caesar). *All authors with literary ambitions wrote "dedicatory epistles," either in gratitude (as Ben Jonson was to do – see document 8.6) or in hopes of gaining patronage (as was the case for North).*

To the Most High and Mighty Princess Elizabeth, by the Grace of God of England, France, and Ireland Queen, Defender of the Faith, etc.

Under hope of Your Highness' gracious and accustomed favor, I have presumed to present here unto Your Majesty Plutarch's *Lives*, translated as a book fit to be protected by your Highness and meet [*suitable*] to be set forth in

English. For who is fitter to give countenance to so many great states than such an high and mighty princess? Who is fitter to revive the dead memory of their fame than she that beareth the lively image of their virtues? Who is fitter to authorize a work of so great learning and wisdom than she whom all do honor as the muse of the world? Therefore I humbly beseech Your Majesty to suffer the simpleness of my translation to be covered under the ampleness of Your Highness' protection. For, most gracious Sovereign, though this book be no book for Your Majesty's self – who are meeter to be the chief story than a student therein, and can better understand it in Greek than any man can make it English – yet I hope the common sort of your subjects shall not only profit themselves hereby but also be animated to the better service of Your Majesty. For among all the profane books that are in reputation at this day there is none – Your Highness best knows – that teacheth so much honor, love, obedience, reverence, zeal, and devotion to princes as these *Lives* of Plutarch do. How many examples shall your subjects read here of several persons and whole armies, of noble and base, of young and old, that both by sea and land, at home and abroad have strained their wits, not regarded their states, ventured their persons, cast away their lives not only for the honor and safety but also for the pleasure of their princes?

Then well may the readers think if they have done this for heathen kings, what should we do for Christian princes? If they have done this for glory, what should we do for religion? If they have done this without hope of heaven, what should we do that look for immortality? And so, adding the encouragement of these examples to the forwardness of their own dispositions, what service is there in war, what honor in peace, which they will not be ready to do for their worthy queen?

And therefore, that Your Highness may give grace to the book and the book may do his service to Your Majesty, I have translated it out of French, and do here most humbly present the same unto Your Highness, beseeching Your Majesty with all humility not to reject the good meaning but to pardon the errors of your most humble and obedient subject and servant, who prayeth God long to multiply all graces and blessings upon Your Majesty. Written the sixteenth day of January 1579.

Your Majesty's most humble and obedient servant, Thomas North

8.4   Grace Mildmay's Advice to her Children (before 1620)

From Northamptonshire Central Library Westmorland (Apethorpe) Miscellaneous Volume 35, 1:1–4, 2:29–31.

Disinherited by her father, largely abandoned by the husband her parents chose for her, Lady Grace Mildmay developed an active interior life. She compiled voluminous scientific papers with diagnostic information as well as recipes for medicinal oils, powders, and pills. James VI, who dined at her house when traveling from Scotland to London to assume the English throne, praised her as "one of the most excellent confectioners in England." Her memoir reveals little of the unhappiness she experienced privately. It is highly conventional in recommending reading for moral instruction. Omitted from this extract are Mildmay's many marginal references to relevant Biblical passages.

I have found by experience (and I commend unto my children as approved) this to be the best course to set ourselves in from the beginning unto the end of our lives. That is to say: first, to begin with the Scriptures, to read them with all diligence and humility, as a disciple, continually every day in some measure until we have gone through the whole book of God from the first of Genesis unto the last of the Revelation and then begin again and so over and over without weariness. To the end that our heart, soul, spirits, and whole inner man may first be seasoned with it and receive the true stamp and lively impression thereof. Whereby we may the better judge of all learning whatsoever, and be able to make true use and good application of all men's judgments and educations, and be confirmed in this constant resolution: never to receive any doctrine from men which proceedeth not from God according to the truth of his word in all sanctity and true holiness. . . .

Also to make ourselves expert in the knowledge of the histories contained in the book of *Acts and Monuments* of the church [*John Foxe's* Book of Martyrs, *excerpted in 4.6*], whereby our faith may be increased and strengthened and our hearts encouraged manfully to suffer death and to give our lives for the testimony of the truth of God wherein we are thus confirmed and sealed by the death and blood of Christ.

Also to make ourselves expert in the understanding and knowledge of the chronicles of the land, what matters of moment have passed from the beginning under the government of our royal and anointed princes. Whereby we may be instructed to imitate and to follow the good examples of true and faithful subjects and to have their worthy acts and exploits in memory which are registered for the same end, and also whereby we may avoid and shun all treasons and treacherous attempts and all unfaithful combinations with plotters and devisers of evil. . . .

Also to be well instructed in the statutes and laws of this land is very profitable and necessary, whereby they may keep themselves within the compass thereof without controlment or running into danger.

Also the wise and witty sentences of the philosophers being heathen men without the knowledge of God are worthy books to be used sometimes for recreation. For they exhort unto virtue and dehort [*dissuade*] from vice, whereby the excellent gifts of God may be magnified in them. . . .

A mind thus furnished will think all times ill bestowed in books of idle plays and of all such fruitless and unprofitable matter which will pervert and carry the mind from all goodness and [which] is an introduction unto all evil. . . .

My reverend mother . . . thought it ever dangerous to suffer young people to read or study books wherein was good and evil mingled together, for that by nature we are inclined rather to learn and retain the evil than the good. . . . And further, she said that she could give me jewels and pearl and costly apparel but she would not until I were furnished with virtue in my mind and decked inwardly. And [she] willed me first to seek the kingdom of God and the righteousness thereof, and all those things should be given to me.

8.5   Sir Francis Bacon, "Of Studies" (1625)

From *The Essays or Counsels, Civil and Moral, of Francis Lord Verulam, Viscount St. Alban*, STC 1148 (CUL copy), Pp3^r.

Sir Francis Bacon envisioned reading as an active and participatory engagement, not just a means of knowledge-acquisition. In 1597 he published a first collection of short pieces modeled on the genre-bending Essays *of Michel de Montaigne. "Of Studies" was among them. But he continued to refine his ideas, as well as to add chapters; this extract is from the revised and expanded edition of 1625 (see also document 5.11).*

Read not to contradict and confute, nor to believe and take for granted, nor to find talk and discourse, but to weigh and consider. Some books are to be tasted, others to be swallowed, and some few to be chewed and digested: that is, some books are to be read only in parts, others to be read but not curiously [*intensively*], and some few to be read wholly and with diligence and attention. Some books also may be read by deputy, and extracts made of them by others. But that would be only in the less important arguments and meaner sort of books, else distilled books are like common distilled waters, flashy things.

8.6   Ben Jonson, Prefaces to *Catiline His Conspiracy* (1611)

From STC 14759 (BL copy), A3^r.

Jonson wrote two prefaces for the quarto publication of his play about Roman politics. In a sardonic variation on the form, these were far less ingratiating than the usual forewords "to the reader." He dedicated the volume to William, Earl of Pembroke, a patron who gave Jonson £20 annually with which to buy books.

To the Reader in Ordinary

The Muses forbid that I should restrain your meddling, whom I see already busy with the title [*title page*] and tricking [*flipping*] over the leaves. It is your own; I departed with my right when I let it first abroad. And now so secure an interpreter I am of my chance that neither praise nor dispraise from you can affect me. Though you commend the two first acts with the people (because they are the worst), and dislike the oration of Cicero in regard you read some pieces of it at school and understand them not yet, I shall find the way to forgive you. Be anything you will be at your own charge. Would I had deserved but half so well of it in translation as that [*Cicero's oration*] ought to deserve of you in judgment, if you have any. I know you will pretend (whosoever you are) to have that [*judgment*] and more. But all pretenses are not just [*right*] claims. The commendation of good things may fall within a many, their approbation but in a few. For the most commend out of affection, self-tickling [*self-pleasing*], an easiness or imitation; but men judge only out of knowledge – that is the trying faculty [*capacity for judgment*]. And to those works that will bear a judge, nothing is more dangerous than a foolish praise. You will say I shall not have yours, therefore, but rather the contrary: all vexation of censure. If I were not above such molestations now, I had great cause to think unworthily of my studies, or they had so of me. But I leave you to your exercise. Begin.

To the Reader Extraordinary

You I would understand to be the better man, though places in court go otherwise. To you I submit my self and work. Farewell.

8.7 Stephen Gosson, *The School of Abuse, Conveying a Pleasant Invective against Poets, Pipers, Players, Jesters, and such like Caterpillars of a Commonwealth* (1579)

From STC 12097 (HL copy), B3^r, B6^v–B7^r, B8^v–C1^r, C1^v, C2^r, C5^v–C6^r, D3^r.

Stephen Gosson arrived in London in 1577, the same year James Burbage opened the first public theater. Gosson tried playwriting – without success – and finally got into print by instead attacking the popular drama in this tirade. Thomas Lodge published a Reply *in which he suggested it was "no marvel though you dispraise poetry when you know not what it means," but this did not end the debate. Gosson followed up with* Plays Confuted in Five Actions *in 1582, and the Puritan polemicist Philip Stubbes wrote an equally vitriolic antitheatrical tract,* Anatomy of Abuses, *in 1583.*

Plutarch complaineth that ignorant men, not knowing the majesty of ancient music, abuse both the ears of the people and the art itself with bringing sweet comforts into theaters, [which] rather effeminate the mind as pricks unto vice, than procure amendment of manners as spurs to virtue. . . . Cooks did never show more craft in their junkets [*confectionary*] to vanquish the taste, nor painters in shadows to allure the eye, than poets in theaters to wound the conscience.

There set they abroach[4] strange comforts of melody to tickle the ear, costly apparel to flatter the sight, effeminate gesture to ravish the sense, and wanton speech to whet [*incite*] desire to inordinate lust. Therefore, of both barrels[5] I judge cooks and painters the better hearing, for the one extendeth his art no farther than to the tongue, palate, and nose; the other to the eye. And both are ended in outward sense, which is common to us with brute beasts. But these [*i.e., playwrights*] by the privy entries of the ear slip down into the heart and with gunshot of affection gall [*vex*] the mind, where reason and virtue should rule the roost. . . .

O, what a wonderful change is this! Our wrestling at arms is turned to wallowing in ladies' laps, our courage to cowardice, our running to riot, our bows into bowls [*bowling*], and our darts to dishes. We have robbed Greece of gluttony, Italy of wantonness, Spain of pride, France of deceit, and Dutchland of quaffing [*drinking*]. Compare London to Rome, and England to Italy: you shall find the theaters of the one, the abuses of the other, to be rife among us. . . . In our assemblies at plays in London you shall see such heaving and shoving, such itching and shouldering to sit by women, such care for their garments that they be not trod on, such eyes to their laps that no chips [*wood fragments*] light in them, such pillows to their backs that they take no hurt, such masking in [*plugs for*] their ears – I know not what – such giving them pippins [*apples*] to pass the time, such playing at foot saunt without cards,[6] such ticking [*touching*], such toying [*trifling*], such smiling, such winking, and such manning them home when the sports are ended that it is a right comedy to mark their behavior. . . . They that lack customers all the week (either because their haunt is unknown or the constables and officers of their parish watch them so narrowly that they dare not queatch [*solicit*]), to celebrate the Sabbath flock to theaters and there keep a general market of bawdry. Not that any filthiness in deed is committed within the compass of that ground, as was once done in Rome, but that every wanton and [his] paramour, every man and his mistress, every John and his Joan, every knave and his quean [*strumpet*] are there first acquainted and cheapen [*bargain*] the merchandise in that place [which] they pay for elsewhere as they can agree. . . .

God hath now blessed England with a queen in virtue excellent. . . . But we, unworthy servants of so mild a mistress, degenerate children of so good a mother, unthankful subjects of so loving a prince, wound her sweet heart with abusing her lenity and stir Jupiter to anger to send us a stork that shall devour

---

4 *set they abroach*: they introduce or give vent to.

5 *both barrels*: Guns were either single or double barreled; Gosson continues the metaphor with reference to the "gunshot of affection."

6 *foot saunt without cards*: Cent-foot was a card game that presumably involved language with a sexual double meaning. Without cards, only the erotic play remained.

us.[7] How often hath Her Majesty, with the grave advice of her whole Council, set down the limits of apparel to every degree,[8] and how soon again hath the pride of our hearts overflown the channel? How many times hath access to theaters been restrained[9] and how boldly again have we re-entered? Overlashing in apparel is so common a fault that the very hirelings of some of our players . . . jet [*swagger*] under gentlemen's noses in suits of silk, exercising themselves to prating on the stage. . . .

Let us but shut up our ears to poets, pipers, and players, pull our feet back from resort to theaters, and turn away our eyes from beholding of vanity: the greatest storm of abuse will be overblown and a fair path trodden to amendment of life. Were not we so foolish to taste every drug and buy every trifle, players would shut in their shops and carry their trash to some other country.

8.8   Sir Philip Sidney, *An Apology for Poetry* (1595)

From STC 22534 (HL copy), C2^v, G4^v–H1^r, H1^v–H2^r, I1^{r-v}, I2^v, I4^r–K2^v, L2^v–L3^v.

Sir Philip Sidney's literary works included a long prose romance, the Arcadia, *and a collection of 108 sonnets and eleven songs called* Astrophel and Stella. *After his death in battle in the Low Countries in 1586, Sidney's sister, the Countess of Pembroke, completed his translation of the Psalms and also arranged for the publication of this first work of literary criticism in English (sometimes known also as* A Defense of Poesy). *Stephen Gosson had had the temerity to dedicate* The School of Abuse *to Sidney; Sidney here defends poetry as more effective than either philosophy or history for moral education. Especially famous are his criticisms about English drama, though it must be remembered that he did not live long enough to see even the earliest work by Shakespeare, or indeed any of the greatest playwrights of the age.*

Poesy therefore is an art of imitation, for so Aristotle termeth it in this word, *mimesis* – that is to say, a representing, counterfeiting, or figuring forth; to speak metaphorically, a speaking picture with this end: to teach and delight. . . .

That [poets] should be the principal liars, I answer paradoxically but truly – I think truly – that of all writers under the sun the poet is the least liar, and though [*even if*] he would, as a poet can scarcely be a liar. The astronomer, with his cousin the geometrician, can hardly escape when they take upon them to

---

7 *Jupiter . . . that shall devour us*: In Aesop's fable, rebellious frogs petitioned Jupiter to remove King Log as their ruler. Jupiter replaced Log with King Stork, who ate all the frogs.

8 *limits of apparel to every degree*: Tudor sumptuary laws designated the fabrics and colors appropriate to each rank of society (see document 6.6).

9 *access to theaters been restrained*: To prevent the spread of contagion, public theaters were closed during plague times.

measure the height of the stars. How often, think you, do the physicians lie, when they aver things good for sicknesses which afterwards send Charon[10] a great number of souls drowned in a potion before they come to his ferry? And no less of the rest which take upon them to affirm. Now for the poet, he nothing affirms, and therefore never lieth. For, as I take it, to lie is to affirm that to be true which is false; so as the other artists, and especially the historian, affirming many things, can, in the cloudy knowledge of mankind, hardly escape from many lies. But the poet (as I said before) never affirmeth. The poet never maketh any circles about your imagination, to conjure[11] you to believe for true what he writes. He citeth not authorities of other histories but even for his entry calleth the sweet muses to inspire into him a good invention; in truth, not laboring to tell you what is or is not but what should or should not be. And therefore, though he recount things not true, yet because he telleth them not for true, he lieth not. . . .

They say the comedies rather teach than reprehend amorous conceits. They say the lyric is larded with passionate sonnets, the elegiac weeps the want of his mistress, and that, even to the heroical, Cupid hath ambitiously climbed. Alas, Love, I would thou couldst as well defend thyself as thou canst offend others. I would those on whom thou dost attend could either put thee away or yield good reason why they keep thee. But grant love of beauty to be a beastly fault (although it be very hard, sith only man, and no beast, hath that gift to discern beauty); grant that lovely name of love to deserve all hateful reproaches (although even some of my masters the philosophers spent a good deal of their lamp-oil in setting forth the excellency of it); grant, I say, whatsoever they will have granted, that not only love but lust, but vanity, but (if they list), scurrility [indecency] possesseth many leaves of the poets' books. Yet think I, when this is granted, they will find their sentence may with good manners put the last words foremost, and not say that poetry abuseth man's wit but that man's wit abuseth poetry. . . .

Plato found fault that the poets of his time filled the world with wrong opinions of the gods, making light tales of that unspotted essence, and therefore would not have the youth depraved with such opinions. Herein may much be said. Let this suffice: the poets did not induce such opinions but did imitate those opinions already induced. . . . Plato therefore (whose authority I had much rather justly conster [construe] than unjustly resist) meant not in general of poets . . . but only meant to drive out those wrong opinions of the Deity (whereof now, without further law, Christianity hath taken away all the hurtful belief), perchance (as he thought) nourished by the then-esteemed poets. And a man need go no further than to Plato himself to know his meaning, who, in his dialogue called *Ion*, giveth high and rightly divine commendation to Poetry. So

---

10 *Charon*: in Greek mythology, the ferryman who transported the dead over the river Styx.
11 *circles . . . to conjure*: Necromancers were known to draw circles on the ground, defining the area within which their magic was operative.

as Plato, banishing the abuse not the thing – not banishing it but giving due honor unto it – shall be our patron and not our adversary. For indeed I had much rather (sith truly I may do it) show their mistaking of Plato (under whose lion's skin[12] they would make an ass-like braying against Poesy) than go about to overthrow his authority. Whom, the wiser a man is, the more just cause he shall find to have in admiration – especially sith he attributeth unto Poesy more than myself do, namely, to be a very inspiring of a divine force, far above man's wit, as in the aforenamed dialogue is apparent. . . .

Methinks before I give my pen a full stop, it shall be but a little more lost time to inquire why England (the mother of excellent minds) should be grown so hard a stepmother to poets. . . . Chaucer, undoubtedly, did excellently in his *Troilus and Criseyde*. Of whom, truly, I know not whether to marvel more: either that he in that misty time could see so clearly or that we in this clear age walk so stumblingly after him. Yet had he great wants [*things lacking*], fit to be forgiven in so reverent antiquity. I account the *Mirror of Magistrates* meetly furnished of beautiful parts, and in the Earl of Surrey's lyrics[13] many things tasting of a noble birth and worthy of a noble mind. The *Shepherd's Calendar* hath much poetry in his eclogues, indeed worthy the reading if I be not deceived. That same framing of his style to an old rustic language [*archaisms*] I dare not allow [*praise*], sith neither Theocritus in Greek, Virgil in Latin, nor Sannazzaro in Italian did affect it. Besides these, do I not remember to have seen but few (to speak boldly) printed, that have poetical sinews in them: for proof whereof, let but most of the verses be put in prose and then ask the meaning, and it will be found that one verse did but beget another without ordering at the first what should be at the last – which becomes a confused mass of words with a tingling [*tinkling*] sound of rhyme, barely accompanied with reason.

Our tragedies and comedies (not without cause cried out against), observing rules neither of honest civility nor of skillful poetry – excepting *Gorboduc*[14] (again I say, of those that I have seen), which, notwithstanding as it is full of stately speeches and well-sounding phrases climbing to the height of Seneca his style, and as full of notable morality, which it doth most delightfully teach, and so obtain the very end of poesy, yet in troth it is very defectious in the circumstances, which grieveth me, because it might not remain as an exact model of all tragedies. For it is faulty both in place and time, the two necessary companions of all corporal actions. For where the stage should always represent but one place, and the uttermost time presupposed in it should be (both by Aristotle's precept and common reason) but one day, there is both many days and many places, inartificially [*inartistically*] imagined.

---

12 *lion's skin*: Aesop's fable of the ass in the lion's skin moralizes that everyone should content himself with his own achievements and not seek to appropriate the merits of another.

13 *the Earl of Surrey's lyrics*: in "Tottel's Miscellany."

14 Gorboduc: This 1561 play was written by Thomas Sackville (also lead author of *The Mirror for Magistrates*) and Thomas Norton.

But if it be so in *Gorboduc*, how much more in all the rest, where you shall have Asia of the one side and Africa of the other, and so many other under-kingdoms that the player, when he cometh in, must ever begin with telling where he is or else the tale will not be conceived. Now ye shall have three ladies walk to gather flowers and then we must believe the stage to be a garden. By and by we hear news of shipwreck in the same place, and then we are to blame if we accept it not for a rock. Upon the back of that comes out a hideous monster with fire and smoke, and then the miserable beholders are bound to take it for a cave, while in the meantime two armies fly in, represented with four swords and bucklers. And then what hard heart will not receive it for a pitched field?

Now of time they are much more liberal, for ordinary it is that two young princes fall in love. After many traverses, she is got with child, delivered of a fair boy, he is lost, groweth a man, falls in love, and is ready to get another child – and all this in two hours' space. Which, how absurd it is in sense, even sense may imagine. . . . Do they not know that a tragedy is tied to the laws of poesy and not of history, not bound to follow the story but, having liberty, either to feign a quite new matter or to frame the history to the most tragical conveniency? Again, many things may be told which cannot be showed, if they know the difference betwixt reporting and representing. . . . .

But besides these gross absurdities, how all their plays be neither right tragedies nor right comedies, mingling kings and clowns – not because the matter so carrieth it, but thrust in clowns by head and shoulders to play a part in majestical matters, with neither decency nor discretion, so as neither the admiration and commiseration, nor the right sportfulness, is by their mongrel tragicomedy obtained. I know Apuleius did somewhat so [*in the* Metamorphoses], but that is a thing recounted with space of time, not represented in one moment. And I know the ancients have one or two examples of tragicomedies, as Plautus hath *Amphitrio*. But if we mark them well we shall find that they never, or very daintily, match hornpipes and funerals. So falleth it out that, having indeed no right comedy, in that comical part of our tragedy we have nothing but scurrility, unworthy of any chaste ears, or some extreme show of doltishness, indeed fit to lift up a loud laughter, and nothing else: where the whole tract of a comedy should be full of delight, as the tragedy should be still maintained in a well-raised admiration. . . .

So that sith the ever-praiseworthy poesy is full of virtue-breeding delightfulness and void of no gift that ought to be in the noble name of learning; sith the blames laid against it are either false or feeble; sith the cause why it is not esteemed in England is the fault of poet-apes, not poets; sith, lastly, our tongue is most fit to honor poesy and to be honored by poesy, I conjure you all that have had the evil luck to read this ink-wasting toy of mine, even in the name of the Nine Muses, no more to scorn the sacred mysteries of poesy, no more to laugh at the name of poets as though they were next inheritors to fools, no more to jest at the reverent title of a rhymer, but to believe with Aristotle that they were the ancient treasurers of the Grecians' divinity; to believe with Bembus that they were first bringers-in of all civility; to believe with Scaliger that no philosopher's precepts can sooner make you an honest man than the reading of Virgil; to believe with Clauserus, the translator of Cornutus, that it pleased the heavenly Deity, by Hesiod and Homer, under the veil of fables, to give us all knowledge, logic, rhetoric, philosophy natural and moral, and *quid non*? [*what not?*]; to believe with me, that there are many mysteries contained in poetry, which of purpose were written darkly, lest by profane wits it should be abused; to believe with Landino, that they are so beloved of the gods that whatsoever they write proceeds of a divine fury; lastly, to believe themselves when they tell you they will make you immortal by their verses. . . . But if (fie of such a but) you be born so near the dull-making cataphract of Nilus[15] that you cannot hear the planet-like music of poetry . . . thus much curse I must send you, in the behalf of all poets, that while you live you live in love and never get favor for lacking skill of a sonnet, and, when you die, your memory die from the earth for want of an epitaph.

8.9 Sir Stephen Slanye's Letter to the Queen's Privy Council regarding Public Theaters (13 September 1595)

From CLRO *Remembrancia* 2:103 (22ᵛ–23ʳ).

In plague times, city officials closed the public theaters in an attempt to halt the spread of contagion. But playhouses were unpopular with the authorities even in good times; wherever large groups of people gathered, they feared disorder and riots. Royal officers, however, thought of the public theater as a laboratory to work up plays worthy of being performed at court. This means that the city and the Crown were often in conflict. Each year the new Lord Mayor of London complained to the monarch's Privy Councillors, sometimes simply copying the letter of the year before.

Our humble duty remembered to your good Lordships and the rest:

We have been bold heretofore to signify to your honors the great inconvenience that groweth to this city by the common exercise of stage plays, wherein we presumed to be the more often and earnest suitors to your honors for the suppressing of the said stage plays as well in respect of the good government of this city (which we desire to be such as Her Highness and your honors might be pleased therewithal) as for conscience's sake being persuaded (under correction of your honors' judgment) that neither in policy nor in religion they are to be permitted in a Christian commonwealth, specially being of that frame and

---

15 *cataphract of Nilus*: Sidney refers to one of the six famous "Cataracts of the Nile." A cataract was a waterfall; in the case of the Egyptian river, whitewaters or rapids.

making as usually they are and containing nothing but profane fables, lascivious matters, cozening [*defrauding*] devices, and other unseemly and scurrilous behaviors – which are so set forth as that they move wholly to imitation and not to the avoiding of those vices which they represent. Which we verily think to be the chief cause as well of many other disorders and lewd demeanors which appear of late in young people of all degrees, as of the late stir and mutinous attempt of those few apprentices and other servants who we doubt not drew their infection from these and like places. Among other inconveniences it is not the least that the refuse [*worthless*] sort of evil-disposed and ungodly people about this city have opportunity hereby to assemble together and to make their matches for all their lewd and ungodly practices. Being also the ordinary places for all masterless men and vagabond persons that haunt the highways to meet together and to recreate themselves. . . . We are humble suitors to your good lordships and the rest to direct your letters to the Justices of Peace of Surrey and Middlesex for the present stay and final suppressing of the said plays as well at the Theater and Bankside as in all other places about the city. Whereby we doubt not but the opportunity and very cause of so great disorders being taken away, we shall be able to keep the people of this city in such good order and due obedience as that Her Highness and your honors shall be well pleased and content therewithal.

8.10 The Examination of Augustine Phillips regarding the Essex Rebellion (18 February 1601)

From SP 12/278: 85.

The fears of the moralists seemed to have been borne out when followers of Robert Devereux, second Earl of Essex, commissioned a performance of Richard II *at the Globe Theatre on 7 February 1601, the night before they planned to overthrow Elizabeth I. The play about a deposed king may have been the version written by Shakespeare around 1595 (and published in quarto in 1597). Essex, under house arrest for having negotiated an unauthorized truce with the Irish rebel Hugh O'Neill, was wrongly persuaded that the play would inspire citizens of London to rise in support of him. On the basis of testimonies such as that of Augustine Phillips, taken "upon his oath," Essex was executed on 25 February 1601. Phillips was an actor and, like Shakespeare, a shareholder in the Globe.*

He sayeth that on Friday last was sevennight – or Thursday – Sir Charles Percy, Sir Joselyn Percy, and the Lord Monteagle with some three more spake to some of the players in the presence of this examinate to have the play of the deposing and killing of King Richard the Second to be played the Saturday next, promising to get them 40 shillings more than their ordinary [fee] to play it. Where this examinate and his fellows were determined to have played some other play, holding that play of King Richard to be so old and so long out of use as that they should have small or no company at it. But at their request this examinate and his fellows were content to play it the Saturday and had their 40 shillings more than their ordinary for it and so played it accordingly.

8.11   Thomas Heywood, *An Apology for Actors* (1612)

From STC 13309 (FSL copy), F3^r–F4^r, G1^v–G2^r.

Although Thomas Heywood said that his tragicomedy The English Traveller *came "accidentally to the press" (in 1633) and that "it never was any great ambition in me to be in this way voluminously read," these remarks were included in a formal preface to the printed playtext. There, he claimed to have had "either an entire hand or at the least a main finger" in 220 plays. He also authored this defense of the theater – which was not to prevail. An anonymous author responded immediately in 1615 with* A Refutation of the Apology for Actors, *and twenty years later William Prynne renewed the attack on the theater, mentioning Heywood explicitly, in* Histriomastix, The Players' Scourge *(1633). When revolutionary Puritans seized control of the state they also, in 1642, closed the public playhouses.*

Plays have made the ignorant more apprehensive, taught the unlearned the knowledge of many famous histories, instructed such as cannot read in the discovery of all our English chronicles. And what man have you now of that weak capacity that cannot discourse of any notable thing recorded even from William the Conqueror – nay, from the landing of Brute[16] – until this day? Being possessed of their true use, for or because plays are writ with this aim and carried with this method: to teach the subjects obedience to their king; to show the people the untimely ends of such as have moved tumults, commotions, and insurrections; to present them with the flourishing estate of such as live in obedience, exhorting them to allegiance, dehorting [*dissuading*] them from all traitorous and felonious stratagems. . . . If we present a tragedy, we include the fatal and abortive ends of such as commit notorious murders. . . . If we present a foreign history, the subject is so intended that in the lives of Romans, Grecians, or others, either the virtues of our countrymen are extolled or their vices reproved. . . . If a moral, it is to persuade men to humanity and good life, to instruct them in civility and good manners, showing them the fruits of honesty and the end of villainy. . . . If a comedy, it is pleasantly contrived with merry accidents and inter-

---

16 *Brute*: In his eleventh-century *Historia regum Britanniae*, Geoffrey of Monmouth influentially wrote that Britain's earliest settler was Brutus, descendant of the Trojan king Aeneas.

mixed with apt and witty jests, to present before the prince at certain times of solemnity, or else merrily fitted to the stage. And what is then the subject of this harmless mirth? Either in the shape of a clown to show others their slovenly and unhandsome behavior, that they may reform that simplicity in themselves which others make their sport (lest they happen to become the like subject of general scorn to an auditory); else it entreats of love, deriding foolish inamorates who spend their ages, their spirits – nay, themselves – in the servile and ridiculous employments of their mistresses. And these are mingled with sportful accidents to recreate such as of themselves are wholly devoted to melancholy, which corrupts the blood, or to refresh such weary spirits as are tired with labor or study, to moderate the cares and heaviness of the mind that they may return to their trades and faculties with more zeal and earnestness after some small, soft, and pleasant retirement. . . . If we present a pastoral, we show the harmless love of shepherds diversely moralized, distinguishing betwixt the craft of the city and the innocency of the sheepcote. Briefly, there is neither tragedy, history, comedy, moral, or pastoral from which an infinite use cannot be gathered. . . .

It follows that we prove these exercises to have been the discoverers of many notorious murders long concealed from the eyes of the world. To omit all far-fetched instances, we will prove it by a domestic and home-born truth which within these few years happened. At Lynn in Norfolk, the then Earl of Sussex' Players acting the old *History of Friar Francis*, and presenting a woman who, insatiately doting on a young gentleman, had (the more securely to enjoy his affection) mischievously and secretly murdered her husband. Whose ghost haunted her and, at diverse times, in her most solitary and private contemplations, in most horrid and fearful shapes, appeared and stood before her. As this was acted, a townswoman (till then of good estimation and report) finding her conscience (at this presentment) extremely troubled, suddenly screeched and cried out, "Oh! My husband, my husband! I see the ghost of my husband fiercely threatening and menacing me!" At which shrill and unexpected outcry, the people about her, moved to a strange amazement, inquired the reason of her clamor, when presently, unurged, she told them that seven years ago, she, to be possessed of such a gentleman (meaning him), had poisoned her husband, whose fearful image personated itself in the shape of that ghost. Whereupon the murderess was apprehended, before the justices further examined, and by her voluntary confession after condemned. That this is true, as well by the report of the actors as the records of the town, there are many eyewitnesses of this accident yet living, vocally to confirm it.

8.12   Sir Thomas Bodley's Letter to his Librarian Thomas James (21 January 1612)

From *Letters of Sir Thomas Bodley to Thomas James*, ed. G. W. Wheeler (Oxford: Clarendon Press, 1926), no. 221.

Sir Thomas Bodley's private collection formed the basis of a library opened at Oxford University on 8 November 1602. In 1605 the Bodleian had 5,611 books. Of these, 2,456 were on theological topics, most written in Latin; 1,868 were on the arts, with just 36 written in English. In 1610 Bodley gave the London Stationers' Company a piece of plate to complete an arrangement that would be ratified by Star Chamber in 1637: Bodley would receive one copy of each book printed in England, providing that it could be borrowed back by the Company for use in reprinting. Bodley's first librarian was Thomas James. Until 1753, when the British Library was founded, the Bodleian was England's national library, and it remains one of the most important collections in the world.

I can see no good reason to alter my opinion for excluding such books as almanacs, plays, and an infinite number that are daily printed of very unworthy matters and handling, such as, methinks, both the Keeper and Underkeeper should disdain to seek out to deliver unto any man. Happily some plays may be worthy the keeping, but hardly one in forty. For it is not alike in English plays and others of other nations, because they are most esteemed for learning the languages and many of them compiled by men of great fame, for wisdom and learning, which is seldom or never seen among us. Were it so again that some little profit might be reaped (which God knows is very little) out of some of our playbooks, the benefit thereof will nothing near countervail the harm that the scandal will bring unto the library when it shall be given out that we stuff it full of baggage books. And though they should be but a few, as they would be very many if your course should take place, yet the having of those few (such is the nature of malicious reporters) would be mightily multiplied by such as purpose to speak in disgrace of the library. This is my opinion, wherein if I err, I think I shall err with infinite others. And the more I think upon it, the more it doth distaste me that such kind of books should be vouchsafed a room in so noble a library.

8.13   William Shakespeare, *Hamlet* (1603 and 1623)

Version One from STC 22275 (BL copy), D4^v–E1^r; Version Two from STC 22273 (FSL copy), 265.

Early modern printers proofread continuously, as pages came off the press, and made corrections without discarding pages already printed with errors. Thus, no two copies of an early book are identical. In the case of Shakespeare, there can be even greater differences in the multiple versions that survive. One theory is that a printer preparing a "pirated" text may have asked an actor who performed a single part to re-create the entire play from memory. Here, a famous speech from the confused quarto text of the 1603 Hamlet is shown before the Folio version of 1623. Unlike other extracts in this sourcebook, these are shown with original spelling and punctuation.

1603 Quarto

To be, or not to be; I [*aye*] there's the point,
To Die, to sleepe, is that all? I all:
No, to sleepe, to dreame, I mary there it goes,
For in that dreame of death, when wee awake,
And borne before an euerlasting Iudge,
From whence no passenger euer retur'nd,
The vndiscouered country, at whose sight
The happy smile, and the accursed damn'd.
But for this, the ioyfull hope of this,
Whol'd beare the scornes and flattery of the world,
Scorned by the right rich, the rich curssed of the poore?
The widow being oppressed, the orphan wrong'd,
The taste of hunger, or a tirants raigne,
And thousand more calamities besides,
To grunt and sweate vnder this weary life,
When that he may his full *Quietus* make,
With a bare bodkin, who would this indure,
But for a hope of something after death?
Which pusles the braine, and doth confound the sence,
Which makes vs rather beare those euilles we haue,
Than flie to others that we know not of.
I that, O this conscience makes cowardes of vs all,
Lady in thy orizons, be all my sinnes remembred.

1623 Folio

To be, or not to be, that is the Question:
Whether 'tis Nobler in the minde to suffer
The Slings and Arrowes of outragious Fortune,
Or to take Armes against a Sea of troubles,
And by opposing end them: to dye, to sleepe
No more; and by a sleepe, to say we end
The Heart-ake, and the thousand Naturall shockes
That Flesh is heyre too? 'Tis a consummation
Deuoutly to be wish'd. To dye to sleepe,
To sleepe, perchance to Dreame; I, there's the rub,
For in that sleepe of death, what dreames may come,
When we haue shuffel'd off this mortall coile,
Must giue vs pawse. There's the respect
That makes Calamity of so long life:
For who would beare the Whips and Scornes of time,

The Oppressors wrong, the poore mans Contumely,
The pangs of dispriz'd Loue, the Lawes delay,
The insolence of Office, and the Spurnes
That patient merit of the vnworthy takes,
When he himselfe might his *Quietus* make
With a bare Bodkin? Who would these Fardles beare
To grunt and sweat vnder a weary life,
But that the dread of something after death,
The vndiscouered Countrey, from whose Borne
No Traueller returnes, Puzels the will,
And makes vs rather beare those illes we haue,
Then flye to others that we know not of.
Thus Conscience does make Cowards of vs all,
And thus the Natiue hew of Resolution
Is sicklied o're, with the pale cast of Thought,
And enterprizes of great pith and moment,
With this regard their Currants turne away,
And loose the name of Action. Soft you now,
The faire *Ophelia*? Nimph, in thy Orizons
Be all my sinnes remembred.

9

Trade and Exploration

The European voyages of the fifteenth, sixteenth, and seventeenth centuries mapped the whole earth for the first time, expanding western understandings of the natural world and of nonwestern peoples. Still, knowledge was not the first purpose of most early explorers. Their aim was to locate new supplies of precious metals and spices, to develop new markets for western goods, and to identify new products that could be trafficked. Technological advances in navigation and cartography promoted an active, internationalized consumer culture.

At the outset, it follows, English voyagers did not have imperialist ambitions. But the reports of traders and explorers, who chronicled the things that were strange and different about the societies they encountered, created a sense of what was "self" as well as what was "other." Willingness to exploit foreign peoples for economic gain was a first symptom of what would later become a colonializing imperative. Eventually, western historians would call the fifteenth, sixteenth, and seventeenth centuries "the Age of Discovery," a phrase which betrayed their unthinking assumption that Europe was at the center of the universe. The term marginalized the "rest of the world" and denied non-European nations their own integrity, as if their history began only when Europe became aware of them and when they became useful to Europe.

Land and Sea

Early contacts between the West and the East had developed along land routes, including the ancient Silk Road between Rome and China. In the thirteenth century, Marco Polo wrote an account of the court of Kublai Khan, which he and other members of his Venetian merchant family had reached by way of the Silk Road. By the fifteenth century, however, overland travel had grown difficult for European traders, as the Ottoman Empire expanded westwards. In 1452 the Ottoman Turks took control of the key crossroads city of Constantinople and seemed poised to make further inroads west. Because Arabs owned the trade routes, European merchants had to pay to traverse them. Europeans therefore began to seek alternative routes east by sea. Ironically, they did so with ship-building advances, sailing techniques, and mathematical skills they learned from Arabs.

For Europe, the leaders in globalized commerce were Portugal and Spain. Prince Henry of Portugal, who was known as "the Navigator," sponsored the first great maritime initiatives. During his reign, in the early fifteenth century, Portuguese sailors made incremental advances down the west coast of Africa. Finally, in 1487, Bartolomeu Dias turned the southernmost Cape of Good Hope and proved that this was a way east. In 1498 Vasco da Gama sailed further yet and reached India. Ferdinand Magellan led a voyage to circumnavigate the world in 1519. (Although he himself died in the Pacific, his ships went on to complete the trip.) To protect the trade routes it traced, Portugal established forts and colonies in Africa, India, and Brazil. Meanwhile, Spain looked primarily to the west, with the "Catholic Kings" Ferdinand and Isabella funding Christopher Columbus in 1492. The successes of the Spanish conquistadors were largely due to the diseases they carried. Measles and smallpox were deadly to Aztec and Inca peoples.

In 1493, Pope Alexander VI assumed the authority to establish an imaginary demarcation line in the Atlantic Ocean. He decreed that Africa, Asia, and eastern South America would belong to Portugal, while the rest of the Americas would be controlled by Spain. But France, the Netherlands, and England had different ideas. In 1497 the English hired an Italian sailor, John Cabot, to search North America for a "Northwest Passage" that would lead to Asia, and in 1534 Jacques Cartier undertook a similar quest for the French. Despite all attempts to assign ownerships, the map of territorial proprieties was, and would remain, volatile.

England's Exports

In the mid-sixteenth century, England was the least developed of the trading nations of the West. First, while English woolen cloths were in demand in other countries, few other English wares were. Reliance on a single product left England painfully vulnerable to market fluctuations. And even in the cloth industry, many of the proceeds went elsewhere. English manufacturers needed Continental raw materials such as oil, woad, madder, and alum in order to process their wool into cloth. The cloth was then exported in an "unfinished" state, to be dyed in the Netherlands. Because dyeing was the most highly skilled work, Dutch craftsmen earned the larger profits.

Second, England's international trade was concentrated on exchange between London and Antwerp, in the Netherlands. Historically, commerce in London was regulated through such livery companies as the Mercers, the Grocers, the Drapers, the Fishmongers, the Goldsmiths, the Merchant Taylors, and the Skinners (to name just a few). In 1407, the growth of global commerce was recognized with the incorporation of the Merchant Adventurers, a group composed of merchants who were already members of the traditional livery companies but who worked exclusively as wholesalers, primarily by exporting their wares to other countries. In the sixteenth century, the Crown granted the

Merchant Adventurers exclusive rights to sell broadcloth at Antwerp's market. With this monopoly, merchants from other English cities were shut out of Europe's most important trade center. Then came a trade slump at Antwerp in the 1550s. Even as hostilities between England and Spain escalated, English merchants were dependent on a single market that was under Spanish control.

Finally, third, London's Merchant Adventurers were accustomed to employing the ships and trade routes of merchants from other countries. The north Germans of the Hanseatic League maintained an important London post, the Steelyard. English merchants had few maritime programs of their own.

In all three areas, then, diversification was urgently needed. Thus, during the 1560s, the Merchant Adventurers developed outlets for English cloth outside Antwerp, in several German cities. In 1555, merchants searching for additional markets and alternative trade routes created the first joint-stock trading organization, the Muscovy Company. With Portugal defending its route around the Cape of Good Hope and without a "Northwest Passage," England sought a "Northeast Passage" to China. This mission failed, but Russia proved to be an important new market for English cloths, as well as a place to procure furs and other raw materials. From Moscow it was also possible to trace an alternate overland route to Persia. The Eastland Company was constituted in 1579, specializing in trade in the Baltic. The Levant Company, formed in 1581, established English trading posts at Aleppo, Constantinople, Alexandria, and Smyrna. The Barbary Company was formed in 1585. With an English maritime culture well underway, in 1597 Elizabeth I was able to expel the Hanseatic League from London. In 1600, she granted a charter to the joint-stock East India Company.

These trade initiatives did not solve all of England's problems, however. Sir William Cockayne, a London alderman and governor of the Eastland Company, sought to revolutionize the industry in 1614. With an upfront cash payment from Cockayne and promise of increased customs duties in the future, James VI and I agreed to end the monopoly of the Merchant Adventurers and also to ban the export of unfinished cloth. But Cockayne's scheme was a disastrous failure. English dressers and dyers did not have the skill to finish cloths to Dutch standards, and Cockayne lacked the international contacts to establish new trading structures. In 1617 the prerogatives of the Merchant Adventurers were reinstated. Another crisis in the early 1620s, caused by currency devaluations in Germany and eastern Europe, showed England's continuing overdependence on European cloth markets.

Trade Imbalances

For all products, not just cloth, English craftsmanship was generally less accomplished than that on the Continent. This skills gap meant that English men and women themselves grew dissatisfied with English goods. Many sought finer objects, fabrics, and foods that could be imported from abroad. The consumer revolution provoked what seemed like a national crisis: English money was being spent outside the country, where it served to grow foreign economies rather than England's own.

At home, therefore, there were proposals to develop new industries to answer market demands through English production. These projects would also fulfill the good social policy of putting English men and women to work, it was emphasized. England could not compete with Spain in mining precious metals in the Americas, but English privateers took to plundering Spanish ships on their journeys home. The merchants' most successful strategy was to triangulate trade. They bought goods in Italy, for example, and then, for a profit, resold the Italian goods in countries that were even less developed than England, such as Russia. As early as the 1560s, English merchants were also brokering the traffic in human slaves, capturing West Africans and selling them in Spain's New-World settlements.

In 1607 the first English colony was founded, at Jamestown. Soon there were settlements in Bermuda, Maryland, and New England. Some were populated by religious dissidents, but others were formed to exploit trade in tobacco, sugar, and slaves.

Contact Narratives

Facing competition from Portugal and Spain, the East India Company also pursued its interests on the diplomatic front. Sir Thomas Roe was sent to the Mughal Empire as James VI and I's ambassador. Roe kept a journal and sent reports home to the governors of the Company and to the king (see document 9.4). These were subsequently published by the indefatigable anthologizer Richard Hakluyt. From the start, the character of England's contact history was formed in print, polemic, and propaganda.

In 1582 Hakluyt brought out *Diverse Voyages Touching the Discovery of America*; in 1589, the massive *Principal Navigations, Voyages, and Discoveries of the English Nation*; and in 1598, the expanded *Principal Navigations, Voyages, Traffiques, and Discoveries of the English Nation*. Many of the documents excerpted below were contained in these collections (9.2, 9.6, 9.7). Hakluyt did not himself travel extensively, aside from a diplomatic assignment in France. But his zeal to preserve and publish travel reports was one sign of the way ventures captured the early modern imagination. To encourage further exploration, Hakluyt appealed to every conceivable interest: the missionary, the mercantilist, and the imperialist.

In fact, most travel narratives were as propagandistic as they were informational. For a 1585 voyage sponsored by Sir Walter Ralegh, for example, John White and Thomas Harriot were directed to document the plants, animals, and peoples of Roanoke Island (see document 9.9). In watercolor illustrations, White took care to show the natives to be peaceable and welcoming, so as not to discourage potential settlers. Ralegh was also intent on discovering El Dorado, a fabled empire of fantastic riches. Convinced that the legendary city lay in Guiana, in 1596 he urged Elizabeth I to fund the quest. The petition was couched in terms calculated to appeal to a virgin queen: "Guiana is a country that hath yet her maidenhead: never sacked, turned, nor wrought; the face of the earth hath not been torn, nor the virtue and salt of the soil spent by manurance; the graves have not been opened for gold; the minds not broken with sledges; nor their images pulled down out of their temples. It hath never been entered by any army of strength and never conquered or possessed by any Christian prince." The petition succeeded; the expedition did not.

Ralegh declared also that "whatsoever prince shall possess" Guiana "shall be greatest, and if the King of Spain enjoy it he will become unresistable." National pride was another note struck often. This was a rhetorical strategy that had a powerful afterlife, in the impulse to empire that was to dominate so much of Britain's subsequent history.

9.1   Sir Thomas Smith, *A Discourse of the Commonweal of this Realm of England* (1549)

From *A Compendious or Brief Examination of Certain Ordinary Complaints of Diverse of Our Country Men* (1581), STC 23133 (FSL copy), G1ʳ–G2ʳ.

As Secretary of State under Edward VI, in 1548, Sir Thomas Smith succeeded in restoring England's temporarily lost trading privileges at Antwerp. The next year he wrote this Discourse *in the form of a dialogue among a knight, a merchant, a crafts-man, a farmer, and a civil lawyer. In the Renaissance, fiscal problems were commonly blamed on covetous behaviors. It was Smith's revolutionary belief that society did not necessarily have to be organized morally; instead, economic interest could be marshaled to advance the common good – for example, the government might assess taxes on wool to encourage the use of land for farming rather than pasturing sheep. Smith's sophisticated economic analysis, still instructive when it was published for the first time in 1581, was originally attributed to John Hales and to William Stafford.*

We might save much [of] our treasure [*wealth*] in this realm if we would [*wished to*], and I marvel no man takes heed to it. What number first of trifles comes hither from beyond the sea that we might either clean spare or else make them within our realm, for the which we either pay inestimable treasure every year or else exchange substantial wares and necessary for them – for the which we might receive great treasure? Of the which sort I mean as well looking glasses as drinking and also to glass windows, dials, tables, cards, balls, puppets, penners [*pen cases*], inkhorns, toothpicks, gloves, knives, daggers, ouches [*buck-*

les], brooches, aglets [*tags on laces*], buttons of silk and silver, earthen pots, pins, and points [*laces*], hawks' bells, paper both white and brown, and a thousand like things that might either be clean spared or else made within the realm sufficient for us. And as for some things, they make it of our own commodities and send it us again, whereby they set their people awork and do exhaust much treasure out of this realm. As of our wool they make cloths, caps, and kerseys [*coarse cloth*]; of our fells [*animal hides*] they make Spanish skins, gloves, and girdles; of our tin, saltcellars, spoons, and dishes; of our broken linen, cloths and rags, paper both white and brown. What treasure think ye goes out of this realm for every of these things? And then for all together – it exceeds mine estimation. There is no man can be contented now with any other gloves than is made in France or in Spain; nor kersey, but it must be of Flanders dye; nor cloth, but French or frizado [*fine cloth*]; nor ouche, brooch, or aglet, but of Venice making or Milan; nor dagger, sword, knife, or girdle, but of Spanish making or some outward country; no, not as much as a spur, but that is fetched at the Milaners. I have heard within these forty years when there were not of these haberdashers that sells French or Milan caps, glasses, knives, daggers, swords, girdles, and such things, not a dozen in all London. And now, from the [Tower] to Westminster along, every street is full of them, and their shops glitters and shines. . . .

They make us pay at the end for our own stuff again; yea, for the strangers' custom [*foreigners' taxes*], for their workmanship and colors, and lastly for the second custom in the return of the wares into the realm again. Whereas, by working the same within the realm, our own men should be set awork at the charges of strangers, the custom should be borne all by strangers to the queen, and the clear gains remain within the realm.

9.2   Richard Hakluyt of the Middle Temple, "Certain Directions Given . . . to Master Morgan Hubblethorne, Dyer, Sent into Persia" (1579)

From Richard Hakluyt, *The Principal Navigations, Voyages, and Discoveries of the English Nation by Sea or Over Land* (1589), STC 12625 (HL copy), 454.

The great anthologizer Richard Hakluyt wrote that his childhood interest in world travel was ignited by the sight of a cousin's "universal map." In Psalm 107 he read that "They that go down to the sea in ships, that do business in great waters, these see the works of the Lord, and his wonders in the deep." As a student at Oxford, Hakluyt devoured travel narratives in Greek, Latin, Spanish, Portuguese, and French. Much that we know of England's early trade missions comes from the massive compendium of documents he published in 1589. This letter was written by his namesake kinsman, generally called for clarity's sake Richard Hakluyt "of the Middle Temple" (for his legal education).

For that England hath the best wool and cloth of the world, and for that the cloths of the realm have no good vent [*sale*] if good dyeing be not added, therefore it is much to be wished that the dyeing of foreign countries were seen, to the end that the art of dyeing may be brought into the realm in greatest excellency. For thereof will follow honor to the realm and great and ample vent of our cloths, and of the vent of cloths will follow the setting of our poor on work in all degrees of labor in clothing and dyeing. For which cause most principally you are sent over at the charge of the city. And therefore, for the satisfying of the lords and of the expectation of the merchants and of your company, it behooves you to have care to return home with more knowledge than you carried out. . . .

And therefore you must have great care to have knowledge of the materials of all the countries that you shall pass through that may be used in dyeing, be they herbs, weeds, barks, gums, earths, or what else soever.

In Persia you shall find carpets of coarse thrummed [*napped*] wool, the best of the world and excellently colored. Those cities and towns you must repair to, and you must use means to learn all the order of the dyeing of those thrums, which are so dyed as neither rain, wine, nor yet vinegar can stain. And if you may attain to that cunning, you shall not need to fear dyeing of cloth. For if the color hold in yarn and thrum, it will hold much better in cloth. . . .

If any dyer of China or of the east parts of the world be to be found in Persia, acquaint yourself with him and learn what you may of him. . . .

Set down in writing whatsoever you shall learn from day to day, lest you should forget or lest God should call you to his mercy. And by each return I wish you send in writing whatsoever you have learned, or at the least keep the same safe in your coffer, that come death or life your country may enjoy the thing you go for and not lose the charge and travel bestowed in this case.

9.3 William Cecil's Notes on Trade Imbalances (*c.*1581)

From SP 12/41: 58.

William Cecil, Lord Burleigh, was Elizabeth I's principal advisor and Secretary of State from the beginning of her reign. In 1572 he was named Lord Treasurer, responsible for all financial matters. He encouraged fuller employment, promoted the mining industry, and approved the growth of new crops such as flax, hemp, and, for cloth dying, woad. In this memorandum, he identified imported wine as a threat to the economy and social order.

Inconveniences of enlarging any power to bring any more wine into the realm.

It is manifest that nothing robbeth the realm of England but when more merchandises is brought in to the realm than is carried forth. As, for example, if eight thousand pounds' worth of foreign commodities be brought in, and but six thousand pounds' worth of the commodities of England carried forth, the realm must spend upon the stock yearly two thousand pounds, which must be paid with money. And it is manifestly seen already by the customer's accounts in the Exchequer[1] that yearly the foreign commodities do surmount the commodities of the land.

The remedy hereof is by all policies to abridge the use of such foreign commodities as be not necessary for us. Whereof the excess of silks is one, of wine and spice is another. And therefore wittingly to make a law to increase any of these is to consent to the robbery of the realm.

Of all these three excesses none is more hurtful to the realm than wine.

First, it enricheth France, whose power England ought not increase.

Secondly, for the more part, the wines of France, both those that come from Bordeaux and from Rouen, are bought with sending ready money thither. For in Bordeaux they have an ordinance forbidding bartering with Englishmen for wines, so as whatsoever excess groweth in bringing home of wines, thereby the gold which is or should be by merchants brought out of Spain or the Low Countries for the commodities of England is conveyed into France.

Thirdly, the multiplying of taverns, which must needs ensue by repealing the Statute of King Edward the VI, is an evident course of disorder of the vulgar people, who by hasting thereto waste their small substance which they weekly get by their hard labor, and commit all evils that accompany drunkenness.

Fourthly, the excessive drinking of wine diminisheth the use of ale and beer, and consequently decayeth tillage [agriculture] for grain, which of all labors in the realm would be [should be] favored and cherished and preferred before such an unnecessary foreign commodity as wine is. Adding thereto that in time of peace, wisdom would think what may chance in wars, and not to lay down the use of our natural food for the enticement of a foreign that by occasion of wars may be kept from us, and then the time may prove too late to recover our own so soon as our need shall be. And whensoever France shall find this opportunity to pinch us [restrict our supply], as it is no doubt but their policy seeth far in all practices, we may percase smart [suffer] when no remedy will be found to ease our pain.

9.4   Sir Thomas Roe's Reports from the Mughal Empire (1615–19)

From *The Embassy of Sir Thomas Roe to the Court of the Great Mogul, 1615–1619*, ed. William Foster, Hakluyt Society, 2nd ser., 1 and 2 (1899), 1: 97, 118–19; 2: 346–7, 475, 478–9.

---

1 *customer's accounts in the Exchequer*: the records of the government official who collected those customs or import taxes which were deposited in the royal treasury.

*Voyagers who reached India in 1608 and 1612 were so enthusiastic about prospects there
that, with the approval of James VI and I, the governors of the East India Company funded
an ambassador to negotiate trading rights with the Mughal Empire. Sir Thomas Roe was
an experienced traveler, having already sailed three hundred miles up the Amazon River in
1610. In his reports Roe sought to disabuse king and Company of unrealistic hopes. He
recognized how unsophisticated English goods and culture seemed to the Mughals.*

24 November 1615

The presents you have this year sent are extremely despised by those who have
seen them; the lining of the coach and cover of the virginals scorned, being
velvet of these parts and faded to a base tawny [*brown*]; the knives little and
mean, so that I am enforced to new furnish the [knife] case of my own store;[2]
. . . the burning glasses and prospectives [*telescopes*] such as no man hath face to
offer to give, much less to sell, such as I can buy for sixpence apiece; your
pictures not all worth one penny; and finally such error in the choice of all
things, as I think no man ever heard of the place that was of counsel. Here are
nothing esteemed but of the best sorts: good cloth and fine, and rich pictures,
they coming out of Italy overland and from Ormus,[3] so that they laugh at us for
such as we bring.

25 January 1616

At night [the king] having stayed [*detained*] the coachman and musician, he
came down into a court [*courtyard*], got into the coach, into every corner, and
caused it to be drawn about by them. Then he sent to me, though ten o'clock at
night, for a servant to tie on his scarf and sword the English fashion, in which
he took so great pride that he marched up and down, drawing it and flourishing, and since hath never been seen without it. So that in conclusion he
accepted your presents well, but after the English were come away he asked the
Jesuit whether the king of England were a great king that sent presents of so
small value, and that he looked for some jewels.

24 November 1616

You must alter your stock. Let not your servants deceive you: cloth, lead, [ivory],
quicksilver are dead commodities and will never drive this trade. . . . The

---

2 *of my own store*: from my own supplies.

3 *Ormus*: the name of both a kingdom and its fortified capital city, strategically located on the Persian
  Gulf and under Portuguese control; also known as Ohrmuzd, Hormuz, and Ohrmazd.

presents sent are too few . . . although the coach for the form and for a model gave much content, yet the matter [*constituent material*] was scorned, and it was never used until two other of rich stuff were made by it, and that covered with cloth of gold, harness and furniture, and all the tin nails headed with silver or hatched [*with ornamental engraving*], so that it was nine months a-repairing. When I saw it, I knew it not.

14 February 1618

You need not insist upon a contract with the Shah [of Persia], but, having license, trade for as much as you could and by what means you could. But the means to furnish this trade will not arise from England, neither by our cloth nor any other commodity. It is folly to deceive you with hopes that will fail. Of these some may yearly be vented by contract with the Shah, and some tin will sell well, quicksilver and vermilion, but not to compass a tenth part of that by you aimed at. By spices you may well assist yourselves; they give as good profit as in England within 30 percent, as I am informed. Chinaware is in good request, and from India great profit to be made by sugars, cloth, steel, and other commodities, by all which you may raise a good part of whatsoever you contract for. . . . All we can forecast will not raise your stock except only jewels, if you can fit them to profit. . . . They imitate everything we bring, and embroider now as well as we. . . . Many things also, as gloves, will give nothing nor be accepted as gift, but as patterns to pick out work [*copy*].

9.5 Sir Thomas Wentworth's Report of a Debate in the House of Commons on the Shortage of Money (26 February 1621)

From *Commons Debates 1621*, ed. Wallace Notestein, Frances Helen Relf, and Hartley Simpson (New Haven, CT: Yale University Press, 1935), 5: 490–3.

Sir Thomas Wentworth's first year in Parliament coincided with the start of a three-year crisis in cloth traffic. Wentworth wanted the House of Commons both to investigate the deleterious effects of trade monopolies which had been granted by the Crown and also to punish the privileged few who had enjoyed them. When price rises on the Continent eased, however, the public debate in England ended, leaving the commercial economy as vulnerable as it had been all along.

There was a motion made that the House should enter into debate according to His Majesty's pleasure, both of the causes and the remedies of the want of money. That there was great necessity to enter into the consideration thereof, looking into the estates and several possessions of persons in the kingdom. First, the case of the lowest: we should find that they had the inheritance of their hands taken from them through monopolies and restraint of commerce, insomuch that in one place there were two hundred looms laid down, and each loom would have set on work forty persons. These men by these means turned out of their inheritance, which is their trades, and to seek new, which is not only pitiful but fearful, lest, as in Germany, it should cause *bellum rusticum* [*riots in the provinces*]. The state of the husbandman [*farmer*] likewise, that labors for other men, is as lamentable, not that there is a want of corn or cattle but that they yielded no price, and that the fairs stood still. The gentlemen and noblemen that could not maintain their estates but by their rents, were not paid. The merchant and tradesmen could get no ready money for their commodities but were forced to sell them of trust, which was occasion of a great mischief in those professions.

It was further said that whereas formerly there had been £23,000 coined yearly in silver, there was now not a penny; that there was more silver melted into plate in the last seven years of Queen Elizabeth than in these last seven years of His Majesty; that every third shop of goldsmiths in Cheapside was shut up; that money was the measure of trade; that the want thereof causeth cheapness of commodities.

The reasons assigned of the scarcity were these. First: the standing [*stoppage*] of the mint for eleven years now past, whereas in Queen Elizabeth's time there were eight millions and an half coined from *primo* to *tricesimo nono* [*the first to the thirty-ninth years*] of her reign. The second: the loss of the exchange of Spanish rials-of-eight, not being of equal worth as they are in other places, and therefore the low valuation of silver at the mint. By reason our standard was better than that of foreign parts was the reason silver was not imported so as it was in other places. And that there was an agreement in Henry the Seventh's time with all the Princes in Christendom to make the standard equal. The third: melting of silver against the law. The fourth: the patent of [*monopoly on*] gold foil, whereby a great deal of bullion was wasted. The fifth: the East India Company, which had license to carry out £11,000 by year. The sixth: the unequal balance of trade, the goods imported exceeding those that were exported. Which would appear (and means to satisfy the House, not by discourse but by record) . . . by examining the Custom Book, and to see what the merchants carried out and what they brought in. If that which they bring in be of more value than what they carry out, then the balance must needs be unequal, which would appear by demonstration. That in Queen Elizabeth's time, the customs upon wines came but to £15,000. Now they are £42,000, and yet we do not export into those parts from whence we fetch our wines a third part so much as formerly we did. And here it was concluded that the French Company was judged a seventh cause, in regard that all that trade was altogether driven with money and carried forth fourscore thousand pounds a year. Yet it was urged that it was not to be known by the values we set upon foreign commodities when they come hither, by reason the merchant buyeth them much cheaper than they make us pay. An eighth cause was the patent of gold and silver thread, which did waste £20,000 of our coin and stayed the importation of £20,000 more in bullion brought in from Venice in that commodity, which patent to stop importation was against an Act of Parliament. A ninth reason was assigned to be the bringing in of Irish cattle, for which they transported money and did not turn it into commodities. And it was affirmed the number of Irish cattle so brought into the kingdom were yearly 100,000, which were some of them worth twenty shillings, some worth forty shillings, and some worth three pounds. A tenth reason was the bringing in of Scottish cattle in like manner as out of Ireland, and carrying away nothing but money – it being said, the victual always takes away money. An eleventh reason was transportation of money into Polonia for corn. A twelfth: consumption of coin within the kingdom. A thirteenth: that those commodities which came into the kingdom formerly for cloth, now comes for money. A fourteenth: the great quantities of Spanish tobacco which the merchant bringeth out of Spain, where formerly he used to bring money. For a fifteenth: some were of opinion that the withdrawing of the Dutch merchants was the cause of this sudden damp.

All these reasons were reduced into three general heads: 1. want of importation of coin; 2. exportation of our own; 3. and consumption and waste within the land.

9.6 Clement Adams on the Kingdom of Muscovy (1553)

Included in Richard Hakluyt, *The Principal Navigations, Voyages, and Discoveries of the English Nation by Sea or Over Land* (1589), STC 12625 (HL copy), 280, 285–6, 292.

With Sebastian Cabot, Clement Adams helped plan an attempt to find a direct route to China (otherwise accessible only through Portuguese intermediaries). The 1553 search for a "Northeast Passage" failed, but the mission helmed by Sir John Willoughby succeeded in opening Russia as a new export market for England. Willoughby died when his ship, one of three, got trapped in ice; he and his men froze to death. The captain of a second ship, Richard Chancellor, was invited by Ivan IV ("Ivan the Terrible") to travel 1,000 miles inland to Moscow. Using information from Chancellor, Adams reported to the queen in ways calculated to inspire support for additional voyages, praising English customs while emphasizing Russian royal magnificence. Chancellor was authorized to revisit Russia in 1556 but drowned on the return trip, off the coast of Scotland.

At what time our merchants perceived the commodities and wares of England to be in small request with the countries and people about us and near unto us; and that those merchandises which strangers in the time and memory of our ancestors did earnestly seek and desire were now neglected; and the price thereof abated although by us carried to their own ports; and all foreign merchandises in great account and their prices wonderfully raised. Certain grave citizens of London and men of great wisdom and careful of the good of their country began to think with themselves how this mischief might be remedied. Neither was a remedy (as it then appeared) wanting to their desires for the avoiding of so great an inconvenience. For seeing that the wealth of the Spaniards and Portingales by the discovery and search of new trades and countries was marvelously increased, supposing the same to be a course and mean for them also to obtain the like, they thereupon resolved upon a new and strange navigation.

Of Moscow, the chief city of the kingdom, and of the emperor thereof

The empire and government of the king is very large and his wealth at this time exceeding great. And because the city of Moscow is the chiefest of all the rest, it seemeth of itself to challenge [*demand*] the first place in this discourse. Our men say that in bigness it is as great as the city of London with the suburbs thereof. There are many and great buildings in it, but for beauty and fairness nothing comparable to ours. There are many towns and villages also, but built out of order and with no handsomeness. Their streets and ways are not paved with stone as ours are; the walls of their houses are of wood; the roofs for the most part are covered with shingle boards. There is hard by the city a very fair castle, strong and furnished with artillery, whereunto the city is joined directly towards the north with a brick wall; the walls also of the castle are built with brick and are in breadth or thickness eighteen foot. This castle hath on the one side a dry ditch, on the other side the river Volga, whereby it is made almost inexpugnable. . . . As for the king's court and palace, it is not of the neatest, only in form it is foursquare and of low building, much surpassed and excelled by the beauty and elegance of the houses of the kings of England. The windows are very narrowly built, and some of them by glass, some other by lattices, admit the light. And whereas the palaces of our princes are decked and adorned with hangings of cloth of gold, there is none such there; they build and join to all their walls benches, and that not only in the court of the emperor but in all private men's houses. . . .

And there hence being conducted into the chamber of presence, our men began to wonder [*marvel*] at the majesty of the emperor. His seat was aloft in a very royal throne, having on his head a diadem or crown of gold, appareled with a robe all of goldsmith's work, and in his hand he held a scepter garnished and beset with precious stones; and besides all other notes and appearances of honor, there was a majesty in his countenance proportionable with the excellency of his estate.

The conclusion to Queen Mary

These are the things, Most Excellent Queen, which your subjects newly returned from Russia have brought home concerning the state of that country. Wherefore if Your Majesty shall be favorable and grant a continuance of the travel, there is no doubt but that the honor and renown of your name will be spread amongst those nations whereunto three only noble personages from the very creation have had access, to whom no man hath been comparable.

9.7   A Report of Sir John Hawkins's Voyage to the Coast of Guinea (1564)

Included in Richard Hakluyt, *The Principal Navigations, Voyages, and Discoveries of the English Nation by Sea or Over Land* (1589), STC 12625 (HL copy), 527–8.

John Hawkins, a leading strategist of the victory over the Spanish Armada, also revolutionized trade voyages by improving ship construction, reducing crew levels (fewer provisions made longer trips possible), raising pay to attract better recruits, and instituting programs of hygiene and ship repair. Another of his innovations was slave-trading, capturing Africans and exchanging them for New World gold, silver, pearls, sugar, tobacco, and animal hides. In 1562–3, Hawkins trafficked 300 Africans; in 1564–5, 400; in 1567–9, 500.

The two and twentieth [of December 1564] the Captain went into the river called Callowsa with the two barks and the John's pinnace and Solomon's boat, leaving at anchor in the river's mouth the two ships, the river being twenty leagues in where the Portingales rode. He came the five and twentieth and dispatched his business and so returned with two caravels loaden with Negroes.

The 27th the Captain being advertised by the Portingales of a town of the Negroes called Bymba, being in the way as they returned, where was not only great quantity of gold but also that there were not above forty men and a hundred women and children in the town, so that if he would give the adventure upon the same, he might get a hundred slaves. With the which tidings he, being glad because the Portingales should not think him to be of so base a courage but that he durst to give them that and greater attempts, and being thereunto also the more provoked with the prosperous success he had in other islands adjacent (where he had put them all to flight and taken in one boat twenty together), determined to stay before the town three or four hours to see what he could do. And therefore prepared his men in armor and weapon together, to the number of forty men well appointed, having to their guides certain Portingales in a boat – who brought some of them to their death, we landing boat after boat and diverse of our men scattering themselves (contrary to the Captain's will) by one or two in a company, for the hope they had to find gold in their houses, ransacking the same. In the meantime, the Negroes came upon them and hurt many, being thus scattered, whereas if five or six had been together they had been able, as their companions did, to give the overthrow to forty of them. And being driven down to take their boats, were followed so hardly by a rout of Negroes, who by that took courage to pursue them to their boats, that not only some of them but others standing ashore, not looking for any such matter, by means that the Negroes did fly at the first and our company remained in the town, were suddenly so set upon that some with great hurt recovered their boats. Other some, not able to recover the same, took the water and perished by means of the oar. While this was adoing, the Captain, who with a dozen men went through the town, returned, finding two hundred Negroes at the water's side, shooting at them in the boats and cutting them in pieces, which were drowned in the water. At whose coming they ran all away. So he entered his boats, and before he could put off from the shore they returned again and shot very fiercely and hurt diverse of them. Thus we returned back somewhat discomforted – although the Captain, in a singular wise manner, with countenance very cheerful outwardly (as though he did little weigh the death of his men . . . although his heart inwardly was broken in pieces for it), done to this end: that the Portingales being with him should not presume to resist against him nor take occasion to put him to further displeasure or hindrance for the death of our men. Having gotten by our going ten Negroes and lost seven of our best men . . . and we had twenty-seven of our men hurt.

9.8   Richard Hakluyt of the Middle Temple, "Inducements to the Liking of the Voyage Intended towards Virginia" (1585)

Included in John Brereton, *A Brief and True Relation of the Discovery of the North Part of Virginia* (1602), STC 3611 (Michigan copy), D1ʳ–E2ᵛ.

Like his kinsman the anthologizer, Richard Hakluyt of the Middle Temple was a passionate advocate of exploration. This tract displayed both imaginative and practical thinking, on the one hand arguing for the notional benefits of New World settlements, and on the other making detailed plans for their success.

1. The glory of God by planting of religion among those infidels.
2. The increase of the force of the Christians.
3. The possibility of the enlarging of the dominions of the Queen's Most Excellent Majesty, and consequently of her honor, revenues, and of her power by this enterprise.
4. An ample vent [*sale*] in time to come of the woolen cloths of England, especially those of the coarsest sorts, to the maintenance of our poor, that else starve or become burdensome to the realm. And vent also of sundry our commodities upon the tract of that firm land, and possibly in other regions from the northern side of that main.

5. A great possibility of further discoveries of other regions from the north part of the same land by sea, and of unspeakable honor and benefit that may rise upon the same by the trades to ensue in Japan, China, and Cathay, etc.

6. By return thence, this realm shall receive (by reason of the situation of the climate and by reason of the excellent soil) woad,[4] oil, wines, hops, salt, and most or all the commodities that we receive from the best parts of Europe. And we shall receive the same better cheap than now we receive them, as we may use the matter.

7. Receiving the same thence, the navy, the human strength of this realm, our merchants and their goods shall not be subject to arrest of ancient enemies and doubtful friends as of late years they have been.

8. If our nation do not make any conquest there but only use traffic and [ex]change of commodities, yet, by mean the country is not very mighty but divided into petty kingdoms, they shall not dare to offer us any great annoy but such as we may easily revenge with sufficient chastisement to the unarmed people there.

9. Whatsoever commodities we receive by the Steelyard merchants,[5] or by our own merchants from Eastland, be it flax, hemp, pitch, tar, masts, clapboard, wainscot, or such-like, the like good[s] may we receive from the north and north-east part of that country near unto Cape Breton, in return for our coarse woolen cloths, flannels, and rugs fit for those colder regions.

10. The passage to and fro is through the main ocean sea, so as we are not in danger of any enemy's coast.

11. In the voyage we are not to cross the burnt zone, nor to pass through frozen seas encumbered with ice and fogs, but in temperate climate at all times of the year. And it requireth not, as the East Indies voyage doth, the taking in of water in diverse places, by reason that it is to be sailed in five or six weeks, and by the shortness the merchant may yearly make two returns (a factory once being erected there), a matter in trade of great moment.

12. In this trade by the way, in our pass to and fro, we have in tempests and other haps all the ports of Ireland to our aid and no near coast of any enemy.

13. By this ordinary trade we may annoy the enemies to Ireland and succor the Queen's Majesty's friends there, and in time we may from Virginia yield them whatsoever commodity they now receive from the Spaniard. And so the Spaniards shall want the ordinary victual that heretofore they received yearly from thence, and so they shall not continue trade, nor fall so aptly in practice against this government as now by their trade thither they may.

14. We shall, as it is thought, enjoy in this voyage either some small islands to settle on or some one place or other on the firm land to fortify for the safety of our ships, our men, and our goods, the like whereof we have not in any

---

4 *woad*: leaves of the *Isatis tinctoria* plant, powdered and fermented to produce an extremely popular blue dye for cloth.
5 *Steelyard merchants*: merchants of the north-German Hanseatic League with a London trading post.

foreign place of our traffic, in which respect we may be in degree of more safety and more quiet.

15. The great plenty of buff [*buffalo*] hides and of many other sundry kinds of hides there now presently to be had, the trade of whale and seal fishing and of diverse other fishings in the great rivers, great bays, and seas there, shall presently defray the charge in good part or in all of the first enterprise. And so we shall be in better case than our men were in Russia, where many years were spent and great sums of money consumed before gain was found.

16. The great broad rivers of that main that we are to enter into, so many leagues navigable or portable into the mainland, lying so long a tract with so excellent and so fertile a soil on both sides, do seem to promise all things that the life of man doth require and whatsoever men may wish that are to plant upon the same or to traffic in the same.

17. And whatsoever notable commodity the soil within or without doth yield in so long a tract that is to be carried out from thence to England, the same rivers so great and deep do yield no small benefit for the sure, safe, easy, and cheap carriage of the same to shipboard, be it of great bulk or of great weight.

18. And in like sort whatsoever commodity of England the inland people there shall need, the same rivers do work the like effect in benefit for the incarriage of the same aptly, easily, and cheaply.

19. If we find the country populous and desirous to expel us and injuriously to offend us, that seek but just and lawful traffic, then, by reason that we are lords of navigation and they not so, we are the better able to defend ourselves by reason of those great rivers and to annoy them in many places.

20. Where there be many petty kings or lords planted on the rivers' sides, and by all likelihood maintain the frontiers of their several territories by wars, we may by the aid of this river join with this king here, or with that king there, at our pleasure. And may so with a few men be revenged of any wrong offered by any of them or may, if we will proceed with extremity, conquer, fortify, and plant in soils most sweet, most pleasant, most strong, and most fertile, and in the end bring them all in subjection and to civility.

21. The known abundance of fresh fish in the rivers and the known plenty of fish on the seacoast there, may assure us of sufficient victual in spite of the people, if we will use salt [*to preserve them*] and industry.

22. The known plenty and variety of flesh of diverse kinds of beasts at land there may seem to say to us that we may cheaply victual our navies to England for our returns, which benefit everywhere is not found of merchants.

23. The practice of the people of the East Indies, when the Portugals came thither first, was to cut from the Portugals their lading of spice, and hereby they thought to overthrow their proposed trade. If these people shall practice the like, by not suffering us to have any commodity of theirs without conquest (which requireth some time), yet may we maintain our first voyage thither till our purpose come to effect by the sea-fishing on the coasts there and by dragging for pearls which are said to be on those parts. And by return of those commodities

the charges in part shall be defrayed, which is a matter of consideration in enter-prises of charge.

24. If this realm shall abound too, too much with youth, in the mines there of gold (as that of Chisca and Saguenay), of silver, copper, iron, etc., may be an employment to the benefit of this realm. In tilling of the rich soil there for grain and in planting of vines there for wine or dressing of those vines which grow there naturally in great abundance; olives for oil, orange trees, lemons, figs, and almonds for fruit; woad, saffron, and madder for dyers; hops for brewers; hemp, flax; and in many such other things, by employment of the soil, our people void of sufficient trades may be honestly employed, that else may become hurtful at home.

25. The navigating of the seas in the voyage and of the great rivers there will breed many mariners for service and maintain much navigation.

26. The number of raw hides there of diverse kinds of beasts, if we shall possess some island there or settle on the firm, may presently employ many of our idle people in diverse several dressings of the same. And so we may return them to the people that cannot dress them so well, or into this realm, where the same are good merchandise, or to Flanders, etc. Which present gain at the first raiseth great encouragement presently to the enterprise.

27. Since great waste woods be there of oak, cedar, pine, walnuts, and sundry other sorts, many of our waste people may be employed in making of ships, hoys,[6] buses,[7] and boats, and in making of rosin, pitch, and tar, the trees natural for the same being certainly known to be near Cape Breton and the Bay of Menan and in many other places thereabout.

28. If mines of white or gray marble, jet, or other rich stone be found there, our idle people may be employed in the mines of the same and in preparing the same to shape. And, so shaped, they may be carried into this realm as good ballast for our ships and after serve for noble buildings.

29. Sugar-canes may be planted as well as they are now in the south of Spain, and besides the employment of our idle people, we may receive the commodity cheaper and not enrich infidels or our doubtful friends of whom now we receive that commodity.

30. The daily great increase of wools in Spain, and the like in the West Indies, and the great employment of the same into cloth in both places may move us to endeavor, for vent of our cloth, new discoveries of peopled regions where hope of sale may arise. Otherwise in short time many inconveniences may possi-bly ensue.

31. This land that we purpose to direct our course to, lying in part in the 40 degree of latitude, being in like heat as Lisbon in Portugal doth, and in the more southerly part as the most southerly coast of Spain doth, may by our diligence

---

6 *hoys*: small vessels used for sailing short distances along a coastline.
7 *buses*: harquebuses, or small, portable cannons.

yield unto us, besides wines and oils and sugars, oranges, lemons, figs, raisins, almonds, pomegranates, rice, raw silks such as come from Granada, and diverse commodities for dyers, as anil and cochineal[8] and sundry other colors and materials. Moreover, we shall not only receive many precious commodities besides from thence, but also shall in time find ample vent of the labor of our poor people at home by sale of hats, bonnets, knives, fish-hooks, copper kettles, beads, looking-glasses, bugles, and a thousand kinds of other wrought wares that in short time may be brought in use among the people of that country, to the great relief of the multitude of our poor people and to the wonderful enriching of this realm. And in time such league and intercourse may arise between our stapling seats[9] there and other ports of our Northern America, and of the islands of the same, that incredible things, and by few as yet dreamed of, may speedily follow, tending to the impeachment of our mighty enemies and to the common good of this noble government.

The ends of this voyage are these:

1. To plant Christian religion.
2. To traffic.
3. To conquer.
Or, to do all three.

To plant Christian religion without conquest will be hard. Traffic easily followeth conquest; conquest is not easy. Traffic without conquest seemeth possible and not uneasy. What is to be done is the question.

If the people will be content to live naked and to content themselves with few things of mere necessity, then traffic is not. So then in vain seemeth our voyage, unless this nature may be altered, as by conquest and other good means it may be, but not on a sudden. The like whereof appeared in the East Indies, upon the Portugals seating there.

If the people in the inland be clothed and desire to live in the abundance of all such things as Europe doth, and have at home all the same in plenty, yet we cannot have traffic with them, by mean they want not anything that we can yield them.

Admit that they have desire to your commodities and as yet have neither gold, silver, copper, iron, nor sufficient quantity of other present commodity to maintain the yearly trade: what is then to be done?

The soil and climate first is to be considered, and you are with Argus eyes[10] to see what commodity by industry of man you are able to make it to yield that England doth want or doth desire. . . . But how the natural people of the country may be made skillful to plant vines and to know the use or to set olive trees

---

8 *anil and cochineal*: one, the indigo shrub used for a deep blue dye; the other, the dried bodies of a Mexican insect used for a brilliant scarlet dye.

9 *stapling seats*: places where export goods were weighed and inspected.

10 *Argus eyes*: In Greek mythology, Argus Panoptes was described as having a hundred eyes.

and to know the making of oil and withal to use both the trades – that is a matter of small consideration. But to conquer a country or province in climate and soil of Italy, Spain, or the islands from whence we receive our wines and oils and to man it, to plant it, and to keep it, and to continue the making of wines and oils able to serve England, were a matter of great importance both in respect of the saving at home of our great treasure now yearly going away and in respect of the annoyance thereby growing to our enemies. . . .

Sorts of men which are to be passed in this voyage:

1. Men skillful in all mineral causes.
2. Men skillful in all kind of drugs.
3. Fishermen to consider of the sea-fishings there on the coasts, to be reduced to trade hereafter, and others for the freshwater fishings.
4. Salt-makers to view the coast and to make trial how rich the seawater there is, to advise for the trade.
5. Husbandmen to view the soil, to resolve for tillage in all sorts.
6. Vineyard men bred to see how the soil may serve for the planting of vines.
7. Men bred in . . . south Spain, for discerning how olive trees may be planted there.
8. Others for planting of orange trees, fig trees, lemon trees, and almond trees, for judging how the soil may serve for the same.
9. Gardeners to prove the several soils of the islands and of our settling places, to see how the same may serve for all herbs and roots for our victualing, since by rough seas sometimes we may want fish and since we may want flesh to victual us, by the malice of the natural people there. And gardeners for planting of our common trees of fruit, as pears, apples, plums, peaches, medlars [*small apple-shaped fruit*], apricots, quinces for conserves, etc.
10. Lime-makers to make lime [*mortar, cement*] for buildings.
11. Masons, carpenters, etc., for buildings there.
12. Brickmakers and tilemakers.
13. Men cunning in the art of fortification, that may choose out places strong by nature to be fortified, and that can plot out and direct workmen.
14. Choice spademen to trench cunningly and to raise bulwarks and rampires [*ramparts*] of earth for defense and offense.
15. Spade-makers that may out of the woods there make spades like those of Devonshire and of other sorts, and shovels from time to time for common use.
16. Smiths to forge the irons of the shovels and spades, and to make black bills and other weapons, and to mend many things.
17. Men that use to break ash trees for pikestaves, to be employed in the woods there.

18. Others that finish up the same so rough-hewed, such as in London are to be had.
19. Coopers to make cask of all sorts.
20. Forgers of pikesheads and of arrowheads, with forges, with Spanish iron, and with all manner of tools to be carried with them.
21. Fletchers to renew arrows, since archery prevaileth much against unarmed people and gunpowder may soon perish by setting on fire.
22. Bowyers also to make bows there for need.
23. Makers of oars, since for service upon those rivers it is to great purpose for the boats and barges they are to pass and enter with.
24. Shipwrights to make barges and boats and bigger vessels, if need be, to run along the coast and to pierce the great bays and inlets.
25. Turners to turn targets [*shields*] of elm and tough wood for use against the darts and arrow of savages.
26. Such also as have knowledge to make targets of horn [*animal horn*].
27. Such also as can make armor of hides upon molds, such as were wont to be made in this realm about an hundred years since and were called Scottish Jacks. Such armor is light and defensive enough against the force of savages.
28. Tanners to tan hides of buffs, oxen, etc., in the isles where you shall plant.
29. Whittawers [*leather-makers*] of all other skins there.
30. Men skillful in burning of soap-ashes and in making of pitch and tar and rosin to be fetched out of Prussia and Poland, which are thence to be had for small wages, being there in manner of slaves. . . .
31. A skillful painter is also to be carried with you, which the Spaniards used commonly in all their discoveries to bring the descriptions of all beasts, birds, fishes, trees, towns, etc.

9.9 Thomas Harriot, *A Brief and True Report of the New-Found Land of Virginia* (1588)

From STC 12785 (HL copy), E1^v, E2^r–E3^r, E4^r, E4^v–F1^r, F1^v–F2^r.

Harriot was a young mathematician when he was chosen by Sir Walter Ralegh to join a mission to Virginia in 1585. The Roanoke settlement failed, and subsequent reports of the harshness of the New World were discouraging. But, like Ralegh, Harriot believed it to be full of possibility, promising such "merchantable commodities" as flax, hemp, sassafras, cedar, grapes, walnuts, bear oil, deer skins, copper, pearls, and tobacco. Harriot, who was to die of a cancer of the nose undoubtedly caused by his use of New-World tobacco, wrote this promotional tract to encourage continued efforts at settlement and trade.

Figure 12 Title page from Thomas Harriot's *Brief and True Report of the New-Found Land of Virginia* (1588). Courtesy of The British library.

The first edition of Thomas Harriot's report from Virginia was a small quarto volume without illustrations. Two years later, in 1590, a folio-sized version appeared, with drawings by John White that introduced England to the images of a new world: the differing costumes of native Americans, views of the Virginia towns of Pomeiooc and Secota, and illustrations of "their manner of carrying their children," "the manner of making their boats," "their manner of fishing," "the broiling of their fish over the flame," "their seething of their meat in earthen pots," "their sitting at meat," "their manner of praying with rattles about the fire," "their dances," and the tomb of their "chief lords." For this volume, an impressive title page was devised in the Renaissance manner, with an architectural framework featuring, above the pediment, a native conjurer, a carved wooden "idol" named Kiwasa, and a priest of Secota. Below are a "prince" of Secota and a "chief lady" of Pomeiooc. The rank of the subjects is iden-tified in terms that may not have made sense in native culture but that would have seemed reassuringly familiar to Europeans.

You may know how that they [*native Americans*], in respect of troubling our inhabiting and planting, are not to be feared, but that they shall have cause both to fear and love us that shall inhabit with them.

They are a people clothed with loose mantles made of deer skins, and aprons of the same round about their middles, all else naked; of such a difference of statures only as we in England. Having no edge tools or weapons of iron or steel to offend us withal, neither know they how to make any. Those weapons that they have are only bows made of witch hazel and arrows of reeds, flat-edged truncheons also, of wood about a yard long. Neither have they anything to defend themselves but targets made of barks and some armors made of sticks wickered together with thread. . . .

If there fall out any wars between us and them, what their fight is likely to be, we having advantages against them so many manner of ways – as by our discipline, our strange weapons and devices else, especially by ordnance great and small – it may be easily imagined. By the experience we have had in some places, the turning up of their heels against us in running away was their best defense.

In respect of us they are a people poor and, for want of skill and judgment in the knowledge and use of our things, do esteem our trifles before things of greater value. Notwithstanding, in their proper manner, considering the want of such means as we have, they seem very ingenious. For although they have no such tools nor any such crafts, sciences, and arts as we, yet in those things they do, they show excellency of wit. And by how much they upon due consideration shall find our manner of knowledges and crafts to exceed theirs in perfection and speed for doing or execution, by so much the more is it probable that they should desire our friendships and love and have the greater respect for pleasing and obeying us. Whereby may be hoped, if means of good government be used, that they may in short time be brought to civility and the embracing of true religion.

Some religion they have already, which, although it be far from the truth, yet being as it is there is hope it may be the easier and sooner reformed. They believe that there are many gods, which they call *montóac*, but of different sorts and degrees: one only chief and great god, which hath been from all eternity, who, as they affirm, when he purposed to make the world, made first other gods of a principal order to be as means and instruments to be used in the creation and government to follow. And after, the sun, moon, and stars as petty gods and instruments of the other order more principal.

First they say were made waters, out of which by the gods was made all diversity of creatures that are visible or invisible. For mankind they say a woman was made first, which by the working of one of the gods conceived and brought forth children. And in such sort they say they had their beginning. . . .

Most things they saw with us, as mathematical instruments, sea compasses, the virtue of the loadstone [*magnet*] in drawing iron, a perspective [*magnifying*] glass whereby was showed many strange sights, burning glasses, wild fireworks, guns, books, writing and reading, spring clocks that seem to go of themselves, and many other things that we had, were so strange unto them and so far exceeded their capacities to comprehend the reason and means how they should be made and done that they thought they were rather the works of gods than of men, or at the leastwise they had been given and taught us of the gods. Which made many of them to have such opinion of us as that if they knew not the truth of God and religion already, it was rather to be had from us – whom God so specially loved – than from a people that were so simple as they found themselves to be in comparison of us. . . .

One other rare and strange accident, leaving others, will I mention before I end, which moved the whole country that either knew or heard of us to have us in wonderful admiration. There was no town where we had any subtle device practiced against us, we leaving it unpunished or not revenged (because we sought by all means possible to win them by gentleness), but that within a few days after our departure from every such town the people began to die very fast, and many in short space. In some towns about twenty; in some, forty; in some, sixty; and in one, six score, which in truth was very many in respect of their numbers. This happened in no place that we could learn but where we had been, where they used some practice against us and after such time. The disease also so strange that they neither knew what it was nor how to cure it. The like by report of the oldest men in the country never happened before, time out of mind. . . . This marvelous accident in all the country wrought so strange opinions of us that some people could not tell whether to think us gods or men, and the rather because that all the space of their sickness there was no man of ours known to die, or that was specially sick.

They noted also that we had no women amongst us, neither that we did care for any of theirs. Some therefore were of opinion that we were not born of women, and therefore not mortal, but that we were men of an old generation many years past, then risen again to immortality.

9.10 William Keeling's Journal of African Voyages (1607)

From Samuel Purchas, *Purchas his Pilgrims* (1625) STC 20509 (Illinois copy), 189; and *Narratives of Voyages Towards the North-West in Search of a Passage to Cathay and India, 1496–1631*, ed. Thomas Rundall, Hakluyt Society (1849), 231.

William Keeling was appointed general of the third voyage of the East India Company, a voyage with three ships. The Consent, *captained by David Middleton, sailed to the Moluccas, and the* Hector, *captained by William Hawkins, reached India. Off Sierra Leone, Keeling's own* Red Dragon *was becalmed by storms and crew resistance. Later, Keeling was to discover the Cocos Islands in the Indian Ocean; these are also known as the Keeling Islands. The early modern anthologizer of his journal, Samuel Purchas, omitted entries about onboard entertainment (added here from the later edition by Thomas Rundall).*

The seventh [of August 1607], there came Negroes of better semblance aboard with my boat (for whom, as for all other, we were fain to leave one of my men, for two of them in hostage), who made signs that I should send some of my men up into the country, and that they would stay aboard in hostage. I sent Edward Buckbury and my servant William Cotterell with a present, viz., one coarse shirt, three foot of a bar of iron, a few glass beads, and two knives. They returned towards night, and brought me from the [Negro] Captain one small earring of gold, valued at seven, eight, or nine shillings sterling. And because it was late, the hostages would not go ashore, but lay aboard all night, without pawn [*hostages*] for them. . . .

4 September.   Towards night the king's interpreter came and brought me a letter from the Portingale, wherein (like the faction) he offered me all kindly services. The bearer is a man of marvelous ready wit and speaks in eloquent Portuguese. He laid aboard me.

5 September.   I sent the interpreter, according to his desire, aboard the Hector, where he broke fast and after came aboard me, where we gave the tragedy of *Hamlet*.

[7 September.]   And in the afternoon we went all together ashore, to see if we could shoot an elephant. We shot seven or eight bullets into him and made him bleed exceedingly, as appeared by his track. But, being near night, we were constrained aboard without effecting our purposes on him.

30 September.   Captain Hawkins dined with me, where my companions acted *King Richard the Second*.

31 September.   I invited Captain Hawkins to a fish dinner and had *Hamlet* acted aboard me, which I permit to keep my people from idleness and unlawful games or sleep.

10

Science and Medicine

The "Scientific Revolution" of the sixteenth and seventeenth centuries can be attributed in part to such technological inventions as microscopes and telescopes; they were the conditions of possibility for new observations. But the Revolution was also produced by hypotheses, analogies, and academic arguments. Nicolaus Copernicus, for example, made no astronomical "discoveries": he speculated from a geometrical model that it might be possible that the earth orbited the sun. Early scientists were called "natural philosophers" because their work involved the application to a subject of the theoretical mind, rather than the collection, examination, and recording of empirical evidence. The new precision devices for studying the planets and navigating the earth were at first called "philosophical instruments."

Those who had revolutionary ideas were expected to demonstrate that they built upon received knowledge. Under the influence of humanism, this was largely classical knowledge. Copernicus, for example, declared himself to be working in the tradition of Ptolemy. However, the wisdom of the ancients had powerfully inhibiting effects. There were limits to how much it was possible to understand about the human body so long as the starting point was Galen and his belief in the centrality of the liver and its "humors." Aristotle had an especially stultifying impact on practical advancement, because he was convinced that nature could not be improved upon. One of the leading thinkers at Oxford University in the late sixteenth century, John Case, was a dedicated Aristotelian.

Another constraining factor was faith. Oxford and Cambridge were understood to prepare their matriculants not for a life of the mind but instead for a life in the church. The first arithmetic text published in England, *De Arte Supputandi* (1522), was written by Cuthbert Tunstal, who would go on to be named Bishop of London (and who would forbid William Tyndale to publish an English translation of the Bible). There was a religious understanding behind Sir Richard Barckley's *A Discourse of the Felicity of Man* (1598), which stated that because the sun was moving continuously closer to the earth, all plants and animals, including man, were declining, growing weaker, and living shorter lives.

Thus, the "Scientific Revolution" was not a matter of steady progress in knowledge. Too often, there were theological, political, and intellectual reasons for natural philosophers to maintain old and erroneous belief systems. Moreover, for every scientific milestone that contributed to a better understanding of the physical world, such as that of Copernicus, there were "breakthroughs" and hypotheses that led nowhere, such as that of Barckley. Much that we now know about mechanics, gravity, and light, for example, can be attributed to Sir Isaac Newton. But Newton also devoted himself to alchemical projects, in a vain attempt to turn base metals such as lead into gold.

A European "Revolution"

Like the artistic "Renaissance," the "Scientific Revolution" began outside England. In Poland, Copernicus proposed that the sun rather than the earth might be the center of the known universe (1543). In Belgium, Andreas Vesalius dissected corpses to produce detailed illustrations of human anatomy (1543). In Flanders, Gerardus Mercator developed a system of global cartographic projection and published a world atlas (1569, 1585). In Denmark, Tycho Brahe observed a supernova in his planetary observatory and argued that the heavens were not static (1572). In the Netherlands, Zacharias Janssen invented a compound microscope (1590). In Italy, Galileo Galilei built a telescope and discovered the craters of the moon, the moons of Jupiter, and the stars of the Milky Way (1609, 1610). In Germany, Johannes Kepler proposed his first, second, and third laws of planetary motion (1609, 1619). In Scotland, John Napier developed a method for calculating logarithms (1614, 1617). The discourses of western knowledge were highly internationalized. Information circulated across the borders of European countries not only by means of university and patronage circles but also in the new medium of print.

The path for England to join this "Revolution" was laid by such men as Robert Recorde, who disseminated already-established arithmetical, geometric, and algebraic knowledge in the reassuringly narrativized form of English-language dialogues (1543–57). Independently, Recorde invented the "equal" sign for mathematical notation. Thomas Digges translated the work of Copernicus and defended the idea of heliocentrism. He himself suggested that the star-filled space that extended beyond the known universe was boundless (1576). Edward Wright proved Mercator's projections by using Euclidean geometry. Even without integral calculus, he was able to solve the problem of how to proportionately increase the distance between parallels of latitude in order to produce the first serviceable chart of the Azores (1599). But the sciences of the time were no more specialized or professionalized than were the arts. All these men were also involved in matters of practical navigation, and Recorde was an administrator of Crown mints in Durham, Bristol, and Dublin; Digges was a Member of Parliament and developer of plans for a standing army; Wright was tutor to James's older son Prince Henry.

By the seventeenth century, English inventors were contributing in a more focused and sustained way to western knowledge. Thomas Harriot used a telescope to map the moon (1609). William Harvey described the heart as a pump continuously recirculating a finite supply of blood (1628). Later in the 1600s, leading English scientists included Robert Hooke, Isaac Newton, and Robert Boyle.

Patronage and Profit

In the Renaissance, as now, there was no such thing as "pure" science. One important impetus for new ideas was provided by patronage. On the Continent, there was the model of Galileo's relationship with the Medici family and Kepler's association with Rudolph II. In England, Digges hopefully dedicated his work to Robert Sidney, Earl of Leicester. Both Sir Walter Ralegh and Henry Percy, Earl of Northumberland, demonstrated their willingness to underwrite research by natural philosophers and mathematicians. However, benefactors generally expected practical returns from their investments. Just as Kepler was required to cast horoscopes for Rudolph II, so there were expectations of John Dee. Dee was the most renowned English mathematician and geographer of the sixteenth century. He studied in Louvain and lectured in Paris, provided an important "Mathematical Preface" to an English translation of Euclid's *Elements* (1570), and also wrote *General and Rare Memorials Pertaining to the Perfect Art of Navigation* (1577). Dee was asked to cast the horoscope of Elizabeth I in order to advise her of an auspicious day for her coronation.

For the nobility and gentry, advances in navigation and mapping held out the promise of imperial expansion. When Thomas Harriot traveled to the New World for Ralegh in 1585, he returned with a remarkable compendium of the unusual flora and fauna of the Americas, *A Brief and True Report of the New-Found Land of Virginia* (1588; see document 9.9). The report included observations on Algonquian beliefs, customs, and language. But Ralegh's motives were not those of the disinterested naturalist, the anthropologist, or the linguist; he appreciated the promotional value of the tract and expected it to encourage further investment in exploration and colonization. Merchants did not themselves have ambitions for territorial conquest, but they were equally concerned with the immediate practical benefits of developments in mathematics (for accounting), spherical geometry (to calculate travel routes and distances), astronomy (to set courses and identify locations), and mapping and surveying. New skills and instruments enabled them to expand their export markets, find sources for raw materials, establish new commercial partnerships, and compete with the traders from other European countries.

Science and Magic

The dividing line between science and superstition was murky. John Dee, for example, is now better known for his purported conversations with angels than for his mathematical interests. For this aspect of the "Scientific Revolution," few careers are as enlightening as that of Robert Fludd. Fludd was educated at Oxford but also spent six years traveling and studying in France, Italy, Germany, and Spain. He was made a fellow of London's College of Physicians (in 1609) and had a successful career as a London doctor. Fludd also published extensively on the Continent. In one tract, *Anatomiae amphitheatrum*, he expanded on the Paracelsian theory of a weapon-salve – that a wound can be cured if the weapon that caused the wound is coated in a mixture containing the patient's blood, some moss that has grown on a human skull, and flesh removed from a hanged man (known as "mummy"). The idea was that there is a sympathetic relationship between the weapon and the wound. Meanwhile, according to Fludd, the wound itself required no treatment other than application of the patient's own urine as a disinfectant. Believing also that sexual abstinence was important to hermetic learning and that all disease follows from sin, Fludd declared publicly that he was himself "virgo immaculata" till his death.

In many ways, Fludd was a radical thinker. He developed an alchemical account of creation from a close reading of the first book of the Bible, Genesis. His first request for a place in the College of Physicians was denied, and his license to practice medicine was withdrawn – all because he dared to challenge the precepts of the Galenic theory of the bodily humors. Fludd held the unacceptable belief that blood circulates in the body. But if William Harvey is generally credited with this advancement in knowledge, rather than Fludd, it is because Fludd's research was not observational. Instead, Fludd argued by analogy from the macrocosm to the microcosm: even as the sun revolves around the earth and provides the earth with heat and light, he said, so the blood circulates in the body and vivifies man.

Although he held ideas that seem outlandish today, Fludd was a life-long interrogator of received wisdom. Thus he helped create the culture of inquiry that was a necessary precondition for the "Scientific Revolution." Because many of the brightest intellects of the Renaissance were believers in hermetic and occult philosophies, much scientific knowledge was a byproduct of magical theory.

The Mechanical Universe

The famous names connected with the Scientific Revolution belonged to men who were among the intelligentsia. Outside these rarefied circles, people continued to think about the natural world in superstitious ways. For them, there were no knowable or discernible laws of operation. Things were unpredictable, best brought under control by prayers and charms.

The real "Revolution," thus, was not a matter of discoveries or inventions. Instead, it was a way of thinking about the world and about the place of rationality in human understanding. In 1619, the French philosopher René Descartes argued for a supreme skepticism, saying that nothing should be considered known until it could be proven through deductive reasoning. In 1620, the English philosopher Francis Bacon developed a concept of scientific method based in empirical observation and inductive logic. Bacon was one of the first Englishmen to believe that nature operated not according to divine purpose but instead by its own rules – and that these rules could be discovered by men. Descartes hailed the work of Bacon because, despite their differing methods, both advanced the concept of a mechanical universe.

These insights turned natural philosophy upside down. In 1662, the Royal Society of London for Improving of Natural Knowledge was founded on the principles not only that natural scientists *can* discover the laws of the universe but also that they *should* discover the laws of the universe. It was a profound vindication for the controversial philosophy of Bacon. By the time the world came around to him, though, Bacon was long dead. While he had never himself been associated with discoveries and experiments, the (probably apocryphal) legend goes that, while traveling, he had a sudden intuition that salt might not be the only way of preserving meat. Perhaps, he reasoned, cold would, too. He is said to have caught a fatal chill while stuffing a hen with snow.

10.1 Heinrich Cornelius Agrippa von Nettesheim, *Of the Vanity and Uncertainty of Arts and Sciences* (1569)

From STC 204 (HL copy), B1^r, B4^r, C1^r.

Agrippa's was a name to conjure with – for some, literally, as he was famously the author of the master work, Three Books of Occult Philosophy. *His celebrity spread across Europe (he was born in Germany) and long outlasted his death in 1535. For example, a book of demonic magic published in 1559 was given the title* Fourth Book of Occult Philosophy *and falsely attributed to him. Despite his notorious public identity, however, Agrippa's belief system is difficult to recover. The first draft of* Occult Philosophy *was written in 1510, and he continued to revise and expand his ideas for making magic a useful human science until its publication between 1531 and 1533. Meanwhile, though, in 1526 he wrote* Of the Vanity and Uncertainty of Arts and Sciences. *In this book Agrippa directly attacked the argument of* Occult Philosophy *and, even while flaunting his own learning, vigorously contended that all the sciences were useless and, worse, harmful. The last published version of* Occult Philosophy *includes this self-condemnation as its own appendix. Agrippa's polemic against knowledge was widely influential; James Sanford translated it from the Latin in 1569.*

It is an ancient and almost an agreeable and common opinion of all the philosophers . . . that every science doth bring unto man some divinity, according to the capacity and value of them both. . . . Notwithstanding, I, being persuaded with other kind of reasons, am of opinion that there can chance to the life and salvation of our souls nothing more hurtful and pestilent than these arts and sciences. Wherefore, I think good to entreat with a contrary order, and my opinion is that the sciences ought not to be extolled with so great praises but rather for the most part to be despised. . . .

Nothing can chance unto man more pestilent than knowledge. This is the very pestilence that putteth all mankind to ruin, the which chaseth away all innocency, and hath made us subject to so many kinds of sin and to death also; which hath extinguished the light of faith, casting our souls into blind darkness; which, condemning the truth, hath placed errors in the highest throne. Wherefore Valentianus the Emperor seemeth not to be despised, who (as it is reported) was an enemy to learning. Neither Licinius the Emperor, who was accustomed to say that learning was a poison and a public pestilence. But which is more: Valerius saith that Cicero himself, the most abundant wellspring of learning, despised it at length.[1] And so large is the liberty of the truth, and the largeness thereof so free, that it cannot be perceived with the speculations of any science, nor with any strait [*narrow*] judgment of the senses, nor with any arguments of the art of logic, nor with any evident proof, with no syllogisms of demonstration, nor with any discourse of man's reason, but with faith only. . . . There is nothing more noisome [*injurious*] nor more hurtful to the public weal than learning and sciences, wherein if there be men endowed with erudition and knowledge, matters are, for the most part, executed at their will, as those which know most. And trusting in the simplicity of the people and in the ignorance of the multitude, they take to themselves against right and reason all the authority of office, whereupon the state of the commonwealth passeth from the peoples' rule to the rule of a few, and afterward, divided into parts, doth soon turn to tyranny, which no man is read at any time in all the world to have obtained without science, without doctrine, or without learning. . . . All sciences are nothing else but the ordinances and opinions of men so noisome as profitable, so pestilent as wholesome, so ill as good, in no part perfect, but doubtful and full of error and contention.

10.2   Sir Francis Bacon, *The Advancement of Learning* (1605) and *The Great Instauration* (1620)

From *Of the Proficiency and Advancement of Learning, Divine and Human*, STC 1164 (CUL copy), A4ʳ–B2ʳ, B3ᵛ–B4ʳ, C1ʳ, C3ᵛ–C4ʳ; *The Works of Francis Bacon*, ed.

---

1 *Valentianus, et al.*: The Roman emperor Valentianus (364–75 CE) was illiterate (though he was known for founding schools); the emperor Licinius (307–24 CE) was notoriously anti-intellectual. Valerius Maximus was the author of *Factorum et Dictorum Memorabilius*.

James Spedding, Robert Leslie Ellis, Douglas Denon Heath, vol. 8 (Boston, MA: Taggard and Thompson, 1864), 41–5, 53.

Sir Francis Bacon's intellectual ambition can be judged by the fact that he published most of his philosophical works in the lingua franca of the day, Latin. The Advancement of Learning *was an exception (though he attempted to have it translated into Latin for wider accessibility in the learned circles of Europe). The book has two parts: first, a forceful defense of the importance of knowledge; second, a survey of the contemporary state of knowledge (with suggestions for areas of exploration). The project Bacon regarded as his magnum opus,* Novum organum, *was never completed, though he published some sections of it and, in a preface titled "Instauratio magna," or "great renewal," outlined the whole. Sending a copy to the king, Bacon summarized that he propounded "a new logic" which would "make philosophy and sciences both more true and more active." It was an eloquent argument against the Aristotelian notion that there was nothing more to be known.*

The Advancement of Learning *(1605)*

To have the true testimonies concerning the dignity of learning to be better heard without the interruption of tacit objections, I think good to deliver it from the discredits and disgraces which it hath received – all from ignorance, but ignorance severally disguised, appearing sometimes in the zeal and jealousy of divines, sometimes in the severity and arrogancy of politiques [*politicians*], and sometimes in the errors and imperfections of learned men themselves.

I hear the former sort say that knowledge is of those things which are to be accepted of with great limitation and caution, that the aspiring to overmuch knowledge was the original temptation and sin whereupon ensued the Fall of man, that knowledge hath in it somewhat of the serpent . . . that experience demonstrates how learned men have been arch-heretics, how learned times have been inclined to atheism, and how the contemplation of second causes doth derogate from our dependence upon God, who is the first cause.

To discover then the ignorance and error of this opinion and the misunderstanding in the grounds thereof: it may well appear these men do not observe or consider that it was not the pure knowledge of nature and universality, a knowledge by the light whereof man did give names unto other creatures in Paradise (as they were brought before him, according unto their proprieties) which gave the occasion to the Fall. But it was the proud knowledge of good and evil, with an intent in man to give law unto himself and to depend no more upon God's commandments, which was the form of the temptation. Neither is it any quantity of knowledge, how great soever, that can make the mind of man to swell, for nothing can fill, much less extend, the soul of man, but God and the contemplation of God. . . . God hath framed the mind of man as a mirror or glass, capable of the image of the universal world and joyful to receive the impression thereof, as the eye joyeth to receive light, and not only delighted in beholding the variety of things and vicissitude of times, but raised also to find out and discern the ordinances and decrees which throughout all those changes are infallibly observed. . . . If then such be the capacity and receipt of the mind of man, it is manifest that there is no danger at all in the proportion or quantity of knowledge, how large soever, lest it should make it swell or outcompass itself – no, but it is merely the quality of knowledge, which, be it in quantity more or less, if it be taken without the true corrective thereof, hath in it some nature of venom or malignity, and some effects of that venom which is ventosity [*pomposity*] or swelling. This corrective spice, the mixture whereof maketh knowledge so sovereign, is charity. . . . To conclude therefore, let no man upon a weak conceit of sobriety or an ill-applied moderation, think or maintain that a man can search too far or be too well-studied in the book of God's word or in the book of God's works, divinity, or philosophy, but rather let men endeavor an endless progress or proficience in both. Only let men beware that they apply both to charity and not to swelling, to use and not to ostentation, and again, that they do not unwisely mingle or confound these learnings together.

And as for the disgraces which learning receiveth from politiques, they be of this nature: that learning doth soften men's minds and makes them more unapt for the honor and exercise of arms; that it doth mar and pervert men's dispositions for matter of government and policy in making them too curious and irresolute by variety of reading, or too peremptory or positive by strictness of rules and axioms, or too immoderate and overweening [*presumptuous*] by reason of the greatness of examples, or too incompatible and differing from the times by reason of the dissimilitude of examples; or at least it doth divert men's travails from action and business and bringeth them to a love of leisure and privateness, and that it doth bring into states a relaxation of discipline, whilst every man is more ready to argue than to obey and execute. . . .

And for matter of policy and government, that learning should rather hurt than enable thereunto is a thing very improbable. . . . For that other conceit that learning should undermine the reverence of laws and government, it is assuredly a mere depravation [*vilification*] and calumny [*slander*] without all shadow of truth. For to say that a blind custom of obedience should be a surer obligation than duty taught and understood, it is to affirm that a blind man may tread surer by a guide than a seeing man can by a light. And it is without all controversy that learning doth make the minds of men gentle, generous, maniable [*tractable*], and pliant to government, whereas ignorance makes them churlish, thwart [*resistant*], and mutinous. And the evidence of time doth clear this assertion, considering that the most barbarous, rude, and unlearned times have been most subject to tumults, sedition, and changes.

The Great Instauration *(1620)*

In the ordinary logic almost all the work is spent about the syllogism.[2] Of induction,[3] the logicians seem hardly to have taken any serious thought, but they pass it by with a slight notice and hasten on to the formulae of disputation. I, on the contrary, reject demonstration by syllogism as acting too confusedly and letting nature slip out of its hands. For although no one can doubt that things which agree in a middle term agree with one another (which is a proposition of mathematical certainty), yet it leaves an opening for deception, which is this: the syllogism consists of propositions, propositions of words, and words are the tokens and signs of notions. Now if the very notions of the mind (which are as the soul of words and the basis of the whole structure) be improperly and overhastily abstracted from facts, vague, not sufficiently definite – faulty, in short, in many ways – the whole edifice tumbles. I therefore reject the syllogism, and that not only as regards principles (for to principles the logicians themselves do not apply it) but also as regards middle propositions, which, though obtainable no doubt by the syllogism, are, when so obtained, barren of works, remote from practice, and altogether unavailable for the active department of the sciences. Although, therefore, I leave to the syllogism and these famous and boasted modes of demonstration their jurisdiction over popular arts and such as are matter of opinion (in which department I leave all as it is), yet in dealing with the nature of things I use induction throughout, and that in the minor propositions as well as the major. For I consider induction to be that form of demonstration which upholds the sense, and closes with nature, and comes to the very brink of operation (if it does not actually deal with it). . . .

Nor is this all. For I also sink the foundations of the sciences deeper and firmer, and I begin the inquiry nearer the source than men have done heretofore, submitting to examination those things which the common logic takes on trust. For, first, the logicians borrow the principles of each science from the science itself; secondly, they hold in reverence the first notions of the mind; and, lastly, they receive as conclusive the immediate informations of the sense, when well disposed. Now upon the first point, I hold that true logic ought to enter the several provinces of science armed with a higher authority than belongs to the principles of those sciences themselves and ought to call those putative principles to account until they are fully established. Then with regard to the first notions of the intellect, there is not one of the impressions taken by the intellect when left to go its own way but I hold it for suspected and no way established, until it has submitted to a new trial

---

2 *syllogism*: an argument proceeding from two principles containing a common term, used to derive a third proposition thus believed to be proven. For example: (a) All animals are mortal. (b) Man is an animal. Therefore, (c) All men are mortal.

3 *induction*: the process of inferring a general principle from the observation of particular instances; as opposed to deduction, the process of drawing a conclusion from a principle already known or assumed, or of reasoning from generals to particulars.

and a fresh judgment has been thereupon pronounced. And lastly, the information of the sense itself I sift and examine in many ways. For certain it is that the senses deceive. But then at the same time they supply the means of discovering their own errors – only the errors are here; the means of discovery are to seek.

The sense fails in two ways. Sometimes it gives no information; sometimes it gives false information. For, first, there are very many things which escape the sense, even when best disposed and no way obstructed, by reason either of the subtlety of the whole body, or the minuteness of the parts, or distance of place, or slowness or else swiftness of motion, or familiarity of the object, or other causes. And again, when the sense does apprehend a thing its apprehension is not much to be relied upon. For the testimony and information of the sense has reference always to man, not to the universe. And it is a great error to assert that the sense is the measure of things.

To meet these difficulties, I have sought on all sides diligently and faithfully to provide helps for the sense – substitutes to supply its failures, rectifications to correct its errors – and this I endeavor to accomplish not so much by instruments as by experiments. For the subtlety of experiments is far greater than that of the sense itself, even when assisted by exquisite instruments – such experiments, I mean, as are skillfully and artificially devised for the express purpose of determining the point in question. To the immediate and proper perception of the sense, therefore, I do not give much weight. But I contrive that the office of the sense shall be only to judge of the experiment, and that the experiment itself shall judge of the thing. And thus I conceive that I perform the office of a true priest of the sense (from which all knowledge in nature must be sought, unless men mean to go mad) and a not unskillful interpreter of its oracles, and that while others only profess to uphold and cultivate the sense, I do so in fact. Such then are the provisions I make for finding the genuine light of nature and kindling and bringing it to bear. And they would be sufficient of themselves if the human intellect were even and like a fair sheet of paper with no writing on it. But since the minds of men are strangely possessed and beset so that there is no true and even surface left to reflect the genuine rays of things, it is necessary to seek a remedy for this also. . . .

All depends on keeping the eye steadily fixed upon the facts of nature and so receiving their images simply as they are. For God forbid that we should give out a dream of our own imagination for a pattern of the world; rather may he graciously grant to us to write an apocalypse or true vision of the footsteps of the Creator imprinted on his creatures.

10.3   *The Book of Secrets of Albertus Magnus* (1560)

From STC 258.5 (Bodleian copy), A3^r–A5^v, C1^r–C2^r, C4^{r-v}.

This compilation of practical and magical information represents the popular science that Sir Francis Bacon and other early moderns inherited. The collection was credited to Albertus Magnus, a famed thirteenth-century scholastic who worked to reconcile the scientific philosophy of Aristotle with the Christian religion. As was true for Agrippa's supposed Fourth Book of Occult Philosophy, *however, the attribution was based not in fact but instead in a calculated attempt by anonymous publishers to gain associational prestige.*

Of the virtues of certain herbs

The first herb is called . . . (with Englishmen) *marigold*, whose interpretation is of *helios* (that is, the sun) and *tropos* (that is, alteration or change), because it is turned according to the sun. The virtue of this herb is marvelous, for if it be gathered, the sun being in the sign [of] Leo (in August), and be wrapped in the leaf of a laurel or bay tree, and a wolf's tooth be added thereto, no man shall be able to have a word to speak against the bearer thereof but words of peace. And if anything be stolen, if the bearer of the things before named lay them under his head in the night, he shall see the thief and all his conditions. And moreover if the foresaid herb be put in any church where women be which have broken matrimony on their part, they shall never be able to go forth of the church except it [the herb] be put away. And this last point hath been proved and is very true. . . .

The fourth herb is named . . . of Englishmen *celandine*. This herb springeth in the time in the which the swallows and also the eagles maketh their nests. If any man shall have this herb with the heart of a mole, he shall overcome all his enemies and all matters in suit and shall put away all debate. And if the before-named herb be put upon the head of a sick man, if he should die he shall sing anon with a loud voice; if not, he shall weep.

The fifth herb is named . . . of Englishman, *periwink*. When it is beaten unto powder with worms of the earth wrapped about it and with an herb called *semperviva* (in English, houseleek), it induceth love between man and wife if it be used in their meats.

Of the virtues of certain stones

If thou wilt know whether thy wife is chaste or no: take the stone which is called *magnes* (in English, the loadstone). It is of sad [*dark*] blue color, and it is found in the sea of Inde, sometime in parts of Allemagne, in the province which is called East France. Lay this stone under the head of a wife, and if she be chaste she will embrace her husband; if she be not chaste, she will fall anon forth of the bed. Moreover, if this stone be put brayed [*crushed*] and scattered upon coals in four corners of the house, they that shall be sleeping shall flee the house and leave all. . . .

If thou wilt provoke sorrow, fear, terrible fantasies, and debate: take the stone which is called *onyx*, which is of black color. And the kind is best which is full of white veins. And it cometh from Inde unto Araby, and if it be hanged upon the neck or finger, it stirreth up anon sorrow or heaviness in a man, and terrors and also debate. And this hath been proved by men of late time. . . .

If thou wilt overcome thy enemies: take the stone which is called *adamas*, in English speech a diamond, and it is of shining color and very hard, insomuch that it cannot be broken but by the blood of a goat, and it groweth in Arabia or in Cyprus. And if it be bounden to the left side, it is good against enemies, madness, wild beasts, venomous beasts, and cruel men, and against chiding and brawling, and against venom and invasion of fantasies.

10.4   John Gerard, *The Herbal or General History of Plants* (1597)

From STC 11750 (HL copy), Pp4^r–Pp6^v, Qq1^r–Qq3^v.

John Gerard was a gardener employed by William Cecil, to whom this collection of detailed botanical information was dedicated. Gerard was said to have had a thousand different herbs in his own London garden, and in the book he describes and provides illustrations for over eighteen hundred plants, many native, but some also imported. To compare the marigold of The Book of Secrets *with Gerard's descriptions of German marigolds, African marigolds, Peruvian marigolds, and ten different English marigolds – just one is represented below – is to witness the beginning of a scientific method of observation and classification. The book was republished with additions and emendations by Thomas Johnson in 1633 and again in 1636.*

Of Marigolds

The kinds: There be diverse sorts of marigolds, differing in many notable points. Some are great and very double; some smaller and yet double; some of the garden likewise and single although it was sown of double seed (so list [*pleases*] nature to play with her little ones); others wild or of the field; and some of the water. . . .

The description: The greatest double marigold hath many large, fat, broad leaves springing immediately from a fibrous or thready root. The upper sides of the leaves are of a deep green and the lower side of a more light or shining green, among which rise up stalks somewhat hairy and also somewhat jointed, and full of a spongeous pith. The flowers in the top are beautiful, round, very large and double, something sweet, with a certain strong smell, of a light saffron color, or like pure gold, from the which follow a number of long crooked seeds, especially the outmost, or those that stand about the edges of the flower which, being sown, commonly bring forth single flowers, whereas contrariwise those seeds in the middle are lesser and for the most part bring forth such flowers as that was from whence it was taken. . . .

The time: The marigold flowereth from April or May even until winter – and in winter also, if it be warm. . . .

The temperature and virtues: The flower of the marigold is of temperature hot, almost in the second degree. Especially when it is dry, it is thought to strengthen and comfort the heart and to withstand poison, as also to be good against pestilent agues, being taken any way. . . . Being drunk with wine, it bringeth down the terms [*menstrual discharge*] . . . the fume thereof expelleth the secondine or afterbirth. . . . If the mouth be washed with the juice, it helpeth the toothache. The flowers and leaves of marigolds being distilled, and the water dropped into red and watery eyes, ceaseth the inflammation and taketh away the pain. Conserve made of the flowers and sugar taken in the morning fasting cureth the trembling of the heart and is also given in time of plague or pestilence or corruption of the air. The yellow leaves of the flowers are dried and kept throughout Dutchland against winter, to put into broths, in physical potions, and for diverse other purposes, in such quantity that in some grocers or cellars of spice houses are to be found barrels filled with them, and retailed by the penny more or less, insomuch that no broths are well made without dried marigolds.

Of French Marigold, or African Marigold

The description: The common French marigold hath small, weak, and tender branches trailing upon the ground, reeling and leaning this way and that way, beset with leaves consisting of many particular leaves indented about the edges which, being held up against the sun or to the light, are seen to be full of holes like a sieve, even as those of Saint John's Wort. The flowers stand at the top of the spriggy branches forth of long cups or husks, consisting of eight or ten small leaves, yellow underneath, on the upper side of a deeper yellow tending to the color of a dark crimson velvet, as also soft in handling. But to describe the color in words, it is not possible, but this way: lay upon paper with a pencil a yellow color called masticot which, being dry, lay the same over with a little saffron steeped in water or wine, which setteth forth most lively the color. The whole plant is of a most rank and unwholesome smell, and perisheth at the first frost.

The place: They are cherished and sown in gardens every year. They grow everywhere almost in Africa of themselves, from whence we first had them. . . .

The time: They are to be sown in the beginning of April if the season fall out to be warm. Otherwise they must be sown in a bed of dung, as shall be showed in the chapter of cucumbers. They bring forth their pleasant flowers very late, and therefore there is the more diligence to be used to sow them very early, because they shall not be overtaken with the frosts before their seed be ripe.

The temperature and virtues: The unpleasant smell, especially that common sort with single flowers . . . doth show that it is of a poisonsome and cooling quality, and also the same is manifested by diverse experiments. For I remember [saith Dodonaeus[4]], that I did see a boy whose lips and mouth when he began to chew the flowers did swell extremely, as it hath often happened unto them that playing or piping with quills or kexes of hemlocks do hold them a while between their lips. Likewise, he saith, we gave to a cat the flowers with their cups, tempered with fresh cheese; she forthwith mightily swelled, and a little while after died. Also mice that have eaten of the seed thereof have been found dead. All which things do declare that this herb is of a venomous and poisonsome faculty, and that they are not to be hearkened unto that suppose this herb to be an harmless plant. So to conclude, these plants are most venomous and full of poison, and therefore not to be touched or smelled unto, much less used in meat or medicine.

Of the Flower of the Sun, or the Marigold of Peru

The description: The Indian Sun, or the golden flower of Peru, is a plant of such stature and tallness that in one summer, being sown of a seed in April, it hath risen up to the height of fourteen foot in my garden, where one flower was in weight three pound and two ounces, and cross overthwart the flower by measure sixteen inches broad. The stalks are upright and straight, of the bigness of a strong man's arm, beset with large leaves even to the top. . . . At the top of the stalk commeth forth for the most part one flower, yet many times there spring out sucking buds which come to no perfection. This great flower is in shape like to the camomile flower, beset round about with a pale or border of goodly yellow leaves, in shape like the leaves of the flowers of white lilies. The middle part whereof is made as it were of unshorn velvet or some curious cloth wrought with the needle, which brave work, if you do thoroughly view and mark well, it seemeth to be an innumerable sort of small flowers, resembling the nose or nozzle of a candlestick broken from the foot thereof, from which small nozzle sweateth forth excellent fine and clear Venice turpentine in sight, substance, savor, and taste. The whole plant in like manner being broken smelleth of turpentine. When the plant groweth to maturity the flowers fall away, in place whereof appeareth the seed, black and large, much like the seed of gourds, set as though a cunning workman had of purpose placed them in very good order, much like the honeycombs of bees.

The place: These plants do grow of themselves without setting or sowing in Peru and in diverse other provinces of America, from whence the seeds have been brought into these parts of Europe. There hath been seen in Spain and other hot regions a plant sown and nourished up from seed to attain to the height of twenty-four foot in one year.

---

4 *Dodoneaus*: a sixteenth-century Flemish botanist whose *Cruijdeboeck* (1554) was translated into French (*Histoire des Plantes*, 1557) and Latin (*Stirpium historiae pemptades sex sive libri XXX*, 1583), and was Gerard's frequent source.

The time: The seed must be set or sown in the beginning of April, if the weather be temperate, in the most fertile ground that may be, and where the sun hath most power the whole day.

The virtues: There hath not any thing been set down either of the ancient or later writers concerning the virtues of these plants. Notwithstanding we have found by trial that the buds before they be flowered, boiled and eaten with butter, vinegar, and pepper, after the manner of artichokes, are exceeding pleasant meat.

10.5   Thomas Digges's Defense of Heliocentrism (1576)

From *A Prognostication Everlasting of Right Good Effect*, STC 435.47 (HL copy), M1^r–M2^v.

Most almanacs were meant for annual consumption, but the version published by Leonard Digges in 1555 was intended to be more lasting, with meteorological information and a defense of mathematics as the source of "more pleasant joy of mind than all thy goods (how rich soever thou be) can at any time purchase." In 1576 Leonard's son Thomas added an appendix that gave the first English translation of the work of Copernicus. Thomas himself devised a diagram that showed the universe to be infinite. In this preface to the reader, he endorsed heliocentrism.

Seeing the continual errors that from time to time more and more have been discovered, besides the infinite absurdities in their theorics which they have been forced to admit, that would not confess any mobility in the ball of the earth, [Copernicus] hath by long study, painful practice, and rare invention delivered a new theoric or model of the world, showing that the earth resteth not in the center of the whole world but only in the center of this our mortal world or globe of elements, which environed and enclosed in the moon's orb, and, together with the whole globe of mortality, is carried yearly round about the sun, which like a king in the middest of all reigneth and giveth laws of motion to the rest, spherically dispersing his glorious beams of light through all this sacred celestial temple. And the earth itself to be one of the planets having his peculiar and straying courses turning every twenty-four hours round upon his own center. Whereby the sun and great globe of fixed stars seem to sway about and turn, albeit indeed they remain fixed. So many ways is the sense of mortal man abused, but reason and deep discourse of wit having opened these things to Copernicus, and the same being with demonstrations mathematical most apparently by him to the world delivered, I thought it convenient together with the old theoric also to publish this, to the end such noble English minds as delight to reach above the baser sort of men might not be altogether defrauded of so noble a part of philosophy. And to the end it might manifestly appear that

Copernicus meant not (as some have fondly excused him) to deliver these grounds of the earth's mobility only as mathematical principles feigned, and not as philosophical truly averred, I have also from him delivered both the philosophical reasons by Aristotle and others produced to maintain the earth's stability and also their solutions and insufficiency. Wherein I cannot a little commend the modesty of that grave philosopher Aristotle, who [saw] (no doubt) the insufficiency of his own reasons in seeking to confute the earth's motion. . . . If therefore the earth be situate immovable in the center of the world, why find we not theorics upon that ground to produce effects as true and certain as those of Copernicus? . . . Why shall we so much dote in the appearance of our senses (which many ways may be abused) and not suffer ourselves to be directed by the rule of reason, which the great God hath given us as a lamp to lighten the darkness of our understanding, and the perfect guide to lead us to the golden branch of verity amid the forest of errors?

In the midst of this globe of mortality hangeth this dark star or ball of earth and water, balanced and sustained in the midst of the thin air only with that propriety which the wonderful workman hath given at the Creation to the center of this globe, with his magnetical force vehemently to draw and hale unto itself all such other elemental things as retain the like nature. This ball every twenty-four hours by natural, uniform, and wonderful sly and smooth motion rolleth round, making with his period our natural day, whereby it seems to us that the huge, infinite, immovable globe should sway and turn about.

The moon's orb that environeth and containeth this dark star and the other mortal, changeable, corruptible elements and elementate things is also turned 'round every 29 days, 31 minutes, 50 seconds, 8 thirds, 9 fourths, and 20 fifths. And this period may most aptly be called the month.

10.6 John Wilkins, *The Discovery of a World in the Moon* (1638)

From STC 25640.5 (BL copy), P2^v–P4^r.

John Wilkins was a serious theologian (eventually appointed Bishop of Chester), but as a natural philosopher he was a popularizer, making the work of Copernicus, Galileo, and Kepler available to general readerships. In another work, Mathematical Magick, or, The Wonders that may be Performed by Mechanical Geometry *(1648), he showed the powerful capabilities of levers, pulleys, and screws, before going on to present ideas about flying machines and submarines.*

The propositions that are proved in this discourse:

1. That the strangeness of this opinion is no sufficient reason why it should be rejected, because other certain truths have been formerly

esteemed ridiculous and great absurdities entertained by common consent.

2. That a plurality of worlds doth not contradict any principle of reason or faith.

3. That the heavens do not consist of any such pure matter which can privilege them from the like change and corruption as these inferior bodies are liable unto.

4. That the moon is a solid, compacted, opacous [*dark*] body.

5. That the moon hath not any light of her own.

6. That there is a world in the moon hath been the direct opinion of many ancient, with some modern, mathematicians, and may probably be deduced from the tenets of others.

7. That those spots and brighter parts which by our sight may be distinguished in the moon do show the difference betwixt the sea and land in that other world.

8. That the spots represent the sea and the brighter parts the land.

9. That there are high mountains, deep valleys, and spacious plains in the body of the moon.

10. That there is an atmosphere or an orb of gross vaporous air, immediately encompassing the body of the moon.

11. That as their world is our moon, so our world is their moon.

12. That 'tis probable there may be such meteors belonging to that world in the moon as there are with us.

13. That 'tis probable there may be inhabitants in this other world, but of what kind they are is uncertain.

10.7   Nicholas Culpeper, *Galen's Art of Physic* (1652)

From Wing STC G159 (Thomason Collection copy), F2^v–F5^r.

The principal medical beliefs of the ancient Greek physician Galen were so widely known and so intractably established that they seem scarcely to have required translation. There was a Latin version of his work in the 1530s (prepared by Andreas Vesalius), but no English edition until Nicholas Culpeper published one in 1652. Culpeper also translated the Pharmacopoeia *(1649), thus ending the pharmacological monopoly of those who read Latin; he characterized his own treatise,* The English Physician *(1652), as "astro-physical" (that is, astrological medicine). In Galen's physiology, there are four bodily humors (black bile, yellow bile, phlegm, and blood). All diseases and personality disorders are caused by deficits or excesses of one humor or another, and personality types are determined by the dominant humor (sanguine, choleric, melancholic, or phlegmatic). Culpeper also goes on to treat of the choleric-melancholy, melancholy-choleric, melancholy-sanguine, sanguine-phlegmatic, and other "commixtures."*

Sanguine Complexion

Description: A man or woman in whose body heat and moisture abounds is said to be sanguine of complexion. Such are usually of a middle stature, strong composed bodies, fleshy but not fat, great veins, smooth skins, hot and moist in feeling. Their body is hairy. If they be men they have soon beards, if they be women it were ridiculous to expect it. There is a redness intermingled with white in their cheeks; their hair is usually of a blackish brown, yet sometimes flaxen. Their appetite is good, their digestion quick, their urine yellowish and thick, the excrements of their bowels reddish and firm, their pulse great and full. They dream usually of red things and merry conceits [*ideas*].

Conditions: As for their conditions, they are merry, cheerful creatures, bountiful, pitiful [*compassionate*], merciful, courteous, bold, trusty, given much to the games of Venus [*sexual activity*], as though they had been an apprentice seven years to the trade. A little thing will make them weep, but so soon as 'tis over no further grief sticks to their hearts.

Choleric Complexion

Description: We call that man choleric in whose body heat and dryness abounds or is predominant. Such persons are usually short of stature and not fat – it may be because the heat and dryness of their bodies consumes radical [*essential*] moisture – their skin rough and hot in feeling and their bodies very hairy. The hair of their heads is yellowish, red, or flaxen (for the most part), and curls much. The color of their face is tawny or sunburnt; they have some beards; they have little hollow hazel eyes. Their concoction [*digestion*] is very strong insomuch that they are able to digest more than they appetite [*desire*]. Their pulse is swift and strong, their urine yellow and thin. They are usually costive [*constipated*]. They dream of fighting, quarreling, fire, and burning.

Conditions: As for conditions, they are naturally quick-witted, bold, no way shamefaced [*bashful*], furious [*fierce*], hasty, quarrelsome, fraudulent [*deceitful*], eloquent, courageous, stout-hearted creatures, not given to sleep much, but much given to jesting, mocking, and lying.

Melancholy Complexion

Description: A melancholy person is one [in] whose body cold and dryness is predominate; and not such a one as is sad sometimes, as the vulgar [*commoners*] dream. They are usually slender and not very tall, of swarthy duskish color, rough skin, cold and hard in feeling. They have very little hair on their bodies and are long without beards. And sometimes they are beardless in age. The hair of their heads is dusky brown usually and sometimes dusky flaxen. Their appetite is far better than their concoction usually, by reason appetite is caused of a sour vapor sent up by the spleen, which is the seat of melancholy, to the stomach. Their urine is pale, their dung of a clay-ish color and broken, their pulse slow. They dream of frightful things; black, darkness, and terrible businesses.

Conditions: They are naturally covetous, self-lovers, cowards, afraid of their own shadows, fearful, careful, solitary, lumpish [*sluggish*], unsociable, delighting to be alone, stubborn, ambitious, envious, of a deep cogitation, obstinate in opinion, mistrustful, suspicious, spiteful, squeamish, and yet slovenly. They retain anger long and aim at no small things.

Phlegmatic Complexion

Description: Such people in whom coldness with moisture abounds are called phlegmatic, yet are usually not very tall. But very fat – some you shall find almost as thick as they are long. Their veins and arteries are small, their bodies without hair, and they have but little beards. Their hair is usually flaxen or light brown, their face white and pale, their skin smooth, cold, and moist in touch-ing. Both appetite and digestion is very weak in them, their pulse little and low, their urine pale and thick, but the excrements of their bowels usually thin. They dream of great rains, water, and drowning.

Conditions: As for conditions, they are very dull, heavy, and slothful, like the scholar that was a great while alearning a lesson but when once he had it, he had quickly forgotten it. They are drowsy, sleepy, cowardly, forgetful crea-tures, as swift in motion as a snail. They travail (and that's but seldom) as though they intended to go fifteen miles in fourteen days, yet are they shamefaced and sober.

10.8   Thomas Wright, *The Passions of the Mind* (1601)

From STC 26039 (HL copy), B6ᵛ–B7ᵛ, C1ʳ⁻ᵛ, D8ʳ, G1ᵛ–G2ᵛ, H2ʳ–H3ʳ.

Thomas Wright was a Catholic priest who was dismissed from the Society of Jesus when he decided to return to England from self-imposed exile in Italy. Ben Jonson, who may have been converted to Catholicism by Wright, wrote a commendatory poem for the publication of this treatise which, although based in Galenic physiology, was nonetheless important as an early study of human psychology. Wright applies a methodical and learned mind to the subject of the ungovernable aspects of human nature. Despite his heresy (he also wrote the anti-Protestant tract Certain Articles or Forcible Reasons, *and was expelled from England in 1610),* Passions of the Mind *was highly influential and was many times reprinted.*

Three sorts of actions proceed from men's souls: some are internal and imma-
terial, as the acts of our wits and wills; others be mere external and material, as
the acts of our senses (seeing, hearing, moving, etc.); others stand betwixt these
two extremes and border upon them both – the which we may best discover in
children, because they lack the use of reason and are guided by an internal imagination, following nothing else but that pleaseth their senses, even after the
same manner as brute beasts do. For as we see beasts hate, love, fear, and hope,
so do children. Those actions then which are common with us and beasts we call
passions and affections, or perturbations, of the mind. . . .

When these affections are stirring in our minds they alter the humors of our
bodies, causing some passion or alteration in them. They are called perturbations
for that (as afterward shall be declared) they trouble wonderfully the soul,
corrupting the judgment and seducing the will, inducing, for the most part, to
vice, and commonly withdrawing from virtue. And therefore some call them
maladies or sores of the soul. They be also named affections, because the soul by
them either affecteth some good or, for the affection of some good, detesteth
some ill. These passions then be certain internal acts or operations of the soul,
bordering upon reason and sense, prosecuting some good thing or flying some
ill thing, causing therewithal some alteration in the body. . . .

The most part of men resolve themselves never to displease their sense or
passions but to grant them whatsoever they demand. What curiosity the eyes
will see, they yield unto them; what dainty meats the tongue will taste, they
never deny it; what savors the nose will smell, they never resist it; what music
the ears will hear, they accept it; and, finally, whatsoever by importunity, prayer,
or suggestion sensuality requesteth, no sooner to reason the supplication is
presented but the petition is granted. . . . Reason, once being entered into league
with passions and sense, becometh a better friend to sensuality than the passions
were before, for reason straightways inventeth ten thousand sorts of new
delights which the passions never could have imagined. . . . Unto these six –
love, desire, pleasure, hatred, fear, and sadness – all ordinate and inordinate
passions may easily be reduced. . . .

First, then, to our imagination cometh by sense or memory some object to
be known, convenient or disconvenient to nature, the which being known
. . . in the imagination, which resideth in the former part of the brain (as we
prove when we imagine anything), presently the purer spirits flock from the
brain by certain secret channels to the heart, where they pitch at the door,
signifying what an object was presented, convenient or disconvenient for it.
The heart immediately bendeth either to prosecute it or to eschew it, and the
better to effect that affection draweth other humors to help him. And so in
pleasure concur great store of pure spirits; in pain and sadness, much melancholy blood; in ire, blood and choler. And not only, as I said, the heart
draweth, but also the same soul that informeth the heart, residing in other
parts, sendeth the humors unto the heart to perform their service in such a
worthy place. In like manner as when we feel hunger (caused by the sucking

of the liver and defect of nourishment in the stomach) the same soul which informeth the stomach resideth in the hand, eyes, and mouth, and in case of hunger subordinateth them all to serve the stomach and satisfy the appetite thereof, even so in the hunger of the heart: the spleen, the liver, the blood, spirits, choler, and melancholy attend and serve it most diligently. . . . If the imagination be very apprehensive, it sendeth greater store of spirits to the heart and maketh greater impression. Likewise, if the heart be very hot, cold, moist, tender, choleric, sooner and more vehemently it is stirred to passions thereunto proportionated. Finally, if one abound more with one humor than another, he sendeth more fuel to nourish the passion, and so it continueth the longer and the stronger. . . .

The will by yielding to the passion receiveth some little bribe of pleasure, the which moveth her to let the bridle loose unto inordinate appetites, because she hath ingrafted in her two inclinations, the one to follow reason, the other to content the senses. And this inclination (the other being blinded by the corrupt judgment caused by inordinate passions), here she feeleth satisfied. Finally, the will, being the governess of the soul and loathing to be troubled with much dissension among her subjects, as an uncareful magistrate neglecteth the good of the commonweal to avoid some particular men's displeasure, so the will, being afraid to displease sense, neglecteth the care she ought to have over it, especially perceiving that the soul thereby receiveth some interest of pleasure or escheweth some pain. . . . We may compare the soul without passions to a calm sea with sweet, pleasant, and crispling [*undulating*] streams; but the passionate to the raging gulf swelling with waves, surging by tempests, menacing the stony rocks, and endeavoring to overthrow mountains. Even so, passions make the soul to swell with pride and pleasure; they threaten wounds, death, and destruction by audacious boldness and ire; they undermine the mountains of virtue with hope and fear; and, in sum, never let the soul be in quietness, but ever either flowing with pleasure or ebbing with pain.

10.9 Robert Burton, *The Anatomy of Melancholy* (1638)

From STC 4163 (CUL copy), "Democritus Junior to the Reader," K2ᵛ; "The First Partition," B2ʳ.

Although Robert Burton does not mention heliocentrism directly, the idea that the earth was not the center of the universe caused a general sense of gloom that humankind was less important than once believed. Influenced by Thomas Wright, Burton wrote about the kinds, causes, and symptoms of melancholy; cures for melancholy; and the special aspects of love and religious melancholy. No excerpt can do justice to the leisurely, digressive, allusive, citational prose of The Anatomy of Melancholy, *which continued to unfold over six editions between 1621 and 1651. The first edition contained over 353,000 words; the last, over 516,000.*

I had a just cause to undertake this subject, to point at these particular species of dotage [*folly*] that so men might acknowledge their imperfections and seek to reform what is amiss. Yet I have a more serious intent at this time and, to omit all impertinent digressions, to say no more of such as are improperly melancholy, or metaphorically mad, lightly mad, or in disposition as stupid, angry, drunken, silly, sottish, sullen, proud, vainglorious, ridiculous, beastly, peevish, obstinate, impudent, extravagant, dry, doting, dull, desperate, harebrain, etc., mad, frantic, foolish heteroclites [*anomalies*], which no new hospital can hold, no physic [*medicine*] help. My purpose and endeavor is in the following discourse to anatomize this humor of melancholy through all his parts and species, as it is an habit or an ordinary disease, and that philosophically, medicinally, to show the causes, symptoms, and several cures of it, that it may be the better avoided. Moved thereunto for the generality of it and to do good, it being a disease so frequent . . . so grievous, so common, I know not wherein to do a more general service, and spend my time better, than to prescribe means how to prevent and cure so universal a malady, an epidemical disease, that, so often, so much crucifies the body and mind. . . .

Melancholy, the subject of our present discourse, is either in disposition or habit. In disposition is that transitory melancholy which goes and comes upon every small occasion of sorrow, need, sickness, trouble, fear, grief, passion, or perturbation of the mind; any manner of care, discontent, or thought which causeth anguish, dullness, heaviness, and vexation of the spirits; any ways opposite to pleasure, mirth, joy, delight; causing frowardness [*perverseness*] in us, or a dislike. In which equivocal and improper sense, we call him melancholy that is dull, sad, sour, lumpish [*lethargic*], ill disposed, solitary, any way moved, or displeased. And from these melancholy dispositions, no man living is free, no stoic, none so wise, none so happy, none so patient, so generous, so godly, so divine, that can vindicate himself; so well composed, but more or less, some time or other he feels the smart of it. Melancholy in this sense is the character of mortality.

10.10   Helkiah Crooke, *Microcosmographia: A Description of the Body of Man* (1615)

From STC 6062 (HL copy), C1ᵛ–C2ʳ.

The first major anatomical textbook in English was produced by London physician Helkiah Crooke. Himself highly educated (at Cambridge and Leiden), Crooke aimed to make the best and most current medical knowledge available to practicing surgeons. Although the Bishop of London attempted to have Microcosmographia *suppressed for its explicit illustrations of genitalia, the book was a popular success, immediately reprinted in 1616 and 1618. In a prefatory epistle to the king, written in Latin, Crooke complained that most physicians treated the human body with too little reverence.*

It is no doubt an excellent thing for a man to attain to the knowledge of himself, which thing anatomy and dissection of bodies doth teach us, and as it were point out unto us with the finger. But there is another far more divine and useful profit of anatomy than the former, proper and peculiar to us to whom the light of the Gospel hath shined: namely, the knowledge of the immortal God. . . .

He hath framed so many and so diverse particles: above two hundred bones, cartileges yet more, many more ligaments, a number of membranes number-less, the pipes or trunks of the arteries, millions of veins, sinews more than thirty pair, muscles almost four hundred, and, to conclude, all the bowels and inward parts. His incredible wisdom appeareth in the admirable contabulation [*joining*] or composition of the whole, made of so many parts so unlike one to another. Enter thou, whosoever thou art (though thou be an atheist, and acknowledgest no God at all), enter I beseech thee into the sacred tower of Pallas – I mean the brain of man – and behold and admire the pillars and arched cloisters of that princely palace, the huge greatness of that stately building, the pedestals or bases, the porches and goodly frontispiece, the four arched cham-bers, the bright and clear mirror, the labyrinthian mazes and web of the small arteries, the admirable trainings of the veins, the draining furrows and water-courses, the living ebullitions [*effervescences*] and springings up of the sinews, and the wonderful fecundity [*fruitfulness*] of that white marrow of the back which the wise man in the Book of the Preacher or Ecclesiastes calleth the silver cord. From the brain turn the eye of thy mind to the gates of the sun and windows of the soul – I mean the eyes – and there behold the brightness of the glittering crystal, the purity and neat cleanness of the watery and glassy humors, the delicate and fine texture of the tunicles [*enclosing membranes*], and the wonderful and admirable volubility [*quickness*] of the muscles in turning and rolling of the eyes. Mark and observe also the art and curious workmanship appearing in the inward part of the ear, how exquisitely it is made and trimmed with labyrinths, windings, little windows, a sounding tympan or timbrel; three small bones, a stirrup, an anvil, and a hammer; the small muscles, the nerve or sinew of hearing, and the cartilaginous or gristle passage, prepared for convey-ing all sounds unto the sense. Look upon the unweariable and agile motions, the conquering power, the frame and composition, the muscles, the proper and peculiar kind of flesh, the membranes, the veins and sinews, and the bridle, as it were, all easily distinguished within the compass of that little body, or rather, little member of the body, the tongue wherewith we bless God and wherewith we curse men. . . .

Wilt thou not cry out, though it be against thy will, "O admirable architect! O, unimitable workman!" And wilt thou not with the inspired prophet sing unto the creator this hymn: "I praise thee, O Lord, because thou hast showed the greatness of thy wisdom in fashioning of my body"?

10.11   Eucharius Roesslin, *The Birth of Mankind* (1540)

From STC 21153 (HL copy), E4ᵛ–F1ᵛ.

The advent of print played its part in the Scientific Revolution, making new informa-
tion more widely known. In the case of Thomas Raynald's translation from the Latin
of The Birth of Mankind, *it was a case of making old information more widely known.*
Childbirth was a mystery to men, having been in the hands of female midwives and
their assistants exclusively. Midwives were even entrusted to perform emergency
baptisms when delivering children they deemed unlikely to survive. That trust was
eroded, however, as medical treatment was professionalized. In his prefatory dedication
to Henry VIII's fifth wife Katherine Howard, Raynold warns of "rude" and "rash"
midwives; by the seventeenth century, the idea that midwives were ignorant and incom-
petent meant that childbirth was increasingly supervised by male physicians.

When the woman perceiveth the matrice [*womb*] or mother [*uterus*] to wax lax
[*grow slack*] or loose and to be dissolved and that the humors issue forth in great
plenty, then shall it be meet [*suitable*] for her to sit down, leaning backward, in
manner upright. For the which purpose in some regions (as in France and
Germany), the midwives have stools for the purpose which, being but low and
not high from the ground, is made so compass-wise [*round*] and cave [*concave*] or
hollow in the middest that that may be received from underneath which is
looked for.⁵ And the back of the stool leaning backward receiveth the back of the
woman. . . .

The midwife herself shall sit before the laboring woman and shall diligently
observe and wait how much and after what manner the child steereth itself;
also, shall with her hands first anointed with the oil of almonds or the oil of
white lilies rule and direct every thing as shall seem best. Also the midwife
must instruct and comfort the party, not only refreshing her with good meat
and drink but also with sweet words, giving her good hope of a speedy deliverance, encouraging and enstomaching [*encouraging*] her to patience and toler-
ance, bidding her to hold in her breath in so much as she may. Also stroking
gently with her hands her belly above the navel, for that helpeth to depress
the birth downward. . . . But this must the midwife above all things take heed
of: that she compel not the woman to labor before the birth come forward and
show itself. For before that time all labor is in vain, labor as much as ye list.
And in this case many times it cometh to pass that the party hath labored so
sore before the time that when she should labor indeed her might and strength
is spent before in vain, so that she is not now able to help herself. And that is
a perilous case.

---

5 *that . . . which is looked for*: i.e., the newborn child.

10.12 *The Anatomical Exercises of Dr. William Harvey* (1628)

From Wing STC H1083 (HL copy), C6^v–C8^r.

As an examiner for the London College of Physicians, William Harvey tested new doctors for their fidelity to Galenism even while himself occupied with a project that would over-turn it. His observations from human dissection were not well accepted when published in Frankfurt: if the blood circulated, it followed that the humors could be mixed, that no one humor could be isolated for correction, and that there was no medical basis for blood-letting – all beliefs and practices fundamental to the treatments of the time. Despite his own role in revolutionizing medical knowledge, when Harvey lay on his deathbed, unable to speak, he indicated that blood should be let from his tongue in Galenic fashion. This translation from the original Latin of 1628 was published in 1653.

Those things which remain to be spoken of, though they be very considerable, yet when I shall mention them, they are so new and unheard of that not only I fear mischief which may arrive to me from the envy of some persons, but I like-wise doubt that every man almost will be my enemy – so much does custom and doctrine once received and deeply rooted (as if it were another Nature) prevail with everyone, and the venerable reverence of antiquity enforces. Howsoever, my resolution is now set down; my hope is in the candor of those which love truth, and learned spirits. . . .

When I had a long time considered with myself how great abundance of blood was passed through, and in how short time that transmission was done, whether or no the juice of the nourishment which we receive could furnish this or no, at last I perceived that the veins should be quite emptied and the arteries on the other side be burst with too much intrusion of blood unless the blood did pass back again by some way out of the veins into the arteries and return into the right ventricle of the heart.

I began to bethink myself if it might not have a circular motion, which after-wards I found true, and that the blood was thrust forth and driven out of the heart by the arteries into the habit [*system*] of the body and all parts of it by the beating of the left ventricle of the heart, as it is driven into the lungs through the *vena arteriosa* [*arterial vein*] by the beating of the right, and that it does return through the little veins into the *vena cava*, and to the right ear of the heart, as likewise out of the lungs through the aforesaid *arterio venosa* to the left ventricle, as we said before.

Which motion we may call circular after the same manner that Aristotle says that the rain and the air do imitate the motion of the superior bodies. For the earth being wet evaporates by the heat of the sun, and the vapors being raised aloft are condensed and descend in showers and wet the ground, and by this means here are generated likewise tempests and the beginnings of the meteors – from the circular motion of the sun and his approach and removal.

So in all likelihood it comes to pass in the body that all the parts are nourished, cherished, and quickened with blood, which is warm, perfect, vaporous,
full of spirit [*vital*], and, that I may so say, alimentative [*nutrative*]. In the parts
the blood is refrigerated, coagulated, and made as it were barren; from thence it
returns to the heart as to the fountain or dwelling house of the body, to recover
its perfection. And there again by natural heat, powerful and vehement, it is
melted and is dispensed again through the body from thence, being fraught with
spirits as with balsam [*a soothing oil*], and that all the things do depend upon the
motional pulsation of the heart.

So the heart is the beginning of life, the sun of the microcosm, as propor-
tionably the sun deserves to be called the heart of the world.

Further Reading

Original Sources

Some of the materials excerpted in this collection are available in modern editions. To read more from these Renaissance authors, consult the following:

1.3   *The Letters of King Henry VIII: A Selection*, ed. M. St. Clare Byrne (London: Cassell, 1936).

1.5   *England's Boy King: The Diary of Edward VI, 1547–1553*, ed. Jonathan North (Welwyn Garden City: Ravenhall, 2005).

1.7–9 *Elizabeth I: Collected Works*, ed. Leah S. Marcus, Janel Mueller, and Mary Beth Rose (Chicago: University of Chicago Press, 2000).

1.11   *King James VI and I: Selected Writings*, ed. Neil Rhodes, Jennifer Richards, Joseph Marshall (Aldershot: Ashgate, 2003); *Political Writings, King James VI and I*, ed. Johann P. Sommerville (Cambridge: Cambridge University Press, 1994).

2.2   *The Early Records of the Bankes Family at Winstanley*, ed. Joyce Bankes and Eric Kerridge, Chetham Society, 21 (1973).

2.4   *The Journal of Sir Roger Wilbraham . . . for the Years 1593–1616*, ed. Harold Spencer Scott, *Camden Miscellany*, 10 (1902).

3.1   *Certain Sermons or Homilies (1547) and A Homily against Disobedience and Willful Rebellion (1570): A Critical Edition*, ed. Ronald B. Bond (Toronto: University of Toronto Press, 1987).

3.5   *The Polemics and Poems of Rachel Speght*, ed. Barbara Kiefer Lewalski (New York: Oxford University Press, 1996).

3.7   *Two Elizabethan Puritan Diaries*, ed. M. M. Knappen (Chicago: American Society of Church History, 1933).

3.14   *The Notebooks of Nehemiah Wallington, 1618–1654: A Selection*, ed. David Booy (Aldershot: Ashgate, 2007); Paul S. Seaver, *Wallington's World: A Puritan Artisan in Seventeenth-Century London* (Stanford, CA: Stanford University Press, 1985).

4.1   *Two Early Tudor Lives: The Life and Death of Cardinal Wolsey, by George Cavendish; The Life of Sir Thomas More, by William Roper*, ed. Richard S. Sylvester and Davis P. Harding (New Haven, CT: Yale University Press, 1962).

4.2   "The Fall of Religious Houses," ed. A. G. Dickens in *Tudor Treatises*, Yorkshire Archaeological Society, 125 (1959), 122–5.

4.3   See 3.1.

4.4   *The Examinations of Anne Askew*, ed. Elaine V. Beilin (New York: Oxford University Press, 1996).

4.6   www.hrionline.ac.uk/johnfoxe/

4.10   See 3.14.

4.11   *The Witch of Edmonton: A Critical Edition*, ed. Etta Soiref Onat (New York: Garland, 1980).

5.2 See 3.1.

5.4 *The Political Writings of John Knox*, ed. Marvin A. Breslow (Washington, DC: Folger Books, 1985).

5.7 See 1.7–9.

5.9 See 1.11.

5.10 Niccolò Machiavelli, *The Chief Works and Others*, ed. and trans. Allan Gilbert, 3 vols (Durham, NC: Duke University Press, 1965).

5.11 Sir Francis Bacon, *The Essayes or Counsels, Civill and Morall*, ed. Michael Kiernan (Cambridge, MA: Harvard University Press, 1985).

6.1 *The Book of the Courtier*, ed. and trans. George Bull (Harmondsworth: Penguin, 1967).

6.2 Henry Peacham, *The Complete Gentleman, The Truth of Our Times, and The Art of Living Well in London*, ed. Virgil B. Heltzel (Ithaca, NY: Cornell University Press for the Folger Shakespeare Library, 1962).

6.7 "Diary of the Journey of Philip Julius, Duke of Stettin-Pomerania, through England in the Year 1602," ed. Gottfried von Bülow with Wilfred Powell, *Transactions of the Royal Historical Society*, 2nd ser. 6 (1892).

6.8 *The Diary of John Manningham of the Middle Temple, 1602–1603*, ed. Robert Parker Sorlien (Hanover, NH: University Press of New England for the University of Rhode Island, 1976).

6.9 *Dudley Carleton to John Chamberlain, 1603–1624: Jacobean Letters*, ed. Maurice Lee, Jr. (New Brunswick, NJ: Rutgers University Press, 1972).

7.1 *The Description of England: The Classic Contemporary Account of Tudor Social Life by William Harrison*, ed. Georges Edelen (Washington, DC: Folger Shakespeare Library, 1994).

7.8 *The Farming and Memorandum Books of Henry Best of Elmswell, 1642*, ed. Donald Woodward (London: Oxford University Press for the British Academy, 1984).

8.1 Thomas Wilson, *The Art of Rhetoric (1560)*, ed. Peter E. Medine (University Park, PA: Pennsylvania State University Press, 1994).

8.3 *Plutarch's Lives of Coriolanus, Caesar, Brutus, and Antonius in North's Translation*, ed. Ralph Hamilton Carr (Oxford: Clarendon Press, 1938).

8.4 Linda Pollock, *With Faith and Physic: The Life of a Tudor Gentlewoman, Lady Grace Mildmay, 1552–1620* (London: Collins & Brown, 1993).

8.5 See 5.11.

8.6 Ben Jonson, *Catiline*, ed. W. F. Bolton and Jane F. Gardner (Lincoln, NE: University of Nebraska Press, 1973).

8.7 *The Schoole of Abuse, by Stephen Gosson*, ed. Arthur Freeman (New York: Garland, 1973).

8.8 Sir Philip Sidney, *An Apology for Poetry, or, The Defence of Poesy*, ed. Geoffrey Shepherd, rev. edn R. W. Maslen, 3rd edn (Manchester: Manchester University Press, 2002).

8.11 Thomas Heywood, *An Apology for Actors*, ed. Arthur Freeman (New York: Garland, 1973).

8.12 *Letters of Sir Thomas Bodley to Thomas James*, ed. G. W. Wheeler (Oxford: Clarendon Press, 1926).

9.1 *A Discourse of the Commonweal of This Realm of England*, ed. Mary Dewar (Charlottesville, VA: University Press of Virginia for the Folger Shakespeare Library, 1969).

9.2–3   Richard Hakluyt, *The Principal Navigations, Voyages, Traffiques, and Discoveries of the English Nation*, 12 vols, Hackluyt Society (Glasgow: J. MacLeghose, 1903–5).

9.4   *The Embassy of Sir Thomas Roe to the Court of the Great Mogul, 1615–1619*, ed. William Foster, 2 vols, Hackluyt Society, 2nd ser. (1899).

9.5   *Commons Debates 1621*, ed. Wallace Notestein, Frances Helen Relf, and Hartley Simpson, 2 vols (New Haven, CT: Yale University Press, 1935).

9.7   See 9.2–3.

10.2   Francis Bacon, *The Advancement of Learning*, ed. Michael Kiernan (Oxford: Clarendon Press, 2000); Francis Bacon, *Novum Organum, with Other Parts of The Great Instauration*, ed. Peter Urbach and John Gibson (Chicago: Open Court, 1994).

10.3   *The Book of Secrets of Albertus Magnus*, ed. Michael R. Best and Frank H. Brightman (Oxford: Clarendon Press, 1973).

10.8   Thomas Wright, *The Passions of the Mind in General: A Critical Edition*, ed. William Webster Newbold (New York: Garland, 1986).

10.12   William Harvey, *An Anatomical Disputation Concerning the Movement of the Heart and Blood in Living Creatures*, ed. and trans. Gweneth Whitteridge (Oxford: Blackwell, 1976).

Secondary Sources

Airs, Malcolm, *The Making of the English Country House, 1500–1640* (London: Architectural Press, 1975).

Archer, Ian W., *The Pursuit of Stability: Social Relations in Elizabethan London* (Cambridge: Cambridge University Press, 1991).

Barish, Jonas A., *The Antitheatrical Prejudice* (Berkeley: University of California Press, 1981).

Beier, A. L., *Masterless Men: The Vagrancy Problem in England, 1560–1640* (London: Methuen, 1985).

Ben-Amos, Ilana Krausman, *Adolescence and Youth in Early Modern England* (New Haven, CT: Yale University Press, 1994).

Burgess, Glenn, *The Politics of the Ancient Constitution: An Introduction to English Political Thought, 1603–1642* (University Park, PA: Pennsylvania State University Press, 1992).

Bushnell, Rebecca W., *A Culture of Teaching: Early Modern Humanism in Theory and Practice* (Ithaca, NY: Cornell University Press, 1996).

Cahn, Susan, *Industry of Devotion: The Transformation of Women's Work in England, 1500–1660* (New York: Columbia University Press, 1987).

Clark, Alice, *The Working Life of Women in the Seventeenth Century* (London: Routledge, 1919).

Collinson, Patrick, *The Religion of Protestants: The Church in English Society, 1559–1625* (Oxford: Oxford University Press, 1982).

Cressy, David, *Birth, Marriage, and Death: Ritual, Religion and the Life-Cycle in Tudor and Stuart England* (Oxford: Oxford University Press, 1997).

——, *Literacy and the Social Order: Reading and Writing in Tudor and Stuart England* (Cambridge: Cambridge University Press, 1980).

Croft, Pauline, *King James* (Basingstoke: Palgrave Macmillan, 2003).

Dickens, A. G., *The English Reformation* (London: Batsford, 1989).

Dillon, Janette, *Theatre, Court and City, 1595–1610: Drama and Social Space in London* (Cambridge: Cambridge University Press, 2000).

Emmison, F. G., *Elizabethan Life: Disorder* (Chelmsford: Essex County Council, 1970).

——, *Elizabethan Life: Home, Work, and Land* (Chelmsford: Essex County Council, 1973).

——, *Elizabethan Life: Morals and the Church Courts* (Chelmsford: Essex County Council, 1973).

Erickson, Amy Louise, *Women and Property in Early Modern England* (London: Routledge, 1993).

Fletcher, Anthony, *Gender, Sex, and Subordination in England, 1500–1800* (New Haven, CT: Yale University Press, 1995).

——, and John Stevenson (eds), *Order and Disorder in Early Modern England* (Cambridge: Cambridge University Press, 1985).

Girouard, Mark, *Robert Smythson and the Elizabethan Country House* (New Haven, CT: Yale University Press, 1983).

Gowing, Laura, *Domestic Dangers: Women, Words, and Sex in Early Modern London* (Oxford: Oxford University Press, 1996).

Greenblatt, Stephen, *Renaissance Self-Fashioning: From More to Shakespeare* (Chicago: University of Chicago Press, 1980).

Guy, J. A., *Tudor England* (Oxford: Oxford University Press, 1988).

Haigh, Christopher, *English Reformations: Religion, Politics, and Society under the Tudors* (Oxford: Clarendon Press, 1993).

Hoskins, W. G., *The Age of Plunder: King Henry's England, 1500–1547* (London: Longman, 1976).

Houlbrooke, Ralph A., *The English Family, 1450–1700* (London: Longman, 1984).

Howard, Maurice, *The Early Tudor Country House: Architecture and Politics, 1490–1550* (London: G. Philip, 1987).

Ingram, Martin, *Church Courts, Sex and Marriage in England, 1570–1640* (Cambridge: Cambridge University Press, 1987).

Jones, Ann Rosalind and Peter Stallybrass, *Renaissance Clothing and the Materials of Memory* (Cambridge: Cambridge University Press, 2000).

Judges, A. V., *The Elizabethan Underworld: A Collection of Tudor and Early Stuart Tracts and Ballads* (London: Routledge & Kegan Paul, 1930).

Kinney, Arthur F., *Rogues, Vagabonds, and Sturdy Beggars: A New Gallery of Tudor and Early Stuart Rogue Literature* (Barre, MA: Imprint Society, 1973).

Laroque, François, *Shakespeare's Festive World: Elizabethan Seasonal Entertainment and the Professional Stage*, trans. Janet Lloyd (Cambridge: Cambridge University Press, 1991).

Laslett, Peter, *The World We Have Lost* (London: Methuen, 1965).

Levin, Carole, *The Heart and Stomach of a King: Elizabeth I and the Politics of Sex and Power* (Philadelphia: University of Pennsylvania Press, 1994).

Macfarlane, Alan, *Witchcraft in Tudor and Stuart England: A Regional and Comparative Study* (London: Routledge & Kegan Paul, 1970).

Manning, Roger B., *Village Revolts: Social Protest and Popular Disturbances in England, 1509–1640* (Oxford: Clarendon Press, 1988).

Paster, Gail Kern, *The Body Embarrassed: Drama and the Disciplines of Shame in Early Modern England* (Ithaca, NY: Cornell University Press, 1993).

Sharpe, J. A., *Crime in Early Modern England, 1550–1750* (London: Longman, 1984).

Sinfield, Alan, *Faultlines: Cultural Materialism and the Politics of Dissident Reading* (Berkeley: University of California Press, 1992).

Siraisi, Nancy G., *Medieval and Early Renaissance Medicine: An Introduction to Knowledge and Practice* (Chicago: University of Chicago Press, 1990).

Slack, Paul, *The Impact of Plague in Tudor and Stuart England* (London: Routledge & Kegan Paul, 1985).

——, *Poverty and Policy in Tudor and Stuart England* (London: Longman, 1988).

Smith, Bruce R., *Homosexual Desire in Shakespeare's England: A Cultural Poetics* (Chicago, IL: University of Chicago Press, 1991).

Spufford, Margaret, *Contrasting Communities: English Villagers in the Sixteenth and Seventeenth Centuries* (Cambridge: Cambridge University Press, 1974).

——, *The Great Reclothing of Rural England: Petty Chapmen and their Wares in the Seventeenth Century* (London: Hambledon Press, 1984).

Stone, Lawrence, *The Crisis of the Aristocracy, 1558–1641* (Oxford: Clarendon Press, 1965).

Thirsk, Joan, *Economic Policy and Projects: The Development of a Consumer Society in Early Modern England* (Oxford: Clarendon Press, 1978).

——, *Food in Early Modern England: Phases, Fads, Fashions, 1500–1760* (London: Hambledon Continuum, 2007).

Thomas, Keith, *Religion and the Decline of Magic: Studies in Popular Beliefs in Sixteenth- and Seventeenth-Century England* (London: Weidenfeld & Nicolson, 1971).

Tillyard, E. M. W., *The Elizabethan World Picture* (London: Chatto & Windus, 1943).

Underdown, David, *Revel, Riot, and Rebellion: Popular Politics and Culture in England, 1603–1660* (Oxford: Clarendon Press, 1985).

Watt, Tessa, *Cheap Print and Popular Piety, 1550–1640* (Cambridge: Cambridge University Press, 1991).

Westfall, Richard S., *Science and Religion in Seventeenth-Century England* (New Haven, CT: Yale University Press, 1958).

Woodbridge, Linda, *Women and the English Renaissance: Literature and the Nature of Womankind, 1540–1620* (Urbana: University of Illinois Press, 1984).

Wrightson, Keith, *English Society, 1580–1680* (New Brunswick, NJ: Rutgers University Press, 1982).

Web Sources

British History Online
www.british-history.ac.uk/catalogue.aspx

A Celebration of Women Writers
http://digital.library.upenn.edu/women/

CERES, Cambridge English Renaissance Electronic Service
www.english.cam.ac.uk/ceres/

Early Modern English Drama Online
http://onlinebooks.library.upenn.edu/webbin/book/browse?type=lcsubc&key=English%20drama%20%2d%2d%20Early%20modern%20and%20Elizabethan%2c%201500%2d1600

The English Bible (early editions)
www.bible-researcher.com/links02.html#bishops

English Broadside Ballad Archive
www.english.ucsb.edu/emc/ballad_project/index.asp

The English Emblem Book Project at Pennsylvania State University
http://emblem.libraries.psu.edu/catalog.htm

Luminarium: Anthology of English Literature
www.luminarium.org/

Rare Book Room
www.rarebookroom.org/

Index

Page numbers in *italics* denote references to illustrations in the text.